C000099464

Beyond Empire

Beyond Empire

The End of Britain's Colonial Encounter

John T. Ducker

[signature: John Ducker]

Feb 4th 2020

BLOOMSBURY ACADEMIC

LONDON • NEW YORK • OXFORD • NEW DELHI • SYDNEY

BLOOMSBURY ACADEMIC
Bloomsbury Publishing Plc
50 Bedford Square, London, WC1B 3DP, UK
1385 Broadway, New York, NY 10018, USA

BLOOMSBURY, BLOOMSBURY ACADEMIC and the Diana logo are trademarks
of Bloomsbury Publishing Plc

First published in Great Britain 2020

Cover design: Terry Woodley
Cover image © Zoonar GmbH / Alamy Stock Photo

A catalogue record for this book is available from the British Library.

A catalog record for this book is available from the Library of Congress.

ISBN: HB: 978-1-78831-735-1
ePDF: 978-1-78673-624-6
eBook: 978-1-78672-618-6

Typeset by Deanta Global Publishing Services, Chennai, India
Printed and bound in Great Britain

To find out more about our authors and books visit www.bloomsbury.com and
sign up for our newsletters.

Contents

Preface

In the July 1950 edition of the journal *African Affairs*, Earl De La Warr, a former Under-Secretary of State for the Colonies and leader of the Commission which visited East Africa in 1937 to study the need for tertiary-level education in that region, asked the question, 'Is the principle of self-government of such intrinsic moral merit that in comparison with it development and happiness do not really matter?'[1]

In 1956, the American journal *Foreign Affairs* carried an article by Vernon MacKay who wrote,

> The speed of this political transformation (of African countries) provides new perspective on a wide range of problems and raises anew the question of whether Africa is going too fast or too slow. Too slow or too fast for what? Too slow to satisfy African aspirations? Or too fast to create economically viable and politically stable states?[2]

These questions, posed before the event, go to the nub of the issues surrounding decolonization and the timing of the independence of the British territories. The purpose of this book is to look at the record in the case of individual colonies and seek to understand the outcome in them at the time of their independence. By looking at a number of territories, the approach is comparative which helps in reaching a broader understanding. However, we cannot generalize. There were common issues but each colony had its own characteristics and problems.

Richard Dowden, writing recently, observed 'in countries which had few European settlers and no removals from the land, there were almost no nationalist movements. Independence came to their inhabitants as a surprise, not as liberation. Here political pressure from the United States was more important than African agitation . . . their inhabitants were told they were going to become independent before they had expressed any demand for it. A group of French territories wanted to remain part of the French empire'. . . . Some local rulers or chieftains in treaty relationship with Britain had a similar preference.

This book is intended for the general reader or student interested in the history of the British colonies in the forty or so years in which their future as independent nation states was determined. It is intended especially for those with relatively little prior knowledge of these events. There is a large literature and there are scholarly tomes on this history, which most will not have the time to read; and an enormous official archive. I have drawn extensively on the archives in particular, but I limit myself mainly to the events and outcome in individual territories. To provide the context for events in individual colonies I have also found it necessary to summarize the evolving position, policies and role of the British Government on decolonization; and the impact of other countries, especially France and the United States, and of the United Nations. I have sought to bring the situation and the debate on colonial events and policies to life by the use of many contemporary quotations and comments. I have also included a review of the coverage by the British press of colonial matters, which serves to convey some of the dynamics and the tension in the process of decolonization. Necessarily I have had to omit much and I seek the indulgence of readers with greater knowledge and understanding of individual countries or events. I hope these omissions did not lead to a misrepresentation of events and outcomes.

The book does not concern itself with the imperial dimension, with strategic questions of importance to Britain itself. Much has been written of the causation of the passing of the British Empire – the rise of two huge and powerful continental powers, the losses from and the impact of the two world wars, the increasingly wide dispersion of the technologies, skills and resources which previously underlay and sustained the British Empire, the emergence of the notion of self-determination as one of the ruling ideologies of the time, and the creation of the League of Nations and the United Nations. I take note of these factors where they are germane to an understanding of some more limited event but do not address these overarching factors at a policy level.

In 1947 British India became independent, as the two states of India and Pakistan. In 1948, Ceylon became independent as Sri Lanka and Burma as Myanmar. Between 1956 and 1966, twenty-four British colonies and the Anglo-Egyptian Condominium of Sudan became independent states, most of them in Africa. Taken together, these accomplishments amounted to an event of historical proportions. Furthermore these events happened largely with consent and with relatively limited conflict, though the partition of India was a bloody affair. At the time everyone directly involved – colonial officers in the field, officials at the Colonial Office, politicians, academics, commentators in the Press – were aware of the speeding up of constitutional change and the implicit timetable of independence. Though there was no explicit official timetable, it was quite evident to all involved that events were following each other much more rapidly than anyone had expected. This was well reflected in a Colonial Office Minute of 1953 – 'the speed of constitutional advance has far outstripped the rate of Africanization'.[3] This was a significant concern as it was widely feared that there would be too few qualified indigenous people to take senior positions in the Public Service at independence of the colonies, and that those who were qualified were unlikely to have the experience needed to take over the complex responsibilities of running a country. Few colonies chose or were able to slow down the speed with which the transfer of power took place. In most it occurred well before anyone expected; or indeed before many considered it sensible.

Looking back fifty years later we are in a position to assess, or reassess, the process of decolonization and consider its effectiveness in creating viable states. There have been significant accomplishments, some of which are summarized in Annex 1, and more recently the economic growth of Africa as a whole has begun to rise in a rather impressive fashion – the Sub-Saharan African economies as a whole are now expanding by about 5 per cent per annum. Perhaps most significantly there has been time for two generations to complete their schooling and university studies and move into public life, business and the professions. Nevertheless, much of the last fifty years in many former colonies has been characterized by misrule and maladministration, by conflict and insecurity, tyranny in some cases, by widespread venality and corruption, by poverty and famine and in some cases the total collapse of public order. This remains the case in some countries. Many high hopes have been disappointed.

The ending of most empires has been followed by conflict with the lifting of imperial controls and policies which had previously kept the peace and limited communal antagonisms. In the early nineteenth century, the ending of the Spanish and Portuguese empires in America was accompanied by revolutions, wars and civil conflict. Within the last century, both the Ottoman Empire and the Austro-Hungarian Empire collapsed as a consequence of the First World War, reflecting a loss of the energy and capacity which created them. The subsequent Versailles Treaty not only recognized numerous new states in Eastern Europe and the Middle East but also planted the seeds of future conflict. The collapse of the Russian/Soviet Empire in the late 1980s created fourteen new republics, in addition to Russia. Several of these republics have experienced domestic conflict and some lack democratic legitimacy. Russia still weighs heavily in their affairs. The member countries of the former British Empire, now independent, have succeeded in retaining significant links with each other through the Commonwealth, with its habit of consultation, though major divergences have also occurred on many issues. Within Africa there have been cross-border conflicts on the fringes of Ethiopia, South Africa and Angola and there have been domestic conflicts of significance in Sudan, Nigeria, Uganda, Sierra Leone, Southern Rhodesia/Zimbabwe, the Congo/Zaire and elsewhere.

During the fifty-year-long period since most of the colonies achieved independence, Africa especially has been the recipient of financial and technical assistance from many sources on a scale never before equalled. Much of it has been put to good use; some projects and programmes may not have been very well conceived, designed or implemented; and some assistance has been wasted or misappropriated. Anyone who has been associated with programmes of assistance in Africa will have had successes to reflect on but many will also have been disappointed, not to say disillusioned, by the setbacks and missed opportunities, and sometimes by sheer incompetence or venality. This disappointment has been shared by Africans; maladministration, war and insecurity have had their biggest impact on the poor and the marginalized in African societies. Some prominent Africans – Ahmedu Oud Abdallah of Mauretania and Ali Mazrui of Kenya, for example – have acknowledged this and even toyed with the reintroduction of a form of colonialism to rectify the situation in individual countries.[4]

In considering this history, we must recall that the world we live in is a world of 'nation states'. The nation state emerged in its current form in late medieval Europe. Some of the European states – especially Portugal, Spain, Holland, Britain, France and Russia – extended their influence and control overseas, in the process acquiring empires. Empires existed in previous eras – in Europe, China, Persia, India, Egypt, in Mexico and South America, in the Middle East and elsewhere. However, at the time of the growth of the European empires from the sixteenth century onwards, large parts of the world had no such empires, or even nation states with the capacity to withstand their impact. In Africa south of the Sahara desert, there were no nation states, though there were a few 'city states' in West Africa and Abyssinia had an ancient identity. Local tribal groups prevailed and loyalty to their tribe was often the only relationship Africans had outside their immediate family.

Britain had over the centuries evolved forms of representative government at home which had an impact on the way in which it perceived and administered its overseas territories. It expected each 'colonial territory' to become largely self-sufficient. From the beginning of the seventeenth century British territories were endowed with legislative assemblies, executive councils and progressively more complex constitutions, legal systems and administrations. As a result they began to acquire some of the attributes of 'nation states' themselves – beginning with the North American colonies, the West Indies, Newfoundland and Canada, and then progressively Australia, New Zealand, India, Ceylon and so on. The United States broke away, adopting approaches to sovereignty, representation and government of its own. Thus when Britain acquired territories in Africa and elsewhere in the nineteenth century, it had much experience to draw on. These new colonial territories, also, acquired legislative bodies and administrative systems. However, in these territories there were not to be found the educated and trained people required to administer them on modern lines and the Colonial Service was expanded to perform these functions. For periods ranging from 60 to 120 years, the Colonial Service ran these countries, which themselves gradually acquired some of the attributes of 'nation states'. By the 1920s the notion of 'Trust' had re-emerged in relation to these dependent territories (see the following text) and by the late 1930s 'self-government' had become the declared objective of British policy for them. In 1955 Sir Ivor Jennings explained what this entailed in a series of BBC lectures (Annex 2).

The period I deal with is broadly from the 1920s to the mid-1960s. I look back at a very general level to India and Ceylon (Sri Lanka) to note the measures taken there under British rule to achieve self-government and independence. Though these Asian countries had many differences from Africa, the timing and process of achieving independence in them offer something of a benchmark when considering events in Africa and elsewhere. To limit the size of the book I have excluded some colonies from consideration, specifically the three Mediterranean colonies of Gibraltar, Malta and Cyprus where there were special considerations; Hong Kong and some of the component parts of Malaysia; and most of the island territories. I also excluded Egypt, which was not a colony though Britain had much influence there for sixty years, and the League of Nations–mandated territories of Palestine, Iraq and Jordan, where again there were special considerations. I did include Sudan, which was administered by the Sudan Civil Service, for historical reasons, rather than the Colonial Service. Events in Malaya and the West Indies are also covered because they were contemporaneous and had relevance to events in Africa.

The first chapter is introductory. In the second chapter I summarize the evolution of colonial policy within the British Government itself. The events and policy decisions of the 1920s, the 1930s and the years of the Second World War in regard to the process of decolonization are little known except by specialists. However, they are critical to understanding subsequent events, including the timing of decolonization, and deserve to be better known.

The third chapter looks at the state of education in the individual colonies at the time of independence. Important for the purpose of this book was the state of tertiary education, for without fully educated people the conduct of government and the professions would have been impossible. How far had the creation of universities and professional training gone by the time of independence? Had the colonies succeeded in building up a cadre of trained men and women to fill posts in the professions and the Public Service, without which no modern government can work?

In the fourth and fifth chapters I look at the process of political and constitutional change which took place, country by country, as independence approached, and also at the extent of 'localization' (largely 'Africanization') achieved in the Public Service by the time of independence. Written constitutions prepared with such care and debated so vigorously in the negotiations leading to self-government sought to protect the freedom of the individual and create a structure of the evolving state. These objectives and the institutions created to achieve them required defenders if they were to prove suitable and durable; and they required procedures and the tolerance to amend them after adequate debate and preparation. The attacks on these constitutions were going to come from politicians and soldiers who felt constrained by them, or ignored them, and from the Press, which was often controlled by those in power. Who was going to defend them? There had been little time for the legal and judicial professions to acquire the status and professional detachment to resist the arguments of impatient politicians. Civil society was still thin, weak and inexperienced. It is important for the purpose of this book to assess the extent to which the Public Service in the new states had, or was likely to have, the capacity to discharge this role.

Finally I add a short reflective chapter giving some personal views on the successes and failures of the decolonization process.

I spent seven years as a member of Her Majesty's Overseas Civil Service, the successor to the Colonial Service, from 1960 to 1967, though my service was in Arabia, not Africa. Subsequently I spent twenty-three years on the staff of the World Bank, for all but seven of those years involved directly or indirectly with Africa. In the 1990s I spent time in Central Asia and was able to observe the post-Soviet republics grappling with their newly independent status. I was stimulated to write this book mainly by my own observations, experiences and thoughts, but also partly by speeches delivered in Lagos, Nigeria, in 1990 by Robert McNamara, former president of the World Bank (see Annex 11) and in 1991 by Kim Jaycox, then vice president of the World Bank responsible for its activities in Africa. In his speech Jaycox explained what he understood by the phrase 'good governance', which he viewed as a prerequisite for economic and social development.

He challenged African nations and leaders to recover the capacity to carry out their duties effectively and with probity. It struck me as ironic that of the five elements of 'good governance' Jaycox identified, at least four of them could be said to have characterized British colonial rule in its later phases. They included the rule of law, accountability, openness, including in particular the freedom to publish and assemble peacefully, and predictability. The fifth element – transparency – may not have been conspicuous in the colonies themselves though, being subject to Parliament in London, colonial administrations were anyway required to account publicly for their actions and respond to questions raised in Parliament.

Was the extent of educational accomplishment at the time of independence insufficient to support a modern representative state? Was the competence and standard of administration provided by the localized Public Service equal to the task, able to resist the challenges it faced? Were functionaries experienced and independent enough to resist being swayed by sectional or personal influences? Were the social changes taking place in these new African states so great that time was always going to be needed to establish strong civilian and representative forms of government?

I hope this book will shed new light on aspects of colonial history at the local level which have perhaps been neglected. I would be pleased if the book arouses the interest especially of younger generations in the history of the colonial era which some tend to view as a blot on our history, perhaps best forgotten, despite the profound mutual impact of the colonial experience and the drama involved in the creation of all these new states.

Sources, acknowledgements and abbreviations

In writing this book I have relied on the official records held at the National Archives, on published government papers, private and published memoirs, journal articles and numerous books. I had nearly finished the book, very much assisted by Frank Heinlein's valuable publication 'British Government Policy and Decolonisation 1945-1963 (Scrutinising the Official Mind)', before I became aware of the compendium of British Documents on the End of Empire (BDEE) prepared with scholarly thoroughness by several specialists in the field. Nevertheless the volumes of the BDEE have been most helpful and have broadened the spectrum of official documents on which I have drawn. The British Library's newspaper depositary at Colindale and the Times-online were the source of most of the newspaper extracts. For the American perspective I used some official correspondence between the British and US governments, as well as the journal *Foreign Affairs*. Analogies with decolonization of French and other colonies have been drawn on the basis of published material in journals and newspapers. I made use of some of the material deposited with the erstwhile British Empire Oral History. Annex 1 is based on the UNDP's Human Development Report 2010; Annexes 2, 3 and 10 are based on material held by Rhodes House, Oxford. The conversion of sums of money to 2012 values was carried out with the advice of the Office of National Statistics using the Composite Consumer Prices Index, which has a long time series.

I am particularly grateful for the skilled help and assistance I received at the National Archives at Kew, the British Library at both St Pancras and Colindale, Rhodes House, the library of the School of Oriental and African Studies, the Office of National Statistics and for the always helpful staff of the Swindon and Cirencester Public Libraries and the Inter-Library Loan Service. At an early stage I benefited from a discussion with Anthony Kirk-Greene at Oxford. I am also grateful for permission to use photographs retained in the Colonial Photographic Archive made available to me by the National Archives.

Finally, I am deeply indebted to my wife, Patricia, for her patience support and understanding during the long time it took to complete this book.

Abbreviations used

ACB	African Continental Bank (Nigeria)
AG	Action Group (Nigeria)
AJUF	Anti-Japanese United Front
ANC	African National Congress
AUB	The American University of Beirut
BDEE	British Documents on the End of Empire
BPP	British Protected Person
CDC	Colonial Development Corporation
CDSC	Civil Defence and Supply Council (East Africa)
CD&W ACT	Colonial Development and Welfare Act, 1940, and successors
Cmnd	Abbreviation used, with a unique number in each case, to identify British Government policy papers
CO	Colonial Office
CPC	Colonial Policy Committee (of the British Cabinet)
CP(O)C	Colonial Policy (Officials) Committee
CPP	Convention People's Party (Gold Coast)
CRO	Commonwealth Relations Office
CROWN AGENTS	Crown Agents for Overseas Governments & Administrations
EACSO	East Africa Common Services Organization
EAHC	East Africa High Commission
EALF	East African Land Forces
EXCO	Executive Council
FCDC	Future Constitutional Development of the Colonies (HMG policy paper)
GOC	General Officer Commanding
HDI	Human Development Index (UNDP)
HMOCS	Her Majesty's Overseas Civil Service
HMG	His/Her Majesty's Government
IBRD	International Bank for Reconstruction and Development
ICS	Indian Civil Service
IG	Inspector General of Police (Nigeria)
IMF	International Monetary Fund
JAC	Joint Advisory Council (Bechuanaland)
JIC	Joint Intelligence Committee (of HMG)
KADU	Kenya African Democratic Union
KANU	Kenya African National Union
KAR	King's African Rifles

LEGCO	Legislative Council
MI5	The Security Service
MI6	The Secret Intelligence Service
NCNC	National Congress of Nigeria and the Cameroons
NLM	National Liberation Movement (Gold Coast/Ghana)
NPC	Northern People's Congress (Nigeria)
OAS	Organisation of African States
PAFMECA	Pan-African Freedom Movement of East and Central Africa
PAP	People's Action Party (Singapore)
PDCI	Parti Democratique de Cote d'Ivoire
PSC	Public Service Commission
RDA	Rassemblement Democratique Africain (West Africa)
SCAC	The Standing Closer Association Committee
SEAC	South-East Asia Command (Admiral Mountbatten)
SOE	Special Operations Executive
SPS	Sudan Political Service
SSA	Sub-Saharan Africa
TANU	Tanganyika African National Union
TEMO	Tanganyika Elected Members Organisation
UMNO	United Malays National Organisation
UN	United Nations
UNDP	United Nations Development Programme
UNIP	United National Independence Party
UTP	United Tanganyika Party
ZANC	Zambian African National Congress

The file numbers of British government papers held at the National Archives consist of one of the abbreviations given below plus a unique number and in some cases the number of the item in the file:

BW	British Council files
CAB	Cabinet Office files
CO	Colonial Office files
DO	Dominions Office files
FO	Foreign Office files
PREM	Prime Minister's Office files

Illustrations

Plates

All images courtesy of the National Archives

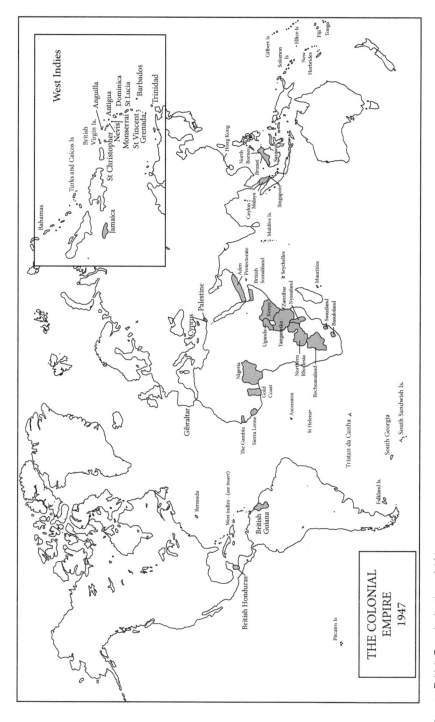

Map 1 British Decolonization of Africa.

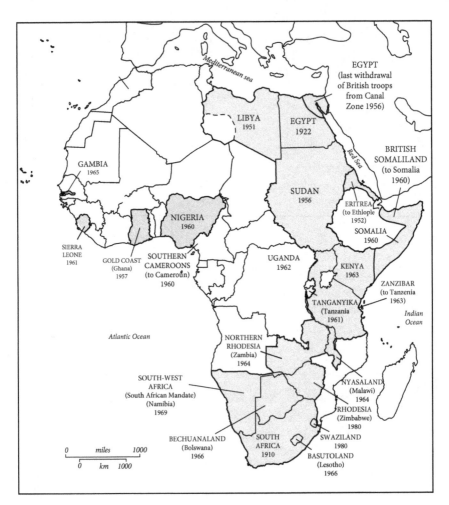

Map 2 British Dependencies in Africa with Dates of Independence.

Chapter 1

Historical background to decolonization

The British colonies of North America and the West Indies in the seventeenth and eighteenth centuries were established by a variety of people with a variety of motives. They were escaping from religious conflict, insecurity resulting from the civil war of 1640–45, poverty and unemployment and attracted by the demand for labour in the colonies. All of them in various ways acknowledged and depended upon the Crown. There were several reasons for this, including fear of other European colonial powers, such as Spain, Portugal, Holland and France, which forced colonies to identify with Britain; and dependence upon the person or company financing the colony – men such as Sir Walter Ralegh, Sir George Calvert (Lord Baltimore) and William Penn – and chartered companies such as the Hudson Bay Company and the New England Company (and later, for example, the Royal Niger Company or the New Zealand Company), which were established in Britain. When trade became possible, during an era of mercantilism, most goods were sold to British markets or to other British colonies. Later as Britain adopted free trade, multilateral trade became possible, but by then the habit and relationships of trade and finance with Britain were strongly established.

Authority in the colonies was exercised directly in the name of the Crown. Simple institutions and administrative arrangements were set up by royal decree or charter or by statute of the British Parliament. The governor was the representative of the Crown, and there was an appointed council and an elected legislature on a restricted franchise. The acts of the colonial legislatures were reviewed by the Privy Council in London, which also heard petitions and legal appeals. Where there was an indigenous people, the colonial government was expected to respect the local laws and practices, an approach endorsed by the Quebec Act of 1774. However, this did not prevent many conflicts with native peoples in North America, Australia, New Zealand and Africa.

Some of the chartered companies, like the Hudson's Bay Company, also exercised limited authority of a quasi-governmental nature in their depots in accordance with the provisions of their charters. There were many of these companies which were a convenient form for raising in London the capital required to establish and sustain the various colonies. Though relations with West Africa did not, for many years, involve settlement or colonization, trade in goods and slaves grew rapidly in the seventeenth century. British involvement in India also began in the seventeenth century following establishment of the East India Company (the Company) in 1600, which at first focussed entirely on the Company's commercial operations. The Company sought a relationship with the various states and rulers it encountered which would enable it to trade successfully. Initially these were a limited number of powerful states – the Ottomans in the West, the Safavids in Persia, the Mughals in India, the Thai king of Siam and the imperial authorities in China. The Company had to adapt to the conditions in the places in which it traded. The Company developed a large fleet of armed ships to facilitate its trade in the face of competition from Dutch and French interests. It took a long time for this trade to become significant – most of the seventeenth century – but by 1700 the Hooghly River near Calcutta had become the major port and entrepôt.

By 1730 the East India Company was being drawn, almost against its will, into the affairs of the various rulers and into matters of revenue and contract enforcement. This was a fundamentally different situation from that in North America and the West Indies at that time, as the Company was engaging with existing native authorities and systems of revenue in India, which were absent in America and the West Indies. As the Mughal Empire in India went into decline in the eighteenth century, especially after the Battle of Plassey in 1759, and power fragmented, Company officials became increasingly involved in the processes of government, of law enforcement and security with the local rulers. Sometimes there was a subsidiary but important objective of excluding French influence. A clear conflict of interest arose between the trading interest of the Company and its increasing involvement in the affairs of the government. The British government was forced to intervene and supervise the Company more closely, to put a stop to abuses. Pitt's East India Act of 1784 created a Board of Control which asserted a greater degree of government control over the Company. Subsequently, there began to grow up the system of administration which became familiar in India and was mirrored in many ways throughout the British colonial territories. The trial of Warren Hastings, the former governor general of Bengal, beginning in 1788, epitomized this re-examination of the Company's operations and served to put pressure on the Company to make itself more publicly accountable.

From another perspective, Britain's combative relationship with France in North America and India at that period served to reinforce the notion that the colonies should be largely self-sufficient financially and not become dependent on Britain, which was meeting the large expense of maintaining the Royal Navy. This policy of colonial self-sufficiency was to fundamentally distinguish British practice from, for example, the French approach to its colonies and form the backdrop to the relationship between a colony, with its governor and legislature, and the government in London, though in the notable case of the American colonies the policy eventually backfired and became an important contributory cause of the American War of Independence and the subsequent Declaration of Independence of the United States.

By and large colonies viewed themselves as being part of the British nation and were content to observe its laws and practices provided the freedom some of them sought to pursue particular religious or cultural practices was not threatened. By the end of the Seven Years War in 1759, French and Spanish forces had been largely expelled from the eastern part of North America, though France remained active in Canada and allied itself with some Indian tribes; and Spain was influential in the South West. Statesmen in London considered that as British forces were helping to defend the colonies in North America against attacks by French and Indian forces, the colonists ought to help meet the costs, and various taxes were proposed or levied – for example, the Quartering Act of 1765 required the colonial residents to provide quarters and provisions for British troops. The issue became one of Sovereignty and Authority. John Locke had contended that whereas a soldier might be commanded by his superior 'to march up to the mouth of a cannon', yet he could not be deprived of 'one penny of his money' without his consent. Pitt (Lord Chatham) and Burke argued that this consent ought to be obtained from the colonial assemblies in each colony or from an assembly representative of the colonies acting together. However, the Quartering Act, the Stamp Act of 1765 and the Tea Act of 1774 were measures taken by the British Parliament. With different ministers and a little more wisdom, the British government of the day could have avoided the clash which followed.

Over the next century, British involvement in India deepened and a strong administration grew up which kept the peace and enabled the economy to expand. As a prerequisite to the success of the policy, an expansion of modern education and training occurred such that by the time of independence in 1947 there was a considerable body of educated, trained and experienced Indians who had already assumed responsibility in the administration, the judicial system, technical organizations and in the police and the armed forces (see the following chapter). From the time of the debate in the 1820s and 1830s between the Orientalists and the Anglicists as to whether the Indian education system should be based on Oriental texts and languages or English texts and language, Indian schools and universities had generally adopted British curricula and education systems. The Cambridge Overseas Certificate and similar examinations conducted by examination boards in Britain became the qualifications sought by many Indian colleges and students. By the 1940s there were 140,000 students at 18 universities in India and the rapid growth of these institutions periodically led to graduate unemployment.

Ceylon (Sri Lanka) followed a similar evolution from 1802 onwards, though under the Colonial Office rather than the East India Company and the India Office. Following the First World War, Ceylonese had progressively moved into positions of responsibility in the Public Service so that by 1941 many senior positions in the administration, the medical services and accountancy were held entirely Ceylonese, as were most technical posts concerned with public works. The country became independent in 1948.

No African colony had reached anywhere near to this stage of development by the mid-1940s, nor indeed were they able to do so by the time of their own independence in the 1950s and 1960s. Their education systems in the 1940s were still principally at the primary level, were simple and staffed by teachers who in many cases had received little training themselves. As recently as 1945, an estimated 95 per cent of children at school in Africa attended schools run by the Christian missionary societies. By the 1920s these societies had themselves realized that the task was getting well beyond their resources and increasingly the colonial administrations and the home government began to take responsibility for education. In 1925 the Colonial Secretary issued a first strategy document on education in the African colonies. A commission visited Eastern Africa in 1937 to study the education system and to assess the need and timing for secondary- and tertiary-level education; a similar commission visited West Africa in 1943/4 and the Asquith Commission of 1943 looked at higher education in the colonies generally. Lord Hailey and Sir Philip Hartog, who had both contributed to the growth of the education system in India, gave evidence to these commissions. The dynamic of creating an education system from the bottom up is such that to get good teachers at one level, you need graduates from the level above; and to get those you need graduates from the level above that. It is a genuine case of chicken and egg; which comes first? In any event it cannot be done quickly.

Thus it was not until 1954 that the first university graduates were to emerge from Makerere College, situated in Uganda but serving all four East African territories. Gordon College in Khartoum became a university college in the late 1940s; the University of Ibadan in Nigeria produced its first thirty-two graduates in 1952, only eight years before independence. The university colleges in the Gold Coast (Ghana) and at Salisbury in Southern Rhodesia (Zimbabwe) also came into being in the late 1940s/early 1950s. For many specializations there was no alternative to studying in Britain especially, as well as in Canada and the United States. A very important decision was to insist that entrants to African universities should take the same level of entry examination as those used in Britain – anything less was considered to be inferior. British universities, especially the University of London, undertook to support the colonial colleges, as Durham had done with Codrington in the West Indies and Fourah Bay in Sierra Leone since the nineteenth century. An Inter-University Council for Higher Education Overseas was created in 1944 and run within the University of London.

All colonies also initiated a process of 'localizing' the Public Service prior to self-government and independence. This normally required the creation of a Public Service Commission (PSC) which influenced or decided on senior appointments and set criteria which sought both to maintain recruitment standards and to give priority to local over expatriate recruitment. This put pressure on those holding vacancies to seek suitable local recruits and on the local colleges to produce suitably qualified graduates. A PSC was established in India in 1886, sixty years before independence. The localization process began in a systematic manner in the Gold Coast (Ghana) in the 1920s, in the Sudan in 1944 and in Nigeria in 1950. Sir Sydney Phillipson, who had been involved in this activity in Ceylon, assisted the Nigerian government in establishing its localization programme in 1951/2 – only eight years before independence. In East Africa a review of the public services in 1947/8 concluded that it was premature to adopt a localization policy per se. The Royal Commission on East Africa of 1953/4 concluded that 'the East African territories were not yet in sight of being able to staff their public services entirely from their own resources'.

The localization policies and programmes were important and necessary. However, the timetable actually adopted for self-government of the colonial territories was in no case linked to or synchronized with the localization programmes. In all cases the timing of self-government was determined principally by local political factors and the British government's reaction to them. Except in the cases of India and Ceylon, self-government and independence came earlier than anyone expected so that no colonial territory had anything like a fully trained, experienced and 'localized' Public Service at the time of independence. The very rapid promotion of inadequately educated and inexperienced staff to take the place of departing British staff at independence, and their replacement by even less well-qualified staff, meant that the Public Service in these countries was almost bound to be weakened for years to come; and so it was.

The long process of creating a governing structure for India and Ceylon (Sri Lanka), over a period of 150 years, was expected to be followed in the other British colonies. In 1945, both British and colonial governments were still talking in terms of decades before self-government and independence. For various reasons, which I will try to describe, those decades were not available and the process was speeded up to the point where most colonies had become independent by the mid-1960s. There was insufficient time to complete the task of creating viable nation states. Instead of 150 years for these territories to acquire the experience and skills needed to govern a modern state, only twenty to thirty years were available. I shall look into the reasons for this. Arguably, these newly independent countries never had a chance.

In this book I propose to examine the ways in which decolonization occurred, especially in Africa: the policies adopted, the actual accomplishments and the stage reached by the various countries by the time they became independent.

I shall look at the state of the education system prior to independence and the supply of trained officials, ministers and technicians available at independence. We are so used to thinking of education, and for that matter medical services, as being functions of the state that it requires an effort of mind to recall that in most countries this became the case only quite recently. By and large, education and medical work, other than public health measures, were not thought of as a function of government, even in much of Europe, until the mid-nineteenth century. In Africa and many other colonies these services were provided by the missionary societies at a basic level until well into the twentieth century. In 1953/5 the East Africa Royal Commission concluded that 'the missions have in many places been so long established and have so identified themselves with African interests that they are regarded as African institutions'. Their impact has been fundamental and long-lasting, though the multiplicity of Christian churches has got in their way and some post-colonial theorists dispute their influence.

Initially the revenues of most colonial governments were in any case totally insufficient to meet the running costs of schools or colleges, or respond as required to the demand for more trained people. The priority for the limited available resources was law and order, followed by public infrastructure. The economic growth of the territories, which would in the future generate larger resources for the public sector, was viewed mainly as a function of the private sector. Some colonial loans raised in the London market had been guaranteed by the British government. But direct funding of the colonies by the British government really only began (very tentatively) with the Colonial Development Act of 1929 and was expanded somewhat with the Colonial Development and Welfare Act of 1940. It only became substantial with the CD&W Act of 1945. The focus of these measures initially was mainly on capital investment rather than recurrent costs. I shall look at the quality and staffing of public administrations, the way in which they grew and the extent to which there was a conscious policy of transferring them into local hands, over what time frame and with what results.

It is not enlightening in considering African history, as sometimes happens, to urge that things should have been done differently or at an earlier stage; that education should have been expanded immediately after the creation of the colonies; that the localization programmes should have been commenced earlier. We cannot ignore the state of the African territories when European powers first began to penetrate and lay claim to them. There were no schools; indeed unlike the situation in India, indigenous languages had not yet been written down, nor dictionaries created; communication between tribes was limited by the multiplicity of languages; while there were oral tribal traditions, in the absence of writing there was no written history. The wheel, the plough and draught animals were largely unknown. Superstition, witchcraft, human sacrifice and mutilation were practised by many people; and slavery was widespread. Among some tribes, seasonal warfare was the custom. Disease of humans and domestic animals was ubiquitous and sometimes devastating. Economies were simple with little trade and often only a precarious ability to supply food. Famine was common, especially in areas subject to drought, and together with the various diseases limited population growth. There were no nations as such, but tribes of various types and complexities, as had indeed been the case in all early societies.

In the absence of coherent state structures in Africa and elsewhere, Britain evolved the system of indirect rule – referred to as the Dual Mandate – under which it recognized and relied on the traditional leaders to help maintain law and order and the traditional social structures, and to provide support for implementing the objectives and policies of government. Where tribal leaders did not exist, for example, among the Ibo in Nigeria, the colonial administrators identified leading personalities on whom they could rely to fulfil these roles. The Colonial Service officers were initially assigned mainly to the principal tribal leaders to assist them in creating and operating coherent local governmental systems.

The impact of contact with the outside world was very disruptive of African society and in some places was stubbornly resisted. The colonial powers had either to persuade the tribal leaders to collaborate by entering into an agreement with them or to defeat them in battle. In practice, most colonies were established by treaty between the relevant tribal leaders and Britain. Once it had established control various notions and practices alien to Africans began to be employed and in time were adopted by Africans. They learnt to take advantage of what the colonial powers offered. The states we see today have an artificial appearance to them, but we should recall that most international boundaries in other continents were also formerly zones of conflict or disagreement and the fixing of African boundaries at the Congress of Berlin in 1885, while certainly peremptory and in some cases arbitrary, did at least serve to reduce conflict over boundaries in Africa through the subsequent period of colonial rule and beyond. The Congress of Berlin also endorsed the principle of 'furthering the moral and material well-being of the Native population', and gave a further boost to the suppression of slavery.

Difficulties occurred in all African countries where there was significant settlement by foreigners – largely by British/Europeans, Indians and Arabs. Unlike North America and Australia, where the indigenous populations were small and gradually submerged under successive waves of British and European immigration, settlement by Europeans in Africa was on a relatively small, local scale, except in South Africa and Algeria. On the other hand, the economic contribution of the settlers was large, as they brought with them technology, skills and marketing contacts, in addition to investment funds. They generated most of the public revenues in the early stages. Soon after its creation, the United Nations adopted the objective of creating multiracial societies in colonies where there were immigrant settlers. This approach repudiated the policy stance enunciated in the Devonshire policy in regard to East Africa. The Africans by and large repudiated the multiracial approach and were not keen to share control. Though understandable, it is rather tragic that multiracialism failed nearly everywhere it was attempted. The costs to the former colonies of such failure were often substantial.

The documents and papers used as source material for this book do not serve to convey in full the views of dissonant voices in regard to colonization and the growth of empires. They do nevertheless describe and articulate many arguments and debates occurring both within official circles and between colonial officials and the people of the colonial territories during the life of the colonies. Necessarily, colonial governments and the Colonial Office in London were engaged in highly practical work and decisions; most of the time they were under much pressure of time, and they often did not have the luxury of reflecting at leisure on matters arising. Post-colonial literature and approaches are by definition ex post facto and not necessarily better informed. In most cases there were no consequences for those articulating dissonant views in later years, a luxury not available to those, both African or non-African, engaged in the rapidly moving events of the late years of the colonial era. In any case, the purpose of this book is to describe and seek to understand the events themselves as seen through the eyes of those directly involved and the accomplishments, country by country, by the time of independence.

Chapter 2

The British government and colonial policy

In order to set the historical context of colonial policy, we should recall that Britain first acquired colonies in North America and the West Indies, starting in the early part of the seventeenth century. Initially the government itself had little involvement other than through the provision of the necessary charter, including a constitution providing for a governor, a nominated council and an elected House of Assembly, roughly comparable to King, Lords and Commons at home. It was intended that the assemblies in these colonies would confine themselves to voting taxes to meet the costs of their own government, and to making local by-laws. Otherwise they were expected in all important matters to obey and implement the laws of the Parliament in England. From the beginning the colonists also took with them their common law rights and began to create institutions of local government. It is also worth noting that these colonies required of the British government consideration of the relations between the native people of these colonies, the European settlers and the British government.

In 1660 the British government established a 'Committee of the Privy Council for the Plantations'. This committee continued in being in various forms until the loss of the North American colonies, when the needs were reconsidered. In 1801 a secretary of state was appointed, initially with responsibility for both war and the colonies. At the end of the Napoleonic Wars in 1815, this office became largely preoccupied with the colonies and the secretary of state's office became the Colonial Office. At that time the office was responsible for Canada, Newfoundland, Australia, New Zealand, Cape Colony in South Africa, Ceylon, Mauritius, Trinidad and the other West Indian islands, Malta, Sierra Leone, the Straights Settlements (which in due course became part of Malaya) and numerous other islands and small territories. In 1854 a secretary of state for war was appointed for the first time and from then until its abolition in 1966, the Colonial Office was concerned solely with the colonies. In addition to the colonies mentioned here, the Colonial Office later took responsibility for more than a dozen African territories and various colonies such as Aden, British Honduras and Guiana and numerous islands. Excluded from this list is Sudan, which was handled by the Foreign Office, for historical reasons, and Palestine Jordan and Iraq, which were League of Nations mandates for a few years. In 1925 a separate dominions office was set up to handle the affairs of the independent dominions – Canada, Australia, New Zealand, the Union of South Africa and Newfoundland.

We cannot avoid recognizing that the early years of British contact with Africa, before the creation of African colonies, were besmirched by the development of the slave trade whose purpose was to supply cheap labour to planters in the West Indian and American colonies and which cast a grim shadow forward until and beyond the abolition of slavery. The triangular trade, taking goods and money to West Africa to buy slaves and various goods; the delivery of the slaves to the West Indian and the American colonies; and the return voyage carrying sugar, molasses, rum and other tropical products to Britain was very profitable, but soon gave rise to the movement for abolition. Slavery had always been essentially forbidden in Britain subsequent to Magna Carta when anyone holding a person against their will could in principle be subject to a writ of Habeus Corpus issued in the King's name. Granville Sharpe argued that slavery was inconsistent with Habeus Corpus. Lord Mansfield's judgement of 1772 in a specific case essentially agreed. Abolition of the slave trade in the British Empire occurred in 1807 and for fifty years thereafter the Royal Navy patrolled the coast of Africa to prevent the continuing trade in slaves to Brazil, the United States and other countries. Ships were stationed at Freetown and Fernando Po, and later on in East Africa at Zanzibar and Mombasa.

India is not mentioned here on account of its scale and because it was handled separately within the British government. Britain began to trade with India by means of the East India Company (the Company) established in 1600. Initially the Company was merely concerned to see its trade prosper. It established 'factories' at various places as points of concentration for its trade. Initially Bombay (Mumbai) and Madras (Chennai) were the most important stations. Money and goods from Britain were used to finance local and regional trade and to purchase materials or goods for despatch to Britain. Later, Calcutta became a hub of this trade. As time went on and the Mughal Empire in India went into decline in the eighteenth century, especially after the Battle of Plassey in 1759, and power fragmented, Company officials became increasingly involved in the processes of government, of law enforcement and the security and affairs of the local rulers. This was a fundamentally different situation from that prevailing in North America and the West Indies at that time as the Company was engaging with existing native authorities and systems of revenue in India which were absent in North America, creating a clear conflict of interest between its trading activities and the responsibility it was assuming for government; and leading to abuses. The Regulating Act of 1773 was intended to address this situation by giving Parliament some control. This did not work very effectively and in Pitt's East India Act of 1784 a Board of Control was established to give Parliament direct control over the Company. Pitt said that his object was 'to give the Crown the power of guiding the politics of India, with as little means of corrupt influence as possible'.[1] By this act the British government became directly involved in the Government of India. The trial of Warren Hastings, the former governor general of Bengal, beginning in 1788, epitomized this re-examination of the Company's operations and activities and served to put pressure on the Company to make itself more publicly accountable. With the abolition of the Company in 1858, after the Mutiny, a Secretary of State for India was appointed.

In settled areas of India, 'Collectors' were appointed to carry out tax collection and revenue management. They were drawn into codification and enforcement of the tax laws, the cadastral surveying of land and, as a corollary, resistance to arbitrary taxation by the rulers. The judicial arm of the Indian service gradually expanded its jurisdiction accordingly and set standards which attracted those seeking justice. In the less settled areas, residents or political officers were appointed to influence the rulers in the direction of more predictable and enlightened government. Thus by the early decades of the nineteenth century, Company officials were engaged as much in running the country as in trading.

The subsequent reform and maturing of the Indian administration was marked by major reforms every decade or so – under Bentinck in the 1820s, Macaulay and Trevelyan in the 1830s and Dalhouse in the 1850s. Statesmen and administrators began to articulate a theory of government of dependencies and began to foresee their future evolution. Following the 1857 Mutiny and the abolition of the Company, there were further administrative and judicial reforms; additionally 1857 ought to be remembered as much because that was the year when the universities of Bombay, Madras and Calcutta were established, which were to have a profound impact on the future of the country. The Morley-Minto reforms of 1908 extended the role of representative institutions; the introduction of 'dyarchy' as part of the Montagu/Chelmsford reforms of 1917 devolved greater powers on provincial authorities and the 1935 Government of India Act established and delimited a federal structure between the state and the provinces creating a state capable of exercising full authority at independence. Over this period, the quality of Indian administration became a standard to be emulated to varying degrees in the other British dependencies. These measured and pragmatic steps towards self-government in India over a period of 150 years were the result both of proposals for such change on the part of British officials in India, demands on the part of native Indians and a policy adopted by successive British governments to the effect that such evolution should be permitted to happen, be anticipated and be gradually carried out. India became independent as the two states of India and Pakistan in 1947.

Colonial policy in Africa and elsewhere in the nineteenth century grew out of this long experience in North America, the West Indies and India. The goal, which at first was hardly articulated at all, was the gradual conferment of self-government. The essential point is that at an early stage Britain had an approach to decolonization, developed over many years. The eventual end of British control was not only accepted but set as a goal of British colonial policy.[2] The exchange of experience between India and the other colonies is brought out in the later chapters dealing with education, political and constitutional reform and the process of localization of the public service. This chapter seeks to describe the evolution of colonial policy within the British government itself from the 1920s onwards.

As in India and North America, trading companies played an important initial role in Africa – for example, the British South Africa Company, the Imperial British East Africa Company and the Royal Niger Company. They established links with African rulers, became familiar with the geography of unexplored and un-mapped areas, pushed their way into large, sparsely populated areas, created infrastructure, dug mines, bought, produced and processed agricultural produce such as sugar, rubber, cocoa, cotton, coffee and palm oil, generally promoted trade and settlement and, as a by-product, began to generate the revenues required by colonial governments to discharge their essential public services, especially the establishment of law and order. The activities of the trading companies were influential in bringing the territories affected into the larger world, which had hitherto in many cases passed them by. Abuses other than the slave trade occurred in the trading companies' relationships with Africans, as in India, and induced the British government gradually to assert greater control. Free trade reached its apogee towards the end of the nineteenth century, encouraging British investors to deploy their resources worldwide, including the colonies. The discovery of rich mineral deposits gave rise to very rapid economic development in some territories, and increased revenues to the colonial governments concerned, though such development was often highly localized. However, as Peter Burroughs points out in his 1978 article,[3]

Obviously an interrelationship existed between free trade and responsible government; commercial policy had always been reserved to imperial control and the constitutional privileges of the colonists had been settled independently of it, according to their ability to operate forms of government that political men in Britain accepted for themselves; the growth of free trade eliminated what had hitherto been a handy commercial weapon available to imperial policy.

The Colonial Office was quite content to see economic development of this kind, but in the light of constitutional developments taking place elsewhere, especially in India, and in the aftermath of the First World War and the creation of the League of Nations in 1919, British government policy gradually changed. From treating colonies as self-sufficient financially and being essentially non-interventionist, the Colonial Office became more assertive. It was alert to the need to ensure that the interests of the Africans were not prejudiced; in 1923 this objective was made explicit in respect of East Africa. Cmnd 1922 stated inter alia 'the interests of the African Natives must be paramount. ... HM government regard themselves as exercising a trust on behalf of the African population, and they are unable to delegate or share this trust'.

The notion of 'trust' in public policy had a long history. In his notable speech on India in 1783, Edmund Burke, reflecting earlier writings by John Locke, reminded Parliament that 'political power might only be exerted in the interest of the subjects' and that 'rights and privileges were untenable if they contradicted that trust'. He said the East India Company had been set up by Parliament as trustee and must act accordingly. In modern times the notion of 'trust' had emerged from the Round Table and was embodied in the Versailles Treaty.[4] On 30 July 1919, Leopold Amery said in the House of Commons, 'Britain is obliged to set up a new and more positive standard of our duty and obligation towards the peoples to whom this House is in a position of trustee'.[5] The notion of trust was increasingly accepted and used in public statements and documents. Apart from Cmnd 1922 in respect of East Africa referred to earlier, see also the constitutions of Southern Rhodesia (1923) and Northern Rhodesia (1924), respectively, though subsequent equivocations in implementation raised questions about their governments' willingness to adhere to the commitments made in their constitutions. Individual colonial officials used the term in describing their role and sometimes referred to certain actions or decisions of government as being 'breaches of trust'. Lord Lugard used the term in his 'Dual Mandate in Tropical Africa'.

A group of talented and forward-looking Colonial Office ministers modified colonial policy during the 1920s and the 1930s. They included Leopold Amery, secretary of state for the colonies from 1924 to 1929, together with W. Ormsby-Gore (later Lord Harlech), his parliamentary under-secretary and later also secretary of state from 1936 to 1938; Sir Philip Cunliffe-Lister (later Lord Swinton), secretary of state from 1931 to 1935. Ramsay MacDonald, then prime minister, was sympathetic to their initiatives. They all gave the Colonial Office new direction so that it increasingly gave policy recommendations to governors drawn from broad experience in all the colonies and became the means for mobilizing the resources of science and imperial policy in the service of the colonies. The Colonial Office appointed expert advisers in education (1925), medicine (1926), agriculture (1929) and later labour (1938) and economics (1939). Policy initiatives were advanced in various fields. The 1925 parliamentary statement on Education in British Tropical Africa (Cmnd 2374) is a case in point (see the following chapter).

The Colonial Development Act (CDA) of 1929 was enacted (very much in the teeth of Treasury opposition) on the initiative of Amery, Ormsby-Gore and Ramsay MacDonald to provide access to official funds (£1 million [2017 £60 m]) per annum for the supply of goods to the colonies which would, reciprocally, benefit the British economy. In 1932 Swinton initiated an economic survey of the colonial empire which was published in 1934. This was followed by the establishment of an Economic Department in the Colonial Office in 1935. In 1936 the Commission on Higher Education in East Africa reiterated the view that the notion of 'trusteeship' was the policy of HMG in its dependencies and that the period of trusteeship would in due course come to an end. By the end of the 1930s public opinion in Britain had become more engaged with the colonies, partly in the light of discontents and violence in the West Indies, which gave rise to the Royal Commission on the West Indies (Cmnd 6607). In 1938 the Colonial Office prepared a comprehensive report on the state of the colonies (Cmnd 5760).

Some important evolutionary changes also took place in the relationship between Britain, the dominions and colonies during the 1920s and 1930s which were to have long-term effects. We should look at these in greater detail. As a consequence of the First World War, the collapse of the Ottoman Empire and the Versailles Treaty, Britain became the mandated authority to administer Palestine, Jordan, Iraq, Tanganyika and parts of Cameroon and Togo. It accepted the notion of 'trust' in its relationship with the people of these territories. Article 22 of the Covenant of the League of Nations stated the dominant principle of the Covenant to be 'the well-being and development of the peoples not yet able to stand by themselves in the strenuous conditions of the modern world'. Ormsby-Gore pointed out that these principles were in practice identical with the principles by which HMG was guided in its general administration of the colonies. Importantly, in 1930 the Statute of Westminster was enacted, ending the notion of Imperial Unity and confirming that the dominions were in fact self-governing – the Imperial Parliament had no power over them except with their consent. This statute created the constitutional basis on which in the future the British Commonwealth was to grow.

In regard to economic relations, even before the First World War, colonial secretary Joseph Chamberlain had signalled Britain's intention to abandon free trade in favour of stronger economic links with the rest of the Empire. This move reflected both the growing economic power of Germany and the United States and a concern to stimulate trade and exchange within the British Empire. The Great Depression of the years 1929–33, when exports and the prices of primary commodities collapsed, provided a strong push towards protection internationally and in Britain there emerged the notion of an 'Empire Economic Union', very much encouraged by Leopold Amery who chaired the Executive Committee of the Union. The Union submitted economic papers to the Imperial Conference of September 1930. At the Ottawa Conference of 1932 Imperial

Preference was adopted by the countries attending. In practice, prior British commitments in regard to trade with Holland (1871) and France (1898), together with commitments made at St Germains (1918) and in the Congo Basin Treaty, as well as long-standing preferences for sugar producers in the West Indies, Fiji and Mauritius, limited the impact of Imperial Preference on commodities produced within the colonies. As D. J. Morgan pointed out[6] the dominions and the colonies at that time were debtors of Britain and, taken with the collapse of prices of all commodities, this explains the severity of the impact of the Depression on them. There was also dissatisfaction with the achievements under the CDA 1929 Act in stimulating the growth of the colonial economies, mainly because HMG could not initiate projects and the sums involved were insufficient to make a significant impact.

In the second half of the 1930s, relations with the totalitarian powers became a major source of strategic anxiety but, additionally, there was a growing feeling, articulated by among others, the governor of Nigeria, Sir Bernard Bourdillon, and by Malcolm MacDonald and Lord Dufferin, that more should be done to promote economic development in the colonies. Bourdillon argued that Britain had failed in its duty to promote the economic welfare of the people. Thus at this time of rising anxiety about relations with Germany, Italy and Japan, colonial matters also rose up the public agenda. Morgan has shown[7] that between July 1936 and February 1938, nineteen papers on colonial policy were discussed by the cabinet's foreign policy committee, twelve in 1937 alone. Debates in the House of Commons on colonial matters also proliferated – eleven in 1937 alone. German objections to the loss of its colonies as a consequence of the Versailles Treaty were a factor, but also influential was the economic and social impact of the Great Depression on the colonies leading to disturbances, especially in the West Indies and Northern Rhodesia, which stimulated the debate about economic development of the colonies. In the case of the West Indies a Royal Commission was appointed under Lord Moyne to study the causes of the disturbances and to make recommendations. The British Cabinet concluded before the commission had actually carried out its work that further expenditure on development in the West Indies was unavoidable.[8] The commission found 'deplorable standards of health and housing, and social conditions generally, among the working population in the West Indies' and numerous reasons to be dissatisfied with policy and its implementation. These findings reinforced the argument made by W. M. Macmillan in his book *Warning from the West Indies*.[9]

Colonial policy was formulated, like any other government policy, against the backdrop of the interests and aspirations of the British government as they were perceived from time to time. During the time we are considering here – that is, from the 1920s to the 1960s – the government had to give attention to various overarching strategic and other national interests. During the early 1930s it was preoccupied with the Great Depression, when demand for manufactured exports and primary products fell sharply, unemployment rose to catastrophic levels, protectionism became rife around the world and Sterling went off the Gold Standard. As mentioned earlier, in 1932 the British Empire adopted Imperial Preference which was of some benefit to the colonies. In the late 1930s the growing threat from Nazi Germany, Italy and Japan became the government's principal preoccupation. With the Second World War access to raw materials became a matter of life and death, which for those colonies which supplied goods to Britain resulted in the accumulation of what were referred to as 'Sterling Balances' held in London for the credit of the dependencies. Britain's relations with the United States were also a vital interest and American views of the dependent colonies became a matter of concern to British governments. In the post-war world, when Britain was economically weak, seeking to repair its productive capacity and put millions of men and women coming out of the armed services back into work, its ability to purchase materials from the colonies with Sterling was very valuable, as were the dollar earnings of the colonies as contributions to the Sterling Area. From the late 1940s the Cold War emerged as the major strategic preoccupation of the Western World. It then became a preoccupation of the Colonial Office and the government generally to prevent the seizure of power by communist-inspired groups in the colonies, notably in Malaya and British Guiana but also more generally.

As David Goldsworthy concluded, 'changing governmental assessments of how best to promote Britain's strategic and economic interest were major determinants of the character of colonial policy. Sometimes these assessments produced an impulse towards accelerating the rate of change ... at others, their main thrust was towards containment'.[10] He went on

> to mention these factors is not to assert that the policies and plans put together on a day-to-day basis by officials and ministers had no internal dynamic of their own, premised on notions of what colonial policy was, ought to be and ought to encompass – that is 'good government', 'development', 'constitutional evolution'. But it does recognize the complexity of causation and motivation impinging on policy formulation.[11]

Goldsworthy articulated another important perspective on the way in which colonial policy was formulated. Describing the attitude of the leaders of the Conservative Party in the 1950s he went on:

> Both Colonial Secretaries (Oliver Lyttleton and Alan Lennox-Boyd) sometimes found themselves rather in advance of general cabinet sentiment on the quintessential colonial policy issue of constitutional change. This was, in a sense, inherent in their very role as colonial secretary ... an ultimate demission of power was settled policy ... from time to time the colonial secretary had

necessarily to argue that now was the moment for a further instalment of devolution and it needs to be said that on all the occasions when such matters came up to cabinet level in the period 1951-59, the colonial secretary got his way ... the cabinet accepted that the judgement of the responsible minister had to be respected.[12]

An important influence on the handling of constitutional change in Africa was the experience of the Colonial Office in Ceylon (Sri Lanka) in the 1920s/30s. Elections to the Ceylonese Legislative Council (LegCo) were first held in 1910 though those elected were still in a minority. But by 1920, with the appointment of non-officials, a kind of 'semi-representative government' was arrived at, which led by 1924 to a genuine, elected representative government, with the franchise extended to both men and women over the age of twenty-one (actually earlier than in Britain in the case of women). However, the British government still retained considerable power and could overrule majority decisions on matters of 'paramount importance', a situation with a built-in contradiction. Furthermore, Ceylon was not a 'national' entity composed of a body of people of the same race, religion, language and tradition; but different communities – especially the Sinhalese and the Tamils. The Donoughmore Parliamentary Commission of 1927 sought to resolve the matter by making a decisive step from representative government towards responsible government, though not in the parliamentary sense – the governor still had reserved powers and Britain was still in control of foreign policy. However, Britain had taken the critical step of surrendering most executive powers – now British constraints could only be maintained by agreement with the Ceylonese.

In 1938 the new colonial secretary, Malcolm MacDonald, summarized the official British approach to colonial policy:

The great purpose of the British Empire is the gradual spread of freedom among all His Majesty's subjects in whatever part of the world they live. That spread of freedom is a slow evolutionary process. In some countries it is more rapid than in others. ... In the Dominions that process has been completed, it is finished. Inside the Colonial Empire the evolutionary process is going on all the time. In some countries, like Ceylon, the gaining of freedom has gone very far. In others it is necessarily a much slower process. It may take generations or even centuries, for the people in some parts of the Colonial Empire to achieve self-government. But it is a major part of our policy, even among the most backward peoples of Africa, to teach them and encourage them always to be able to stand a little more on their own feet.[13]

After the Munich crisis of September 1938, the Colonial Office hesitated for a while to seek funding for the proposed Colonial Development and Welfare Fund in view of the government's other critical preoccupations. However, in December 1938, the secretary of state decided to approach the Chancellor of the Exchequer for funding on grounds that 'It was an essential part of her defence policy that (Britain's) reputation as a colonial power should be unassailable ... and that it would be of no less importance over the next ten years than any other branch of policy'.

In the same year Lord Hailey produced his monumental African Survey.[14] Hailey had taken on this immense task on his retirement from the Indian Civil Service. The survey had its origin in a suggestion made by General Smuts in 1929 and taken up by Lord Lothian and the Royal Society for International Affairs. The Survey was funded by the Carnegie Corporation and the Rhodes Trustees. This seminal work contributed to and strengthened the intellectual basis for formulating colonial policy in Africa and the drafting of the White Paper on Colonial Development and Welfare (Cmnd 6175) issued in February 1940 by Malcolm MacDonald. The Colonial Development and Welfare Act, to provide £5 million per annum (2017 £269 m) for the development of the colonies, was enacted by Parliament in May 1940 just as the German Army was streaming over Northern France towards Dunkirk – a far-sighted decision at a time of peril for Britain. This measure was to provide regular and increasing government funds in the future for economic development of the colonies. Undoubtedly, the criticisms contained in the report of the West Indies Royal Commission, which was actually suppressed at the time by decision of the War Cabinet for reasons of national security, spurred the cabinet on to approve the CD&W Bill at such a critical moment in the life of the nation. Simultaneously, a Controller was appointed to oversee the government of the West Indies and ensure the reforms recommended by the Royal Commission were implemented. The first grant approved under the 1940 CD&W Act was for the West Indies.

Hailey's Survey drew attention to an aspect of colonial government structure and staffing which was by then already becoming pressing, namely the future role of the local and municipal councils which had grown up under the rubric of 'indirect rule', widely introduced in Africa and elsewhere. The system had grown up empirically as a result of negotiations with existing tribal authorities by hard-pressed and understaffed Colonial Officers; but also following Lord Lugard's publication of 'The Dual Mandate', which advocated 'indirect rule' as the best way to govern the colonies at that stage. However, even as the system was becoming normal and widely used, new influences were raising questions about the capacity of 'indirect rule' to deliver an adequate system and quality of government. These influences included the availability of increasing, though still small, numbers of citizens of the colonies themselves with the education and training required to begin to fill senior positions in the public service; the need for increasingly skilled and technically trained staff to fulfil roles in the technical departments; the growth of the cities and other areas of increasingly dense population where the obligations and constraints of tribal life were being eroded and new government structures were required; the need for different systems of land tenure to facilitate more predictable and productive systems of agriculture; in the towns, the provision of improved public utilities; and more broadly an increasing interest in policy, politics and forms of representation.

The African Survey stimulated discussion about these issues, discussions which were given impetus by the impact of war. Thus, immediately following the outbreak of war in 1939, we find the Colonial Office organizing discussions on the subject in London and writing to governors warning them to think about the danger of native authorities and legislative councils developing upon divergent lines. As a consequence of these considerations and exchanges, Lord Hailey was asked in late 1939 to visit Africa again to look in more detail at the issue, country by country, not with a view to making proposals but to produce a dispassionate consideration of the issue to assist in future decisions. As we shall see subsequently, his report was produced in 1942 and was to become an important forward-looking basis for consideration of government structures in the colonies.[15]

Thus by the time of the Second World War Britain was strongly committed to the promotion of constitutional and economic development of the colonies. Though the financial stringency of the war years inevitably was to delay some interventions, we will see in later chapters that the war did not stop serious work on colonial administration and policy and also stimulated political and social change in several colonies. Some significant individual steps were taken during the war. Notable among these were the Asquith Commission on Higher Education in the colonies, the Elliot Commission on Education in West Africa and constitutional changes in the Gold Coast and Nigeria. Within Britain, thinking about the colonies continued during the war. In Winston Churchill's wartime coalition government, the colonial secretary was always a member of the Conservative Party – for three years Colonel Oliver Stanley – and some of their statements are referred to in the following text. Within the Labour Party, much detailed thinking was also done, which became important when the Labour Party came to power after the 1945 post-war election.

In August 1941, before the United States entered the war, Prime Minister Winston Churchill met President Roosevelt in Placentia Bay, Newfoundland, and, inter alia, agreed to the text of the Atlantic Charter.[16] This conference was mainly concerned with bilateral relations between Britain and the United States, with the political strategy for the war and military collaboration. But the charter also included clauses addressing the future of the states occupied by the belligerents. The two countries pledged themselves, first to 'no aggrandisement, territorial or other', as a result of the war, second to 'no territorial changes that do not accord with the freely expressed wishes of the people concerned', and third Britain and the United States pledged themselves to 'respect the right of all peoples to choose the form of government under which they will live; and they wish to see sovereign rights and self-government restored to those who have been forcibly deprived of them'. It is clear from the context of the meeting and subsequent exchanges about it that these statements were directed at the countries occupied during the course of the war. However, Churchill became concerned that the wording might be interpreted to apply to the British and other dependencies and eight days after the statement was issued he noted in a minute to Leopold Amery, then secretary of state for India, that in his view the application of this particular pledge 'would only arise in such cases when transference of territory or sovereignty arose'. It was surely not intended, he wrote, 'that the natives of Nigeria or of East Africa could by a majority vote choose the form of government under which they live, or the Arabs by such a vote expel the Jews from Palestine'. It was 'evident', Churchill added, 'that prior obligations require to be considered and respected, and that circumstances alter cases'. Churchill was right to be concerned that the charter might be used for purposes which were not intended, and it was. Some of those living in the colonies chose to interpret the statement as applying to them also (see also[17]).

British ministers with an interest and responsibility for colonial policy during the war found it necessary from time to time to assert Britain's position vis-à-vis the United States government. Malcolm MacDonald spoke in Detroit in November 1942 stressing the progress made in the colonies in recent years; Lord Cranbourne, while briefly colonial secretary, also spoke in December 1942 to assert the prerequisites for the attainment of self-government 'the process of development I have tried to describe has no fixed limits. It is a continuing process, sometimes rapid, sometimes slow … I see the Colonial Empire moving along the same road (as the Dominions) … playing an ever-growing part in the British Commonwealth of free nations'; Colonel Oliver Stanley, when colonial secretary, expressed his view that the notion of 'trust' given so much prominence pre-war was somewhat static in connotation; he hoped to see a more dynamic interpretation of Britain's responsibilities for the colonies. Though self-government for the colonies seemed premature, in July 1943 Stanley stated in Parliament that the government was pledged 'to guide Colonial peoples along the road to self government within the framework of the British Empire'.[18] In November 1944, Stanley submitted a proposal to the War Cabinet, subsequently approved, that provision be made to increase the spending limit of the CD&W fund to £120 million (2017 £5,659 million) over ten years. In 1945, he set out again the policy objectives for the colonies when preparing for the San Francisco Conference.

We are pledged to guide the colonial people along the road to self government … we are pledged to build up their social and economic institutions, and we are pledged to develop their natural resources … it is up to us to see that circumstances as soon as possible justify political advances and to ensure that as soon as possible people are trained and equipped for Self-Government.

It is also interesting to note the attitude of Lord Swinton, a former colonial secretary, when he was the resident minister in West Africa during critical war years. In his paper on economic policy in West Africa of 24 February 1942, he urged

> pressing on with the things that matter to the common man – agricultural and industrial development, cooperative farming and marketing, health, education; staffing the services concerned with Africans as quickly as they can be trained; assigning to African local administrators more and more responsibility for these services. The more Africans are playing their part in the things that really matter, the less they will bother about constitutional reforms.[19]

The needs of war and the impetus to foster economic development after the war required of the Colonial Office some new thinking and expertise. Sydney Caine, CO, financial adviser, consulted Lord Keynes at the Treasury. Caine anticipated the need for a semi-commercial organization (such as the Colonial Development Corporation [CDC]) became to take the initiative in investment and was instrumental in creating the Colonial Economic Advisory Committee in October 1943 which was to become an important agency in considering priorities in the allocation of CD&W and other resources in the colonies.

In April 1944 Colonel Stanley addressed a letter to all officers administering the colonies summarizing the then current view of the Colonial Office on the nature of economic and social planning and the weight to be given to different sectors. He said, inter alia, 'Without belittling the need for welfare expenditure, the basic objective of sound development must be the improvement of productive and earning power … the ultimate objective being to place the dependency in a better position to support itself adequately.' He further emphasized the necessary partnership required between the state and the private sector and the need to think ahead to the transition from a wartime to a peacetime economy, which might take several years. The more active role envisaged for the state, of which the CD&W Act was emblematic, after many years of colonial self-sufficiency, is striking. Attached to Stanley's letter to the governors were copies of two Papers on Colonial Affairs – C.M. No 3, The Planning of Social and Economic Development in the colonial empire, and C.M. No 4, The Effects of Wartime Changes in Colonial Economic Structure and Organisation. The CDC was established in 1947 with borrowing powers of up to £110 million (2017 £4,092 million) to assist in providing capital for desirable projects of development and enterprise.

As mentioned earlier, Labour politicians and analysts also devoted much time and attention to colonial issues which had the advantage that the Labour Party was well prepared for the time in July 1945 when they found themselves in office. Rita Hinden, secretary of the Fabian Colonial Bureau 1940–50, articulated the dilemmas for socialists from the Fabian perspective:

> The fact is that, even before the entry of imperialist powers, the colonial territories were poor and economically backward. The act of withdrawal would not, of itself, open the gateways to prosperity. On the other hand – and this is how those who would accept the burdens of trusteeship have argued – if the imperial powers remained, at least for a time, and instead of exploiting these lands, acted as trustees to develop and enrich them for the sake of their own people, then the crushing problems of poverty and backwardness might be overcome. New nations might be built on the strength of the best we have to give. Only then would they be able, on their own, to stand erect and take their place in the modern world. If this 'sacred trust' were to be neglected, and socialists simply sloughed off their responsibilities, the result would only be a reversion to political barbarism and economic chaos. ... This is the train of thought, with all it implies of idealism, self-sacrifice, and service to others, which has placed many British socialists among the greatest Empire reformers.[20]

Thus it was that when Arthur Creech Jones became colonial secretary in 1946 it was with very clear ideas of his responsibility and with many plans for reform. His under-secretary, Andrew Cohen, was of a similar mind. There are many allusions to their statements and perspectives in the following chapters of this book. They are summarized in an official report issued in 1948 (Cmnd 7433) in which the Labour Party's approach and policy were reiterated: 'The central purpose of British colonial policy is simple. It is to guide the colonial territories to responsible government within the Commonwealth in conditions that ensure to the people concerned both a fair standard of living and freedom from oppression from any quarter.' This policy was in fact subscribed to by all three principal British political parties and it is fair to say that for a period of nearly ten years, there were no serious differences of policy between them. However, although Creech Jones was knowledgeable on colonial affairs and energized many aspects of the administration, with the appointment of many additional administrative and technical staff in the colonial service, he has been criticized for being slow to recognize the force of the emerging African nationalism and the impact this was likely to have on 'the slow work of nation-building' and the likely timing of political transfer. Half a century of 'indirect rule' had indeed left a residue of goodwill and understanding with the mass of Africans, but there was also an increasing perception that this could not support a modernizing state.

    A problem which did arise in the immediate post-war period was the morale of the colonial service. Many officers had been away from home and separated from their families since before the war began six years earlier; the number of serving officers had been reduced by war service; yet the number of new recruits would be low until men coming out of the armed forces had been recruited and trained, which would take a considerable time. (Recruitment in 1946 rose sharply to 1,673.) There was also increasing awareness, following Hailey's second tour of Africa, that colonial government reforms implemented at the central level during the war and in the immediate post-war period were only supported by weak local government institutions, which is where most of the District Officers and District Commissioners spent much of their time. 'Half a century of "indirect rule" had indeed left a residue of goodwill and understanding with the mass of Africans', but there was also an increasing perception that this could not support a modernizing state. Local government was therefore to be given wider powers, be made responsible for carrying out development programmes that would improve the living standards of the ordinary Africans, and be given the credit for their success.[21]

But this was not all. To engage the better-educated Africans, the existing central institution of colonial administration – the chief secretary's office – would have to be broken up into departments or groups of departments and 'unofficials' would gradually begin to take charge of these departments and begin to serve on the executive councils. Either by statute or by custom, the governor would begin to take the advice of the majority on the executive council. Since the unofficials 'would be persons commanding the confidence of the legislative council, the executive council would become increasingly responsible to the Legislature'. In due course, the members of ExCo would become ministers in a cabinet collectively responsible to LegCo, whose members would be chosen by the people through direct or indirect elections. The number of departments controlled by the governor would gradually decrease. The timing of this plan would depend upon two simultaneous processes: the Africanization of the public service and the development of the 'chain of representation', probably by a series of indirect elections, reaching from the lowest district through regional or provincial councils to the central legislature. Creating the 'chain of representation' would require the development of local government, which should in due course become more than a mere agency of the central authority. It must become the base on which would rest an efficient and democratic political system serving the people of a self-governing country and be truly responsible to them. Thus the whole process would require modification or evolution of the 'indirect rule' system at the local level and creation of functioning and accountable local governments.[22]

On the initiative of the Colonial Office, Andrew Cohen drafted two very similar statements of the policy on local government: a paper for the 1947 governor's conference and the Creech Jones despatch of 25 February 1947. The latter read in part 'In the development of an efficient and democratic system of local government, defined in the broadest possible sense, lies the best hope of success. I wish ... to emphasise the words efficient, democratic and local.' Not that these terms implied any sweeping change in the techniques or objectives of administration. But they seemed 'to contain the kernel of the whole matter; local because the system of government must be close to the common people and their problems, efficient because it must be capable of managing the local services in a way which will help to raise the standard of living and democratic because it must not only find a place for the growing class of educated men, in addition to the traditional rulers, but at the same time command the respect and support of the mass of the people'. In this document, Cohen considered again many of the arguments and issues raised by Hailey in 1939 in his meetings with Malcolm MacDonald following his Survey of Africa; and by G. F. Seel of the Colonial Office in a minute in which he considers the way in which indirect rule would be integrated into a parliamentary system of government in Africa. Since the outbreak of the war, increasing numbers of educated Africans had been brought into the central government machinery of several colonies – especially the Gold Coast and Nigeria. But this policy carried the danger that it might result in the creation of a class of professional African politicians absorbed in the activities of the centre and out of direct touch with the people themselves. The danger of dictatorships, tyrannizing the people instead of serving them, was all too obvious.[23]

In his July 1949 appearance before the Colonial Affairs subcommittee of the House of Commons Supply Committee, Creech Jones gave a review of the activities of the Colonial Office and the colonial service in the year 1948–9. He emphasized the extent to which powers were being devolved from the Colonial Office to colonial administrations:

While this House must exercise responsibility in regard to the shaping and development and application of policy in the territories overseas, we are at the same time devolving to those territories and their local governments a great deal of responsibility, and consequently they are in charge of the detailed administration of policy in their own countries. We cannot unduly interfere with that administration without to some extent weakening the extent of that devolution ... I would add that most of our Colonial Territories are going through a period of transition in regard to political, economic and social changes, and we cannot expect that those changes will be carried through without trouble, difficulty or disturbance. ... What is the broad purpose we have in mind in regard to colonial policy? ... Our effort is to bring stability, good order and mutual prosperity to the world; to do this with the cooperation of the colonial peoples by building up in the Colonial Territories' responsibility and the conditions of good living ... we wish the colonial peoples to appreciate the values which actuate us in our own affairs. ... In the years since the end of the war (1945), we have recruited for the administration and technical staffs of the Colonial Service no fewer than 5000 men and women ... In addition the Crown Agents have recruited about 3,500 ... Currently we need 163 doctors, 150 agriculturalists, 38 veterinary officers, 160 teachers and 170 engineers; and we are sometimes in despair as to when some of the work in the Colonies can go forward because of this shortage of the necessary skills and technical knowledge ... we are working hard to improve conditions of service and to fill these gaps. ... We are also doing everything possible to ... open new courses and provide new opportunities for study in this country ... for instance for labour officers, for cooperative officers, for police officers; ... I should like to express our sincere thanks to the universities in this country for the tremendous enthusiasm with which they have entered into the training of our cadets and members of the technical staffs.[24]

(It is of interest that the British representatives at the United Nations at this period had frequently to remind members of the anti-colonial lobby that HMG's ability to determine policy in the colonies was gradually being circumscribed by the progressive devolution of authority to the colonial governments themselves.)

In commenting on Creech Jones's testimony, a Labour member of the committee, Thomas Reid, remarked,

We have provided in the Colonies an administration unsurpassed anywhere for ability, integrity and humanitarian feelings. But in spite of that, a very small intelligentsia grows up. ... It is made self-conscious by education and in spite of all the benefits our Government bestows on these Colonies, those people become discontented and then move for self-government; further, whatever their ancestors' way of life may have been, they desire a Western standard of living. But the Western standard of living cannot be provided by a man working with a hoe or a buffalo ... science has to be applied ... which will require very large sums ... in spite of that, the intelligentsia demand self government straight away, regardless of their country's poverty. ... 'Ceylon has got self-government' they say; 'why should we not have it?'... Yet Ceylon is not as large as Ireland and has had 140 years to learn the arts of government; Nigeria alone is nearly as big as Europe; self government must be based on a stable and prosperous economy. ... It is only by investment of capital on a large scale and a radical change in the economic life of these countries that starvation can be avoided ... their birth rate is 40 per 1000; ours is 13 per 1000 ... the colonies are moving towards famine, starvation and epidemics ... education is the answer; but we have 50 million people in this country; there are 60 or more millions in the colonies; I ask the Committee, is it the intention that in addition to providing education for our own people, we should supplement the revenues of the colonies to educate 60 million people there as well; I do not think it can be done.[25]

Similar concerns were expressed elsewhere. The following year the journal *African Affairs* carried a short article by Earl De La Warr, who had served as under-secretary for the colonies and chaired the Commission on Higher Education in East Africa in the 1930s, and who was among those who worried that the pace of change in the colonies was becoming too rapid:

> Political developments that involved centuries of work, struggle and hard experience for this country are being compressed into a few years. Promises are being made and assurances of self-government are being given with an almost tragic lack of any sense of how little tradition or training for Government really exists amongst even the few educated Africans that there are. The policy may be right or wrong. It is certainly being pursued with great sincerity by quite a number of estimable people; but one cannot help wondering – have we really thought out where it is taking us all? Do we honestly think that, for some considerable time at any rate, Africa will be better developed and its millions of inhabitants be the happier under African rule than under British rule. Or do we say that the principle of self-government is of such intrinsic moral merit that in comparison with it, material development and happiness do not really matter?
>
> On my Commission in 1937, we reported in favour of concentration in the first instance on training men for the jobs that really needed to be done, and should be done by Africans, but that now have to be done by Europeans. We spoke especially of agricultural advisers, vets, doctors, elementary engineers, teachers and traders. We did so because we thought ... Africa had to solve quite a large number of severely practical problems before becoming distracted by politics. ... This may seem to be rather a material approach to our problems, but it is not a reactionary one.
>
> We have no right, having gone into Africa, having broken up the tribal life and beliefs of her people, having taught them Western values and having embarked on social and material developments that once started cannot be left uncontrolled; we have no right, I say, to just walk out. And what right have we in the name of self-government to hand millions of simple Africans over to the tender mercies of a small number of frequently aggressive-minded intelligentsia who are to a large extent as yet only half-educated.[26]

Similar points were made by Elspeth Huxley in her Foreign Affairs article of 1949, British Aims in Africa.[27]

> 'We do not always realise how much must be destroyed in order to rebuild, or how drastic that destruction must be to the human beings involved in it.

The customary way of life of the African ... is incompatible with westernism. It must go ... what will replace it? The strength of tribal life was discipline, loyalty, faith and the sense of community, of working together for common ends ... in the new generation now we see froth and nobody; it is easily led, ignorant yet arrogant, undisciplined and above all self-seeking and unstable ... their first need is to raise the pitifully low productivity of their peasant holdings and to arrest a hastening decline of soil fertility. The yield from a scientifically managed plot is four times that of the peasant holding; I have visited an experimental station where this has been demonstrated for 15 years and Africans can see the difference by looking over the fence; but they still follow the old ways – superstition, suspicion and conservatism are formidable; "tropical inertia" and lack of "technical discipline" prevail ... the process of achieving self-government was seen as one of gradual evolution, allowing time to learn from experience and to build up a healthy economy and a well-informed public opinion ... estimates of time required were shunned, but it was universally expected to be slow ... train the few who would then become leaders of the many. But the plan has gone wrong ... the time to be allowed has been drastically cut. People no longer think in centuries but in decades or even in single years. ... African politicians, new-hatched and raw, repeatedly told that self-government is to be "pressed on with" naturally start to demand it not for their children, but for themselves, here and now ... thus the elite cease to be co-operators but become sour and lose no chance to inject venom, aided and abetted by the British tradition of free speech'. ... The rising tempo of events has hastened matters ... Nigeria has had two constitutions in three years ... 'history has much to say of the results of handing over to a small minority of privileged persons all the powers of government before there is a body of citizens with critical judgement and independent views to keep them in check ... this is the road not of democracy but of tyranny'.

As Margery Perham pointed out at the time,

These fears are not groundless. There is no precedent for the sudden grant of the parliamentary franchise to a large, illiterate, tribal population, utterly remote from the political experience of the Western peoples. ... A perilously small fraction of the African people have any knowledge of the arts or sciences by which the modern welfare state they demand is conducted. With an electorate at once so ignorant, so expectant and so racially sensitive, and with none of the conditions present for the development of a party system, the invitation to demagogy seems certain to be accepted ... the aim should be to distribute rather than concentrate power. No hope of easy achievement should be cherished.

She quoted Roy Welensky, then leader of the Northern Rhodesian colonials, commenting on the Gold Coast election,

> The Government of the United Kingdom is not going to judge self-government for the colonies on the ability of the people to govern themselves: the whole thing will be a matter of political expediency. To the British Socialist Government, the ills of the colonies are dispelled by the provision of the ballot box and a trade union. This is a travesty of development.[28]

Another feature of the immediate post-war colonial policy and the earlier CD&W Acts, reflecting also the need for careful use and deployment of goods and resources engendered by the need for rationing, was the injection into the colonial economies of a degree of socialist-style planning. This is well described in the 1948 Foreign Affairs article ascribed to Britannicus.[29]

> The notion of financial self-sufficiency in the colonies came to an end with the Great Depression and the Second World War. With the 1929 Colonial Development Act and the 1940 CD&W Act, Britain began to take responsibility for the fostering of economic and social development, previously left mainly to the private sector. The 1945 expansion of the CD&W scheme from £5 million per annum (2017 £269 m) to £120 million (2017 £5,659 m) over ten years made it possible for territories to contemplate long-term and large-scale schemes of public works, social services, and agriculture, supplemented by their own locally-generated funds. Each colony prepared flexible and realistic programmes of expenditure, making use of local expertise, supplemented by specialists supplied by the Colonial Office. The Office created a Colonial Economic and Development Council to advise the Secretary of State on these plans and programmes and expanded the range of technical programmes to include for example geological and topographical surveys. Expertise was made available to encourage the development of varied resources, expansion of basic utilities and the creation of additional social capital such as schools and medical facilities.

Without dissenting from the policy objectives enunciated by ministers, Lord Hailey's report issued within the Colonial Office in 1942 on the state of Native Administrations in Africa, and published in 1951,[30] which analysed in great detail the strengths and weaknesses of these administrations, drew attention to the difficulties to be expected in superimposing on these relatively weak administrations the additional fundamental functions required for self-government on a national scale (see Annex 6). In particular:

(i)   There existed a major problem of personnel with sufficient training to take on higher-level duties in accordance with the institutions of self-government. He proposed appointment of African assistants to district officers so they could acquire greater experience of the work involved.

(ii) A system of self-government based on 'selected' or 'elected' representatives pre-supposed that the African public would be willing to modify the role of their local leaders or chiefs; experience in municipalities had not been encouraging in this respect as they did not seem to attract Africans of standing and municipalities showed little willingness to increase taxation to meet additional expenditure. Furthermore, representatives have to be held to account. How was this to be done?

(iii) The magisterial function of the Native Administrations would probably have to be assigned to other bodies once local administrations became involved in the quasi-political task of finding representatives.

(iv) The form of self-government proposed had not been set out in detail, nor the stages by which it was to be attained. How was indirect rule to be reconciled with the inevitable growth of a large, educated native population? He very much feared essential stages would be either rushed or omitted in order to meet political deadlines.

In order to address all these matters and attain the capability within local authorities required to sustain self-government, time was going to be needed. This was well understood by officials in the colonies and at the working level in the Colonial Office. In her Foreign Affairs article referred to earlier, Marjory Perham wrote: 'It is not a very bold speculation to believe that *the African colonies may become fully self-governing nation states by the end of the century – i.e. AD 2000*' (emphasis added). However, with the dynamic inserted into colonial policy as described earlier, and with the default American standpoint on colonies, it gradually became evident that neither the emerging political leaders in the colonies, nor the Trusteeship Committee of the UN, nor indeed the United States, were inclined to acquiesce in HMG's clear preference to allow such time. Nearly all British colonies were in fact to become independent by 1965.

A very difficult issue which cropped up in various ways in the various territories was the issue of the franchise. Who should be able to vote and should there be a simple franchise – one person, one vote; or a qualified franchise requiring landownership (freehold or tenancy), or a minimum income, or a minimum level of educational attainment, or a minimum residential qualification; or should there be separate franchises for different racial groups or reflecting the scale of contribution of groups to the nation? If we compare for a moment a semi-nomadic people scratching a living on the edge of the desert with a farmer producing crops for export; or those with a modern education with those with no formal education. In the end the only defensible franchise is one man or woman one vote. But introduced quickly this could threaten the social situation or status of all residents and traditional social structures. Most colonies found they had to go in the direction of a simple franchise in a step-by-step manner and by no means all attained a satisfactory outcome. These complexities are looked at further below in the country-by-country sections of Chapters 4 and 5.

The return to power of the Conservatives

In the election of 1951, the Labour Party lost power and the Conservative Party was returned to office under Winston Churchill. They remained in power until 1964. It was during this period that most of the colonies achieved first a state of self-government and then independence within the Commonwealth. As mentioned earlier, there was little difference in the policy objectives of the Conservative administration from those of the Labour administration. There was a greater propensity to expect more time to pass before the colonies achieved self-government, but the overall policy did not change. Most of what follows concerns implementation of the policy.

It is of interest that a committee assembled by the permanent under-secretary of the foreign office, which reported in June 1952, addressed itself in some depth to what it described as 'the problem of nationalism'. Reviewing the FO paper Sir Thomas Lloyd, permanent under-secretary of state at the Colonial Office, wrote:

> Nationalism takes two forms – destructive when based on xenophobia and fear of alien domination, and constructive when motivated by legitimate aspiration to self-government and a place in the comity of nations. It is the former type with which the paper is chiefly concerned, but it is the latter type which is more important in the colonies, even though it may be marred by feelings of race. Its existence both arises from and underlies our basic Colonial policy; namely, the guidance of the Colonial peoples to self-government within the Commonwealth.

He went on,

> In dealing with this situation it is necessary to realise that the outlook of settled European groups in the Colonies is not the same as the outlook of the U.K. public. These groups are themselves potentially nationalist and their nationalism necessarily conflicts with that of other racial groups in the territories concerned. The problem which faces us here is that of fusing the different nationalist demands into one.[31]

The general conclusion of the study was that

> there is nothing new in nationalism ... it is a logical stage in the continuing historical process by which nations of the world have been formed and in which Britain has played a leading role ... this process cannot be stopped .... Britain was bound to swim with this tide but we can hope to exert influence on the speed at which the tide runs.

Sir Ivor Jennings noted in his BBC talks in the 1950s (see Annex 2), 'The real problem in any country, and not least in a country which is moving towards self-government, is not to draft a Constitution or to make laws, but to find men and women capable of running the machinery of government'; and 'It is not always appreciated that what Britain is trying to do (in such countries) is to overcome the local difficulties in the way of "freedom" and "independence".' This is what Britain was engaged in during the rest of the colonial period. In many ways there were remarkable accomplishments. However, serious problems also occurred and there was precious little time to complete the task; in no case were there sufficient men and women 'capable of running the machinery of government'.

Seven matters especially preoccupied Oliver Lyttelton (later Lord Chandos), colonial secretary from 1951 to 1954 – the approach to self-government and independence of the Gold Coast (Ghana) and Nigeria; the communist-inspired insurrection in Malaya; the Mau Mau emergency in Kenya; the creation of the Central African Federation; the attempt by Jagan in British Guiana to bring a communist government to power and the organization of a conference on the possibility of creating a federation of the West Indies.[32] Lyttelton was concerned to support the governor of the Gold Coast in the phased approach to independence, which was achieved in 1957. This turned out to be perhaps the most deliberate handling of the pre-independence period of any African colony. There were three elections, with a steadily widening franchise, though within the short period of eight years. The Gold Coast had a number of experienced and able political leaders, lawyers and administrators and a satisfactory financial situation. More time would have been desirable for the territory to work out how to accommodate an Opposition to hold the government to account. But when the country became independent in 1957, it was reasonable to be modestly optimistic about its future. Lyttelton was also much involved at a key moment in 1954 when Nigeria was considering and adopting a new constitution arrived at with the benefit of wide consultation within the country (See Chapter 4).

Lyttelton had an important role in getting the right balance of military and civil/police response to the Malayan insurgency, which required a mature understanding of the nature of government and the experience and confidence to take difficult measures. It also fell to Lyttelton to handle the outbreak of Mau Mau terrorism in Kenya, which required draconian emergency measures to isolate the

Mau Mau gangs from the rest of the Kikuyu and the other Kenyan tribes they tried to subvert. Large forces had to be mobilized to catch or kill those still engaged in the revolt (see Chapter 4 for more details). Lyttelton also commissioned and set the terms of reference of the East Africa Royal Commission, which produced an excellent and comprehensive analysis of the social, economic and land issues facing Kenya, especially, which it was felt might have contributed to the outbreak of the Mau Mau rebellion. Lyttelton launched the Central African Federation in 1953, after many years of British government equivocation on the subject. It was a peculiar federation between a virtually self-governing colony, Southern Rhodesia, and two protectorates which remained under the Colonial Office. It could have worked if the settlers had made a serious effort to make it attractive to the Africans, but they didn't do enough for that purpose.[33] These matters are examined in greater detail in later chapters.

Lyttelton's successor from 1954 to 1959 was Alan Lennox-Boyd (later Lord Boyd), his under-secretary, who presided over significant steps towards self-government in many colonies and oversaw the writing of perhaps more constitutions for these nascent new states than any other single person. Lennox-Boyd had interested himself in imperial and colonial affairs since the 1920s and had accumulated a depth of knowledge on the subject which few equalled. He brought considerable authority and much personal charm to his duties and was much respected by many in the colonies. There are numerous references to his role in this book, especially in a country context. But I wish to refer to one country issue he faced which ramified across the whole region and into relations between Britain and other countries.

This concerned British Somaliland, a relatively small, poor country in the Horn of Africa.[34] The neighbouring Somalia, formerly Italian Somaliland, had become a Trust Territory of the United Nations in 1949, with Italy as the administrator. The UN took a decision to bring Somalia to independence in 1960. Britain did not set such dates for the independence of its colonies on grounds that there were too many uncertainties to be taken into account, and because a date fixed in this manner tended to spur a competition between aspirants of power, which was not helpful in achieving a good result. The issue for HMG had numerous facets:

Relations with Ethiopia, in which the United States had significant interests.

Relations with Somalia and with the Italian administrators and the UN.

Relations with other countries with Somali minorities (Kenya and French Somaliland, which the French government was keen to retain)

Policy with regard to other East African countries and Aden.

HMG began to think seriously about this matter at the time of Lord Lloyd's visit to British Somaliland in 1956 (see Chapter 4). In January 1957 a report[35] was produced by officials to provide a starting point for decision-making. By the end of 1958, HMG and the governor of British Somaliland had come to the conclusion that they could not postpone much longer a public statement of policy about the future of the country and the possibility of a merger with Somalia, as the Somalis themselves were agitating on the matter. HMG considered that negotiations could be arranged as soon as the Somali LegCo had an unofficial majority, envisaged for 1960. HMG sought the views of the US government, France and Italy; and also those of the governors of the East African colonies. The latter were most concerned as they felt, with good reason, that if British Somaliland could be given authority to negotiate with Somalia, despite the retarded state of development of both countries, the East African territories, which were in some ways well ahead in terms of education and training, could be destabilized and demand a similar freedom earlier than thought desirable. The Kenya government feared ramifications among its Somali citizens. The governor of Uganda was blunt in his comment to the Colonial Office about the lack of warning and the likelihood of heightened pressure for early independence. The governor of Aden said he would have preferred HMG not to make the statement.

The secretary of state made his statement of policy on this matter in Hargeisa in February 1959, which described the steps to be taken to prepare for further constitutional changes. A commission would be created to study all aspects of the matter with a view to an unofficial majority in the legislative council by the end of 1960. This would require all the steps leading to self-government to be compressed within a period of two years at a time when the number of well-educated Somalis available for public service was still tiny, and at a time when elsewhere policy was to spin out the process. Lennox-Boyd also outlined the future financial support Britain could provide. There were demonstrations by the Somali National League and pressure in regard to the traditional grazing lands which currently lay within Ethiopia under the Treaty of 1897. The US and Italian governments were fully supportive of the statement. The French government was opposed. The Ethiopian government was very sceptical and the foreign secretary argued for a major effort to be made to encourage direct talks between the Somalis and the Ethiopians, with a view to enhancing good relations between the two countries before HMG handed over to the merged state.[36] Certainly, British Somaliland, by British standards, was ill-equipped for self-government in 1960.

Lennox-Boyd's departure from office after the 1959 General Election was coloured by the Emergency in Nyasaland and the death of Mau Mau prisoners at the Hola Camp in Kenya, which are examined later in the chapter.[37] In retirement, Lennox-Boyd was formally interviewed at Oxford by several people engaged in writing on colonial affairs. A synopsis of his remarks to the interview panel is to be found in Annex 4.

The Afro-Asian conference at Bandoeng, Indonesia

This event came before the British cabinet because the Colonial Office and Foreign office disagreed on whether British colonies should be 'encouraged or discouraged' from attending the conference. The CO advocated discouragement on grounds that a conference of Asian prime ministers should not be seen as competent to pronounce on the affairs and destinies of Africa. The cabinet endorsed the foreign secretary's proposal that we should do nothing to encourage attendance but help with advice if asked; and invited the Commonwealth and Colonial Secretaries to take discrete steps to discourage any governments invited to attend.

Study of future constitutional development of the colonies (FCDC)

Soon after Harold Macmillan became British prime minister in 1957, he commissioned a study titled the 'Future Constitutional Development of the Colonies (FCDC)', divided into 'Political & Constitutional Prospects' and 'Economic & Financial Considerations'. This was completed in May–July 1957.[38] The study was not made available to Parliament but was drawn on for purposes of discussion with the US government at the 1957 Bermuda Conference; and with the French government, with whom the prime minister was keen to have understanding. The study both addressed the impact of the colonies on Britain and the future of the colonies themselves, and seems to have been a key document in developing Macmillan's thinking on the subject. By this time the Gold Coast was near to independence, as Ghana, and was not addressed in the study. The Rhodesias and Nyasaland were also omitted from the study.

At the Bermuda Conference, which was focussed mainly on strategic matters, the colonial issue was raised out of concern that the Sino-Soviet bloc was turning its attention to Tropical Africa. British ministers tried to persuade US policy-makers to overhaul their traditional attitude to and rhetoric in respect of 'colonialism' (see more detailed treatment in Chapter 6). In the preparatory talks for the conference, officials of the colonial and Foreign Offices prepared the note to be found at Annex 7, which is probably the best summary statement of Britain's colonial policy at that time and indicates why Britain was concerned by the way in which US officials sometimes spoke on colonial matters. Additionally, a joint UK/US study titled 'Communist Influence in Tropical Africa' was carried out just prior to the Bermuda Conference. At the general level, this study considered that there was 'conclusive evidence that the leaders of the Sino-Soviet Communist bloc have the long-term objective of dominating Tropical Africa. Although their ultimate aim was the Sovietization of the continent, their purpose in the present phase was to detach Tropical Africa from the West, both economically and politically'. The study concluded that the best counter to Soviet aims was to pursue systematically the constructive policy of leading dependencies *as rapidly as is practicable* towards stable self-government or independence in such a way that these governments are willing and able to preserve their political and economic ties with the West.

> The Sino-Soviet policy is likely to pursue the same direction as in Asia, towards the political neutrality inspired by Chou En-lai's Five Principles ... they must also be expected to offer markets for African products on favourable terms ... they may be expected, as in Asia, to work indirectly as well as directly ... through for example the strong French Communist Party and Communist-controlled trade unions.

The FCDC study itself contained some quite detailed country-by-country notes. The following notes do not attempt to indicate the full content of the study, but draw out a few points considered significant. The Colonial Balance of Payments with Britain was positive overall though negative in East Africa and the West Indies; the Sterling Area Assets of the Colonies were large, exceeding £1,350 million (2017 £30,944 million), but they were expected to decline as countries became independent. The paper also addressed the level of British financial assistance under CD&W which for the five-year period from 1955 amounted to about £86 million (2017 £1,971 million). Colonial loans to be raised in the London market were expected to amount to £30–35 million (2017 £688–802 million) per annum though some would have to be underwritten by the British government.

Colonial economic policy and development

This book does not attempt to address this large topic. However, we should take note of a few aspects which assist us in understanding the situation in which colonies found themselves during the years prior to independence. Historically, the search for primary commodities and markets for goods had been a stimulus for colonization in some places. Mineral development required railways, as did the bulk carriage of products such as groundnuts and grains. The railway development occurred quite early, financed privately or with government backed loans. Plantations were relatively few at that time – cotton in Sudan, cocoa in

West Africa and some trading companies also fostered peasant-like producers by providing credit and inputs.

There was a dramatic change during the Second World War when nearly all commodities were in demand. This led to intervention by the colonial governments to ensure attractive prices for commodity producers and the creation of publicly owned Marketing Boards and measures to boost the supply of labour and agricultural inputs. This increased demand continued after the war, especially at the time of the Korean War, which also coincided with the increased availability of CD&W funds. Over time, the marketing boards became controversial – they came to be viewed as a de facto fiscal mechanism at the expense of the primary producers. At a time of increased socialization of the economies of most colonial powers, the effect was to encourage in governments a much increased controlling role in the colonial economies. The economies of most colonies became quite heavily centralized. In due course there was a reaction. The Structural Adjustment Programmes supported by the IMF and the World Bank in the 1980s/90s were part of the response to this over-centralization of the economies of the former colonies.[39]

The Tanganyika decision

On 10 April 1959, the secretary of state, Alan Lennox-Boyd, submitted to the Cabinet's Colonial Policy Committee, chaired by the prime minister, a memorandum on Future Policy in East Africa, which had been prepared following discussions he had held with the governors of Kenya, Uganda, Tanganyika and the British resident in Zanzibar.[40] He recalled that up to the present time it has been possible to make notable constitutional advances in East Africa (such as generally increasing the degree of unofficial representation in the legislatures, associating unofficials – in some cases as ministers – with the executive work of government, introducing direct elections), while still maintaining official control. The existence at present of government majorities in the Executive and Legislative bodies of all four territories means that HMG still retained full control. But the time is approaching, certainly in Tanganyika and Uganda, when constitutional advance will start the process in earnest of tipping the balance of power in favour of unofficials. So long as the territories are not allowed to advance beyond the stage of self-government, HMG's control in vital matters (defence, external affairs, law and order and the internal security side of the work of the Provincial Administrations) will remain more or less unimpaired. But experience elsewhere suggests (a) that once the balance moves in favour of the unofficials, rapid progress to internal self-government is difficult to check; and (b) that thereafter it is not likely that the state of internal self-government itself can be maintained 'intact' for more than a very few years.

In its decision paper, the Committee noted that over the last 200 years we had tended to follow the same pattern in our Colonial policy, i.e. leading Colonial territories by gradual stages from a purely direct rule by British officials to a system of parliamentary democracy based on that practised in the UK. It was open to question whether this process of evolution was appropriate in present circumstances, and furthermore whether the UK's political system was necessarily the best form of democratic government for these territories and especially for those where difficult racial problems were likely to persist.

The Committee decided as follows:[41]

(i) Our policy should be one of step-by-step constitutional advance. Recent development in other countries had raised the question whether our form of parliamentary democracy was necessarily the best for these territories or whether some other form of democratic government might lead to their acquiring greater stability when they become independent of the UK. But the arguments were evenly balanced.

(ii) The secretary of state should bring before the committee the text of the governor of Tanganyika's proposed public statement at a subsequent meeting.

This was the moment when Lennox-Boyd could have used his influence to persuade the governor to find ways to stretch out the process longer, to give the Tanganyika more time to acquire the necessary experience in government. However, he was not able to take the issue further before he left office for personal reasons at the time of the 1959 General Election.

Iain McLeod[42]

Soon after this measured decision had been taken, and following the British election, Iain McLeod became colonial secretary. He had had no prior experience of colonial matters, never having visited any of the colonies. However, he had a brother, Rhoderick, who had served in Africa during the war and had taken up farming in Kenya afterwards. Rhoderick had gradually moved towards the liberal end of the political spectrum in Kenya, becoming a founder/member of the New Kenya Group led by Michael Blundell, just as McLeod was on the liberal wing of the Conservative Party in Britain. Undoubtedly this liberal bias was an important factor in McLeod's approach to colonial policy and issues.

McLeod was an exceptional minister and was much admired by the civil servants working with him. He set a tremendous pace of work, was clear-minded and decisive – at one time chairing five constitutional conferences in London simultaneously, in addition to his other ministerial duties in the cabinet and parliament. But forcing the pace, despite the progress described earlier, meant that he also stimulated opposition from the right wing of the Conservative Party and the cabinet and from some European political leaders in Africa who deplored his lack of patience and disagreed with his approach and timing. For some he became a threat.

It so happened that McLeod's appointment closely followed two grim events in African colonial history, the death in detention of eleven Mau Mau detainees at the Hola Camp in Kenya and the declaration by Governor Armitage of Nyasaland of a State of Emergency. The cause of this emergency was agitation against Nyasaland's membership of the Central African Federation. It resulted in some sixty-five deaths and the detention within Northern Rhodesia of over a thousand Nyasas – an event which gave rise to the appointment of a commission under Lord Devlin to study the causes of the agitation and the State of Emergency (see Chapter 4).

McLeod was deeply unhappy at these events and later stated, 'It became clear to me that we could no longer continue with the old methods of government in Africa and that meant inexorably a move towards independence.' This was a strange thing to say as by then Ghana was already independent and Nigeria about to become so. The countries of East Africa were making steady progress, but needed more time. However, McLeod had set out to be the last colonial secretary. He later wrote in the *Spectator*, 'It has been said that after I became colonial secretary there was a deliberate speeding up of the movement towards independence. I agree. There was. And in my view any other policy would have led to terrible bloodshed in Africa. This is the heart of the argument.' As significant was a remark he made regarding Africanization, land schemes and so on.

> One went ahead all the time with things like planning the Africanisation of the civil service, getting agreement from the Treasury and from the Cabinet, land schemes for Africans in the White Highlands and elsewhere, but these matters were less in one's own control than the question of constitutional advance and the calling of a constitutional conference. And therefore to some extent they lagged behind.

In other words he was keen to press ahead with the things he could do himself, and not be held back by the inevitably slower-moving process of giving Africans the chance to learn the arts of government and develop their economies. He lacked the perception that more time was needed.

McLeod convinced himself that in the absence of decisive steps towards self-government, there was a danger of serious bloodshed in East Africa, though the evidence for this is not persuasive. He decided that it was time for a breakthrough in Kenya to African majority rule, to end the Kenya emergency, and to support Governor Turnbull in Tanganyika in placing increasing responsibility on Julius Nyerere and his supporters. In fact, it was 'Max' Webber's suggestion in the Colonial Office that the Kenya constitutional conference (actually called by Lennox-Boyd before he stepped down) was the time to make a move towards majority African representation in the Kenya legislature. Additionally, Webber had been instrumental in persuading Lennox-Boyd that Governor Turnbull in Tanganyika was running ahead of the agreed timetable for the country and should be checked. This carefully nuanced approach, reflecting the situation on the ground in each territory, did not appeal to McLeod who was eager to press ahead everywhere. It remains puzzling that the measured approach followed throughout the 1950s was suddenly abandoned after the 1959 election. Lennox-Boyd reflected on this later and seems to have believed it was a combination of an impetuous McLeod and a change of mind on the part of Macmillan, one which the latter soon came to regret. (See Annex 4 which provides a synopsis of Lennox-Boyd's Oxford interviews).

An interesting indicator of McLeod's attitude became apparent when he learnt during the course of a meeting with Michael Blundell of Kenya that the Belgians had decided to leave the Congo in June 1960. According to Blundell, McLeod's only concern was that Britain would be the last colonial power to leave Africa rather than the first. Perhaps this was a jocular remark, but it did also match his general attitude. Forcing the pace was certainly necessary to achieve an outcome from some of the independence negotiations, but as an attitude to the timing question was unfortunate, with long-term malign consequences for the countries concerned.

McLeod became colonial secretary at a time when Prime minister Macmillan, following the FCDC study, was already interested in the future of colonial Africa. In May 1959, McLeod received a visit from Colonel David Sterling, a distinguished soldier who had lived in Central Africa since 1950 and founded the Capricorn Society, whose members were dedicated to the sharing of power between Africans and Europeans in Central Africa and the rejection of apartheid as practised in South Africa. Also in May 1959 as mentioned earlier he met Michael Blundell, the Kenya minister, who was visiting London, who reinforced his view that policy changes in Kenya were required. In the course of the censure debate on the Hola incident, the government had been strongly attacked by members of its own party, especially by Enoch Powell, giving yet more emphasis to the need for careful attention to colonial policy.

At the end of the day, McLeod's energy and pressure to get ahead almost certainly accelerated the timing of self-government and independence in several of the remaining African colonies. It has been argued since that he managed thereby to facilitate the end of British colonial rule without significant bloodshed, avoiding catastrophes such as in the Congo and the inter-communal violence in North Africa. But it is equally arguable that British policy was already proceeding satisfactorily according to a long-held and well-understood policy, that some countries had already achieved independence amicably and that more time was needed to see this policy through to completion in the other parts of Africa. It would have required careful negotiation to keep the goodwill of the rising political classes, but that had been possible elsewhere (not least in Nigeria) and there was no reason to be pessimistic about the future elsewhere.

Colonel David Sterling and Dr Nkrumah – Proposals for a declaration of principles in respect of Central Africa

During a meeting with McLeod, Colonel David Sterling advocated a rather vague idea for a declaration about the future of Central Africa. With McLeod's concurrence, Sterling passed his proposal to the prime minister; McLeod suggested to the prime minister that he should not reject the idea but modify it into something more practicable. The prime minister and Lord Home, the Commonwealth secretary, met Colonel Sterling on 11 June 1959. The note of the meeting is interesting in that it records the prime minister's approach to the difficult pending negotiations on the Central African situation:

> The Prime Minister thought it useful to keep the objectives in front of us rather than at this stage to try and say what we were going to do. Our objective was to induce the Europeans to accept something that was going to happen anyhow and to assure the Africans that progress would be made towards the inevitable. The timing depended entirely upon a proper situation having been achieved.

Sterling reiterated that he felt a declaration of Britain's objectives would nevertheless ease the necessary negotiations.

On 1 June 1959 Lord Home circulated a note of discussions he had had with Dr Nkrumah, the Ghanaian president, on colonialism in Africa. Visiting Ghana, Home had told Nkrumah that he felt the anti-colonial campaign in Ghana, associated with the African Congress, could lead to strained relations between Britain and Ghana and he wished to find ways to avoid this. Nkrumah, while expressing regret for excesses, said that he was bound to go on speaking in favour of two principles – first that the African colonies should become independent and second that elections should be based on one man one vote. Home argued that in some colonies there is justification for a qualified franchise as an interim measure to avoid bloodshed; Nkrumah agreed that measures are needed to avoid hatred and bloodshed and asked if a declaration of principles could be made, to which others could contribute. Home expressed his concern about the pressure on the timetable; to which Nkrumah responded that while he felt the pace should be quickened, 'in fact, though the Europeans might find it difficult to believe it, if the Africans were given power they wouldn't want to exercise it – that was the African mentality'. Home recorded that he found it almost impossible to decide whether Nkrumah was sincere in his desire to find a peaceful solution in East and Central Africa. Others had found him insincere, including recently Sir Arthur Lewis, the West Indian economist. Home wrote that 'Nkrumah sees himself as a Messiah sent to deliver Africa from bondage' – on his statue in Accra is written 'Seek ye first the political kingdom and the rest shall be added unto you' – a perversion of the Biblical quotation. Home concluded that the emergence of Nigeria as a full and independent nation would serve to limit Nkrumah's influence.

Home followed up this exchange with a draft of an outline of a declaration which could be made, along the lines of those suggested by both Sterling and Nkrumah, which was circulated to the prime minister and a few other members of the cabinet. So far as I could find out, the draft was never followed up. Was an opportunity missed, or was it redundant or already too late? Probably not, for by then the prime minister may well have already been thinking ahead to his visit to Africa at the end of the year during which he intended to address all these issues publicly.

Prime Minister Macmillan's visit to Africa

In January 1960, the British prime minister Harold Macmillan did an unusual thing. He embarked on a month-long visit to six countries in Africa – Ghana, Nigeria, Northern and Southern Rhodesia, Nyasaland and South Africa. He had previously visited the Asian members of the Commonwealth. Only Winston Churchill before him had made such extended visits abroad while prime minister. Macmillan wanted to meet those responsible for taking important decisions in those countries and make public statements to clarify British policies for all concerned. There had earlier been signs of greater interest on the part of the prime minister with the situation in the colonies; emblematic of this was his decision to assume the chairmanship of the Cabinet's Colonial Policy Committee in November 1958. The cabinet secretary, Sir Norman Brook, accompanied the prime minister to Africa and prepared detailed records of the visits and the prime minister's statements.[43]

Brook recorded,

In Africa the Prime Minister was concerned throughout with the problem of race relations – a problem of immense intellectual difficulty and one which can quickly arouse strong prejudice and bitter controversy. In the Federation he had to engage in delicate private discussions on matters which threatened to divide the Governments of the Federation and the United Kingdom – e.g., the substance and procedure of the Monckton Commission, the future prospects of the Federation and the security position in Nyasaland. And in South Africa he had to make plain to the Union Government the attitude of HMG on such difficult questions as racial policy and the future of the High Commission Territories. In these countries, therefore, he had difficult business to transact in his private discussions with ministers. But the problem of public reference to these controversial issues was even more difficult. Almost anything he said about them in public was likely to give offence in some quarters; and if he said nothing, he would be thought by public opinion at home to have failed in his duty. Finally there was the additional difficulty that, with the rising tide of national consciousness in Africa, the problem of race relations was uppermost in men's minds wherever he went – with the result that he was constantly obliged to turn aside questions about it which were pressed upon him in Ghana and Nigeria before he had even reached the countries where he was due to discuss it with those who bear a direct responsibility for finding practical solutions.

Brook went on:

Through all these difficulties, the Prime Minister contrived to steer a steady and consistent course. He did not shirk the controversial issues, but he stressed everywhere the difference between private advice and public criticism; and in his public pronouncements he followed the course of concentrating anything he had to say on these matters in a single policy speech in each country he visited. In those speeches he followed the line of re-stating the policy on the colonies and on racial questions which the British Government was applying in territories for which it was responsible and leaving the hearers to draw what conclusions they chose about his attitude towards the policies of other Governments. Brook felt that everywhere the Prime Minister spoke, he won respect for the policy and point of view of the British Government; even in the Union they seemed to command the assent of a substantial proportion of the European opinion.

The following notes highlight the matters which came up in the prime minister's private discussions in each individual country:

Ghana

One of the most important discussions held in Ghana concerned the contribution Ghana and Nigeria could make, as they were either independent, or near to it, in persuading Africans in the other colonies to be patient and constructive in the measures to be taken before self-government could be achieved. The prime minister urged Dr Nkrumah to help persuade the Africans in East and Central Africa that they had nothing to fear in terms of British policy or the ultimate goals; but that patience and flexibility of approach would be needed on the part of all concerned if differences of view on objectives or timing were to be bridged.

The second important discussion was with members of the Opposition parties. Dr Danquah and Messrs Dombo, Sodamtten and Appiah said that Ghana was already tending to become a one-party state and key institutions, such as the Electoral Boundary Commission, were being abolished. They felt that democracy would be more secure in Ghana if there were two parliamentary chambers (favoured by most Commonwealth countries); Dr Nkrumah had rejected this idea. They were concerned that Ghana might become a republic on the American pattern, but without the checks and balances built into the American constitution. In response the prime minister said that it had taken a long time to get the rule of law established in Britain and it needed a continual effort to keep the system in balance. It was up to the Opposition in Ghana to fight for their ideals by trying to win votes and to seek power in an honourable way.

(As we know, the fears of the Ghana Opposition were born out; by the following year all the careful safeguards for minorities built into the constitution had been swept away and the members of the parliamentary opposition were in prison. The Nkrumah government could then put anyone in prison without trial for five years. Ghana did become an autocracy, which was only ended when the Army overturned the government. However, that was not the end of the matter; it was to be years before Ghana regained a system of government by consent.)

Nigeria

The visit occurred in January 1960, only months prior to the agreed date of Nigerian independence. The Nigerian prime minister said that the government was concerned about its long, open frontiers and asked if Britain would come to Nigeria's assistance if it came under threat. The prime minister said he would have to consult his colleagues in London about this, but he expected that a defence agreement could be arrived at. Nigeria also expressed concern about Ghana, which seemed to attract all the extremists. The prime minister expressed the hope that the newly independent states of West Africa would try to avoid unilateral territorial expansion. Macmillan urged the new federal council of ministers to adopt the principle of collective responsibility in regard to their deliberations, as the council was the body, above all others, which had the responsibility of fostering national unity within the federal constitution. To this end he also urged that the council's decisions be accurately and promptly recorded so that at times of stress there was no ambiguity about the decisions taken. Ministers who had reservations about the record should bring them up equally promptly so that they did not fester unaddressed.

In a meeting with the leaders of the Opposition, the latter all paid tribute to the work of Sir Frederic Metcalf in his role as Speaker of the House of Representatives. They had learnt much from the manner in which he had conducted the debates in the House.

The governor general of Nigeria, Sir James Robertson, told the prime minister that he considered the country was becoming independent at least five years too early. There were plenty of Nigerians in the public service with adequate formal qualifications, but far too few with the experience required to take over the senior posts. Thus, for some years to come the administration would continue to depend on the retention of British officers. He expected to be asked to continue in post for a year after independence and he would recommend that Dr Azikiwe become governor general after he left.

The Federation of Rhodesia and Nyasaland

The federal ministers were concerned to know the views of the British government regarding the future of the federation; they felt the current uncertainty was prejudicing its future. Macmillan sought to allay these doubts by not only giving strong expressions of support for the idea of federation but also reaffirming the determination of the British government to fulfil its obligations to the Africans. He praised the concept of partnership. These discussions went well but the goodwill generated by them was somewhat marred by differences over the release of Dr Banda of Nyasaland, which could not be resolved in the time available. It was arranged that the Commonwealth secretary, Lord Home, would follow up the prime minister's visit to continue the discussions.

Macmillan devoted much effort to countering suspicions about the forthcoming Monckton Commission whose purpose it was to lay out the options for the future evolution of the federal relationship and the federal institutions. The sensible course was to get full value from the commission by ensuring that cogent evidence was put in support of the thesis of the United Federal Party; that the commission should be properly prepared in advance and that it should be enabled to lay out all the evidence and arguments for all to ponder. They should remember that one function of the commission was to make the arguments for the federal concept within the body politic in Britain, which was also divided on the matter, and which would have to legislate about it. Macmillan found it necessary to engage in detailed discussions about the modus operandi of the commission to reassure the federal and Southern Rhodesian ministers and to ensure that the approaches taken to the commission were harmonized before its arrival.

Sir Edgar Whitehead told the prime minister that when Southern Rhodesia had entered the federation, it thereby surrendered some of its separate powers under the 1923 constitution; and that the feeling was growing that if a good outcome was not arrived at soon, it was not impossible that Southern Rhodesia would itself withdraw from the federation. Macmillan found the Southern Rhodesian Africans had as yet scarcely any organized political machinery for the expression of their views.

In Northern Rhodesia, the prime minister met with the officials and politicians and, in particular, held a long meeting with members of the United Federal Party and the Central Africa Party. As articulated by Gondwe,

> He had found recently ... when touring his constituency ... that wherever he went, the Africans thought of Federation as synonymous with Salisbury and Sir Roy Welensky. They were indignant at the way things had gone. If Federation had an economic purpose, there need be no hurry to take irrevocable political steps. The fact that there appeared to be a rush in implementing Federation made the Africans even more suspicious.

Some argued that it had been a great mistake to put the federal capital in Salisbury; it would have been much better placed in Northern Rhodesia. Macmillan travelled widely in the country, and heard many expressions of resentment about the attitude of some Europeans, who took the view that it would be decades before there would be sufficient educated and trained Africans to fill senior and ministerial posts.

In Nyasaland, Macmillan met with the executive council, none of whom had been elected. He heard that secondary education had lagged in Nyasaland, that uncertainty about the future of the federation was making it difficult to recruit and retain expatriate officers. He encountered views which suggested that the prospects of Nyasaland remaining in the federation were low; opinion had been almost totally poisoned against it.

South Africa

Macmillan's visit to South Africa had a somewhat different purpose from the other visits. South Africa had been a Dominion within the Commonwealth since 1931 and there were and are many bonds of family and friendship between the European residents there and people in Britain. Two-thirds of foreign investment in South Africa at that time was of British origin. The government and people of

South Africa had shown great loyalty to the British cause in the two world wars and Prime Minister Macmillan was determined to give expression to the bonds which these deeds in war had built up. At the same time, he could not, and did not wish to, disguise or avoid the differences between the Union of South Africa and Britain in regard to the future of Africa and South Africa's role in it, nor to the tolerance required on the part of the Commonwealth members if South Africa was to continue as a member of it.

The speech he gave in Cape Town has proved to be a landmark event and a synopsis of it appears at Annex 7. It is often referred to as the 'Wind of Change' speech and this metaphor was indeed used in the course of the speech. But more significant for our purposes was the philosophical explanation Macmillan gave for the path Britain had taken in decolonization and was taking in bringing about that 'change' in the African countries for which it was responsible; and in regard to the responsibilities it still had for the colonies. In brief he re-emphasized the evolution of policy in accordance with the values espoused in British public life, in response to events in the international context and the situation in individual territories.

The end of the Central African Federation[44]

The Monckton Commission, whose full title was 'The Advisory Commission on the Review of the Constitution of Rhodesia and Nyasaland', assembled at Victoria Falls in mid-February 1960. It spent three months in the federation taking evidence. The report was to form the briefing and agenda for the Federal Review Conference, which had been planned since the creation of the federation in 1953, and which was to be held in London, commencing in December 1960. The commission's report, submitted to the British government in September 1960 was comprehensive but its impact was weakened by several Notes of Reservation and one Minority Report. Only eight of the commissioners signed the report without reservation. The main report drew attention to the significant economic advantages of federation, in which all three member countries shared in various ways, and which offered much for the future. But the commission could not avoid pointing to the 'widespread, sincere and long-standing hostility' of the Africans in Northern Rhodesia and Nyasaland to the federation.

The crucial conclusion was that the 'Federation cannot, in our view, be maintained in its present form'. After recommending far-reaching constitutional and legislative changes at both federal and territorial levels, the commissioners, who included some white Rhodesians, were obliged to acknowledge that the British government retained the right to consider requests for secession, and should announce its willingness to do so. The size of the bridge to be crossed in establishing relations of mutual trust between the communities involved is shown by the fact that Sir Roy Welensky and several other European participants had never met Kenneth Kaunda of Northern Rhodesia or Dr Banda of Nyasaland before they met at the Review Conference. They had not sought to understand their concerns or to negotiate with them. In the absence of a serious effort on the part of the European settlers to gain the confidence of the Africans in the federal idea, the notion withered and died in the face of the Africans' experiences of the past and fears for the future.

The Federal Review Conference was not successful and the proposed revisions of the constitution had to be postponed. There followed long and complex negotiations of new constitutions for Northern Rhodesia and Nyasaland which took much of 1961. Meanwhile Southern Rhodesia enacted significant changes to its own constitution which, among other things, increased African representation in LegCo, incorporated a Bill of Rights and created a Constitutional Court, measures which, if they had been enacted earlier, might have garnered greater African support for the federal idea.

John Hargreaves summarized the end of the federation as follows:

The Nyasaland emergency had not only ensured that Monckton's review could not be the simple technical exercise which Welensky desired; it restored the initiative in British policy-making to the Colonial Office, the department responsible for public order in the protectorates, as against those ministers who still cherished federation as a part of a grand design ... for Southern Africa. Macleod ... quickly reached the conclusion that restoring the confidence and collaboration of Africans in Nyasaland and Northern Rhodesia was the essential condition for maintaining the federation. For him, Banda was the essential partner, but to secure his release in the face of opposition from Governor Armitage, Sir Roy Welensky and some members of the British Cabinet he had to threaten resignation. ... Macleod argued that any long-term British commitment to suppress African nationalism was politically as well as morally unacceptable, and that negotiation with the Congress leaders was the only realistic course. ... He advised Banda and the new Governor of Nyasaland, Glyn-Jones, to expect an early conference. ... In Northern Rhodesia, the militant nationalists of the Zambian African National Congress (ZANC) regrouped as the United National Independence Party (UNIP) which, after Kaunda's release, became a highly organised mass party. Kaunda personally was deeply committed to non-violent methods, but there were signs of increasing violence latent within the country. ... In July and October 1962 conferences were held in London on the future constitutions of both Nyasaland and Northern Rhodesia, respectively, the outcome of which tended to prejudice the survival of the federation. These conferences were followed by the re-activated Federal Review Conference in December 1962, which was itself interrupted by further meetings on the constitutions of both Northern and Southern Rhodesia.

McLeod was then assigned to other duties by the prime minister and Mr R A Butler was persuaded to accept responsibility for Central African affairs. ... He attempted to discover from Banda and Kaunda whether these leaders would allow some looser relationships to succeed federation to avoid disrupting the existing administrative and economic relationships between the three countries. However, new elections in Southern Rhodesia brought Winston Field's Rhodesian Front to power in December 1962, thus ending any chance of a negotiated reform of the Federal Constitution. By March 1963, both Nyasaland (Malawi) and Northern Rhodesia (Zambia) were in a position to become independent on the typical basis of African majority rule. Both countries then faced the future alone with a very limited capacity to fulfil their countrymen's aspirations. Southern Rhodesia inherited the bulk of the federation's military, the University College and various other assets, including the switches which controlled the Kariba power station.

Chapter 3

Education in the colonies

It goes without saying that the government and administration of a modern state require educated, trained and experienced men and women to fulfil the diverse needs both of the state, the professions and the economy. This chapter traces the measures taken by the colonial authorities to address the growing educational needs prior to independence, especially from about 1920 onwards, and to assess the availability of suitably educated personnel at the time of independence.

In such a large field, I have sought to describe the main policies as they evolved, to describe some of the most important analyses of progress made, to illustrate some of the difficulties faced, to give some illustrative factual information and to indicate broadly the status of educational institutions at the time the various countries became independent. I make some remarks about the progress achieved in generating a cadre of men and women with the education required to take on the responsibility of running these newly independent countries.

The dynamic of the growth of an education system is such that it cannot be created quickly. Progress at the higher levels depends on the supply of students reaching those levels; progress at the lower levels depends on the supply of teachers from the higher levels. Truly, it is a chicken and egg dilemma. Furthermore, if the education system is expanded too fast, in advance of the growth of the state and the economy, unemployment can become widespread. This is what happened in India (see the following text). We are so used to thinking that education is a function of the state that we forget how recent that has been the case, at least in Britain. The first time the British government allocated budget funds for education was probably in 1835, and that was for schools in India. Prior to that, it was not considered to be a function of government, either in Britain or abroad, and schools were created and maintained by the churches, by charities and by the private sector. Universal primary education was only introduced in Britain by the Elementary Education Act of 1870, with funding by the state where necessary, but it was not achieved for two decades despite the fact that there already existed an education system which had grown up over centuries. Universal secondary education was made available in Britain in 1918 with responsibility given to local education authorities, but did not become compulsory until the Butler Education Act of 1944.

In Africa all education was provided by the Christian missions, private agencies or public subscription until well into the twentieth century. The first schools were established in West Africa more or less contemporaneously with the abolition of the slave trade by Britain in 1807. The missions continued to run and develop schools in Sierra Leone, the Gambia, the Gold Coast and Nigeria with the encouragement and some Grants-in-Aid provided by the local administrations throughout the nineteenth century. By 1900 there existed a well-educated minority in the Gold Coast. Education in Uganda was provided entirely by the missions from 1877 until 1924. The Gordon Memorial College in Khartoum was founded by public subscription in the Empire in 1902; a School of Medicine was opened in Sudan in 1924 largely with private funds. Necessarily the schools created by the missions, which were predominantly at the primary level, were limited by the availability of trained missionaries willing to work in Africa at a time when disease was ubiquitous and conditions of life poor, and by the financial resources of the missions. Despite these limitations, the accomplishments of the Christian missions in inculcating a desire for education and launching a basic system, especially of primary schools, over huge areas of Africa, and in the teeth of every conceivable difficulty, were extraordinary.

However, by the end of the first two decades of the twentieth century, the economies of the colonies and government revenues had grown to the point at which they could begin more systematically to allocate funds for education, and Departments of Education were being created in many colonies. By the end of the First World War in 1918, it was accepted that government had an important role and ought to pay more attention to it. There had been signs of this sense of responsibility earlier – as early as 1847 the Privy Council Office in London sent to the Colonial Office a considered statement on educational policy for Africans. But there were few British colonies or protectorates in Africa at that time. Furthermore, the sheer lack of budgetary resources in the early days of African colonization would have prevented much expenditure on education. The priority was establishing law and order and enabling investors to pursue their enterprises.

In 1921, the Phelps-Stokes charity of New York funded a review of the state of education in West Africa and followed this up with a review of the state of education in East, Central and Southern Africa in 1924. This was a collaborative exercise between the charity and those responsible for the education systems. For example, the 1924 Commission comprised two distinguished American educationists, including the chairman of the Commission, Dr Jones and Dr Dillard, the president of the Jeanes Fund, Dr Aggrey from the Gold Coast, Dr Williams of the Church Missionary Society in London, Dr Loram from the Union of South

Africa and Major Hans Fischer of the Colonial Office.[1] The Directors of Education in the various colonies participated in the Commission's activities during their visits. The Commission's reports contributed both a good description of the state of education at that time and made recommendations for future developments.

A number of key steps occurred about that time, in some cases stimulated by the Phelps-Stokes Commission. For example, an Education Ordinance was enacted in Kenya in 1924, providing for effective supervision and control of all schools by the Department of Education and for a Central Advisory Committee on Education. Similarly, a Department of Education was established in Uganda and Hussey, previously Inspector of Schools in the Sudan, was appointed director; this department was established at Makerere, which ultimately became the site of the first university in East Africa. In Tanganyika (Tanzania), which was a German colony until 1918, a new start had to be made with education after it became a Trust Territory of the League of Nations, with Britain as the administrator. The former director of Education in Zanzibar, Rivers-Smith, was appointed as director of the newly established Department of Education in 1920.

The Commission found the situation in Nyasaland (Malawi) to be different. There was no Department of Education, though the administration was making Grants-in-Aid to mission schools. The Commission was much impressed by the quality and extent of craft instruction being given which enabled many of the young men to travel abroad to South Africa and Rhodesia to work in the mines and elsewhere. The Director of Education in Southern Rhodesia (Zimbabwe) was making Grants-in-Aid to mission schools. Northern Rhodesia (Zambia) had no Department of Education, but it was under consideration and grants were being made to mission schools anyway. A proclamation made in Northern Rhodesia in 1921 gave considerable powers over education to local administrators. The director of Education in Basutoland (Lesotho) also had responsibility for education in Bechuanaland (Botswana).

In June 1923 the secretary of state for the Colonies in London established an Advisory Committee on Education in the Colonies, chaired by the under-secretary and including people with experience of India and Africa, and educational missionaries. In March 1925 the Committee recommended adoption of a Parliamentary Paper providing a statement of principles and policy to guide all those engaged in the expansion and improvement of education in Africa.[2] By then directors of Education had been appointed in most colonies and they appreciated the guidance provided. The paper reserved to government the general direction of education policy and the supervision of all educational institutions. It promoted cooperation between government and other educational agencies, including especially the Christian missions. It required the establishment of Advisory Boards of Education in every territory, including officials of the medical, agricultural and public works departments. It expected that education 'would be adapted to the mentality, aptitudes, occupations and traditions of the various peoples'. Its aim was to 'render the individual more efficient in his or her condition of life ... and contribute to advancement of the community as a whole'. Reflecting the importance of the missionary organizations in this sector, the paper stated that 'both in schools and training colleges, religious and moral instruction should be accorded an equal standing with secular subjects'. It stated that 'a policy which aims at the improvement of the condition of the people must be a primary concern of Government and one of the first charges on its revenues'.

It added that 'the status and conditions of service of the Education Department should be such as to attract the best available men, both British and African'. Voluntary organizations should be encouraged through Grants-in-Aid 'to schools which conform to the prescribed regulations and attain the necessary standards'. Attention was to be paid to the vernacular languages at the primary level and teachers 'should be adequate in numbers, qualifications and character, and should include women'. It was indispensable for teachers 'from time to time to be brought back for further periods of training'. Apprentices and learners were to be 'attached to every Government department and should as a rule sign a bond to complete their training for the prescribed period'. Technical training was to be provided in government agencies and workshops. With regard to the education of women and girls the paper stated, 'it is almost impossible to overstate the delicacy and difficulties of the problem'; in fact there is not one problem but many as the situation varies from tribe to tribe.

This paper was followed in 1930 by a Memorandum on Native Education Policy in East Africa which declared the objective to be 'the spread of education in the widest sense', for adults, for children and youths, not merely to raise the quality of clerical or handcraft activities, but to raise the standard of knowledge and intelligence of the whole community with a view to effecting a transformation in the daily lives of the people.[3]

In June 1932, the directors of Education in East Africa met in Zanzibar and discussed at some length the nature of the courses leading to matriculation by means of the University of London's School Examination.[4] They noted with satisfaction that it was intended to start at Makerere in January 1933 a course of this nature. The discussion of the directors addressed more broadly the question of University Education for Africans and made the following points:

(i)   The number of secondary schools in Africa is increasing and their standards are improving. Increasing numbers of Africans are meeting the requirements for admission to university, but most have to leave Africa to attend university.

(ii) Within British Africa, five institutions aim to provide educational facilities roughly up to a university standard, namely Fourah Bay in Sierra Leone, Achimota in the Gold Coast, Yaba in Nigeria, Makerere in Uganda and

Gordon College in Khartoum. Some of these facilities are for one or two faculties only.

(iii) These institutions will have to expand to be able to admit more students and broaden their course offerings. This is desirable on grounds of cost and because courses in British universities are simply not geared to the needs of students from Africa in some subjects.

(iv) It is therefore high priority to create more university-level course offerings at African institutions.

(v) There is much to be said for African colleges to be linked to British universities in the same way as the newer British universities have been linked with the older ones.

(vi) Women's education is retarded by the understandable reluctance of women to proceed overseas. For them African universities are essential.

Experience over the next ten years modified the position taken on girls' education in the 1925 paper, as African societies increasingly pressed for more such education and Dr Mary Blacklock pointed out in her 1936 paper on the Welfare of Women and Children in the Colonies that the policy was leading to a dangerous disequilibrium between the care of men and the neglect of women. Dr Blacklock's report[5] was accepted by the Advisory Committee and circulated by the secretary of state to all colonial governments. It was found that even in Muslim areas such as Zanzibar and Northern Nigeria there was an increasing demand for girls to be educated.

Another issue with which the Colonial Office grappled actively at this time was the question of the language of instruction for schools. Many vernaculars were not yet written down and some were only used very locally. Though it was recognized that the local vernacular must be used in the first stages of primary education, encouragement was given to the displacement of some vernaculars by dominant or union languages such as Swahili in East Africa and Hausa in Northern Nigeria. English was, however, regarded as a necessity in all intermediate, secondary or technical schools and 'if it is a necessity in these, its inculcation would have to commence in the higher standards of the elementary schools'. This policy was endorsed by a resolution of the Council of the International Institute of African Languages and Cultures.[6] This was not the end of the matter however and the issue continued to crop up in all countries and at all levels. There are further references to it in the chapter.

The 1925 policy paper was a major step which gave direction and stimulated the expansion of the educational system in nearly all dependencies. However, it was soon followed by the Great Depression of the 1930s, with the associated economic, fiscal and financial retrenchment. Thus progress was not as rapid as might have been hoped for. In some colonies financial resources and qualified staff were so few that very little was accomplished even by the late 1930s. In British Somaliland, for example, an Education Commission in 1936 found that the only schools in existence were Koranic schools and private institutions of a similar type, some of which received monetary aid from government. A proportion of the pupils reached a low standard of literacy in the Arabic language. The Somali language, which had not yet been written down, was to be used in the initial years of schooling, followed by Arabic. The Commission proposed to establish a Station school in one of the larger towns, to be followed by others later. These would aim to provide a sound elementary standard in reading and writing Arabic, arithmetic and geography, besides a knowledge of the Muslim religion. In due course a boarding school would be created for a few boys selected from the Station schools. A European Superintendent of Education was to be appointed. Teachers were for the time being to be trained in Sudan at the new Bakht a Ruda teacher training centre.[7]

However, in some other dependencies progress was more rapid. In northern Sudan, unusually for Africa, education was for the most part in the hands of the government. By 1938[8] there were intermediate schools in all the most important towns, a teacher training centre at Bakht a Ruda, Gordon College at the secondary level, the School of Medicine, a small School of Law and small schools in veterinary science, general science and arts were in the process of being created. In southern Sudan, education was provided by four missionary societies and comprised three intermediate schools, fifty-seven elementary schools and 600 substandard 'bush' schools. Secondary education for Southerners was also available at Gordon College in Khartoum. (NB. Intermediate schools were attended by children who had already had four years of schooling; Junior Secondary schools were the lower four years of secondary education; Senior Secondary schools were the equivalent of the Sixth form in England. There was debate about the value of the 4+4+4 years of education, as opposed to the 6+6 years pattern of schooling, but in many territories the former was adhered to for many years.)

The De La Warr Commission

In 1936 a commission was appointed by the secretary of state to look into the question of Higher Education in Eastern Africa.[9] It was chaired by Earl De La Warr, under-secretary of state at the Colonial Office, and had a good diversity of expertise among its members. It was asked:

1. To examine and report upon the organization and working of Makerere College and, so far as may be considered necessary, of the institutions

or other agencies for advanced vocational training connected with it in relation to:

(i) the society which they are intended to serve, and

(ii) the educational systems of the territories from the which the students are drawn

2. Having in mind the declared policy of His Majesty's Government to promote the establishment of facilities for higher education in East Africa, to make recommendations for the development and administrative control of Makerere College and its allied institutions to this end, within the limitations imposed by the ability of the Governments concerned to meet the cost, whether of endowment or annually recurrent charges.

3. In making such recommendations to consider:

(i) the effect of the development of the College upon the educational organization of the territories concerned:

(ii) the general interest and needs of the communities from which the students are, or may in the future, be drawn;

(iii) the educational needs of women.

The Commission reiterated the view that the notion of 'trusteeship' was the policy of HMG in its dependencies; and that the period of trusteeship would in due course come to an end. Thus education in Africa was not only inevitable, but right. It quoted the secretary of state:

"One of the essential aims not only of every university but of every school should be to preserve and enhance indigenous local tradition and culture. What mankind has done for himself is always better in the long run than what has been imposed upon him by others. We must develop local pride in achievement and this achievement if it is to last and contribute to the richness and variety of human experience must not be merely imitative. Education in effect must always aim at being creative.

The Commission made estimates of the numbers of college-educated and secondary school graduates required over the next ten years. On plausible assumptions it arrived at 1,255 college graduates and 4,364 secondary school graduates (girls and boys) for the four territories of Uganda, Kenya, Tanganyika and Zanzibar. It concluded that to meet this demand, 'large expansion and improvement will be required at all stages of education, primary, secondary and post secondary, for both boys and girls'. The Commission therefore took the view that the governments would be wise clearly to announce a policy offering facilities for training Africans in due course to full university standard and of giving them opportunities thereafter to rise in the Public Service to the highest responsibilities commensurate with their abilities. Though in due course the need for Europeans might decline, there was so much room for the expansion of all services that to talk of the replacement of anyone at that time would have been irrelevant. In allocating the limited resources it was essential to ensure some higher education took place as without it there would be no supply of trained secondary school teachers, doctors, scientists, lawyers and administrators. The provision of these skills would soon pay for itself by improved schooling, health, agricultural production and administration.

The Commission looked at the language issue, the scarcity of teaching materials in the numerous vernacular languages and the dire need for better trained teachers, at both the primary and the secondary level (many of the missionaries did not have teacher training qualifications); it endorsed the model adopted in the Native Administration Schools in Tanganyika which were closely associated, geographically and technically, with health and maternity work, afforestation and anti-erosion control measures, agricultural demonstration and training, and animal husbandry and veterinary work; and it gauged the time needed to get all the secondary schools up to an adequate standard to provide entry to university education at a good level. It considered that one of the weakest elements in the school system of East Africa was the backwardness of girls' education, despite the near universal demand for it. The Commission was keen to see girls' education brought up to the same standard as boys by the time they entered university. It insisted that candidates for Makerere when it became a university should be dealt with impartially, whether they came from mission or government schools.

The Commission considered the need for and availability of teachers from Britain for the secondary schools and university, and the pay and conditions required to attract them. It stressed the need to apply the same standards as were in use in Britain, that is, a degree or a teaching certificate for secondary school teachers and graduate degrees for university teachers. It pointed out that co-education was a new idea in Uganda and it encouraged the spread of co-education at primary level to get people used to the idea. It also considered how to provide for technical training which is always much more expensive than academic studies.

The Commission was very impressed by Makerere College which they found to be a most dynamic institution. Since its creation in 1921 it had reached the stage where some boys had secured exemption from the London Matriculation. The Commission formed a high opinion of both the schooling received by the boys and their general character. This progress had made the College a magnet for the other schools in East Africa. In 1938 the headmaster of Marlborough College in England became head of Makerere. Despite this progress, the College had not received funding at a level comparable with that allocated to Achimota College in the Gold Coast and Gordon College in Khartoum. The Commission recommended that the secondary education being given at Makerere should be continued but that a separate institution be created, to be named the Higher College of East Africa, with departments of Arts, Science, Agriculture, Medicine, Education, Veterinary Science and Engineering. In due course this would become the university college of East Africa. They proposed that an endowment be created for the College and that the governments should make available annual funds for recurrent costs. They thought the example of Achimota College, Gold Coast, in gaining recognition from London University in respect of its faculty of engineering was a helpful example of how to proceed in upgrading the various faculties to full university level.[10]

In a minority, dissenting report, John Murray, a member of the Commission, argued that the role proposed for government by the Commission was excessive and that the success achieved by the Protestant and Catholic missions in creating an indigenous education system in two generations should be perpetuated by limiting the role of government to provision of funds, establishment of standards and inspection.

The Commission's report was also criticized by the Roman Catholic Church, in particular for not acknowledging adequately the achievements of the missionaries, not making sufficient use of the missionaries' experience in preparing the report and not retaining the equal emphasis given in the 1925 Parliamentary Paper to religious and moral teaching with secular subjects.[11] From a reading of the report, it is difficult to agree with these criticisms. Arguably, what Murray and the Catholic Church had difficulty coming to terms with was the fact that government was inevitably becoming much more influential in setting policy for the education system, in which tax revenues, not merely the donations of the missions, were going to be deployed in creating and expanding this new system.

An African Survey

The publication in 1938 of *An African Survey*, by Lord Hailey was a major event in improving the understanding of the history, culture and the general situation of Africa. In respect of education, the Survey provided a description of the current educational situation in both British and non-British dependencies and addressed many of the issues referred to earlier.[12]

The Asquith Commission

In August 1943, the Colonial Secretary appointed another Commission on Higher Education in the Colonies more generally, under Mr Justice Asquith (the Asquith Commission.[13] The Commission consisted of seventeen persons with experience in the colonies and India, and with educational expertise. The Colonial Secretary invited cooperation from the vice-chancellors of all universities in Britain in contributing expertise and providing support for implementation of the recommendations which would emerge from the Commission. The Commission was

> to consider the principles which should guide the promotion of higher (post secondary) education, learning and research and the development of universities in the Colonies (read as including all forms of British dependency); and to explore the means whereby universities and other appropriate bodies in the United Kingdom may be able to cooperate with institutions of higher education in the Colonies in order to give effect to these principles.

A separate but related Commission (the Elliot Commission) was also appointed to study ways to enhance higher education specifically in West Africa, with some commissioners serving on both commissions. A further, separate enquiry was also to be made of the situation in the West Indies.

At that time there existed four universities in British dependencies administered by the Colonial Office, in addition to those in India. These were in Malta (dating from 1769), in Palestine (the Hebrew University in Jerusalem), in Ceylon (now Sri Lanka), which grew out of a university college founded in 1921 and medical schools of earlier vintage, and in Hong Kong, founded in 1921 and at that time under Japanese occupation. These territories were viewed by the Commission as being in a separate category from the colonies where there was no university-level college and it did not give much attention to them.

Elsewhere there existed a number of colleges which were either approaching university level or higher-level secondary schools. In the West Indies, Codrington dated from 1710 and was affiliated with Durham University; the Imperial College of Tropical Agriculture in Trinidad trained staff for the Colonial Agricultural Service. In West Africa Fourah Bay College in Sierra Leone, founded by the Church Missionary Society in 1827, had also been affiliated with Durham University since 1876. Prince of Wales College in Achimota, Gold Coast, which had been founded in 1924 as a secondary school, by the early 1940s had a 'university department' which prepared a few boys for London External examinations. In Nigeria the Hope Waddell Institute was founded in 1895 by a Presbyterian mission in Calabar as a secondary institute; several post-primary schools were created by the missions around Lagos, and in 1909 King's College, Lagos, was established by the government. Queen's College, Lagos, for girls was established in 1929, the Medical School in 1930 and the Yaba Higher College in 1934, focussed on technical and scientific training. In East Africa Makerere College, founded in 1921, was in the process of becoming a university college following the De

La Warr Commission's recommendations, and Gordon College in Khartoum in the Sudan which had been founded in 1902 similarly was also in the process of becoming a university college. In South Africa there was Fort Hare College, whose students emanating from both South Africa and the neighbouring British dependencies sat exams of the University of South Africa. In Malaya there was Raffles College, Singapore, opened in 1928 and the Medical and Dental Schools, which a separate Commission in 1939 had recommended should be merged to become a full university, though these colleges were still in 1943 occupied by the Japanese. It was anticipated that all these colleges could provide the nucleus of some of the new universities then envisaged.

In approaching their task, the main consideration in the minds of the Asquith commissioners was that the British government had entered upon a programme of social and economic development for the colonies through the CD&W scheme not merely out of a desire to fulfil their moral obligations to the colonial peoples but also designed to lead to the exercise of self-government by them. For this purpose, people trained at university level were a prerequisite. It was hoped that the universities would serve both to produce men and women with standards of public service and capable of providing leadership and to counteract the influence of local racial differences and sectional rivalries which would otherwise impede the formation of institutions on a national basis. Considerations of policy and finance alike made it essential that as large a proportion as possible of those entering the various professions be educated, trained and recruited locally. Thus universities were viewed as an inescapable corollary of any policy which aimed at the achievement of colonial self-government. No antithesis was seen between a liberal and a vocational education and indeed both practical and financial advantages were expected in combining them. Such centres of higher education would attract better teachers and motivate students.

The commissioners saw the need to produce not only well-trained people in the main specialist subjects but also the teachers required to train assistant-level staff in a wide array of fields and teachers to man the various levels of the education system. Thus almost all the colleges and universities would contribute to teacher training. They felt that whatever the long-term requirements, in the short term all colleges and universities should be residential in view of the diverse origin of the students who would come from all over the countries and be of different tribal and religious background. It would permit greater opportunity for adequate supervision of the students' health and well-being. It was also true that no other arrangement could contribute more effectively to a spirit of unity in a situation where communities were divided and had been separated not only by distance and other natural barriers to travel but also by racial, tribal or sectional differences. The universities should be open to all classes, without distinction of wealth and without discrimination on the ground of race, sex or creed. The entrance criteria should be academic achievement and personal suitability to profit by the courses offered. The entrance tests and scholarship system should be directed at securing the general principles already described. Lastly, the staff responsible for teaching the students and for the tutorial duties essential in a residential institution had to be adequate in number and of high quality.

The Commission addressed the difficulty of attracting and retaining good teachers, most of whom were expected to come initially from Britain. In the immediate aftermath of the Second World War, when millions of men and women would be coming out of the Armed Services, the demand for teachers in Britain at university or equivalent level was expected to be such that there would be a shortage. The situation was expected to change after a few years. The Commission also expressed the hope that when it came to proposing cooperation with new colleges and universities in the colonies, their recommendations would also be sympathetically considered by the authorities in the British Dominions (Canada, Australia, New Zealand and South Africa), and in India, as well as in Britain. They addressed the conditions of service and living, including the means for teachers from Britain to retain the option of reintegration into the home universities, the danger of academic isolation, the role of part-time teachers, the need for expatriation allowances, secondment of some staff and local recruitment. They also argued strongly that the universities could play a valuable role by becoming centres of local research, especially of the applied sciences in the initial years.

The Commission addressed the many issues involved in establishing universities such as the nature of the governing authority, the period of transition from college to full university status, the entrance requirements and the degree-giving possibilities and so on. The existence of the external degree system of London University was particularly helpful in adding flexibility to both students and institutions in the colonies. The Commission was conscious that the decisions taken in regard to the universities would have repercussions right down through the education system. In general, it was considered that the new universities should aim for the same standards of entry and graduation as in Britain though it was understood that it would take time to achieve that standard. It was also recognized that most students in colonial universities would need bursaries to cover their financial needs, though the Commission was also keen to see that scholarships awarded as a mark of academic distinction should be available from the beginning, to help raise academic standards. The Commission also addressed the situation of older students, a system of indenture for students sponsored by employers and the acute need for improved methods of teaching English as a second language up to the level required for study at university.

The Commission proposed the creation in Britain of an Inter-University Council for Higher Education in the Colonies. This body would be a cooperative organization of the universities in Britain charged with the task of cooperating with existing colonial universities and of fostering the development of new colleges in their advance to university status. It would have a particularly important task in mobilizing university teachers in Britain to go and work in the new colleges and universities. It would assist in placing students from the colonies in British universities. The Commission also recommended the creation of a separate body, parallel to a similar body then existing in Britain, to render advice on the allocation of British Government funds for the new universities. This became the Colonial University Grants Advisory Committee. The creation of these two bodies within London University was acceded to by the Senate of the University in May 1944. They were to play a crucial role to which reference will be made in this chapter.

Expenditure by Britain on these new universities was expected to come mainly from the Colonial Development and Welfare (CD&W) Fund and was expected to meet most of the capital costs, though some colonies (the Gold Coast, for example, which had accumulated substantial financial reserves) were expected to be able to meet some of the costs themselves. As far as possible, it was expected that recurrent costs would be met locally from fees, donations and colonial or local governments. There was support for the creation of an endowment for universities as soon as possible to help smooth their income, through recognition that this would take many years to have a significant impact.

On 5 September 1945, the Principal of Makerere College wrote a note on the implications of the Asquith Report for his college. He said this confirmed the conclusions of the De La Warr Commission of 1938, few of whose recommendations had been implemented due to the outbreak of the Second World War in 1939. After six years of war, there was still a wide gap between the present attainment of Makerere and the status of a university college. There was a need for strong recruitment of teachers; extension of the premises; and a rapid improvement and extension of secondary school education. There were currently only ten secondary schools in East Africa, with an average enrolment under 200 each. Five were in Uganda, two in Kenya and three in Tanganyika. With the exception of two schools in Tanganyika, all were mission schools and prepared the students for the Cambridge School Certificate. The numbers were grossly insufficient for the needs of the countries and the College. Makerere graduated only about twenty teachers each year, most of whom did not go into teaching, but sought entry to other professions, where prospects and pay seemed better.

The Elliot Commission

This commission focussed solely on the educational situation and needs in West Africa.[14,15] It described the multiplicity of languages in which children grew up; the impact of the Koranic schools in the Muslim areas and the accomplishments and limitations of the schools created by Christian missions; the strains and stresses caused by the interaction between the two great religions and the pagans living among them (Some Nigerian Emirs found to their consternation that there were pagan teachers working in some of the Koranic schools); the strikingly different position of women and girls in the societies along the coastal regions of West Africa and in the Muslim interior; the fact that at that time no education in West Africa was free, so many children were excluded by inability to pay their share; the fact that practically everyone living in West Africa was exposed to malaria, sleeping sickness and other debilitating diseases. They acknowledged that it was possible to contemplate higher levels of education in West Africa only as a consequence of the dedicated work of the Christian missions over many years, who had also implemented the first Africanization programmes as part of their creed.

The post-secondary schooling situation in 1945 was that while there were many accomplishments, there remained many challenges. At the post-secondary level, the small Fourah Bay College in Sierra Leone, which had been affiliated with Durham University for seventy years, drew its students from both Sierra Leone and other parts of West Africa. They normally numbered between twenty-five and forty students and followed a course leading to a pass BA degree of Durham and in some cases to the university's diploma of theology or education. The College had been maintained principally by the Church Missionary Society for nearly 120 years, in the face of great difficulties. In the Gold Coast, a 'University Department' was opened at Achimota school in 1929, preparing 100 or so students (including both boys and girls) mainly for the external examinations of London University in arts and sciences, including engineering which received some emphasis. The College was subsequently separated from the local secondary school. The European members of the staff worked as missionaries and were unpaid, though supported by the Church Missionary Society. In Nigeria, post-secondary education began with the opening of the Medical School in 1930 and the Higher College at Yaba in 1934, which accepted about forty-five students annually. Both of these colleges were financed by the Nigerian government. The students at Yaba studied for local qualifications in science, engineering, survey, agriculture, forestry and animal health and in general were expected to serve in the various government departments. Students could then go on to specialized schools in agriculture and forestry at Ibadan, medicine at Lagos hospital, surveying at Oyo and animal health at Vom.

The Commission struggled with the question how to allocate resources effectively at the post-secondary level – how to avoid diffusion of the limited available resources over too many institutions; how to avoid giving Nigeria an excessive share of resources on account of its size. In the end this dilemma could only be resolved after independence. The Commission endorsed the proposal to create a substantial university college at Ibadan with faculties of medicine, engineering, arts and general sciences, agriculture and forestry, animal health (pre-clinical, with clinical training and specialized subjects to continue at Vom) and teacher training. Some of the courses and students at Yaba were to constitute the nucleus of some of the new faculties at Ibadan, Yaba being focussed thereafter on diploma/specialized courses. They recommended that Social Sciences should be developed at Achimota with the assistance of the London School of Economics. General sciences, engineering, general arts would also be provided at Achimota, as well as an educational institute to serve the four British dependencies in West Africa. The Cocoa Research Institute being supported by a separate CD&W grant would also be sited near Achimota. The recommendations for Fourah Bay College were more limited by the smaller size of the populations of Sierra Leone and Gambia. There were difficulties of comparison with the larger-scale teaching facilities being built up in the Gold Coast and Nigeria and in nearby Dakar in French West Africa. Though there were clear advantages in focussing resources on a limited number of institutions to create universities of quality, the consequence was remoteness from these places of most of the people of the British dependencies. This problem could not be overcome within the time frame being used by the Commission.

The Commission recommended the creation of a West African Advisory Committee on Higher Education to watch over the various colleges and guide further development of them. The Commission also laid considerable emphasis on the creation of research programmes at the colleges focussed on the needs of West Africa.

Five members of the Commission prepared a minority report which disagreed with the recommendations about the proposed distribution of the new facilities which they considered would still diffuse the funds and teachers in a way which would delay expansion of the required higher-level education. This minority wanted to see a single university college for all of British West Africa, supplemented by territorial colleges in the three largest countries whose function it would be to teach up to the Sixth form level so as to become feeders to the university college, train teachers and social welfare workers and provide adult education and extra-mural studies. These proposals had similarities with proposals being made at that time for the West Indies, which did not survive independence either. They were quite rational but did not take adequate account of the local wish for autonomy.

The sociological impact of education

The sociological context for the introduction of modern education into the tribal societies of Africa was not conducive to education, whatever the demand for it. Most students had spent their childhood in environments in which Western learning and the effect of applied science on the material setting of everyday life had been practically non-existent, where many forms of action had been determined by custom and where, in the acquisition of new knowledge, verbal memory was apt to take the place of understanding. In this complex situation and however much British officials or non-officials might wish to push ahead, there was also recognition that modern education was going to engender considerable strains and stresses in the traditional, tribal societies. Britain had in many Indian states, and most of the rest of the colonial empire adopted, a system of 'indirect rule' whereby the traditional tribal or state authorities were retained and discharged local functions under the guidance of District Officers or Commissioners, within a system of government which gave final authority to mainly British officials at the national level. Most African tribal rulers in the 1920s and 1930s had had no formal education at all, so the appearance of school and college leavers within these societies was almost certain to lead to a challenge to the traditional authorities. Christian missions had begun teaching largely in the local vernacular and most dictionaries and grammars of these languages were prepared by missionaries. However, it was not long before they started teaching in English and, as in India (see the following text), demand on the part of the Africans was for an English curriculum to enable them to achieve higher-level qualifications. The exception was in the teaching of Muslim children. Knowledge of the Koran required knowledge of Arabic and reading and writing in Koranic schools were typically in Arabic. Sir Philip Hartog, a distinguished educator in India, who had been the first vice-chancellor of Chittagong University, testified to the Elliot Commission that in Bengal, where he taught for many years, Muslim children were almost always two or three years behind Hindu children on account of the heavy language component of the curriculum in Muslim schools (Arabic and often Persian and/or Hindi/Urdu, as well as Bengali). The consequences of this were manifested in the difficulty Muslim children often had in getting into college after school, especially in technical and scientific subjects, in which they generally had no grounding at all. The same phenomenon was facing Muslim communities in Africa, such as Sudan, Somaliland, Northern Nigeria and Gold Coast. For example, in the Northern Province of Sudan, most people spoke Nubian and this was the first language taught in schools. Arabic followed and English then was a third language to acquire before children could gain access to the modern world.

The situation in regard to girls and women was also complex. Girls typically married at about fifteen years of age and the social pressure to do so was strong. Yet a primary education system without women teachers was not feasible and if women were ever to climb further up the educational ladder, the societies would have to accept the notion that either they would not marry until later or would continue in schooling after marriage. This came easier in some societies than others. The administrators of mission schools sought to maintain celibacy among the students until after they left school, but were not always successful given the societal pressures on the students.

The testimony of Lord Hailey and Sir Philip Hartog to the Elliot Commission, based on their long experience in India, was fascinating and full of sage advice. In 1833, the British government declared that in making appointments in India there should be no discrimination on account of colour, race or religion and it looked forward to the large employment of Indians in the administration. The question then was whether children were to be educated in the classical languages of the East or in English. The majority of Indian authorities were in favour of English, with very long-term and profound consequences for India and, subsequently, for Pakistan and Bangladesh. The first modern universities in India were founded at Calcutta, Madras and Bombay in 1857, ninety years before the first universities in colonial Africa. By 1943, when Hailey and Hartog gave their testimony, there were eighteen universities in India with a total student body of 140,000. Lord Hailey stressed the profound change this availability of graduate entrants to the civil service had made, replacing a system of promotion from among the relatively poorly educated staff in the lower grades by appointment of new, better-qualified graduates. He warned the Commission that Africa faced the same difficulty. Until university graduates were available, promotion within the civil service would have to be from the less well-educated lower grades, tending to block access to graduates when they became available. He also said that the rapid expansion of university education in India had had two malign consequences – first, it had not been possible to maintain entry and graduation standards and second, because the economy had not expanded and modernized as quickly as the universities, there was much graduate unemployment. In some states, the failure rate at graduation exceeded 50 per cent, an enormous waste of resources, and as many as 70 per cent of graduates had inadequate employment, a cruel delusion to aspirant students and their families. Furthermore, he counselled that in India the balance between arts and scientific/technical teaching had been all wrong, mainly because the arts subjects are cheaper to provide. Against the 140,000 university students, there were only 21,000 students at professional and technical colleges, including 6,700 in law, 5,000 in medicine and only 2,100 in engineering. This was partly a consequence of a most pernicious feature which was the prevailing opinion that bookish studies were more profound and prestigious than scientific and practical subjects. He counselled the Elliot Commission to avoid that outcome in West Africa. Sir Philip also warned that it is not possible, even if the potential students and the necessary funds are available, which is rarely the case, to create a good university from scratch in less than fifteen to twenty years. Further he warned that during his educational career in India he had never seen so much waste of time and poor teaching than in the teaching of English. It was essential to devote resources and skilled teachers to working up good methods for English teaching, and insist on their use. Finally, he warned against allocating excessive resources for sending students to England or elsewhere except for teacher training and a few subjects not available locally.

Allocation of CD&W funds

An important moment in the development of university education in the colonies was the decision taken by the Colonial University Grants Advisory Committee in 1947 to allocate the £6 million (2017, £223 million) made available under the CD&W legislation to seven colonial universities, as follows:

Allocation of CD&W Funds for Colonial Universities 10 October 1947

West Africa	University College, Ibadan	
	University College, Gold Coast	£1,750,000 (2017 £65 m)
East Africa	Makerere College	£1,150,000 (2017 £43 m)
Mediterranean	University of Malta	£ 135,000 (2017 £5 m)
West Indies	Univ. College of the West Indies	£1,750,000 (2017 £65 m)
Far East	University of Malaya	
	University of Hong Kong	£ 950,000 (2017 £35 m)
General	London Univ. special services	£ 265,000 (2017 £10 m)
	Total	£6,000,000 (2017 £223 m)

Examination standards and curricula

When African schools, whether conducted by missions or governments, felt it desirable to enter their pupils for public examinations, they followed the obvious course of asking the examination boards in Britain to extend their work to Africa. The consequence initially was that the curriculum was in some subjects (e.g. botany) unsuitable for African schools and modifications were necessary to make them more suitable and relevant. To help deal with this matter, the Colonial Office took an initiative of great importance in the formation of a Joint Advisory Board for Examinations in the Colonies and Dependencies, with participation by the various boards, especially the London and Cambridge boards, as well as others offering their services in the colonies. In due course, examination boards began to appear in individual colonies, such as the Joint East African Examining Board in Medicine.

An important influence was the work of Dr Jeffery, director of the Institute of Education at London University, who visited West Africa in 1949. In recommending the creation of a West African Schools Examination Council he stressed the need for the Council to assure itself that all examinations held in the four British West African colonies, whether under the aegis of examining bodies in Britain or instituted in West Africa, whether qualifying or competitive, general or specialized, should in every case promote educational practice which, while it is of such a standard as to earn respect outside Africa, is African in character – such that children at school did not live in an artificial world of book-learning. He went on 'the adaptation of the curriculum is much more radical than is commonly supposed ... for there is hardly an examination paper set in any subject which does not refer to things outside the personal experience of the African child. This fosters the prevalent sense of unreality to which reference has already been made. There is the still deeper problem of developing secondary education which has its roots in African life and ways of thinking. This can be solved only by careful reconsideration of syllabuses and curricula in which the teaching profession in Africa must play a leading part ... I envisage the work of the Council in this connection as extensive and continuous.'

He also saw a need to 'promote the steady growth of a more informed educational outlook so that the educated man is not equated with the certificated man'. He further promulgated the view that 'the work of universities should be based fairly and squarely on the secondary schools in the same country' through allowing some schools to reach for higher standards similar to the best in Britain or elsewhere. The Advisory Committee on Education in the Colonies circulated Dr Jeffery's report to other colonies as they considered the reasoning applicable elsewhere.[16]

Employment of non-graduate teaching staff in the colonies

In September 1951, the Colonial Office sought the views of the various colonies on the employment of non-graduate teaching staff in view of the difficulty of filling all the necessary posts with graduates. The requirements of the education authorities for teaching staff in Britain, opportunities available in many other professions and the growing specialization of the teaching profession were reducing the availability of graduate teachers for the colonies. The responses varied from outright rejection of the suggestion to imaginative approaches to make use of all available skills, which would depend upon the experience and willingness of non-graduates to work as assistant teachers.[17]

Colonial Office annual report to Parliament 1948/9, educational achievements

The Colonial Office made annual reports to Parliament and it is instructive to note some of the points made in the report for 1948/9, as an example. The report referred to the work of the Inter-University Council for Higher Education in the Colonies, the appointment of a library adviser for colonial colleges and enactment of Legal Instruments securing the full autonomy of the universities and colleges established in the colonies, as recommended by Asquith. It reported the creation of the University of Malaya and the appointment of its first vice-chancellor; the first full session of the University of Ibadan under its new vice-chancellor, Dr Mellanby, and a CD&W grant of £1.5 million (2017 £55.8 million) for construction, the inauguration of the University of the Gold Coast, the commencement of medical teaching in the new University of the West Indies and so on.[18]

African education: A study of educational policy and practice in British Tropical Africa

This study was funded by the Nuffield Foundation and the Colonial Office and carried out in 1953. It was discussed at a well-attended conference held at Cambridge.

It was the first comprehensive survey of the state of education in Africa since the 1924 Phelps-Stokes review. There is an excellent and objective review of the report in African Affairs.[19] All the issues and controversies mentioned earlier reappear and a few conclusions of the report are worth noting:

- There was a difference of opinion between African and British participants at the conference in regard to the splitting of the school age, with Africans favouring the traditional 6+6 years, the British 4+4+4 years, because, they argued, permanent literacy could be achieved within four years; and the level of wastage is reduced by the shorter segments.

- The generally high level of wastage – long distances between schools and home, dark, damp dilapidated buildings, dull teaching and overcrowding, the poor quality of many teachers and so on.
- Technicians need eight years of schooling to reach an adequate standard.
- The need for schools to be both an instrument of stability and an instrument of change.
- The primary school system has been more successful in preparing a few for secondary schools than in preparing the many for life.
- The report praised the Gold Coast policy of encouraging individual good schools rather than the policy in Eastern Nigeria where education was so diluted that there were few growth points.
- The school curricula were still exposed to absolute subservience to the Cambridge School Certificate and to the examination fetish.
- The pressing requirement for adult education in order to reduce the tensions arising from uneducated parents and siblings.

Colonial Office management of the education programmes

The Colonial Office accumulated considerable expertise in the management of the diverse education programmes in the colonies. Among the many who contributed to this work, two stand out – Sir Christopher Cox and Freda Gwilliam. Cox, who had been the Dean of New College Oxford, was appointed the director of Education in Sudan in 1939. In due course he became the secretary of state's Education Adviser and continued in that post until the mid-1960s. His dynamic energy and positive approach, mixed with realism, were of great benefit to all colonies. Miss Gwilliam was for many years the secretary of state's Adviser on women's education, a task which she discharged essentially by extensive travel which gave her an unrivalled knowledge of what worked and what didn't; she was always welcomed by education administrators. The author of this book interacted with both of these people during their visits to the Aden Protectorate in the 1960s. In an article in African Affairs in April 1958, Miss Gwilliam summarized many of the difficulties faced by educational administrators in the colonies[20]:

For a long time now, our overall policy, however mixed its origins, has had self-government as its objective and fundamental to the policy as a nation-building agency has been education ... if political advance is the aspiration and economic development is the dynamic, then social development is needed to grease the wheels of change ... all these are a function of education ... yet only a half of the children in the colonies get to school, possibly for only one or two years ... all colonies want 100% attendance ... the challenge to education comes from all directions ... first finance and cost, which are always limiting ... is it the cost of what people want, or what people need or what people can afford ... second, nothing can make it less than ten years for a child to grow from the age of five to fifteen ... every year in this country (England) about a quarter of a million children get the General Certificate of Education (GCE); there are 50% more people in the African colonies than in England, and they graduate 10,000 children at GCE ... .Some say 'for goodness sake let every child have a chance' ... but the people we are going to look for are the people who are able to replace the Europeans who are working with them ... we have got to have a system of education which at every stage provides enough people from which to select for the next stage ... that is the dilemma of quantity versus quality.

Comments by country

This section gives a brief picture of the educational situation in individual dependent territories to illustrate the progress, policies and issues which arose. Necessarily, I have had to omit much.

Sudan

Expansion of the Sudanese education system continued throughout the period of the Second World War. In 1945 secondary education, which had been centralized at Gordon College, was moved to two new schools at Wadi Seidna and Hantub, Gordon College becoming a university college, which would grow into the principal university in the country. Both schools prepared boys, who numbered about 650, for the Cambridge School Certificate at the end of four years. The Teacher Training Institute of Education at Bakht a Ruda had broadened its teaching from primary teacher training to encompass both intermediate and secondary-level teacher training. Technical training was taking place at Omdurman Technical School and at the Atbara Technical School of Sudan Railways. In Southern Sudan, expenditure by both missions and government increased by creating two primary teacher training institutes and six further Station Schools. Recruitment of experienced teachers from Britain had improved, though by now half the teachers at Hantoub were Sudanese and three were Egyptian.

During 1947 a review led to the decision to open another boys secondary school near el Obaid in Kordofan and a girls secondary school in Omdurman. Recruitment of expatriate teachers continued to expand with twenty-one in 1946 and thirty in 1947, mainly from Britain. In addition, there were by then seventy-six Sudanese students in Britain and thirty-three in Egypt.[21]

The physical scale of Sudan, the largest country in Africa, and the wide dispersion of its people had always created difficulties in making education available. A World Bank Education project in 1975 (twenty years later), which was accompanied by an ILO/UNDP study of Growth, Employment and Equity, noted that the level of illiteracy in the country as a whole was still 85 per cent among adults, while in the rural areas it was as high as 95 per cent. In Southern Sudan only about 10 per cent of children were in primary education compared with 47 per cent in the rest of the country where all the cities were situated. The author of this book recalls at that time seeing children pouring out of school long after dark near Sennar in Blue Nile Province, where obviously double shift teaching was taking place to make up for lack of school facilities. On the other hand the Bank project found that post-secondary enrolment was relatively high compared with other developing countries, though less than 5 per cent of children in secondary education were receiving technical or vocational training. In sum there were major imbalances in the educational structure between rural and urban populations, between academic/literacy and technical/vocational needs, and there was a need for greater attention to adult literacy.

Sierra Leone

As elsewhere in Africa, the earliest schools were created by the missionaries, but there were significant differences. As mentioned earlier, an early start was made in education in the colony of Sierra Leone, linked to the return of manumitted, de-tribalized slaves who fled the United States during the War of Independence, following Lord Mansfield's judgement of 1772; and of men of slave origin discharged from the British army and navy at the end of the War. These 'Creoles' spoke Creole or Pidgin at home and English at school. They lived mainly in Freetown and their children were expected to go to school. The significance of Freetown as a base of the Royal Navy during the fifty years spent in putting a stop to the slave trade meant that the colony advanced constitutionally earlier than elsewhere in West Africa. In addition, grammar schools were opened for boys in 1845 and for girls in 1849. Elsewhere in the colony, but outside Freetown, the inhabitants were indigenous Africans with representatives of the tribal chiefs among them. In the protectorate, which accounted for more than 95 per cent of the total population, the inhabitants were indigenous Africans, living in their tribal units and speaking the local vernaculars, principally various forms of Mende. When it came to education, those living in the colony used English from the beginning; those in the protectorate used Mende in most primary schools and only began to use English as they moved up the educational pyramid. Over time, the early progress achieved in Freetown was somewhat diluted by the larger population in the protectorate and by resource constraints. Thus the progress made and the standards reached were very variable.[22]

Gold Coast/Ghana

Participation rates of children in the schools grew rapidly in the coastal province of the Gold Coast, and along the trade routes towards the interior. When the Department of Education was established in the late nineteenth century the department had the effect of gradually increasing governmental influence over curricula, teaching standards and so forth. This caused some tensions with the missions which had fewer resources, but by 1945 the role of government in the education programme was fully established, though participation by missions in individual schools continued for some years.

Achimota College became the predominant education centre in the Gold Coast. Important initiatives were taken, especially with regard to teacher training. This entailed the bonding of school leavers to the Department of Education for five years as teachers after intermediate education; various scholarship schemes at teacher training establishments; selection of promising students for higher education, prior to subsequent bonding as teachers and so on. As CD&W funds became available from 1946, better-designed and more structured systems were adopted to expand and upgrade the whole standard of school education.[23]

University College of the Gold Coast, Achimota

The College was created in 1948 under sponsorship of the Inter-University Council and was admitted on its foundation to the scheme of special relationship with the University of London. By 1952–3, there were faculties in Arts, Classics, English, French, Geography, History, Mathematics, Philosophy, Social Sciences, Theology, Physical Sciences, Biological Sciences, Agriculture and Education. By then there were 330 students, expected to rise rapidly to 1,000, and a teaching staff of 88. Most of the residential accommodation had been built with grants from the Cocoa Marketing Board, the government and the CD&W fund. An additional expenditure of £3 million (2017 £111 million) had been recommended; 85 per cent of the recurrent expenditure was born by the government. Just before independence in 1957, the number of students qualified for degree-level education was still not keeping pace with the expansion of the new university. For example in 1955 the total output of secondary-level schools was 650 students versus the 1,000 entry places planned for the university. This was partly accounted for by the fact that the government and the Cocoa Marketing Board were still sponsoring students for study abroad in subjects which could have been taught in the new Gold Coast University. But the shortfall was partly accounted for by the closure of some streams leading to secondary education in order to release resources for the new university.[24]

Nigeria

By February 1955, serious consideration was under way as to the desirability of creating two more universities in Nigeria, one in the Eastern Region, the other in the Northern. Though Ibadan University College was a federal institution, political opinion in these two regions professed to regard it as an appurtenance of the Western Region. In fact the scale and population of the country were such that further university-level institutions would certainly be required. The question was when could these be justified, how could the necessary funds (both capital and recurrent) be raised and where would the teachers be found. The number of children with an education approaching university-entry level was rising steadily:

Nigeria Secondary School Passes 1957/58[25]

	1957	1958
Lagos	208	Na
Southern Cameroon	55	Na
Eastern Region	1,093	1,182
Northern Region	185	Na
Western Region	1,011	1,124

The charismatic Premier of the Eastern Region, Dr Azikiwe, was drawn to an American-type university and he had already been eyeing the new buildings created outside Enugu for girls' education and teacher training. The Catholic Church was also proposing a university to be staffed mainly by Jesuits with a possible link with Fordham University in New York State for purposes of post-graduate work. The Inter-University Council for Higher Education in Britain had been engaged in discussions about a university in Eastern Nigeria with US authorities and the University of Michigan had prepared a scheme for a university at Nsukka. The Government of Nigeria had set aside £4 million (2017 £95 million) for the capital costs and £1 million (2017 £23.8 million) for running and maintenance. The United States had undertaken to supply some of the initial teaching staff. CD&W funds were available for some staff in 1960 but not after

Nigeria became independent. In the event the University of Nsukka was opened in 1960, just as Nigeria achieved its independence. The Inter-University Council said it would continue to provide assistance in the form of advisers and some teachers and there would be additional technical assistance. The British Council expected to play a supportive role. The Regional Government would also help to meet the costs.[26]

In the North, educational development was so much further behind that it could not yet be foreseen when a university would be justified. Those Northern students who had managed to get into Ibadan had found the cultural differences problematical and sometimes found themselves virtually ostracized. In 1954, not a single Northerner entered Ibadan University College. Nevertheless, the collection of institutions which had grown up around Zaria, partly on account of its geographical situation, was already such that it was becoming the obvious place for such an institution when the time came. This is where Ahmedo Bello University was eventually established.

The Ashby Report[27]

Nigeria became independent in 1960. A year earlier a commission headed by Sir Eric Ashby, Master of Clare College, Cambridge, visited Nigeria 'to conduct an investigation into Nigeria's needs in the field of post-School Certificate and Higher Education over the next twenty years', its costs being met by the Carnegie Foundation (The Ashby Report). Several of the commissioners were Nigerian or employed at Ibadan University. The Commission found that at that time, a year before independence, there was an acute lack of balance in the education system and crippling shortages of nearly all forms of education and training. There were still only 1,800 students enrolled in Ibadan University and the Nigerian College of Arts, Science and Technology at Yaba. The quality of higher education in Nigeria (Ibadan and Yaba) was high, mainly as a result of their entering into a special relationship with London University. In addition it was estimated that there were about 1,000 students at universities abroad. However, of the 25,000 young people in teacher training institutes in Nigeria, many of them were themselves poorly educated. Of the 82,000 teachers in primary schools in Southern Nigeria, where universal primary education was within sight, nearly three-quarters were not properly trained for the job and were un-certificated; two-thirds had had only a primary education themselves. Similarly, there was a totally inadequate supply of trained and educated secondary school teachers – 80 per cent were neither graduates nor certificated as teachers. On the other hand the enthusiasm for education was such that there was much part-time study in progress. Thus Ibadan had over 1,000 applicants with the necessary qualifications for entry, while they could still only take in 300 per annum (less than Achimota).

Ashby reiterated the point made by Lord Hailey twenty years earlier that the lack of prestige of technology, agriculture and the other science-based studies was such as to be a crippling handicap for the country.

In Northern Nigeria, the Ashby Report found the educational level was far behind. On account of the strongly held Muslim traditions, primary education was largely in Koranic schools, whose curriculum was generally focussed on learning the Koran and Arabic and training in the life of a good Muslim. The Christian missions had had very little impact and by 1960, only about 9 per cent of the children in Northern Nigeria were in primary schools – in some districts the percentage was as low as 2 per cent. Although there were about 2 million children of secondary school age in Northern Nigeria, only about 4,000 were enrolled in such schools. The only university-level education taking place in the North was an engineering school at Zaria and the Veterinary School at Vom. There were only fifty-seven Northern students at Ibadan and a few overseas.

The Commission devoted a large part of their report to the educational needs of the North. Among other things, the Commission gave careful attention to a study carried out in parallel to the Commission by Professor Harbison of Princeton into the needs for post-secondary manpower in the country. Though recognizing that it would be short-sighted to allow an education system to be controlled solely by manpower needs, one thing an education system had to do was to satisfy those needs. In round figures, he estimated the minimum need to be about 80,000 people with post-secondary education within the next ten years – by 1970. This implied at least 6,000 graduates per annum from the universities, versus the then current number of 300, plus perhaps 600 per annum from overseas, clearly an impractical target. In addition the country needed 50,000 people with diploma/technician qualifications.

On the basis of these numbers, taking together the rate of population increase of some three-quarters of a million per annum, Ashby prepared a plan for Nigeria to produce a flow of at least 8,000 young people per annum with some post-secondary education within twenty years – by 1980. He found a need for a substantial expansion of primary education in the North, an additional 4,850 secondary school teachers, greatly enlarged technical institutes, special programmes of remedial training for primary and secondary school teachers, the compulsory addition of manual and/or technical training in all secondary schools and a sevenfold increase in university places. In addition, there was a great need for more, and more diverse, training of agricultural staff and farmers and training for various other professions. These proposals were daunting, just to get the country to a level where it could begin to supply trained men and women in something like the necessary numbers. There could be no assurance that all the funds and teachers required could be mobilized, though the first Nigerian oil well had begun production in 1959.

Uganda

The Carr-Saunders Report on Makerere College in 1946 indicated that progress since the De La Warr Commission in 1937 had been limited by the impact of the war. However, the campus facilities had expanded satisfactorily, there were twenty-two teachers (of whom only one was African and most of the others were recent graduates from British universities) and 176 students, of which twenty were engaged in higher-level teacher training, thirty-five in medicine (with clinical training taking place in the nearby medical school adjacent to Mulago hospital), six in veterinary science and six in agriculture. The report indicated that the development had been very unequal, being much further advanced in medicine and agriculture.[28]

Following the deliberations of a committee under de Bunsen in 1953, the Government of Uganda endorsed proposals to:

- reorganize and expand the system of teacher training to produce an additional 1,100 teachers per annum in order to accommodate an additional 23,000 primary school places per annum;
- improve the conditions of service of teachers of all categories;
- expand and upgrade the quality of secondary education to produce 500 school leavers per annum;
- expand the primary and secondary facilities for girls' education;
- lengthen the period normally spent by pupils in primary education.

The committee did not address the needs of technical and commercial education as a £2 million (2017 £50.1 million) programme had already been adopted for this purpose. The government allocated a further £2.5 million (2017 £62.8 million) for school and college buildings and accepted a total cost estimate of £7 million (2017 £175.7 million) over five to six years. Recruitment of teachers from Britain was still expected to present problems. The committee made numerous recommendations for reforming and devolving the system of educational administration. It also had sections on girls' education, urban education and Muslim education.

Tanganyika

In 1950, the government produced a Ten-Year Plan for African Education,[29] which received considerable criticism in the Colonial Office. Primary education was based on an assumption of fifty children per teacher, double sessions in the first two years (morning and afternoon) and full-day sessions for the third and fourth years. However, wastage between the first and second years was assumed at one-third, and it was assumed that less than a half of the cohort would ever get beyond the second year. Furthermore, the post-primary education plan proposed was found to be inadequate by the Colonial Office on the grounds that those able and willing to progress beyond the primary level were to be held back until the primary system was further expanded. The Tanganyika government was asked to focus on reducing the level of wastage, reducing the enormous primary classes, 'selling' the notion of further education and setting higher targets for middle and secondary school attendance. This would demand additional resources but it was felt that the government would have to face this. The Colonial Office also considered the plans for girls' education to be too timid, both in and of itself and because without more educated women, the primary school system would never be able to expand towards universal participation. Furthermore, they were keen to see teacher training concentrated in larger centres where there would be economies of facilities and where parallel streams would stimulate each other.

A major difficulty faced by the Tanganyika government was the prior dependence on the missions for schooling, and the fact that the schools were geographically very dispersed – unlike Nigeria, for example, with its large population centres, there were few significant towns. In the case of girls' education, there was considerable reluctance among Africans to allow girls to live away from home and the number of girls' schools was still very limited. However, the Colonial Office was becoming dissatisfied that these transitional problems continued to impede progress. As the following figures show, the number of children in the middle and senior secondary schools was quite small in 1949 and, though the percentage increase was quite large in some years, the total increase proposed by the government over the seven years to 1956 was modest[30]:

	Middle Schools						
	1949			Planned for 1956			%
Level	Boys	Girls	Total	Boys	Girls	Total	Increase
V	6,600	1,270	7,870	7,760	1,640	9,400	19
VI	4,630	680	5,310	7,760	1,640	9,400	77
VII	757	275	1,032	5,690	960	6,650	544
VIII	599	215	814	5,690	960	6,650	717
Total	12,586	2,440	15,026	26,900	5,200	32,100	113

	Secondary Schools						
	1949			**Planned for 1956**			**%**
Level	**Boys**	**Girls**	**Total**	**Boys**	**Girls**	**Total**	**Increase**
VII*	686	-	686	800	70	870	27
VIII*	520	-	520	800	70	870	67
IX	372	25	397	700	60	760	91
X	279	-	279	700	60	760	172
XI	72	-	72	200	30	230	218
XII	72	-	72	200	30	230	218
Total	2,001	25	2,026	3,400	320	3,720	84

*These classes overlapped those at the Middle Schools.
The numbers of those in teacher training was expected to increase by 92 per cent in the case of
    men, but by only 34 per cent for women.

A revision of the Ten-Year Plan was submitted to the Colonial Office in August 1951,[31] but still found to be inadequate on grounds that the proportion of children in primary education was expected to reach only 36 per cent and the proportion going on beyond primary education was expected to be only 20 per cent. The 1952 Cambridge Conference on African Education served to inform educationalists in all the colonies, but when a Five-Year Plan for Tanganyika was produced in 1956, it was again criticized by the Colonial Office for being too limited. A letter to the Governor, Sir Edward Twining, dated 16 November 1956 stated:

> The most salient feature of education in Tanganyika at the present time is the pitifully small number who are eligible to sit the Cambridge School Certificate examination. If Africans are to play a part in the development of the country within the next generation, the expansion of the secondary school system is urgent and to this end we feel that the proposals made under Section V of the Plan are the minimum. ... Both Kenya and Uganda have followed the principle of a balanced system of primary and secondary schools and have accepted the view that a system which concentrates on primary education is economically and educationally unsound.[32]

In February 1958, Julius Nyerere, the leader of the Tanganyika African National Union, also criticized the growth of the education system as being 'shamefully slow'. The Government of Tanganyika responded in a statement titled 'The Truth about Education in the Last 40 Years', summarized in the Tanganyika Standard, to the effect that it had in fact grown rapidly since 1920 and that the slow rate of growth could be ascribed to the absence of growth prior to 1920. Pressure on the government continued, as indicated by a House of Commons question put in July 1959. In reply, the minister had to reply with the following figures[33]:

Tanganyika: Children in School 1959		
(i)	Primary, 382,144	43% of age group
(ii)	Middle, 39,753	4.5% of age group
(iii)	Secondary, 4,220	0.47% of age group
(iv)	Technical, 1,799	0.02% of age group
General aims of next planning period ending 1966:		
(i)	Primary	50% of age group
(ii)	Middle, continued expansion towards ultimate target of eight-year course for all entering primary schools	

By 1960 the government in Dar es Salaam had reconsidered the educational programme and begun to implement an accelerated expansion of secondary education over the years 1961–3 with places for 9,653 pupils. The announcement of this expansion coincided with discussions with a Visiting Mission of American educationalists (Thurston and Morrill) prompted by UN agencies, which both encouraged and worried British administrators. Thurston, funded by the Ford Foundation, produced a good report on human resources and manpower plans which among other things pointed out that of c4000 senior positions in the Public Service, only 500 were held by Africans. Thurston identified two immediate priorities – first, 'the almost exclusive concentration upon teachers for secondary schools for the next two years ... and; second, a large increase in well-trained farm extension workers'.[34] He was keen to see training be as near to the job as possible, to get immediate results.

The additional resources potentially available from the United States would obviously help to meet the increasing costs. However, a proposal for a 'University of East Africa' (a somewhat idealistic concept when each state wanted its own university) and a so-called airlift of students, teachers and promising employees in the economy to attend courses in the United States were on such a scale as to threaten to disrupt existing new educational institutions, such as Makerere and The Royal College, and siphon off the very staff required to run the growing institutions of government which were already thinly staffed with trained Africans. A conference to discuss all this was planned at Princeton and Colonial Office staff prepared a note on 'Tactics and Objectives' for the conference designed to secure American financial and technical support but within the existing framework of educational institutions in East Africa and on a scale which did not weaken the government and the teaching institutions.[35]

The first step in the creation of a university in Tanganyika was taken in 1961/2 when a five-year allocation of funds for the creation of the University College of Dar es Salaam was made by the government.[36]

Kenya

Agricultural education began in the primary schools and was emphasized at all subsequent stages of education. Specialist agricultural education was provided at farmer's training centres (especially after the land consolidation exercise in the 1950s), at three centres for the training of extension workers and at diploma level at Makerere. When it commenced agricultural training at degree level in 1957, Makerere decided to phase out the diploma course in 1965. In the event, it had to stop the diploma course in 1959 due to staff shortages, forcing the four governments to devise their own agricultural training at this level.[37]

In 1958 a further review of Higher Education in East Africa generally and the status of the Royal Technical College of East Africa was carried out under Sir Alexander Carr-Saunders.[38] These reviews were used to inform a White Paper issued in 1958 by the Governments of Kenya, Tanganyika, Uganda and Zanzibar which made recommendations for the future of Higher Education in the four territories. These were reviewed by a Working Party of educationalists appointed by the secretary of state, headed by Dr John Lockwood, Master of Birbeck College, London.[39] The issues to be considered included:

(i)   Makerere College. The College had entered into a special relationship with London University in 1949 permitting students to sit for London degrees in the Faculties of Arts and Sciences. The number of students in 1958 was 800, enrolled from all four East African countries and Central Africa, and the plans provided for this to rise to about 1500–1800 'soon after 1965'. But this pre-supposed the continued expansion of secondary education. The recurrent costs were met principally by equal grants from the three larger states. It was not yet in the plans for the College to become a full university.

(ii) Royal Technical College of East Africa, Nairobi. This college was founded in 1954 by the East Africa High Commission, was inter-territorial like Makerere, did not offer degree courses, but 'facilities for higher technological training, professional training, research and vocational training'. Under an agreement with the Gandhi Memorial Academy Society, however, courses were also being offered in arts, science and commerce, leading to degrees. By 1958 the College had 270 students. The Working Party recommended turning the College into a second university college offering both degree courses and professional training especially in technological subjects.

(iii) The Working Party also endorsed the proposal to create a university college in Tanganyika by about 1965/6, with faculties specializing in subjects not available at Makerere and Nairobi. It described the steps to be taken to bring this about. A Higher Education Trust Fund Ordinance had been passed by the Government of Tanganyika in 1956 as a first step towards the creation of a university college 'when the number of students completing secondary education justifies it'. In 1956, the number of Tanganyikan students passing the Cambridge School Certificate was 142. Of these, thirty-seven had been accepted by Makerere, fifteen by the Royal College and fifty-seven were under consideration for other further education.

The four governments established a grants committee to carry out a quinquennial review of higher education as a whole and make recommendations for expansion and development. They also asked the Governing Councils of Makerere and the Royal Technical College to create an academic liaison committee to ensure that un-economic duplication was avoided. They wanted to be sure that all the branches of education developed in proportion to one another and in proportion to the other social services for the community as a whole.

It should be noted that at that time there was still the expectation that the East Africa High Commission (EAHC), which provided services to all four East African territories, would continue in some form after independence and therefore a degree of specialization at any College would not be at the expense of any one of the four territories. There was also an underlying assumption that the supply of funds and teachers could be rationalized to make this possible. In the event the idea of federation died and the EAHC did not survive independence, becoming instead the East Africa Common Services Organization. None of these colleges could realistically have expected, even under favourable assumptions with regard to the availability of funds and teachers, and the growth of the secondary schools, to become fully fledged universities before 1970–5.

Southern Rhodesia (Zimbabwe)

Southern Rhodesia initially had a system whereby the majority of the African schools were provided by the missions. By the 1950s government Grants-in-Aid accounted for about 65 per cent of the recurrent costs. In the mid-1950s, about 65 per cent of the total school-age population was in school, of which about half were in the lower standard schools. By 1953 there were twelve African schools providing secondary education, with a total enrolment of about 1,100. There were a number of adult education centres. In March 1956, the government announced a five-year plan for provision of education for all African children by 1960. Simultaneously, the government initiated a campaign to produce 4,000 adequately trained teachers by 1960 and to double the number of pupils in the higher levels of the primary system. In addition to the existing twelve secondary schools, a further three were to be added in 1959. These targets were well ahead of similar targets elsewhere among the British colonies in Africa, other than Ghana. The education of European settlers was financed on a separate budget, and at more generous levels, which became a major source of dissension.

In August 1961, the government issued a paper on the state of African Education in Southern Rhodesia.[40] By then, 85 per cent of children were in primary school, probably the highest percentage in Africa other than in the Union of South Africa. At the post-primary level the immediate objective was 'to effect a general raising of academic standards, to eliminate the untrained teacher from the system, to provide teachers of higher academic standards and to train specialists in the fields of building, carpentry, agriculture, hygiene and commercial subjects'. The majority of head-teachers were African, and the rest would soon be so. At the secondary level over 5,000 pupils enrolled. There were also fourteen Technical and Vocational Schools with 1,400 pupils, also at the post-primary level. By the time of this report, 66 per cent of primary school teachers were fully trained and certified to work at the primary level and the output of additional trained teachers was 1,230 per annum, and rising. In addition there were 123 Community and Evening Schools with 13,500 adult students attending. There were also eight Homecraft Schools and four special schools for the handicapped.

Northern Rhodesia (Zambia)

Here too, the early history of African education was associated with the work of Christian missions and began even before the British South Africa Company extended its activities and influence north of the Zambezi at the end of the nineteenth century. From 1885 onwards, various missions established themselves. In 1925, soon after the administration of the territory was transferred from the Company to the Colonial Office, a sub-department of Native Education was established within the Department of Native Affairs, following a recommendation of the Phelps-Stokes Commission. By 1937, there were 413 maintained and aided schools, which increased to 1,226 by 1947, 1,522 by 1957/8 and 1,693 by 1960/1. By then enrolment was about 290,000, with the proportion of boys and girls in school being about the same. In addition there were separate schools for European and Asian children numbering about 19,000. Although this expansion is striking, most of the primary schools were substandard, and this problem was reflected all the way up the educational pyramid. The capital investment required to meet the physical needs of the expanding education system was well beyond the government's revenues and there was an acute need for more and better teachers.

Nevertheless, in 1956 the African Advisory Board recommended a rapid expansion of both upper primary and secondary education. The number of children taking the secondary school entry exam doubled between 1955 and 1956 from about 2,000 to about 4,000, of which about 20 per cent were girls. In addition the mining companies were making significant use of the Adult Education Facilities to train their employees in craft and technical skills. The Federal Government was making funds available for bursaries to study abroad, which averaged fourteen per annum, tenable at Fort Hare, Durban, Makerere and in Britain. In addition, children completing the normal secondary schooling were being encouraged to stay on to qualify for entry to the Rhodesian University.[41,42]

Nyasaland (Malawi)

The missions were particularly active in Nyasaland for 100 years, partly on account of the prior presence and teaching of Dr David Livingstone. Primary-level education expanded quite rapidly and participation levels were quite high. This was followed by the introduction of effective vocational training which equipped boys to go and work in the Rhodesias and South Africa, especially in the mines. However, a crisis was reached by the end of the Second World War, which precipitated the appointment of a new Director of Education, Miller, with experience in Northern Rhodesia and Basutoland.

The Advisory Committee in London reported in November 1948 after twelve meetings that

> it has found the educational problems of Nyasaland unusually urgent and intractable; urgent because, in spite of its history and early promise, education has yielded such meagre results; intractable because, after years of discussion, Government has not succeeded in giving firm direction to educational policy. We are impelled to contrast the neighbouring territory of Northern Rhodesia where educational development has been rapid and vigorous.

Government had not played a sufficient part in education; the missions had been mainly interested in extending a rudimentary level of education as widely as possible. Secondary education and teacher training had been neglected. 'In effect, Nyasaland has not succeeded either in giving an adequate basic education to the masses or in training African leaders. Teacher salaries had been far too low to attract talent to the profession. The local Advisory Committee had been dominated by European missionaries with inadequate African participation'. There had been a debilitating dispute with the missions over the creation, staffing and curricula of the secondary schools. There were inadequate numbers of full primary schools, though these were now increasing rapidly. There were too many older students, a disruptive influence in the primary schools. Girls' education had lagged, though the Colonial Office expert, Miss Gwilliam, had made firm recommendations which were to be implemented. Craft training, based on departmental institutes, had been effective, but was now outmoded in standard and approach. A central technical training centre was required. Miller was encouraged to ensure that available funds were devoted to high-quality schools and not spread around thinly on all schools.[43] By 1955, secondary education had made considerable progress within the country and additional students were being sent to schools in Southern and Northern Rhodesia.[44]

Central Africa – universities

The creation of institutions of higher education in the three Central African countries of Southern Rhodesia (Zimbabwe), Northern Rhodesia (Zambia) and Nyasaland (Malawi) was inextricably linked up with the creation in 1953 of the Federation of Central Africa, which was eventually abandoned ten years later in 1963. The proposal for this federation was rejected by the Royal Commission of 1938 under the chairmanship of Lord Bledisloe. Nothing was then done to implement the idea during the Second World War, except that in 1943 the Central African Council was created to promote closer links between the three countries. Under the federation created in 1953 primary and secondary education were territorial responsibilities; higher education was a federal responsibility, which the federal government exercised through the Inter-Governmental Liaison Committee on Education and the Federal African Scholarship Board. In general, the principle was that no child who showed the ability to enter a university should be prevented from doing so by the absence of financial means.

In 1949 the Central African Council commissioned a study under Sir Harold Cartmel-Robinson to consider the need for higher education facilities for Africans in Central Africa. Impetus to implement the study recommendations was given when in 1950 the Union of South Africa announced that after 1953 it would no longer admit students from the three Central Africa countries to its universities. This decision had the effect of reactivating the study team as a Commission on Higher Education for Africans in Central Africa. This Commission, chaired by Sir Alexander Carr-Saunders, urged the creation without delay of a university college 'worthy to take its place by the side of those instituted with such success in the past decade in the West Indies, East Africa, Nigeria and the Gold Coast'. The commission gauged that at that time the secondary schools could produce about 100 entrants per annum with the Cambridge Overseas School Certificate required for entry to the college, and that there was sufficient demand for graduates in the countries to absorb a rising output from the college. As recommended by Asquith, the Commission considered that the university should be autonomous and be established by Royal Charter to ensure this, though initially it could be linked to London University. It should be multiracial and the site should be capable of expansion to 1,250 acres. It recommended that the teaching staff should reach about seventy-five in the principle faculties within five years.[45]

However, the situation was complicated by the earlier creation in 1946 of the Rhodesian University in a European part of Salisbury on an attractive though limited site. Arrangements had been made for the Queen Mother to lay the foundation stone of this university, which made the situation even more delicate. Carr-Saunders thought there would only be resources for one such college, not two; Dr Alexander Kerr, the former Principal of Fort Hare College in South Africa, who served on the Commission, stated in a note of reservation 'that nothing in the past history of these or neighbouring territories justifies the expectation that an inter-racial policy of admission would be allowed to proceed to the point when the numbers of Africans would exceed the numbers of Europeans'. He therefore proposed that the new college should be sited at Lusaka, in Northern Rhodesia, not in Salisbury. Further, since the Rhodesian University would be dependent by statute on the Government of Southern Rhodesia, it could not be as autonomous as Carr-Saunders considered necessary for the new College.[46,47]

The Colonial Office agonized over this issue, partly because by this time (1953) London University felt it was carrying as large a load as it could in supporting the creation of the colonial universities and was not keen to take on another; partly over the means to ensure that the proposed university was fully multiracial in a country where formal or informal segregation still prevailed; partly on account of the uncertainties surrounding the future of the Central African Federation; and partly over the financing of the new university. Nevertheless, the University College of Rhodesia and Nyasaland was opened near Salisbury in 1957, the Federal Government accepting that it should be multiracial, though with separate accommodation initially. London University agreed to provide facilities and advice as with the other new universities.[48] Progress in the creation of a multiracial university in the Federation was endangered by criticism of the separate living arrangements on the part of British politicians, including Hugh Gaitskell, leader of the Labour Party, which threatened to cause European Rhodesians to go to college in South Africa instead.[49] However, the University continued in its relationship with London University and established a link between its medical faculty and Birmingham University. The Southern Rhodesian government took over responsibility for the maintenance and development of the college, with a system of triennial grants. Britain continued to support the establishment of the university in its early years.[50]

As a consequence of the decision to locate the university in Salisbury, when the break-up of the Federation occurred and Zambia and Malawi became independent states, they were without any university college of their own and dependent on admission to universities in other countries, including Southern Rhodesia. The growing isolation of Rhodesia after its declaration of independence, as a civil war broke out, exacerbated the problem of access to university-level education for both countries. It is of interest that Philip Murphy, biographer of Colonial Secretary, Alan Lennox-Boyd, recorded hearing Lennox-Boyd regret that he had not insisted on the Central African university being located in Lusaka.

In 1961, a review of Technical Education in Northern Rhodesia was carried out by Sir David Lindsay Keir, Master of Balliol College, Oxford. The Federal and Territorial governments and the Copperbelt Technical Foundation agreed that courses of instruction should be open to students of all races who complied with the admission requirements. Colleges would have the capacity to provide remedial teaching to those who were not up to standard in specific subjects. Since the number of students was not expected to be large, students were to be concentrated in a few centres so that viable classes could be created. Duplication of colleges created at the Federal level was to be avoided.[51]

In due course a university college was created in Zambia at about the time the country achieved its independence in 1964. It was to be a four-year course, the first year being the equivalent of the Sixth form course, which was to be abandoned in the schools for a while. The first vice-chancellor was a Canadian and one or two existing institutions (The Rhodes-Livingstone Institute and the Oppenheim Institute of Social Science, established with funds from the mining family of that name) served as initial constituents of the university. Britain offered to provide personnel for several key positions and a relationship was established with Keele University in Britain.[52]

Since Northern Rhodesia had substantial mining and related industrial enterprises, careful attention was given to the nature of the new university and its relationship to technical training colleges. The matter was reviewed carefully by the Council for Technical Education and Training in Britain in their review of the report by Dr Lockwood on the proposed new university. It was felt that a single institution could not do both jobs – provide both a good university education and technical training linked into the needs of industry.[53]

Southern Africa

The countries of Basutoland (Lesotho), Bechuanaland (Botswana) and Swaziland were administered from the 1880s until independence by a British high commissioner, who was responsible to the Colonial Office in London. From 1830 Christian missions had begun to establish schools in all three countries, with varying degrees of support from the traditional authorities. By 1954, there were

946 schools in Basotoland, of which eight were controlled by the government, the rest by the missions. Fourteen of these schools were secondary or junior secondary, and the total enrolment was 103,000, of which 63 per cent were girls. It was estimated that by that time, school enrolment was approaching 100 per cent. From 1949 onwards, the Basuto authorities began setting aside funds for post-secondary schooling, mainly for the provision of bursaries. In Swaziland the first school was opened somewhat later, in 1880, though the authorities began to make Grants-in-Aid to the mission schools in 1903. By 1954, there were 225 schools, 195 controlled by the missions, the remainder by tribal or national bodies. Enrolment was 16,500, with a majority of girls. By 1963, this had risen to 50,000, but only 20 per cent of schools were government aided. By the end of 1962, only 450 students had completed five years of secondary education and only seventy had graduated from a university. Wastage from the schools was still high, particularly after primary education when many children began work on family farms.

Bechuanaland had a small, dispersed population very difficult to gather together for the creation of schools, and unusually, the growth of education depended less on the missions than on the local tribal authorities. By 1903, these authorities were setting aside funds for education. By 1953, there were about 20,000 children in school, of which more than 60 per cent were girls, partly because the boys were expected to assist with cattle-herding. Programmes for the period to 1960 included an additional seven secondary schools, including an unusual one at Swaneng Hill which focussed on education with production.

Initially, African students completing a full secondary education could apply to go to Fort Hare College in South Africa or the Medical College in Durban. But in 1953 this was stopped by a decision of the South African Government. As a result, in January 1964, the University of Basutoland, Bechuanaland and Swaziland, was established near Maseru, Basutoland. Entry was by the Cambridge Overseas Certificate, implying two years of additional schooling for many children before undergraduate courses began. By the end of 1964, enrolment was 188 students. It was expected that this number would grow to 240 students within a year and a further 300 by 1967. The ultimate target at that time was about 1,000 students. It was hoped that students from the three countries would be supplemented by students from elsewhere who would help to build a viable institution. Courses were limited in number and included a post-graduate teacher training diploma course. For this reason some students would still have to seek their further education and training elsewhere. CD&W provided most of the funds for the capital investment; USAID provided scholarship funds; the three governments met 56 per cent of the recurrent costs, CD&W the remainder. The UN/UK economic mission of 1965 expressed doubts about the potential viability of the university, but meanwhile accepted that it was the only way to create any institution at the undergraduate level in the three countries in view of their small populations.[54]

West Indies

The report of the Royal Commission on the West Indies (Cmnd 6174 of 1940) contained recommendations on the educational sector. In his letter to the Colonial Secretary of August 1943, Sir F. Stockdale, Governor of Barbados, made proposals for meeting the inevitable cost increases which would accompany the implementation of the Commission's recommendations.[55] He concluded that it was unrealistic to expect to find sufficient funds to pay the salaries for all the additional teachers recommended; he also thought it inadvisable for HMG to begin to pay subventions for teacher's salaries, as this could turn into a permanent requirement which ought to be met by the island budgets. However, he took issue with the recommendation of the Royal Commission to abolish the practice of using pupil teachers until such time as funds for teachers' salaries were more adequate. He argued that the only way forward was to reform the pupil-teacher system by (i) limiting the teaching element to no more than half a day at a time, the balance of the day to be spent as a pupil in an appropriate school; (ii) by forbidding the use of pupil teachers as full-class teachers; (iii) and by using some of the CD&W funds allocated for education to build housing for both teachers and pupil teachers, as housing was poor and in short supply and a house would be a good incentive to attract potential teachers and pupil teachers. Most of the remaining CD&W funds would be used for capital purposes, upgrading school buildings, and for helping meet salaries of some teachers in the secondary schools. He did plan to use some of the CD&W funds for such elements as the cost of grants for teacher training, school books and equipment in elementary schools; and the cost of establishing housecraft and handicraft departments in the senior elementary schools. This is a typical example of the pragmatic way in which budgets were squeezed to maximize the impact of limited funds.

Education in the West Indian islands has a fairly long history, certainly since the abolition of slavery in the early part of the nineteenth century. As in Africa, the task was left mainly to the Christian missions, though initiatives were taken by private persons and various island governments. Codrington College in Trinidad has a long history, dating back to the eighteenth century. In Jamaica, by 1947, there were twenty-four Grant-aided secondary schools, with a total enrolment of 4,541 pupils, with approximately equal numbers of boys and girls. Seven of these schools were offering Sixth form subjects to prepare students for university entrance and some students were taking London external exams at an undergraduate level. Approximately one-third of the funding came from government, two-thirds from pupils or endowment or scholarship funds. This level of accomplishment was better than in some of the other islands and Guyana. However, Trinidad also had the Colonial Agricultural College, partly funded by HMG, which gave it strength in the fields of agriculture, forestry and stock rearing.[56]

The British government hoped that the islands would eventually evolve a federal structure which would maintain the characteristics of the different small islands, and provide for a pooling of resources and collaboration at a federal level for certain functions of government. The Federation was not to be at a political level, but the idea was not totally abandoned in specific fields, including higher education. The growth of tertiary education in the West Indies was complicated both by the search for federal solutions and by differences of view among some talented, if 'awkward' characters, including Dr Eric Williams of Trinidad, Sir Arthur Lewis of Jamaica and Dr Sherlock. In the end, the University of the West Indies was established with two campuses, one in Jamaica and another in Trinidad, with outlier centres in the small islands. Thus about half of the islands eventually had campuses of the University of the West Indies, though a separate university was also established in Guyana. Links with Britain and Canada were maintained and the impact of private students going to the United States under various auspices added a further dimension to the picture. Thus the facilities for tertiary education became quite diverse and varied.[57]

Malaya/Singapore

Just prior to the Second World War, a commission was appointed to address the future of secondary and post-secondary education in Malaya and Singapore, just as in Africa and the West Indies. At that time, the education system was already far ahead of the situation in the African colonies. In 1938, 2,800 students took the School Certificate examination in Malaya. However, the occupation of these two countries by the Japanese in 1941 set back progress by about seven years. In December 1950, the director of Agriculture was still writing to the Colonial Office to the effect that the output from the secondary schools was only just beginning to reflect the post-war reopening of schools; he also said that the terms of service for Agricultural and Research Assistants were inadequate. There was much to be done beyond reconstruction and assembling the teaching and student bodies again. The College of Agriculture at Serdang had the prime function of turning out Technical Assistants for the Rubber Research Institute, the Industrial Development Authority, government departments and the rubber and palm oil estates. It was also to train subordinate agricultural staff. Those aspiring to become professional-level agricultural officers would have to do a science degree at the university and then undertake two years of post-graduate work, with one of these at the College of Tropical Agriculture in Trinidad.[58]

Malaya also had to contend with the communist insurgency. In February 1950, the high commissioner for Malaya, General Sir Gerald Templar, said in an address to the Legislative Assembly:

I have recently written to State and Settlement Governments, as the executive authorities responsible for primary and secondary education, regarding the importance of ensuring that the schools are free of political propaganda ... the proposals for increasing the number of well trained teachers, Malay and Chinese, are urgent and vital. There exists a mental form of slavery quite as real as any economic form. We are pledged to destroy it. If you want human liberty, you must have educated people ... we must remember that the aim of education is to train men and women to understand the world they live in. Their standards and ideals must be raised on the firmest possible foundations of wide knowledge and experience, if they are to be qualified to assist or resist the ruling tendencies of their time.

An important step was taken with the Education Ordinance of 1952 which promulgated an education system and curriculum designed to foster a national identity and address the prevailing racial exclusiveness of Malays, Chinese, Indians and other minorities. The Chinese schools in Malaya were mainly private creations, some dating back to the nineteenth century. Events in China from 1912 onwards were eagerly followed by the Chinese in Malaya and stimulated an expansion in schools with the teaching materials coming mainly from China. However, to avoid their becoming instruments of Chinese propaganda, registration of schools and teachers had been introduced in the 1920s. As government financing of schools grew, precedence was given to schools teaching in Malay and English, but Chinese schools also benefited. The Second World War and the Communist victory in China virtually put an end to the normal movement of Chinese to and from China. The expansion of schooling in the 1950s was rapid and it is of interest that in 1954 out of a total enrolment of 158,000 in the English schools (government, aided and private) 80,000 were Chinese. However, the insistent demand for more education was absorbing an increasingly large proportion of government funds. The Chinese community expanded the Chinese schools accordingly. By 1955, there were 1,160 Chinese schools in the Federation with a total enrolment of 245,000 pupils. It was realized that these schools, particularly the secondary schools, were still open to political influence from the Malayan Communist Party and the Communist Party of China. Curriculum reforms addressed this situation. By 1953 the government budget for Chinese schools was St$37 million (2012 St$875) compared with St$43 million (St$1,017) for Malay schools and St$11 million (St$260 million) for Indian schools (NB: These 2012 figures may not be reliable). Needless to say, the education programme, curricula and budgets became a highly political issue, especially after the Alliance Government came to power in 1955, and the Education Committee of LegCo decided that all secondary education should be in English. Some Malays advocated more Malay education; however, both educational and political leaders drew attention to the limitations of the Malay language in a country hoping to grow quickly.

An imaginative programme to rapidly expand the availability of teachers for Malayan schools was devised in 1951 when a vacant college building at Kirkby, near Liverpool in England, was made available for training teachers from Malaya. The British Council made the arrangements. The first group of 150 trainees arrived in December 1951, a second group in September 1952, for courses lasting twenty months. As part of the programme, the students were to spend time in the Liverpool schools to gain experience.[59]

The rapid progress in Malaya and Singapore was facilitated by the buoyant revenues from rubber and tin production, so that even during the Emergency, adequate funds were available for the expansion and upgrading of education at all levels. In 1947, CD&W funds were allocated for the new university being established. By 1957, the year before independence, plans were being made for the continued recruitment of British teachers and various types of specialist after independence. However, when Tunku Abdul Rahman, Malaya's Chief Minister, visited the Colonial Office in London to make the necessary arrangements, he indicated that recruitment was also taking place in India and he felt the need for recruitment of teachers and specialist staff in Britain would gradually diminish.

Hong Kong

The education system of this territory also suffered badly from the Japanese occupation. By mid-1948 the number of operational schools and students had still not recovered to pre-war levels. One secondary school was by then fully staffed with teachers from Britain, but the other secondary schools had been looted and damaged and they were getting by as best they could with grants from government. A number of private schools had reopened and some of the students were going on to Chinese universities. Following a review in 1935, a local School Leaving Certificate had been adopted and this still had widespread recognition from government, colleges, teachers and the commercial interests. Some students seeking entry to Hong Kong University were avoiding the compulsory Chinese studies by taking the London matriculation exam, which gave exemption. Teacher training at the university had been a success pre-war, but salaries had become inadequate to retain teachers, though the situation was improving again by 1948. Provision of schooling in the New Territories was still minimal.[60]

Arabia

Aden and the Aden Protectorate were administered from India from 1839 until 1928 and by the Colonial Office from then until independence in 1967. In the protectorate numerous Koranic schools were gradually established, many of them supported by charities based in India, the Far East or elsewhere where the people worked and traded. By 1956 there were also 115 government primary schools and 6 intermediate schools. Bedouin children were catered for in special schools. During the 1960s, several more intermediate schools were opened and secondary schools in both Western and Eastern Protectorate. In Aden Colony there were nineteen primary schools, ten intermediate schools and four secondary schools. Aden College was the most notable of these and there was a good Technical Institute. A girl's secondary school was opened in 1956. Revenues in Aden Colony were buoyant so all education was free until the secondary level, when a means test was applied and scholarships provided for those who could not afford the expense. The major problem was finding qualified teachers. Teacher training received much priority from 1945 onward but teachers were also recruited from Britain, Sudan and Jordan. Use of Egyptian teachers was felt to carry with it political risks, and was restricted. Those going on from secondary school attended universities in Britain, Khartoum, Cairo or the American University in Beirut (AUB). The CD&W scheme provided much of the financing for expansion of the facilities, the employment of foreign teachers and scholarships for study abroad. By the time of independence, the level of education achieved was quite respectable in Aden Colony, though there were still insufficient people with full professional qualifications. In the Protectorate, where the population was quite dispersed and budgets very limited, some children were still missing even primary education and facilities for secondary education and technical training were still very limited.[61] The University of Aden was founded after independence.

Summary

To summarize, during the nineteenth century, and well into the twentieth century, education in most colonies was provided mainly by the Christian missions, a true labour of love and dedication, despite their limitations. They were often supported by Grants-in-Aid from the local administrations. By 1920, the British government had accepted responsibility for the growth of education in the colonies and provided policy and technical guidance to the increasingly professional Departments of Education in each colony. By the time of the De La Warr Commission in 1937, it was clearly accepted that educational development was a prerequisite if the objective of self-government was to be attained and by the time of the Asquith Commission in 1943, self-government had become a more explicit objective and the need for more universities was pressing.

With the passage of the 1940 Colonial Development and Welfare Act in 1940, and its successors, a steady flow of funds became available from Britain for educational expansion in the colonies. The creation of the Inter-University Council for Higher Education in the Colonies and the Colonial University Grants Advisory Committee, both located within the University of London, helped to mobilize excellent technical support for policy-makers and administrators in the colonies from the entire educational establishment in Britain. It is difficult to envisage a more distinguished group of advisors than those mobilized by the Inter-University Council between the 1940s and the 1960s, which is testament to the importance given to educational expansion and enhancement in the colonies by the educational and government agencies in Britain.

The accomplishments were substantial at all levels, despite many obstacles including finance, a permanent shortage of adequately qualified teachers and events such as the Great Depression and the Second World War. However, the dynamic of educational expansion was such that the growth of the education systems was bound to be constrained, even if all the resources required had been available. So at the time of independence of the colonies, many children were still not in school, much schooling was still of a poor standard, secondary-level schooling was insufficient in most colonies and most colonies still did not have fully fledged universities to educate school leavers to the professional level.

The truth of the matter is there was inadequate time to complete the job. At the time of the independence of India in 1947, there were eighteen universities in India and some of them were ninety years old. At the time of the independence of the British African colonies, comprising sixteen countries, there were two or three small universities and nine or ten university colleges, on the way to becoming universities. None of them were more than fifteen years old and none of them had by then reached the status of a full-blown university. There was no possibility in the time available to generate the number of people, educated to a full professional level, to create fully adequate cadres of teachers and professional staff, let alone for them to acquire the experience to discharge their responsibilities competently.

Fifteen years later, in 1988/90, the World Bank carried out a review of 'Free-standing Technical Assistance for Institutional Development in Sub-Saharan Africa'. Their assessments were coordinated with those of bilateral agencies from European countries which were carrying out a similar review. The views of African borrowers of the Bank were also elicited through extensive interviews during the field visits as well as at a seminar held in Berlin in April 1988. The review concluded, among other things, that 'many African countries face chronic shortages of qualified personnel. They still depend on foreign personnel even to maintain existing levels of performance'.

University and non-university colonial students in Britain in January 1945[62]

	Law	Medicine	Science & Eng	Arts	Social	Other	Total
London University	26	36	13	7	36	36	167
Oxford University	8	2	5	2	12	12	29
Cambridge University	18	9	13	1	6	6	48
Other English Universities	2	44	20	17	22	22	108
Scottish Universities	-	62	7	6	19	19	95
Irish Universities	1	23	1	-	1	1	26
Non-university Students	47	11	24	2	109	109	193
Total	102	187	83	35	54	205	666

See Attached Table on the state of university education in British dependencies at independence

The state of university education in British dependencies at independence

Country	Date of Independence	College	Date Founded
India	1947	Calcutta	1857
		Madras	1857
		Bombay	1857
		(Plus fifteen other universities)	
Ceylon (Sri Lanka)	1948		1922
Malaya	1957/	ex Raffles	1949
Singapore	1965	College and Medical College	
West Indies	1962–6	U.W.I.	1948 (several campuses on the different islands)

Country	Date of Independence	College	Date Founded			
		Guyana	1962/3 (still doubts about quality)			
Sudan	1956	ex Gordon College	1946 (founded earlier as a boy's secondary school)			
				Number of Graduates in		
				1955	1960	1965
Sierra Leone	1961	Fourah Bay	1876*	Averaged 30 students in the 1930s, half from other West African countries		
Gold Coast (Ghana)	1957	Achimota	1929	Initially just a few Students attended the 'Univ Dept'; Established as University College		
		Legon Hill	1948			
Nigeria	1960	Medical School	1930			
		Yaba Tech.	1934	Initially diploma level; foundation courses for professional training		
		Ibadan	1948	<300		
		Nsukka	1960			na
East Africa**						
Uganda	1962	Makerere	1949	<300		
				From all East Africa		
Tanganyika (Tanzania)	1961	Dar/Morogoro	(1965 planned)	<230		
Kenya	1963	Royal Tech College	1954			
		University College	1963	<270		

Country	Date of Independence	College	Date Founded			
S Rhodesia*** (Zimbabwe)	(1980)	Rhodesia University	1952	na	na	na
		University College of Rhod & Nyasaland	1957		na	na
N Rhodesia (Zambia)	1964	Tech Ed	1961			
Nyasaland (Malawi)	1964	not yet founded in 1965				
Bechuanaland/ Basutoland/ Swaziland (Botswana/ Lesotho/ Swaziland)	1966	University College	1964 1967/8			<188 <300

* This was the year Fourah Bay entered into an agreement with Durham University
**Higher School Certificate entries in East Africa in 1957, 1960 and 1964 (when all three countries were independent) were estimated as follows:

	1957	1960	1964
Kenya	92	148	300
Tanganyika	27	137	180
Uganda	-	70	150
Zanzibar	-	20	20
Total	119	375	650

***Southern Rhodesia African Education in 1961

Secondary Ed.		Tech/Vocational Ed.		Teacher Training Certs Awarded			Community & Evening Schools	
Schools	Pupils	Schools	Pupils	Male	Female	Total	Schools	Pupils
34	5,069	14	1,406	840	390	1,230	123	13,466

Chapter 4

The approach to self-government and independence of colonies

The political and constitutional context

This chapter describes the main political and constitutional events occurring in the various colonies in the years leading up to independence. These provide the local context for all the changes required before the handover of authority from the British government to the local government. The most immediate and significant impact of these political events was on the timing and process of localization ('Africanization' for most countries) of the public service which is addressed in Chapter 5. The countries follow the same sequence as in the previous chapter.[1]

Sudan

Historically, Egypt maintained a claim to the whole of the Nile valley and until its occupation by Kitchener on behalf of the British and Egyptian governments in 1898, Sudan had been very loosely and poorly governed by the Ottoman Turks and Egypt in a manner which permitted religious zealotry, tax farming and slave trading, often by rapacious traders and petty rulers, which left the country very disturbed. By 1898, much of Sudan was in a pitiful condition. Following the Anglo-Egyptian Treaty of 1899, the country was governed as a condominium between Britain and Egypt. However, relations between the co-domini in regard to Sudan were typically uneasy, reflecting the general state of relations between the two countries. Following the 1924 assassination in Cairo of Sir Lee Stack, who was both the governor general of Sudan and the Sirdar (Commander-in-Chief) of the Egyptian Army, Sudan was for all practical purposes administered by Britain, although Britain continued to acknowledge the formal Egyptian rule in the country.

Due to its condominium status, instead of being supervised by the Colonial Office, the country was supervised by the Foreign Office, which handled relations with Egypt. This gave rise to some differences in the way the country was run, by comparison with the colonies. In particular, the governor general of Sudan was required normally to correspond with the Foreign Office in London through the British Ambassador in Cairo. The general function of the Foreign Office is to represent British interests, not to administer territories. The Cairo embassy was concerned with British interests across the Middle East and the Canal Zone military base. This helped in understanding the position being taken on issues by the government of Egypt but did create something of a screen between Khartoum and London. Egypt's influence and the priorities of the Foreign Office sometimes created complications for Britain in Sudan; and was viewed as something of a 'Gordian Knot' entangling the governor general.

The 1899 treaty between Britain and Egypt was revised in 1936 by means of the Anglo-Egyptian Treaty of that year, which was due to run for twenty years and which, among other things, permitted the stationing of a battalion of Egyptian troops in the Sudanese capital, Khartoum. There was much disquiet in Sudan that this new treaty was negotiated without Sudanese involvement. Also in 1936, Italy invaded and occupied Ethiopia. This led during the Second World War to the brief occupation of small frontier areas of eastern Sudan by Italian forces, their repulse by Sudanese and British forces and subsequently to the defeat of the Italian army in Ethiopia by British-led forces in 1941, following a campaign in which Sudanese, other African forces and the Indian Army participated.

Sudan was administered by the Sudan Political Service (SPS). The senior officer in Sudan, under the governor general, was the civil secretary. From 1939 until 1945, most of the period of the Second World War, this post was held by Sir Douglas Newbold. From 1945 until Sudan became independent in 1954 the post was held by Sir James Robertson. The following passages draw extensively on Robertson's memoirs, and also on M. W. Daly's biography of Sir William Luce who played a significant role in the period leading to Sudan's independence as Advisor to the governor general on constitutional and external affairs.[2,3]

In 1938 the Graduates Congress was established in Omdurman as the first stirrings of an educated and politically conscious class in Sudan. In April 1942, the Congress submitted a memorandum to the government calling for self-determination after the war. Surprisingly, no steps had been taken before the Second World War to establish any form of central assembly or legislative council though on local matters town councils and tribal councils existed as consultative bodies throughout the country. Sir Stafford Cripps, who passed through Khartoum during the war, advised Newbold to go ahead and establish a national advisory council . Thus in 1944 Newbold created an Advisory Council for Northern Sudan and in 1945 this was followed up by an administration conference to propose ways of associating the Sudanese more closely in both central and local government. Apart from the Congress' memorandum, another factor influencing Newbold was the Atlantic Charter agreed between the United States and Britain in August 1941, which, inter alia, contained a commitment to the restoration of the sovereignty and self-government of countries occupied during the war. This was interpreted by some, though not by Britain, as being a commitment to self-government of colonies. These and other factors persuaded Newbold that steps were required to facilitate the appointment of Sudanese into higher positions in the administrative service. Newbold also established a Sudanization committee under the advisory council (see Chapter 5).

Meanwhile, Britain was negotiating post-war settlements with Egypt and in private discussions between Ismail Sidky, the Egyptian prime minister, and Ernest Bevin, the British foreign secretary, agreement was reached to modifications in the relations between the two countries (the Sidky-Bevin protocol). This stated that

the policy which the High Contracting parties undertake to follow in the Sudan, within the framework of the unity of the Sudan and Egypt under the common crown of Egypt, will have for its essential objective to assure the well-being of the Sudanese, the development of their interests and their active preparation for self-government and consequently the exercise of the right to choose the future status of the Sudan.

This statement on the one hand acknowledged the unity of Egypt and Sudan under the Egyptian Crown, which most Sudanese rejected, yet also for the first time conceded that Sudan would eventually be self-governing.

Over a period of several months a debate proceeded in the Foreign Office and between ministers in London on this issue.[4] Among the Sudanese, the Umma Party, led by Sayed Abdel Rahman al Mahdi, were utterly opposed to the statement and the purported 'common crown'. The governor general, Sir Hubert Huddleston, and several senior British officers also felt they could not remain in Sudan to enforce a treaty of this nature on the country. Huddleston therefore visited London in November 1946 and confronted Prime Minister Attlee with this view. He insisted on written instructions to stand fast on British policy and the British interpretation of the treaty, to the effect that the Sudanese would have the right to determine the future of their country in due course. He got these instructions and confidence in British intentions among the Sudanese restored. Evidently, Egypt wanted to dominate Sudan and incorporate it within the Egyptian sphere; Britain wanted to develop self-governing institutions and assist in the economic and educational development of the country until it could decide for itself what its future should be.

The next constitutional steps in Sudan concerned the creation in 1947 of a Legislative Assembly and an executive council to replace the existing advisory council and governor general's council. In the discussions about these proposed institutions, the status of Southern Sudan became a major issue. From 1820 until about 1900, the southern provinces of Sudan had been in a state of more or less continuous unrest and strife directed against the Turko-Egyptian government in Khartoum and the depredations of northern traders and slave traders. Thus when the condominium government began to move into the area, from about 1900, they found great fear and suspicion among the people. It took twenty-five years to establish a civil government in the area, with the result that educational, social and economic development was well behind the rest of the country. Meanwhile the area was made subject to a Closed District Ordinance, to protect the people against economic exploitation by northerners. To quote Robertson, 'It was hoped that behind such a barrier the Southern people would develop until they were able to stand on their own feet and meet the northerners on equal terms.' However Robertson concluded that though devoted men and women had worked in the South for many years, they found it difficult to have much impact on such a vast area with their limited resources. Some of the better-educated southerners were actually inclined to hold the Sudan government responsible for the divide between the North and the South.[5]

In the same year, 1947, the advisory council in Khartoum and a meeting of Southerners held in Juba endorsed Robertson's proposal that the South should be represented in the national legislative council, that Sudan should for that reason be administered as a unitary state, but that safeguards should be adopted to ensure the healthy and steady development of the Southern people. Decisions were also made to increase investment in the South to hasten economic development. This was partly facilitated by a grant of £2 million (2017 £74.4 million) from the British government to Sudan in settlement of what it considered were Britain's debts to Sudan following the Second World War.

Later, Robertson wrote of this issue:

Looking back ... I still think the decision of 1947 was the right decision; Southern Sudan had to be opened up ... the tragedy was that political independence impinged on an unsophisticated people before they were adequately prepared, or even fully understood what was taking place, and the early removal of the British District Officers in accordance with the Sudanisation clauses of the Anglo-Egyptian Agreement of 1953 left them without one of the safeguards which I had thought necessary. Few people in 1947 could have foreseen the sudden change in the world situation which led to the rapid emancipation of the 1950s and 1960s. I certainly never guessed in 1947 that the Sudan would be independent less than a decade later.[6]

This sentiment was to be articulated by colonial officials regarding their own countries throughout the colonial empire.

Egypt raised the issue of its sovereignty over Sudan at the United Nations but its arguments were largely dismissed on grounds that not enough was known about the viewpoint of the Sudanese, whom it was felt should have the right of self-determination when they became self-governing.

Creating the legislative and executive councils through discussions in the advisory council posed a whole range of issues such as constituency boundaries, the nature of the franchise, the use of electoral colleges, the residual powers of the governor general under the Anglo-Egyptian Treaty, the role of political parties and so on. Indeed the Egyptian government never signified its assent to the creation of these two councils. It was therefore near the end of 1948 before the councils came into being. It is evident from Robertson's book that it took some time before the councils learned how to work effectively, but there is no question that as time passed the members of the councils expanded greatly their knowledge of the issues facing the country and the difficulties in dealing with them. For example, in a short period of several months, the councils debated and passed a new local government law, a bill amending the Code of Criminal Procedure and a Workshops and a Factories bill. But this work on the constitution and the creation of elected bodies was accompanied by constant pressure from Egypt, both officially and through the press, radio and personal contact. They were not above seditious acts, despite Egypt's position as one of the co-domini states. Though there was much resistance to this pressure on the part of Sudanese independents, in particular Sayed Abdul Rahman al Mahdi and the Umma party, there was also support for the Egyptian position from the Ashigga party and 'Unity of the Nile Valley'.

The period of negotiations on revisions to the Anglo-Egyptian Treaty and the future of the Sudan, taken together with continuous Egyptian propaganda, excited the population, especially students at the University College and the secondary schools. There was also a growth of labour unrest, especially at the Atbara headquarters of the railways, so the government was much preoccupied with introducing comprehensive labour legislation and getting acceptance of this by the trade unions. The reform of local government was finally completed, a major piece of business for the government, for which purpose it received skilled advice from the city treasurer of Coventry in Britain. His report, which specified the nature of the elected councils, their responsibilities and powers, was accepted by the government and they were established in 1950. This proved to be long-lasting reform and did not require significant amendment until 1971, seventeen years after independence. One problem to which this reform gave rise in Sudan, as in most colonies, was that once elected councils came into existence at the level of the district or province, the role of the former British district commissioner and district officers was changed or abolished altogether. This had the effect in Sudan of eliminating the one central government officer who had a role in coordinating government activities in the district and representing the interests of the inhabitants. Though the DC was replaced by a Sudanese political appointee, the remoter regions of the country missed the knowledgeable and neutral role of the district commissioners and officers. A revealing analysis of the impact in the South of these measures is contained in a memorandum from the deputy governor of Bahr al Ghazal Province, T. R. H. Owen, to the governor general, Sir Robert Howe, of March 1951.[7]

The actual independence of Sudan was precipitated by Egypt which in October 1951 unilaterally abrogated the 1936 Anglo-Egyptian Treaty and the 1899 agreement regarding Sudan. King Farouk was proclaimed King of Sudan. The British government did not recognize unilateral abrogation of treaties and this was made clear by the foreign secretary, Anthony Eden, in a statement he made in the House of Commons on 15 November.[8] There was also much opposition in Sudan to the Egyptian claims. However, following the 1952 officer's coup d'etat in Egypt, when General Neguib became president, things improved for he was half Sudanese, had lived in Sudan and spent time at the university college. He was also inclined to come to an agreement with Britain for revision of the 1936 treaty. Nevertheless, his visit to the Sudan sparked anti-British disturbances resulting in loss of some blood, partly due to the inexperience of the new Sudanese cabinet. The position of British technicians seconded to Sudan in March 1953 also became an issue and the foreign office eventually concluded that it would be impossible to resolve the issue until the Sudanese authorities realized that the technicians were actually about to leave the country.

With regard to the administration, as Robertson concluded,

as far as we British in the Sudan were concerned, we did not object to Sudanisation; we had pushed ahead with it as fast as seemed possible, and had certainly promoted to senior posts some Sudanese who were hardly up to the responsibilities which they had to assume. Too rapid Sudanisation of top posts would mean that some of them would be filled by persons who could not carry out the work, and would also mean a gap somewhere down the line, as the number of candidates suitable for selection who were coming forward was inadequate to fill all the vacancies that would occur if every British administrative official left within a short time. ... Our representations along these lines were brushed aside in the negotiations in Cairo and it was decided that the Anglo-Egyptian Agreement should be signed in Cairo on 14th February 1953. ... Criticisms were voiced by some of the expatriate staff, especially in Southern Sudan, against the way in which we celebrated an agreement which was far from satisfactory. I was accused of having sold the pass and handed over the South to the Egyptians and the Northerners, contrary to promises repeatedly made in the past. The 1953 treaty established the terms of self government and the steps to be taken to achieve self-determination within the exceptionally short period of three years. The Condominium was to come to an end, there would be parliamentary elections and the Sudanisation Committee was to be given a Sudanese majority. The Foreign Office and Egypt were pleased with this treaty; the SPS was despondent and critical. Robertson noted that 'some of the SPS criticised the way in which we marked an agreement which was far from satisfactory.' Certainly, the departure of the British officers was precipitate with grossly inadequate time for effective handover. Similar charges were made at the time of independence of other British dependencies, including India in regard to some of the Indian Native States, but also in some of the African colonies.

In July 1953, at the time of his departure from Sudan, Sir James Robertson, spoke at the Royal African Society.[9] He said, 'Sudan still lacks cohesion; there are too many differences; we have not had a long enough time in our 55 years to weld the many tribes and racial groups into one nation, though there are signs of a growing feeling of common nationality.' He identified three major rifts in the Sudanese nation – the rift between North and South; the serious split between town and country (the educated townsman who tended to despise the rural people and their tribal sheikhs) and the serious religious differences. Thus the timing of Sudanese independence was not determined by the readiness of the country to administer itself as a unity and in harmony but by the timing of the 1954 Anglo-Egyptian Treaty, which was in turn driven by diplomatic and strategic considerations.

Control began to be transferred to Sudanese politicians and civil servants. Elections were held to the assembly in December 1953, producing the first all Sudanese administration. The results were something of a surprise to many observers but at least all parts of the country had participated. Ismail al Azhari of the National Union Party (NUP) became the first prime minister. In October 1955, HMG informed al Azhari that it would support a vote for independence in the Sudanese parliament.

Sir William Luce played a crucial role in the period between signature of the 1953 treaty and independence. In his biography Daly described the evolution of Luce's thinking in a rapidly evolving situation involving political parties, Southern Sudan, Egypt and HMG. Unlike many members of the SPS, who considered the 1953 agreement was a betrayal of Sudanese interests, Luce was more inclined and capable of detachment and of taking into account wider concerns. Luce considered it essential for him to demonstrate goodwill towards rising politicians and by mid-1954 had reached the conclusion that the NUP would remain in power until independence – 'I see no reason not to accept Al Azhari's declared views as genuine and representative of the Khatmia and the majority of the educated class on whom the NUP must rely for their votes. ... Mirghani and a number of Khatmia have expressed the same view – but it must not be dominated by Saiyid Abdulrahman al Mahdi ... it is no concern of HMG whether the independence of Sudan is brought about by the NUP or the Umma'.

Sir Robert Howe's term as governor general was due to end soon after the 1953 agreement had been signed. There was an unsatisfactory hiatus in the appointment of his successor, with the result that Luce was holding the fort in Khartoum for some months until Sir Knox Helm was appointed in early 1955. The relationship between the Sudanese political parties became fractious and as time passed, public sentiment and the view of the Sudanese government tended towards full independence. The Sudanese parliament proposed and decided to end the Condominium effective 1 January 1956.

In August 1955, five months before independence and when Sudanization of most posts had been completed, there was a serious mutiny in Torit in Southern Sudan and disturbances in much of the South. The board of enquiry identified a number of proximate causes of the mutiny, some of which could have been avoided, but the overall causes of the mutiny obviously had deep roots in the past and it is regrettable that the northerners did not, or could not, do more to reassure the southerners about the future government of the area after independence. As we know, despite efforts by some politicians and public servants on both sides to address the concerns of the southerners, and some periods of peace (e.g. following the Addis Ababa accords of 1972, negotiated by President Nimeiri, when the situation was in many ways normalized), the province has tragically been subject to repression, insurrection and outright civil war for much of the time since independence – a period of over fifty years. In 2011, Southern Sudan was eventually recognized by the United Nations as a new state, 'Southern Sudan', fifty-five years after the independence of Sudan.

Gold Coast (Ghana)

The constitution adopted for the Gold Coast in 1925 provided for a legislative council with fifteen official and fourteen unofficial members, a considerable advance by the standards of the day, though some of the unofficials were elected by the new provincial councils, acting as electoral colleges, rather than directly. This constitution remained practically unaltered until the mid-1940s. But, following a review, a new constitution was adopted in 1946, which provided for a substantial unofficial majority, the first such constitution in an African colony.

The issue of when the Executive Council (ExCo) should have unofficial, African members had become an issue of importance during the Second World War. The initiative to appoint unofficials to ExCo was first taken by Sir Alan Burns soon after he was appointed as governor of the Gold Coast in November 1941, on the basis of his experience in the West Indies and other colonies. He argued that unofficials often knew more about local conditions and the feelings of the people, and that they would help to lessen the likelihood of friction arising between African nationalists and the administration. He therefore proposed that at least two Africans should be admitted to the Gold Coast ExCo. The secretary of state in London, Lord Moyne,[10] agreed to this but stipulated that Burns should first consult the governors of other West African colonies. Governor Bourdillon of Nigeria in particular agreed with Burns on the basis of his earlier experience in Ceylon. However, with the appointment of Lord Cranborne as colonial secretary in London, ministerial concurrence with the proposal was lost, largely on the advice of Lord Hailey, who was influential with Cranborne. Hailey argued that logically appointments to ExCo had to be of officials holding departmental office, not unofficials with no such responsibilities, and the appointment of Africans to ExCo should come when they were qualified to hold departmental office.

Within the Colonial Office the arguments for and against were put by Fred Pedler, who in an internal memorandum, argued that while this action 'would bring into the inner councils of government men who are not bound by the same ties, either of loyalty or of secrecy, as their official colleagues' and 'might stimulate demands for further constitutional concessions ... it would offer some prospect of identifying with the Government the very persons who, in opposition, would be the most embarrassing opponents ... and on the whole the presence of Africans in ExCo may do as much to help us in dealing with them as to hinder us'. Bourdillon further argued that 'with the rapid growth in political consciousness which had taken place in Nigeria in the last two years, and the equally rapid development of the Trades Union movement, the need for such advice (in ExCo) has become very much more pressing than it had been'. He also pointed out that it was not the case that departmental heads in ExCo carried responsibility for policy, as elected ministers did in Britain, for responsibility for policy lay with the governor. Cranborne eventually accepted the arguments made by Burns and Bourdillon in September 1942. The first such appointments of African unofficials to ExCo were made in both the Gold Coast and Nigeria in the same month.[11] Trade Unions were legalized and recognized in the Gold Coast in late 1941.

Burns continued to press for further changes in the constitution, especially in regard to the level of unofficial representation in LegCo. Oliver Stanley, the colonial secretary, visited the Gold Coast in 1943 and discussed with Burns proposals emanating from the Joint Provincial Council, the Ashanti Confederacy Council and African Un-Officials in LegCo. The principal concern of the Colonial Office was the possible impact of such proposals in other colonies, especially East and

Central Africa, where the level of African education was much further behind and the number of qualified Africans fewer. Nevertheless in 1946 agreement was reached on a revised legislature with more directly elected representatives from coastal areas and also from Ashanti.

The Second World War was a major agent of change in the affairs of most colonies by requiring a greater degree of local reliance, through the experience of men enlisted in the armed forces, in some cases (such as Sudan, British Somaliland, Burma, Hong Kong and Malaya) by becoming theatres of war, and by leading in the case of some British colonies to the accumulation of what were known as 'Sterling balances' in the accounts of colonies which supplied goods or services acquired by the British government during the war. The Gold Coast certainly accumulated substantial sterling balances, but more significant as an agent of change was the experience of men of the Royal West African Frontier Force who participated in the East African and Burma campaigns. Another irritant after the war, as in Britain itself, was the shortage of consumption goods and continued rationing of goods . Perhaps the impact of these factors was not fully appreciated by the Gold Coast administration and in 1948 serious trouble broke out in Accra and elsewhere in the country before the 1946 constitution had bedded down. These troubles led to the appointment of a commission of inquiry under A. K. Watson.[12]

Though not charged with making constitutional proposals, the commission made a number of recommendations which the British government accepted subject to their being submitted to the Gold Coast people for consideration and to the reservation of some powers to the Governor. An All-African Committee under Justice Coussey produced a report in 1949, based on Watson's proposals, recommending conversion of the existing executive council into a body discharging ministerial functions, the abolition of the former central secretariat and its replacement by ministries, and creation of an enlarged Legislative Council to be wholly elected by popular vote. The resulting constitution was published in 1950. Further reform of the local authorities was also provided for. Thus by 1951, the Gold Coast had a new constitution, adopted after serious local consideration, and providing representative organs to take the country up to self-government, though with some powers still reserved to the Governor.

However, the next few years proved to be anything but smooth. The governor of the Gold Coast from 1949 until independence in 1957 was Sir Charles Arden-Clarke. The following passage draws on a speech given in 1957 by Arden-Clarke.[13] In 1949 Dr Kwame Nkrumah returned from his studies in Britain to become the general secretary of the United Gold Coast Convention Party, the principal nationalist party. However, he decided to establish his own more militant party, to be known as the Convention People's Party (CPP) with the slogan 'Full Self-Government Now'. The CPP launched a campaign of 'positive action' in pursuit of immediate self-government, but the government was prepared; within three weeks order was restored and those chiefly responsible were in prison. In early 1951 elections were held in accordance with the new 1950 constitution and the CPP won a substantial majority. Nkrumah was therefore released from prison and following careful, yet bold, negotiations between Arden-Clarke and Nkrumah, a working relationship was established between them which managed to see the country through to independence in 1957.

Much time was then devoted by the elected ministers and the officials to understanding how to govern the country within the provisions of the new constitution; how to make collective responsibility of the government a reality. This is when the inexperience and inadequate numbers of African civil servants made itself abundantly clear to all concerned, even though by comparison with colonies gaining self-government later, the Gold Coast was much better endowed than they were with both well-educated politicians and civil servants. It also became apparent that the increase in powers gained by the new central government was not matched by a similar strengthening of the local administration. Ideally, there should have been more time to address these inadequacies. However, the forward pressure of events did not allow sufficient time for these inadequacies to be made good.

It is of interest that in preparing for his discussions with Nkrumah on future constitutional development, Arden-Clarke was at pains to understand how similar developments were being handled in the Sudan. Though there were significant differences in the relations between Britain and the Sudan, on the one hand, and Britain and the Gold Coast on the other, due to the fact of Egypt being a co-dominus of Sudan, Arden-Clarke received important and subtle advice from the Colonial Office on detailed questions regarding the powers of the new institutions being created, reserve powers prior to independence, and other matters.[14] The governor of Nigeria also followed events closely, from at least January 1952, as they would obviously have an impact on Nigerian politicians, and in March 1953 visited London to express his concern about the possible effects in Nigeria.[15]

Under the Coussey constitution, another election was due to be held within four years. This occurred in June 1954. Participation was 59 per cent of the electorate. The CPP finished with a substantial majority of about 12 per cent of those voting. Immediately afterwards, a National Liberation Movement (NLM) was formed in Ashanti, the proximate cause being dissatisfaction with the cocoa price, which Nkrumah's government had fixed for four years. The movement grew and, beyond the issue of cocoa prices, represented a deep distrust of Dr Nkrumah and the CPP and a wish to preserve some kind of regional autonomy. Many incidents occurred on account of the rivalry between these two movements. A by-election led to the election in Ashanti of a candidate of the NLM, accompanied by a major swing of votes from the CPP to the NLM. Following the election, Nkrumah realized that he had to work hard to bring the country as a whole to acceptance of his approach to self-government.

Underlying the distrust of the CPP was the fear that a strong central government would hasten a decline in the role of the chiefs, among whom the Asantehene of the Ashanti was pre-eminent. Some of the leading members of the Opposition also held sophisticated concerns regarding the freedom of the individual, which were born out by later experience, and which were expressed to the British prime minister when he visited Ghana in January 1960.[16] This clash between the traditional forms of government, which the British authorities had strengthened under indirect rule as an incipient form of local government, and the progressive accretion of power to a central government staffed by the better educated, who generally proved to be much more adept at electoral politics, had been anticipated by Hailey (see Chapter 2), and was to appear in nearly all African and other British colonies. The NLM favoured a more federal structure with a Council of State comprising regional representatives.[17] The CPP favoured a strongly centralized structure. It has to be said that federal structures adopted elsewhere did not prove to be much more effective than unitary ones, though Nigeria was a possible exception and Malaysia a conspicuous one.

A further revised constitution was promulgated in the Gold Coast after the 1954 elections which gave the largest measure of self-government possible, short of complete independence. The new Assembly consisted of members who were all elected under a system of universal adult franchise; the cabinet consisted entirely of African ministers, with an African prime minister. The governor no longer attended cabinet, but he still retained his reserved powers. Further elections were held expressly to resolve the deadlock created by the differences between the government and the opposition parties over the question of federation. They were accompanied by the publication of further constitutional proposals which provided for regional assemblies with limited powers. The CPP, led by Nkrumah, won 72 seats out of the 104; the Northern People's party 12 seats; independent members 15 and the rest were won by minor parties. The turnout at the poll was 50 per cent, of which the CPP won 57 per cent of the votes cast. The CPP won all forty-four seats in the 'colony', eight seats in Ashanti, eleven seats in the Northern Territories and nine seats in Trans-Volta Togoland. Though there remained considerable regional dissent from the CPP's proposed system of government, the British government did not consider it could any longer withhold consent to full self-government within the Commonwealth. The existence of treaties between Britain and the chiefs of the Northern Territories, which comprised a British Protectorate, was not considered by either HMG or the chiefs themselves as being sufficient reason to withhold agreement to self-government, as the chiefs were already participating in the newly created political institutions of the country.

Reference has been made to Togoland, which was formerly a German colony, and was now a Trust territory held under a United Nations mandate by Britain and France. A plebiscite was held in May 1956 to determine the future of the country. The decision was in favour of the integration of the part of Togoland which had been under British administration with an independent Gold Coast.

The Gold Coast economy had benefited considerably from the increased demand for commodities during the war and the prospects as independence approached were encouraging. The level of education was well ahead of most other African countries. Communications were quite well developed and agriculture was quite diverse. The swollen shoot disease of cocoa trees was a worry, but the necessity of attacking it by felling the affected trees was fully accepted. Discussions on the proposed Volta River hydro/mining/industrial project were under way. Approaching independence the issue arose whether the Gold Coast/Ghana would continue to be eligible for CD&W financing. HMG's initial response was negative. We know now that Britain has in fact continued to contribute to Ghana's financing needs.

Corruption in public life became an issue before the independence of the Gold Coast. The practice of giving 'dash' is deeply ingrained in West Africa, going back to the days of tribal rule, though the colonial authorities did their best to eradicate the practice in the public service. A case in point was addressed by the secretary of state in his Memorandum of 29 August 1956 to the cabinet.[18, 19] A recent report of a commission of inquiry into the activities of the cocoa purchasing company clearly established that the company had been used by the Gold Coast government for party political purposes and that both the prime minister and the finance minister had been implicated in and condoned irregularities. Beyond a certain point, it was impractical for Britain to withhold self-government, though it was stressed to Nkrumah that the publication of the Report would have an important impact on public opinion in Britain and the Commonwealth and it was very important that the Gold Coast government demonstrate that they took the matter seriously. The governor persuaded Nkrumah to make a statement in the Legislative Assembly to the effect that the commission's report would be published, together with the government's proposals for implementing its recommendations. The announcement of the date for independence was withheld until after the publication of the Report.

The ten years prior to independence of Ghana permitted three general elections and progressive constitutional change, which was impressive. Nevertheless, it all happened very quickly – between 1949 and 1957 – and allowed little time for the underpinnings of government to be strengthened, especially for the acquisition of experience on the part of the different branches of the civil service, and the broadening of competence in public institutions. The initiative seized by the CPP and Nkrumah had become irresistible but it was not to be long before second thoughts occurred. These were summarized by Dennis Austin in African Affairs.[20] In addressing the means for achieving economic progress in the country, he wrote, 'if one asks how such an aim is to be pursued, the answer is clear – through the party, which dominates the contemporary scene in Ghana. It has remodelled the state in its own image – reducing the power of the Chiefs, centralizing the trade unions, legislating against tribal and regional parties, centralizing power within the constitution through the Constitution (Repeal of Restrictions) Act of November 1958, and the Constitution (Amendment) Act of March 1959, which abolished regional assemblies and empowered the National Assembly to legislate on any matter by a simple party majority. There must be no stress on local, separatist loyalties: "We insist," said Dr Nkrumah at the tenth anniversary of his party in Accra, that in Ghana in the higher reaches of our national life, there shall be no reference to Fantis, Ashantis, Ewes, Gas, Dagembas, "strangers" and so forth, but that we should all call ourselves Ghanaians – all brothers and sisters, members of the same community, the State of Ghana.' The same argument was elaborated by Peregrine Worsthorne in the May 1959 edition of Encounter (Trouble in the Air; Letter from Ghana) into a general critique of the Colonial Office approach to self-government of the colonies, in which he exhibited a somewhat nostalgic preference for rule by Chiefs, which was not actually a possibility if colonies were to evolve into nation states.

This centralization of power came to be quite widely accepted by those concerned with bringing the colonies to independence as inevitable and perhaps for the best at a time when the role of government was being expanded in various ways, when there were often severe limitations in the availability of qualified men and women and in view of the potential for destabilizing tribalism and regional movements. However, Sir Ivor Jennings made a strong case for the necessary checks and balances to limit the power of the state (see Annex 2). The argument for federal structures was eventually rejected in the West Indies, Central Africa and South Arabia, though adopted in Nigeria and, after an interval of time, Malaysia. Even so, the centralization of power in unitary states did not prevent the frequent and damaging intrusion of tribal and regional influences into the national life of many former African colonies following independence.

South Africa was opposed to Ghana becoming a member of the Commonwealth and delicate negotiations were required to make this possible. The Colonial Office had to explain to Dr Nkrumah that membership was not automatic and required the consent of all the current members. Eventually South Africa decided to leave the Commonwealth rather than accept the widening membership which came about in the 1960s.

Nigeria

There are parallels between the experience of Nigeria and Ghana in the years leading up to independence, due to proximity and contact between the people of the two countries, overlap of institutions and other factors. However the experience of Nigeria is unique for many reasons, but notably its scale and diversity. This section again draws on the memoirs of Sir James Robertson who was the last governor general of Nigeria[21] and also on the biography of Sir Bernard Bourdillon, governor from 1937 to 1942.[22]

It was in Nigeria that the system of indirect rule, adopted widely in Britain's African territories, had perhaps reached its apogee under Lugard's direction, but it was also in Nigeria that it had been first and most directly challenged. Under indirect rule, and with the guidance of district officers, the native authorities were strengthened so they could perform local government functions. Undoubtedly, this policy of creating and training local government agencies in all departments affecting the people most closely was of great service to Nigeria. It gave people a sense of responsibility and as the local organizations bedded in, it gave the people themselves a chance of running their own affairs and spending their own money.[23] However, being in some cases dominated by the tribal rulers the authorities tended to ossify and did not respond well to the interventions of younger, better-educated and trained citizens with political ambitions. A danger existed, as pointed out by the Australian W. R. Croker, a colonial official in Northern Nigeria, as early as 1936, that colonial populations could find themselves squeezed between the traditional rulers and Chiefs on the one hand and the newly educated young men and women entering public life on the other. In a critique of indirect rule he said the native authorities could not be a training ground for self-government, for economic and social development, 'if their leaders could neither read nor write'. Representative councils were required.

Some significant progress was made towards the creation of representative institutions in Nigeria before the Second World War. The governor, Sir Bernard Bourdillon, had initiated discussions with various people in 1938, especially with Nnamdi Azikiwe and Dr Abayomi, and with his emollient character, wide knowledge of the territory and decisive manner of administration made substantial progress in working out a system of representation and strengthening the foundations for unity in the country at the expense of the tribal and regional differences. In 1939 he issued a Memorandum on the Future Political Development of Nigeria.[24] While emphasizing the virtues of what Lord Dufferin in India had referred to as 'slow growth and gradual development' and the need for flexibility in the actual measures taken to reflect different local traditions and social structures, he argued that significant steps were now required to strengthen national institutions. Among other things, the Emirs in Northern Nigeria were not represented, and did not seek representation, in the national Legislative Council in Lagos, though it was actually taking financial decisions in respect of Northern Nigeria. This problem was exacerbated by the disloyalty shown by the commissioner for the northern region, Theodore Adams, and other officers, who continued to argue for enhanced regional autonomy and acted with that object in mind. (Adams actually outlasted Bourdillon in office.)

Bourdillon had had to face the consequences of the Second World War for Nigeria which required the wage-employment of many more people, control of production and sale of goods, with consequences for social relations, for inflation and the economy generally, and which stimulated urbanization. These events distracted Bourdillon from issues of constitutional development following his 1939 memorandum. However in 1942 he issued a second paper titled 'A Further Memorandum on the Future Political Development of Nigeria' which urged that decisions be taken and which was discussed in London in the period June–November 1942.[25]

There was general agreement that three regional councils should be created in the Western, Eastern and Northern Regions and that the gradual introduction of unofficials to these councils and to the national legislative council should follow. This was a path-breaking decision as most federal constitutions had hitherto been created by the decision of independent states themselves to merge in a federal form. In this case, it was a matter of dividing up a potential unitary state into regions. The number of regions is important. Bourdillon had also articulated the view, held by some officers, that three regions and their governments would be too large and remote and that a larger number of smaller, more homogeneous regions or provinces might be preferable.[26,27,28] Though Bourdillon did not pursue this alternative in the discussions in the Colonial Office, it is interesting that this argument was also made five years later by Obafemi Awolowo in his small book 'Path to Nigerian Freedom'[29] which, while giving an honest assessment of Nigeria's capacity to govern itself at that time and prodding Britain to get ahead with measures to educate and modernize the country, also argued that 'the federal institutions being created should enable each tribal group to evolve its own political institution. Each group must be autonomous in regard to its internal affairs. Each must have its own Regional House of Assembly'. He acknowledged that at that time there were not sufficient trained staff to handle the affairs of over ten houses of assembly, but he argued that it ought to be the objective. He drew an analogy with Switzerland where in a country of four million, there were twenty-two cantons, each with its own Assembly.

Nigeria like the Gold Coast was much affected by the Second World War, which as elsewhere was a catalyst of change. The Royal West African Frontier Force was much enlarged and was engaged in the East Africa and Burma campaigns. The government bought up the entire cocoa crop and much other produce. After the Fall of France in 1940, Nigeria found itself surrounded by French territories trying to determine whether to adhere to the Vichy authorities or throw in their lot with the Free French and de Gaulle. Bourdillon articulated the issues for the Colonial Office and as the pressures of war increased, Lord Swinton, an experienced British minister and former colonial secretary, was appointed as resident minister in West Africa to oversee wartime operations in the region. After the Japanese occupation of Malaya, Singapore and the Dutch East Indies in particular, Nigeria came under intense pressure to expand rapidly its production of tin, rubber, palm oil, groundnuts, grains, timber and other products. The numbers in paid employment rose rapidly, inflationary pressures gave rise to strikes and other employment problems arose to preoccupy the government. For the period when the Mediterranean Sea was too hazardous for civilian and even naval traffic, Nigeria became a major and strategic route to Egypt and the Eastern Mediterranean. Airfields were built across the region and into Sudan and Egypt. Nigeria like the Gold Coast built up substantial Sterling balances as a result of British purchases in the country. The Colonial Office sent a labour adviser to Nigeria, leading to the creation of the Nigeria Trade Union Congress in July 1942. Thus by the end of the war, the impact on Nigerians was substantial and stimulated interest in the new forms of government under consideration.

By 1942, after thirty-five years in India, Iraq, Ceylon, Uganda and Nigeria, Bourdillon's health had deteriorated to the point that he had to retire. Sir Arthur Richards was appointed to replace him. His appointment coincided with that of a new secretary of state, Colonel Oliver Stanley. Richards was keen to handle constitutional matters himself in consultation with the traditional rulers in Nigeria. In his despatch of July 1944[30] he proposed:

(i) A structure of a national Legislative Council and three regional councils, with a House of Chiefs and a House of Assembly in the north and Houses of Assembly in the west and east, plus the colony (essentially Lagos).

(ii) The membership of the proposed assemblies and LegCo.

(iii) The responsibilities of each level of the councils, with LegCo being the sole legislative body; but substantial delegation of financial responsibility to the regional councils, which would share the proceeds of direct local taxation, and block grants from the central government out of indirect taxation for specific purposes. In addition they would approve budgets.

(iv) Creation of regional deputies to the heads of all principal national departments of state, to facilitate greater delegation of day-to-day decisions.

(v) The existing system of native authorities set up under indirect rule was to be retained.

Bourdillon had been relaxed about the possibility of unofficial majorities in the councils. However, Richards wanted to retain official control in all councils initially to give them stability. The secretary of state reversed this reservation and permitted unofficial majorities in all councils from their creation. Nomination and selection of candidates for LegCo would be by the unofficials only of the Regional Assemblies. The final version of the new constitution was presented to LegCo as Sessional Paper No 4 of 1945 and published in Britain as Cmnd 6599.

Richards travelled extensively in Nigeria in making the case for the proposed constitution and pointed out that most Nigerians were not touched by the arguments of the urban politicians. He spent 1946 trying to force his way through a reluctant legislature and populace. The new constitution came into effect in January 1947. There followed initial sessions of the assemblies and much political activism outside them, especially by the National Council of Nigeria and the Cameroons (NCNC), Azikiwe's party, which managed to antagonize many other political leaders. By 1948 Richards had lost the confidence of the Colonial Office and its new secretary of state, Creech Jones. He retired and was replaced by Sir John Macpherson in April 1948, who had the services of the talented Hugh Foot as chief secretary. They found that despite early criticism and misunderstanding, the new constitution had got off to a good start and had been widely appreciated. They also noted that there had been a remarkable move of opinion in all regions in favour of a policy of regional autonomy within a federal state.[31]

Separately, following Creech Jones important despatch to African colonies of February 1947 on local government reform, which urged an increased elected element in local councils, Eastern Nigeria initiated local government reform by appointment of a select committee of the regional assembly, which reported in August 1948.

The year 1948 was a critical year when the decision was taken to open the Richards constitution to possible modification in the second three-year period after its adoption, instead of after nine years; and to launch a period of consultation 'by allowing time for expression of public opinion … and setting up a Select Committee composed of all the unofficial members of LegCo to review the whole position and make recommendations'. This was on the one hand a departure from Bourdillon's initial centralizing emphasis but on the other hand the manner of negotiating it was very much in the Bourdillon style. This consultation was widespread and involved village councils, local councils and regional councils, culminating in a national Constitutional Conference at Ibadan in January 1950. This major effort to seek and mobilize opinion in support of the revised constitution in 1951/2 served both to mollify those who had been offended by Richards' manner but also to educate the body politic into the different forms of government. A 'county council' with subordinate and elected district and local councils was established experimentally in South-East Nigeria in 1950–1. Boundaries were redrawn, small authorities merged, the tax system reorganized and local government put in charge of education. In South-Western Nigeria, the councils consisted of both elected and traditional members, with the Oba sometimes acting as the head of the council. In the north, the traditional rulers remained firmly entrenched but they were complemented by elected councils, which became effectively a form of cabinet of the Emir. The city of Kano received its own town council. A Colonial Local Government Advisory Panel was convened with participation by two pre-World War Nigerian officials to consider local government proposals, especially in respect of Eastern Nigeria.The new constitution was considered and approved by the British Cabinet in May 1950.[32]

Following the earlier addition of un-officials to ExCo, the new Nigerian constitution introduced in 1951 converted the Council into a true Cabinet. As the members of the Council were either British officials or Africans selected by electoral colleges, it did not gain immediate legitimacy in African eyes. However, the House of Representatives (LegCo), whose design was based on the British House of Commons, did begin effectively to give elected members experience in the art of consensual government. During 1953/4, there were further conferences on the constitutional future of the country, as a result of which the federal character of the country was strengthened. The three regions of the country – North, East and West had their separate areas of authority enlarged. A number of specified subjects were made federal or concurrent responsibilities, but all residual matters were to be under regional authority. This structure on the one hand recognized the three majority tribal groups of Yoruba (West), Hausa/Fulani (North) and Ibo (East), which also dominated the three main political parties, the Action Group (AG) in the West, the Northern People's Congress (NPC) in the north and the National Congress of Nigeria and Cameroons (NCNC) in the East; but on the other hand created a reasonably modern structure of government, within a superior Federal Government. Under pressure from Northern Nigeria, Lagos was cut out of the Western Region and made a federal capital and territory to ensure that access to the port was available to all Nigerians. There were obvious difficulties about implementing this structure, not least ensuring that the smaller tribal groups were not marginalized, but it represented a serious and sophisticated approach. Furthermore, conscious that the North had lagged in developing its educational system and civil institutions, it enabled the Sardauna of Sokoto, on behalf of the northern emirs, to reject the notion, then becoming current in the South, of self-government for Nigeria in 1956.

Robertson's description of the process leading to Nigerian independence on 1 October 1960 suggests that while there were no doubt frustrating and exhausting negotiations, the goodwill on all sides and the acceptance by the Nigerians of the inevitability of the outcome meant that agreement was never in doubt. There were however major difficulties arising from the normal operation of government, especially the prosecution from 1948 of the Zikist movement which articulated a revolutionary approach to the future of the country; concerns about the spread of communism; the response to a tragic loss of life when the police opened fire on striking coal miners in Enugu in 1949; and debates about the status of Lagos. In 1952 there was a serious dispute over the provisions of the constitution in regard to regional governments when Obafemi Awolowo and members of the NCNC made a serious attempt, involving vitriolic exchanges with government officers, to expand their powers in administering the country. Public meetings were held on the subject. A drafting error in the constitution caused legal problems. A split developed within the NCNC. In early 1953 there was pressure from ministers of the central government, who had been operating their ministries with limited powers to be given full powers to direct their ministries, partly for reasons of prestige, partly for reasons of more efficient decision-making. Additionally, a major divide between north and south emerged in LegCo over an AG motion to move towards self-government by 1956, which the northern ministers rejected. HMG concluded from these disputes that there would have to be further amendments to the constitution if the country was to be kept together, as the 1951/2 constitution was giving rise to acrimony.

A conference was convened in London in July 1953 under the chairmanship of the secretary of state, Oliver Lyttleton. The purpose was to examine the defects in the 1951 constitution, propose remedies and to look to the prospect of self-government by 1956. Subject to further detailed study by a drafting commission which was to visit Nigeria and the report of a fiscal commissioner, the conference decided on the following[33]:

(a) The number of regions would not be changed.

(b) Lagos would be excised from the Western region and would be the federal capital.

(c) The federal legislature would be directly elected, with average constituencies of 170,000 electors; but the North would have no more than half of the members. It would legislate on all matters exclusive to the central government and on the concurrent list.

(d) The unofficial members of the federal cabinet would number ten (three from each region and one from Cameroon). Federal ministers would no longer require confirmation by their regional legislature.

(e) There would be all-African legislatures and ministries in the regional governments which would have a greater degree of autonomy.

(f) There would be minimum qualifications for participation in elections but the method of elections would be left for lieutenant governors to decide with the regional ministers.

(g) The conference settled the division of jurisdiction between the Centre and the Regions.

(h)   The federal and regional public services were to remain under the control of the governor and lieutenant governors.

(i)   The financial arrangements were to be studied by a fiscal commissioner and come into effect from 1 April 1955.

(j)   The issue of control of the Police remained for further study.

(k)   Further consideration of the Cameroon issues.

(l)   HMG would in 1956 grant full self-government to those regions which wanted it, but would not coerce any region to move to that stage.

Thus to ensure the national interest was not neglected and to encourage national awareness, the federal legislature was to be directly elected by the whole country, rather than through regional assemblies acting as electoral colleges. Half the seats were to be filled by northerners, half by southerners. Each of the three regions was to be under a British lieutenant governor but effective authority was largely devolved on the Nigerian regional ministers. In the Central Executive Council, chaired by the governor general, there were to be three ex officio members (chief secretary, financial secretary and attorney general) but the remaining ten were Nigerians, three from each region and one from Southern Cameroon (which had decided by plebiscite to become part of Nigeria). They were to become the federal ministers. The Public Service was split between the regions, which had their own service notionally separate from the federal government. The judiciary was similarly divided along regional lines under a Federal Supreme Court, which could hear appeals from the regional courts. While the regions provided many local services, the principal collector of revenue was the federal government with the revenues being divided among the regions in proportion to the amount collected in each region. This federal structure was due for review by 1956 when regions were to be enabled to request full internal self-government in all matters for which they were responsible.[34]

Making this constitutional construct work effectively was difficult on account of the different interests represented, jealousies between regional and federal assemblies and agencies, the complex redistribution of responsibilities required, personality differences and a general fear of the northerners that they could come to be dominated by the better-educated southerners, numbers of whom lived in the north. Opposition parties in one region tended to be dominated by the leading parties in the other two regions. Nevertheless, it was heartening that the surprise results of the first elections to LegCo in late 1954 under the 1954 constitution did not disrupt progress. The results were as follows[35]:

Results of the first elections to LegCo, 1954

Party	North	West	East	South Cameroon	Lagos	Total
Northern Peoples Congress	80	-	-	-	-	80
Nat.Council of Nigeria and Cameroon	-	23	34	-	1	58
Action Group	1	18	7	-	1	27
Kameroon Nat. Congress	-	-	-	6	-	6
Others	11	1	1	-	-	13
Total	92	42	42	6	2	184

This unforeseen result, with the action group very much in the minority, could have upset the balance. However, careful negotiations initiated by the NPC and the governor resulted in a balance in the council of ministers which permitted business to go forward effectively. There was however a tendency initially for civil servants in the federal government to go on giving instructions to their colleagues in the regions as though the country was still a unitary state. Another difficulty was that regional and federal elections sometimes produced different results so that, for example, as Robertson recalled, the AG had a majority in the western regional assembly at the same time as it had no representation at all in LegCo. Robertson devoted considerable energy in persuading ministers of the federal executive that they ought to think nationally, not regionally, to seek ways to strengthen national cohesion rather than undermine it for party political advantage. Another significant difficulty was that the leaders of the political parties often preferred to remain in the regional assemblies, their power bases, rather than join the federal legislature. Thus the latter tended to contain second-string political leaders, who tended to be beholden to the regional leaders. Despite this, it was generally felt that the new constitution was being implemented effectively and with significant support from those involved. The acrimony of the London conference had largely faded away. After the event, Nigerians attending the conference were very positive about the outcome and the role of Oliver Lyttelton in chairing it.

Preparations for the next constitutional conference due no later than August 1956 were thorough and there were almost continuous exchanges between Nigeria and London about the issues to be discussed and settled. In November 1955, the colonial secretary, Alan Lennox-Boyd, held a private meeting with Dr Azikiwe at which he aired and discussed a number of matters including the financial policies of the Eastern region government and the case of the

African Continental Bank, which he said had to be addressed soon if the 1956 conference was to be a success. He also met with Abubakr Tafawa Balewa and Robertson had a productive meeting with Awolowo.

In early 1956, in the middle of all the negotiations about local, regional and national issues, Queen Elizabeth and the Duke of Edinburgh spent three weeks touring Nigeria. Many reports confirm that this was a great success which drew Nigerians together in visits, personal contacts, festivities, durbars and served to demonstrate to Nigerians and Cameroonians, who had not travelled much around the country, that Nigeria was a large and diverse nation with much to be proud of and much to hope for.

Before the 1956 conference could be held the leader of the opposition of the Eastern Regional Assembly tabled a motion criticizing Azikiwe's behaviour in regards to the African Continental Bank. Lennox-Boyd decided that since this was a federal matter the commission of inquiry into the affair should be held before the Constitutional Conference. The commission of inquiry was appointed on 24 July 1956, under the chief justice of Nigeria, Sir Stafford Foster-Sutton. The allegation was that an agency of the Eastern regional government had made £2 million (2017 £45 million) available to the African Continental Bank, in which Dr Azikiwe, the regional premier, was the principal shareholder. The chairman of the agency, who was a rival politician in the NCNC, agitated against the transaction. The inquiry found that Azikiwe's actions had fallen short of the standards required of a public and political figure, though there appeared to be no criminality and Azikiwe himself did not appear to have benefited personally from the transaction. Following the publication of the Foster-Sutton report, Azikiwe transferred all his rights and holdings in ACB to the Eastern region government and asked for a dissolution of the House of Assembly. New elections to the regional assembly were held in March 1957. The NCNC lost a few seats, the Action Group gained twelve seats, which made it the largest of the opposition parties. Dr Azikiwe remained premier.[36]

The postponed 1956 Constitutional Conference was held in London in May–June 1957 under Lennox-Boyd's chairmanship with delegates from all three regions, Cameroon and the federal government. The findings were published in Britain. The most important decisions were as follows[37]:

(i)   The western and eastern regional governments would become self-governing after the conference under interim statutory instruments, pending the drawing up of the final ones, with discretion retained by the governor in respect of any Bill which in his view might impede or prejudice the performance of any of its functions by the federal government.

(ii)   The Northern Region requested that self-government for the North should be introduced in 1959.

(iii)   There would be an enquiry into the possibility of creating new states and the issues governing minorities.

(iv)   The Federal House of Representatives would run its full course until the end of 1959 and then be dissolved for new elections for a membership of 320, or about one per 100,000 electors.

(v)   A second federal assembly, the Senate, would be created with a membership of twelve for each region and the Cameroons (subject to a decision by the people of that country), four for Lagos and four to be nominated by the governor.

(vi)   An office of prime minister and other consequential changes would be made to the senior official positions.

(vii)   The powers of the governor would not be changed until independence.

(viii)   There were some amendments to the functions of federal and regional governments and encouragement to the creation of provincial authorities in some special cases.

(ix)   It was agreed that a date for independence in 1960 would be determined by consultation.

The 1960 date for independence was arrived at by the Colonial Office after agonizing debate among its officials and ministers, and with Robertson and the lieutenant governors in Nigeria, as they all felt that more time was needed to get the country ready for independence. Critical was the position of the north which decided to go for self-government in 1959 partly out of concern at the changing views of younger, better-educated people and partly out of a wish not to hold up the country as a whole. On the part of the Colonial Office, there was a concern to avoid detracting from the excellent relations which then existed between Britain and Nigeria by postponing independence.

In August 1957, the officials in the federal council of ministers were replaced by a prime minister and a minister of finance, both Nigerian. Robertson said he found it much easier to chair a meeting consisting entirely of Nigerian ministers than to arbitrate irritating debates between ministers and officials. The regional lieutenant governors were the main channel for Robertson to influence government in the regions – Sir Bryan Sharwood-Smith who had served for many years in the North, Sir Clem Pleass in the East and Sir John Rankine in the West. They had direct day-to-day relations with the leaders of the political parties, including the Sardauna of Sokoto in the North, Dr Azikiwe in the East and Chief Awolowo in the West, who were all in their own way prima donnas and highly articulate political figures.

Robertson responded to the strengthening of the regional governments by stimulating federal-level agencies to be proactive in providing coordination between the regional bodies, by the creation of a national economic council and similar national bodies. He also gave close attention to the Africanization process in the Public Service on a national basis, including the police and armed forces. He considered that Nigeria had not progressed as rapidly as the Sudan in localizing its Public Service. As the Lidbury Commission observed in regard to the Gold Coast, 'responsibility is the most effective of all teachers and the essential point, if an officer has the necessary quality, is to arrange for his employment as early as possible on responsible work'. Robertson wrote, 'I tried to impress on the Public Service Commission that it was imperative to push on capable Nigerians and get them into the higher segments of the service as soon as they could do the work and take responsibilities, and that risks would have to be taken'. The issue of the creation of more states came up again in early 1955, but there was little sympathy for this notion within the Colonial Office; the papers on this matter seemed to suggest that the federation would be threatened by the creation of more states, though that conclusion was not, and is not, inevitable. Nevertheless, the Nigeria administration sought to follow the discussion on this topic among Nigerian leaders, though they tended to feel that it was only pursued by the AG and the NCNC with a view to weakening the NPC.[38]

The key issues to be addressed after the 1957 Constitutional Conference were as follows:

- The Western and Eastern Regions became self-governing in their regional functions by August 1957; the lieutenant governors ceased to act in an executive manner but provided advice and attended to federal-level business. The Northern Region chose to delay this stage for itself until 1959, by which time they hoped to be better prepared. Meanwhile the regions would take some steps towards self-government before 1959. Thus a great deal of authority was conveyed to the Regional governments ahead of full independence.

- The situation of the minorities, which was looked into by a commission of inquiry under Sir Henry Willink. This commission found that the arguments for additional regional states were evenly balanced by the arguments against, including significant potential administrative complications which could, at that stage, have delayed independence. The issue of minorities was therefore shelved, though it was to re-emerge strongly after independence, and especially after the Biafran War when the federal concept was reconsidered and amended. Even as late as the 1990s additional, though smaller, states were created. Thus over time the federal government became relatively more powerful and the state governments less so.

- The position of the Police. The Regions wished to have the power to maintain law and order in their regions but the minorities were especially concerned that the police should not be subject to the control of the regional politicians. Furthermore, some local police forces were closely identified with the local emirs and chiefs. During the transition to independence, the colonial authorities felt it to be essential for them to retain control of the police and the army. The solution arrived at for the police, which endured well, was that they would remain a federal body under the control of an inspector general (IG). The police commissioners in the regions would be responsible to the IG, but would also keep in close contact with the regional premiers. If the commissioners felt they were being pressured to depart from general federal police policy, they could refer the matter to the IG. A Police Council consisting of the federal prime minister, the Regional Premiers and the IG would be the final controlling authority to which issues could be referred. Until independence, the governor general would act as chairman of the council.

- Distribution of Revenues. This issue was addressed by a commission under Sir Jeremy Raisman who had been finance member of the Government of India from 1939 to 1945. The issues here were partly technical but also a matter of fairness over time. At that stage, oil had not yet been found in Nigeria. The Regions thought the federal government had been generously treated but accepted the commission's recommendations.

- The appointment of a federal prime minister, who would nominate other ministers representative of the entire country. Alhaji Abubakr Tafewa Balewa was appointed and proved to be an excellent first prime minister of Nigeria. Robertson found it was quite easy to agree solutions to issues with him, including matters of foreign policy and defence, which would remain under British control until independence.

- The difficult transition of the government authority in the north from emirs and chiefs who had exercised great authority for centuries to elected bodies and politicians; and the lack of trained northerners to perform governmental and technical functions.

In preparation for independence, and reflecting the changed international situation, the decision was taken to abolish the single command of the Royal West African Frontier Force situated in Kaduna, Nigeria and create three new commands in Ghana, Nigeria and Sierra Leone/Gambia, with three distinct military units. Provision was also made for an Army Advisory Council for West Africa.[39]

Independence was sought by the federal assembly following the election of December 1959 in which the NPC gained 149 seats, the NCNC 89 seats and the AG 72 seats. The British cabinet accepted this result and brought in legislation for the independence of Nigeria effective from 1 October 1960.

East Africa

HMG's policy in regard to the British East African territories was first set out in a considered fashion in the Devonshire White Paper of 1923[40] which, while responding to questions from Asians in Kenya, also dealt with East Africa generally:

> Primarily Kenya is an African territory, and His Majesty's Government think it necessary definitely to record their considered opinion that the interests of the African Natives must be paramount, and that if and when those interests and the interests of the immigrant nations should conflict, the former should prevail. ... In the administration of Kenya His Majesty's Government regard themselves as exercising a trust on behalf of the African population, and they are unable to delegate or share this trust, the object of which may be defined as the protection and advancement of the Native races ... there can be no room for doubt that it is the mission of Great Britain to work continuously for the training and education of the Africans towards a higher intellectual, moral and economic level than that which they had reached when the Crown assumed responsibility for their administration ... as in the Uganda Protectorate, so in the Kenya Colony, the principle of trusteeship for the natives, no less than in the mandated territory of Tanganyika, is unassailable.

The sentiments of this policy had actually been articulated earlier by Ellis in 1908 and also by Lord Peel in 1923.

In July 1927, the colonial secretary circulated a paper to the British cabinet setting out more generally the future policy in regard to Eastern Africa.[41] This started by reiterating the statement of 1923. But it then went on to review the findings of the East African Commission of 1924, which emphasized the common needs and problems of the three territories; differentiated the territories from those of West and South/Central Africa; and outlined the conclusions of a conference of the British East African governors held in Nairobi in early 1926. This conference was the first step taken towards securing better cooperation between the administrations of territories 'whose boundaries are in the main the result of historical accident rather than the expression of ethnological and geographical facts'. The paper referred to the East African Guaranteed Loan Act providing for loans up to £10 million (2017 £552 million) to be guaranteed by HMG, which required proper coordination of policy for the railways and other facilities; the movement in favour of effective cooperation in research into agriculture and human and animal disease; the fostering of identical customs tariffs and a postal union between the territories. It referred to the need for those participating in public administration and policy to focus not merely on the needs of their own communities, but also on the interests of the territories at large. It wanted 'to associate more closely in this high and honourable task (trusteeship) those who as colonists or residents have identified their interest with the prosperity of the country'. The paper discussed the possibility of federation, but viewed that concept as something for the future.[42]

The four East African territories of Kenya, Uganda, Tanganyika (Tanzania) and Zanzibar, though sometimes grouped together for administrative purposes in colonial times, presented different issues of development and administration; in the approach to Africanization of the public service, governments had to take account of their very different character. The following table summarizes the population of the three mainland countries in 1948, when the future of the colonies was becoming a matter of importance:

Population of the three mainland countries in 1948

	African	European	Asian	Other (mainly Arab)
Kenya	5,251,120	29,660	90,528	
Tanganyika	7,407,517	10,648	44,248	
Uganda	4,917,555	3,448	33,767	
	17,576,192	43,756	168,543	53,672

Source: East African Population Census, 1948.

The Africans belonged to many different tribes, with some locally or even nationally predominant such as the Baganda in Uganda and the Kikuyu in Kenya. At that time (1948) they lived predominantly on the land, with only 64,000 Africans in Nairobi, 43,000 in Mombasa and 51,000 in Dar es Salaam. Of the Europeans, about two-thirds of those in Kenya were engaged in farming and the related rural activities. They had created the productive and export-oriented agricultural economy which supported the national economy. Others were engaged in business, teaching and the professions. Most Africans were engaged in subsistence agriculture, though increasingly this could be more correctly described as peasant farming growing coffee, tea, cotton and a few other cash crops. The Asians were widely spread and were engaged in a wide range of activities – agricultural processing, trade and retailing, work on the railways, as artisans, craftsmen, clerks and so on. A distinctive element among the Asians were the members of the Isma'ili sect of Islam under the leadership of the Aga Khan. With this diverse population, most of whom were still living at a subsistence level, there could not fail to be potential difficulties of access to land, representation, the franchise, educational participation, income and social customs. These difficulties arose as early as the 1920s, especially in regard to the situation of the Asian community, but also in response to differences of view between the British settlers in Kenya and the colonial government over the status of the British settlers. Seeking to clarify the situation in Kenya where the problems were most acute, the British government had made the declaration, quoted earlier, in the Devonshire White Paper of 1923.

Though difficulties continued to arise subsequently, right up to the time of, and beyond the time of, independence, in regard to all the issues listed earlier, the statement of principle in the 1923 declaration ensured that the destination of travel was clear and would not be changed. The declaration drew somewhat on the British experience of the Union of South Africa, where settler groups had acquired substantial autonomy, and Southern Rhodesia where something similar was taking place at that time. In principle, the British government was anxious to avoid a similar situation arising in East Africa through inertia, though sometimes their actions were equivocal, in particular in the way they permitted, and even encouraged, settlement by additional British settlers until the 1940s. Thus the issue of land rights became fundamental, especially in Kenya.

On 1 January 1953, an East African Royal Commission was commissioned:

Having regard to the rapid increase of the African population of East Africa and the congestion of population on the land in certain localities, to examine the measures necessary to be taken to achieve an improved standard of living, including the introduction of capital to enable peasant farming to develop and expand production, to make recommendations with regard to the economic development of the land … adaptations or modifications in traditional tribal systems of tenure … taking account of existing obligations incurred by treaty, agreement, or formal declaration of policy in relation to the security of land reserved for different races and groups etc.

The terms of reference of the Royal Commission were widely cast to ensure it could consider all aspects of the problem. One of the fundamental conclusions reached was that the only way to resolve the land issue in Kenya (and also Uganda and Tanganyika, though there it was a less pressing problem) was to view the country as a single, integrated economic unit and abolish the tribal and racial boundaries/reservations. Until 1955 the tribal/racial/communal issue in Kenya predominated and was an important underlying cause of the Mau Mau insurrection among the Kikuyu. Thereafter, it became easier to contemplate changes and greater flexibility in administering the country as a whole. However the commission recognized that replacing the previous ordinances governing land and gaining acceptance of the alternative they put forward, would take time and require consistent application of the new policy. As a result of these deliberations on land issues and the Mau Mau revolt, time was lost before such constitutional issues as representation, the franchise and so on could be addressed effectively in Kenya. Although a similar issue arose in Tanganyika, it did so in only a small part of a much larger country. The land issue did not arise in this form at all in Uganda, though the administration did have to take into account the system of 'Mailo' land among the Baganda, the so-called lost counties and commitments made to other tribes.

In its report,[43] the Royal Commission stressed the poverty of the three East African countries by comparison with other African countries. The per capita net product was among the lowest in Africa. The commission concluded that this poverty was a consequence largely of the fact that subsistence agriculture formed the basis of the rural economy except in the areas settled by Europeans and peasant cash cropping, especially in parts of Uganda; that some areas had been denuded of population due to rinderpest, tsetse fly, locust infestation, the German response to the Maji Maji rebellion in Tanganyika and other factors; and by the absence of significant mineral development; and was intensified 'by the elaborate system of restrictions and inhibitions which pervade the East African economy and which is in part a feature of the tribal order of society and in part a creation of public policy'. In addition, the traditional Arab and Indian traders had gained something of a stranglehold on trade locally, leading to monopolistic practices.

Coordination between the three territories had been encouraged and implemented in various ways for some decades. N. J. Westcott has described the history of this coordination in his comprehensive article of October 1981.[44] The matter was investigated four times in the 1920s and 1930s without conclusion, though economic factors were drawing the three countries together. This led some, including Sir Arthur Dawe, a senior Colonial Office official, to conclude that the forces working for unity would be greater than those working against it. Others articulated the fear that this would benefit the Kenya settlers more than other inhabitants and this was against policy. However the situation changed during the Second World War when much was contributed by all three countries to the war effort and coordination between the three countries became an imperative. The governor's Conference Secretariat became the focus for a number of ad hoc committees, councils and boards created to facilitate the war effort, with the governor of Kenya the permanent chairman. Sir Henry Moore, the governor, felt obliged to authorize the creation of the Civil Defence and Supply Council (CDSC) for this purpose. This encompassed among other things guaranteed crop prices, conscription of labour and an Agricultural Production and Settlement Board, which were managed mainly by European unofficials.

The Colonial Office was concerned that this was leading to domination of East Africa by the Kenya settlers and towards the creation of a 'white' dominion in

East Africa following the war. The colonial secretary, Lord Cranbourne, said that there was no chance of such a proposal being accepted by the war cabinet. Furthermore, and of great interest in view of his key later role in the decolonization process, the Parliamentary under-secretary for the colonies, at that time Harold Macmillan, commented in 1942 that the whites were unlikely to stay in Kenya – 'a clash is bound to come. The whites cannot afford economically to abandon their supremacy. The Government will be torn between the rights of the settlers and their obligations to the natives. Even if the federal solution ... were to be put into effect now, the land hunger and the pressure of the natives will not be relieved'.[45] He advocated buying out the settlers and giving the land back to the natives. This would be expensive but not so expensive as a civil war. (HMG did in due course pay a large sum to Kenya in the 1960s to buy out many of the European settlers.) Governor Moore was recalled to London and told he would have to reform the CDSC, rename it the East African Production and Supply Council and increase the representation of Uganda and Tanganyika. However, the governors of Uganda and Tanganyika were still not happy with this solution, which tended to undermine territorial authority. Colonial Office consultation with the Labour members of the war cabinet also showed how much reluctance there was in Britain to increased control on the part of the settlers. Despite this clear thinking in London at that time, some Kenya settlers continued to believe that they could continue to control events for the foreseeable future.

Post-war, under a new governor of Kenya, Sir Philip Mitchell, a somewhat more flexible body was proposed in the form of a high commission of the three governors of East Africa, which would have complete control over the common services to be run by a central secretariat. Legislation on these matters would be the sole responsibility of a Central Legislative Assembly. This solution also was found unacceptable in London, as centralizing too much authority in Kenya. In August 1946 the new colonial secretary, Creech Jones, and his senior official, Andrew Cohen, visited East Africa and negotiated a compromise which reduced the power of the Assembly and clarified that the territories would be responsible for economic policy. Further, the high commission would be financed by an annual block vote for each service from each territory. Despite this re-emphasis on territorial control, not a single African or Asian voted in favour of this arrangement in the territorial legislatures. The revised scheme was however voted through by the officials. The East African High Commission came into being in January 1948 and in practice (despite continuing Colonial Office fears of overlapping authorities) was essentially an administrative and technical body with little political power. Its remit was limited and quite specific; apart from informal consultation on matters of mutual interest, it was limited to provision of common services, such as the railways and harbours, customs and excise, posts and telegraph, some research functions and disease control. Nevertheless, as late as November 1950, the colonial secretary of the day still felt he needed authority from the Cabinet to assert the territorial authority of the four colonies in the face of continued pressures to address matters on an East African basis.[46]

To jump ahead a little, at the time of the negotiations leading to the independence of Tanganyika in early 1961, Julius Nyerere was keen to see a federation created:

> for the sake of securing the prize of federation, he was ready to defer the date of Tanganyika's independence. ... I think he fully understands that it may not be possible for HMG to make forward moves in Kenya, still less in Uganda ... when advocating federation, Nyerere expressed the view that if the countries deferred coming together until after they had severally gained their independence, the chance of federation would probably be lost. Therefore, his argument was that they must move to federation and independence at one and the same time.[47]

However the three countries were moving forward on such different timetables that despite his earlier remarks, in practice Nyerere showed no willingness to delay the independence of Tanganyika until agreement could be reached between the three territories on federation.

Consideration of the issue continued and during the course of the June 1963 discussions on the future constitution of an independent Kenya, serious consideration was still being given to the notion of federation. In the course of the discussions, the Kenya ministers outlined the progress made in working out the constitution for the proposed East African Federation, which would comprise Kenya, Tanganyika, Uganda and possibly Zanzibar. It was agreed that it was desirable that Kenya should become independent shortly before the inauguration of the Federation, which it was hoped would take place before the end of the year. It is clear that what was being considered here was a federation still focussed on practical, economic relations rather than political relations, since there was little enthusiasm for a political federation to succeed the colonial relationship.

The following sections look at the particular political and constitutional issues which arose and approaches taken in all three mainland East African countries in turn.

Uganda

The general view at the time and among those serving there was that Uganda was the most harmonious of the three mainland territories (Uganda was actually a British protectorate, rather than a colony). A relatively large proportion of the African population had entered the cash economy following a redistribution of land under the 1900 Agreement with Britain, creating an economy based on new patterns of society. Cotton and coffee were the principal cash crops and it is important that this was in the hands of Africans, rather than settler Europeans, of whom there were few. The volume of trade had been rising steadily. By the mid-1950s exports were roughly twice imports, and food production also rose rapidly. By contrast Kenya's balance of trade was negative. There was a growing interest in public policy. Education had made considerable progress and Makerere had already emerged as the principal education centre of East Africa. The progress being made towards self-government was also promising. The people seemed attracted to production and commerce, to education and to Christianity. This does not mean there were no nascent problems, not least the special status of the Baganda with their own assembly, the Lukiko, and their tribal chief, the Kabaka who, subject to certain conditions, exercised direct rule over his tribe under a regime agreed between the Kabaka of the time and Captain (later Lord) Lugard in 1890, an agreement recognized officially by the British government in 1900. This regime was a more sophisticated structure than the usual Native Authority and aroused jealousy among some of the other tribes and tribal chiefdoms. How to fit the Baganda and its traditional structures into a structure for a self-governing state was to be a complex problem, which was never solved.

The system of justice had remained largely in the hands of the Native governments. The Lukiko of the Baganda was the highest court and integration with the colonial legal system was only partial. Colin Legum wrote of the Ugandan justice system: 'The resistance to effective integration is strong and flows from the same causes that have prevented a Western system of parliamentary democracy from taking root in the country.'[48] He went on, 'Having secured a wide measure of internal autonomy under the 1900 Agreement, the Baganda proceeded to develop a porcupine-like defence reaction to any move threatening their right to control their internal affairs.' They resisted 'Closer Association' with Kenya and Tanganyika, initially resisted creation of a Legislative Assembly, welcomed elsewhere, on grounds that LegCo would be dominated by outsiders and represented a possible future threat to their autonomy. A casualty of this mood was the Buganda Land Acquisition Act introduced to permit purchase of land by government for Makerere University and the Empire Cotton Experimental Station, for example. Development of industrial and energy potential also encountered suspicion and resistance.

Into this complex situation, Sir Andrew Cohen was appointed governor in 1953, arriving with the reputation of a progressive reformer and formidable experience in the Colonial Office. He set out to foster rapid expansion in education, community development and industry, democratization of the Buganda constitution and reform of LegCo. He had considerable success in many of these sectors, but not in regard to constitutional reform of the Lukiko and LegCo. In the process he also stirred up opposition to his proposals at significant points. Though progress was made in Buganda, there was opposition to elections to the Lukiko in place of nominations by chiefly status or by the Kabaka. The Lukiko even asked HMG to place Uganda under the foreign office, as it had been at the time of the 1900 Agreement, instead of the Colonial Office. In 1953, the colonial secretary, Oliver Lyttleton, referred in a speech in London to the possible desirability of Uganda becoming part of an East African federation. This was reported in the East African Standard whose reporter went around speculating about the notion and stirring up a hornet's nest of objections. This was particularly sensitive in Uganda which was very concerned about being bounced into close relations with and possible dependency on the Kenya settlers, and in Tanganyika due to its position as a trust territory of the United Nations. In November 1953, the Kabaka wrote to Lyttleton asking for an assurance that there would never be a federation of East Africa, that responsibility for Uganda be transferred from the Colonial Office to the Foreign Office and that Buganda be declared 'independent'.

The opposition to reform of the Lukiko was endorsed by all three ministers in the council, who also endorsed the Kabaka's letter to Cohen stating why he did not agree to Cohen's proposals for the constitution. Faced with this opposition, Cohen returned to London for consultation with the colonial secretary. The British government's response was to accept that if Uganda did not wish to enter a federation of East Africa, the matter would not be pressed. HMG considered the notion of placing Uganda under the Foreign Office to be 'constitutionally inappropriate'. In addition, HMG rejected the notion that Buganda could not be under the purview of the LegCo since this would be in breach of the 1900 Agreement. After various other exchanges and disagreements between the governor and the Kabaka, the governor informed the latter that HMG was withdrawing recognition of him as a Native ruler and an order of banishment was served on him. The Kabaka was deported to Britain. Ex post facto, it would seem that Cohen did not fully comprehend the relationship between the Kabaka and the Lukiko, which was changing and indeed had changed since 1900; and felt he was being stubborn without adequate reason. Successive colonial secretaries, Lyttleton and Lennox-Boyd, felt that Cohen's personality and manner exacerbated the arguments between them, and that he had mishandled the situation, though they were reluctant to overrule the governor.

The following section draws considerably on a speech made by Cohen, then the retiring governor of Uganda, to the Royal Africa Society in 1957.[49] Cohen stressed the comprehensive way in which the protectorate government had pursued a deliberate plan of action in public policy in the 1940s–50s through a series of important policy studies – the Wallis Report on local government, the de Bunsen report on African education, the Watson Report on agricultural productivity, the Maybury Committee on the advancement of Africans in trade and the Frazer Committee on medical and health services. These provided the basis for practical programmes of action and legislation over a decade. In addition, Uganda was the first of the three East African territories to establish a public service commission with the task of promoting appointment of Africans and the maintenance of standards in the Public Service.

To reflect the strength of tribal loyalty in the country, and in order to channel this loyalty into constructive activities, the tribal authorities were given increased powers and responsibilities for the running of provincial services, including local education, medical and health services and the agricultural and veterinary services, all of which were to be run in accordance with the policies of the Protectorate government. At the same time, the tribal authorities were made more representative of the people, with elected majorities in councils. New agreements were entered into in Buganda and Bunyoro in 1955 and analogous arrangements made in most of the other districts. These councils introduced a graduated tax system in the mid-1950s. At the national level, in the mid-1950s a ministerial system was introduced in the Executive Council and the LegCo reformed to ensure that every district of the country was represented. The members were elected mostly through district councils acting as electoral colleges, with the announced objective of moving to direct elections on a common roll in 1961.

HMG was keen that all three East African territories should introduce a qualitative franchise with tests for residence, age, literacy, income and ownership/rental of land. Under the original Uganda proposal for the LegCo elections, a typical case, these required a residential qualification, a minimum age of twenty-one years, completion of Primary IV schooling, net cash income of £100 per annum or property of £500 and freehold or rental of land for at least three years. However, in an act of brinkmanship, the Lukiko rejected this for Buganda in favour of universal adult suffrage. After negotiations and some modifications, the final arrangement was for the residence and age qualifications plus ability to read or write his/her own language, cash income of £100 per annum or property worth £400, registered ownership of Mailo land or a record of paying Crown Land rents for two years, with the additional option of seven years continuous public service or seven years paid employment in agriculture, commerce or industry. The Uganda government estimated that these qualifications would enfranchise 70–80 per cent of men and 10–20 per cent of women in Buganda, and somewhat lower percentages elsewhere. Acceptance would be accompanied by the announcement of a change to universal adult suffrage in 1961 on a common roll, provided adequate representation for the minority communities was assured. This complexity is typical of pre-independence constitutions in many colonies, especially where there were European and Asian settlers. HMG decided to accept this proposal despite the then current decision in Kenya and Tanganyika to insist on a qualitative franchise including completion of Primary IV education.[50] These measures ensured that prior to the drafting of an independence constitution, some experience had been gained by Ugandan politicians and civil servants over a short period of five years in working an elected government.

There were two serious issues which troubled the approach of Uganda towards self-government, which concerned the relationship of the Baganda to the other tribal groups in the country and the position and powers of the Kabaka, Mutesa II, discussed earlier. Once he was banished, the question arose in what circumstances and on what terms he might be permitted to return, an issue which was influenced both by the evolving constitutional situation in Uganda and by the comparable situation of Seretse Khama of Bechuanaland, who was also in exile in Britain. After Cohen's replacement by Crawford, a way was found to allow the Kabaka back and in the independence constitution he became president of Uganda.[51,52]

Not for long however. At the 1962 election, Milton Obote, from one of the northern tribes, became prime minister, while the Kabaka remained president. This relationship ultimately destabilized the country and led to its downfall. After four years, Obote expelled the Kabaka, who had been seeking greater autonomy for his tribe, abolished the other tribal units (such as Bunyoro and Toro) and became president himself, with full executive powers. He created a one-party state and adopted a programme of socialist measures. However, in the process of seizing power he gave the army its head and Amin, its senior officer, proved to have greater support in the army than Obote. Amin also had external support from Israel which was providing support to Southern Sudan's secessionists for its own reasons. In 1971, Amin overthrew Obote, who was out of the country, and began to rule it himself. Amin expelled the Asians in 1972 and became a tyrant who violently resisted any attempt to limit his authority. This was too much for the nascent nationhood of Uganda, which succumbed to the struggle for power between contenders supported by backers from outside the country. The sense of nationhood within independent Uganda was too fragile.[53]

Tanganyika (Tanzania)

(Writing this passage has been greatly eased by Colin Baker's very able and detailed analysis of the Tanganyika negotiations which appears in his biography of Sir Richard Turnbull).[54]

Tanganyika was a German colony until the end of the First World War, when it became a British Mandate of the League of Nations. After the creation of the United Nations in 1945, it became a British Trust territory of the UN. Though this international interest in the territory did not have a large day-to-day impact on the way the country was administered, it remained a factor which the administration had to keep in mind, and the uncertainty of its status probably had a negative impact on investment in the territory in the interwar period. However, Sir Edward Twining, the governor from 1949 to 1958, pointed out at a later date that there were constant dangers of Tanganyikan affairs being dealt with not objectively for the good of the territory, but for purposes of international politics. For this reason one of the first things Twining did as governor was to visit the UN to reiterate and reinforce the policies articulated by the British representatives at the UN that under the Trusteeship Agreement, 'the administering power, that is the United Kingdom, is ultimately responsible ... and if the colonial authorities and HMG do not agree with the views of visiting UN missions and arguments made in the Trusteeship Council, it is our responsibility to decide what was best for Tanganyika'.[55]

Indirect rule, which had been introduced to Tanganyika by Sir Donald Cameron in 1925 based on his Nigerian experience, permitted the large and sparsely populated country to be administered at relatively low cost. Doing so enabled the government to rationalize somewhat the structure of the tribal units into tribal councils for purposes of administration. Despite this measure, it is worth noting that under the Ordinance to make provision for African chiefs and chiefdoms as late as September 1953, the government still recognized no fewer than 380 chiefs of various types and title,[56] which Twining considered excessive. These became the lowest level of the administration with a limited range of duties and powers, but nevertheless the first building blocks of a national administration. Inevitably, difficulties arose over the relations between the new tribal councils and the chiefs, though quite often the chiefs became leaders of the tribal councils. The Tanganyika Executive Council had been established in 1920, soon after Britain accepted the mandate, and the Legislative Council in 1926. Membership was the usual mix of officials and unofficials. It was not until 1958 that elections to LegCo were introduced.

In his speech to the Royal Africa Society in October 1958,[57] Twining gave credit to Sir Donald Cameron for three important accomplishments. First Cameron had recognized the economic value of the country despite its state of undevelopment, and had begun creation of a communications system. Tanganyika is a large country – several times larger than Uganda and more than twice as large as Kenya. It was sparsely populated, partly due to the widespread presence of both types of tsetse fly. Improved communications were necessary to overcome the distances and remoteness of the regions. Second, Cameron introduced the system of indirect rule mentioned earlier. Finally he laid down the foundations of a multiracial policy which had the effect of bringing Africans into the affairs of the country earlier than might otherwise have been the case.

Twining explained the need for provincial councils in terms of permitting greater autonomy for remote regions and enabling the central government to keep in better touch with the regions. The provincial councils were to become electoral colleges for the Tanganyika Legislative Council. After considerable debate, including the findings of a commission set up by Twining in 1950, a scheme was worked out, acceptable to the regions, for parity of representation of the African, Asian and European populations in the unofficial seats in LegCo – eleven nominated members from each racial group (so far as I know, a unique system of representation in colonial history). The first group of African representatives included Julius Nyerere. Since the population numbers in each racial group were so different, this scheme could not be expected to last long, but it may have had the effect of encouraging the people to think in a multiracial manner in regard to public policy. Inevitably, however, the multiracial approach came up against the policy of Africanization of the Public Service and the general political thrust in favour of Africanism.

In early 1956, Twining still felt optimistic about this arrangement, which he expected to be followed by a decade's gradual maturing of the constitution with self-government by about 1970. But by November 1956 he had changed his mind. The reason was the rapid growth of the Tanganyika African National Union (TANU); he had realized that the European and Asian communities were not strong or large enough to play a leadership political role at the national level. Thus, the field was left open to TANU – there were no political forces or pressure groups to balance them. In November 1956 Twining put forward the suggestion to the Colonial Office that some sort of Upper House or Council of State be provided for in the constitution where various notables who might not seek to run for office could be given an honorific position and be available to participate in consideration of difficult issues.[58] It is a pity this notion, similar to the structure later established in Bechuanaland, was not pursued as it could have given greater balance between the old and the new structures of the state.

In the absence of some such body, perforce, government would have to rely solely on African leadership generated through TANU. TANU had been the first political party to emerge in the country. The Tanganyika African Association existed earlier, but was more a lobby for the country than a political party per se. Even TANU was partially a foreign initiative. Julius Nyerere was the founder in 1954 but the constitution was written in the American consulate with official consular assistance and that of a visiting American, Mrs Byers. (The next US consul appointed was instructed by his government to keep out of Tanganyikan politics.) A visiting UN mission also gave much assistance to TANU despite its avowedly Africanist orientation, to which Twining drew attention. Nyerere and TANU also had financial assistance from other sources in Britain, the United States and India. TANU's appeal tended to be strongest in the areas where tribal affiliation was least strong, in the towns and plantations. The United Tanganyika Party was started later essentially by Europeans and did not have much success nationally, though it did have the distinction of being avowedly multiracial.

Another perspective on this period is provided by an interview conducted by Rhodes House with J. Vinter who served in Tanganyika from 1947 to 1963.[59] He considered that the chiefs had been demoralized by the way in which Twining and the British government gave in to pressure from TANU – thus the absence of an African viewpoint at variance with TANU was partly a consequence of Twining's own actions. He said he thought that Twining became hostile to TANU, which was a big mistake. He personally had been reprimanded by Twining for entertaining Nyerere.

Twining's change of mind over the electoral system was received in the Colonial Office as a *volte face* as he had given no warning of it, though in fact there were officials in London who had never shared Twining's optimism about the multiracial approach.[60] Faced with the growing strength of TANU, government sought ways to keep the initiative in constitutional, social and economic development. Through progressively preparing for elections and with the appointment of ministers in departments of state, unofficials began to take responsibility for government business. Direct elections to LegCo were introduced in 1958 and 1959 as the electoral roll was prepared and the elections organized.

As the Colonial Office had accepted Twining's proposals for future constitutional development, Sir Richard Turnbull was faced on appointment as governor in July 1958 with the immediate constitutional decisions having already been taken. Twining had proposed to appoint a post-election committee after the spring 1959 elections to confirm the position ex post facto on parity of representation (there was talk of a 2:1:1 racial ratio) and the timing of a possible move towards responsible government, encompassing responsible ministers. The only item left undecided was the pace of future change after the elections and the Post-Elections Committee. The Colonial Office came back on this and said that they did not want public statements to be made on further such changes of a constitutional nature as they needed more time to consider the consequences, including the time required to develop the country's human and natural resources sufficiently.

In fact the whole tenor of the exchanges in the Colonial Office from September 1958 onwards was 'back-pedalling' to slow down what they had concluded was an over-rapid bandwagon rolling in Dar es Salaam. See, for example, Gorell Barnes's minute of 31 December 1958 to Sir John Macpherson, Macpherson's minute of 2 January 1959 to Lennox-Boyd and Gorell Barnes's letter to Turnbull of 6 January 1959:

> We believe that it would be a complete abdication of responsibility to retreat in the face of Nyerere's sweet reason and acquiesce in the establishment of an unofficial majority as the essential end product of the Post-Elections Committee, let alone the establishment of a government with a majority of unofficial Ministers in 1960 or pretty soon thereafter. ... We take this view in the full realisation that this will probably lead to very serious trouble in the country ... if we cannot convince Nyerere ... then we had better have the showdown at the outset rather than a year or two later.

Turnbull was faced with three challenges on his appointment – TANU's allegations that the government was dragging its feet over the timing of the 1959 elections;

the multiracial policy in regard to the franchise and the elections; and the implications of that policy for African representation. The Colonial Office saw the Post-Elections Committee as being appointed 'to advise on the representative side of LegCo'. But TANU did not want to wait until the September 1959 elections and Turnbull himself also began to argue the case for bringing the elections forward to February; he even toyed with the notion of bringing forward the Post-Elections Committee to sometime before the elections. TANU was already familiar with the timetable outlined by Twining; why did Turnbull want to press ahead with the elections, especially as Gorell Barnes had emphasized to him in his letter of 6 January 1959 that the secretary of state did not visualize more than the bringing of some elected ministers into the government and some expansion of the franchise in favour of Africans. One factor may have been a speech made by Nyerere in September 1958 at Mwanza at which several other African leaders from other countries were present; and where the Pan-African Freedom Movement of East and Central Africa (Pafmeca) was founded. This became a rallying point for TANU and Turnbull became concerned about the possibility of trouble. A government sociologist, Hans Cory, wrote:

> The moment has come to revise Government's policy towards TANU because of (i) the result of the (September) elections; (ii) the subjects discussed at the Pafmeca conference; (iii) the examples of Ghana and Nigeria; (iv) the irresistible strength of TANU's aims ... a party which will occupy nearly all the unofficial seats in LegCo cannot just be considered subversive or be treated with suspicion and a show of force.[61]

However revising government's policy towards TANU on these grounds did not necessarily entail pressing ahead more rapidly with the timetable of constitutional change for there were other prerequisites for a successful independence, not least more African officials in senior positions in the Public Service and adequate time for them and the new ministers to learn how to do their jobs. Turnbull used some of Cory's arguments in seeking to persuade the colonial secretary to allow him to indicate in a speech that the policy in regard to multiracialism was being reconsidered. He followed this up with speculative comments about the possibility of independence by 1965. This set the alarm bells ringing at the Colonial Office.

Turnbull was summoned to a meeting at Chequers in January 1959 with the colonial secretary, Lennox-Boyd, and other Colonial Office ministers and officials, called at short notice and attended by all the East African governors, at which they discussed the immediate and long-term aims in East Africa. There was agreement that they would try to postpone further elections in Tanganyika until 1961 with internal self-government by 1969. There was some concern about the capacity of the police to control political demonstrations or protests. The decisions taken at the meeting were substantially at variance from the arguments Turnbull had been making.

Clearly Turnbull was overruled at the meeting or failed to put across his views with sufficient vigour. An article by former governor Twining in Optima and reported in the Tanganyika Standard at that time also warned that 'events (in Tanganyika) may move too fast ... no-one who knows the country can responsibly state that the territory is anywhere near to being ready for self-government, or even responsible government which must precede it'. However on Turnbull's return to Dar es Salaam, Nyerere indicated to him that TANU now expected him to announce a timetable for responsible government during 1959. Other members of LegCo made the same argument. Turnbull could not budge. Nyerere and his colleagues later returned to Turnbull and suggested a compromise whereby the Africans would get three ministers, the Asians and Europeans one each. The Colonial Office accepted this. That these events had some impact on Turnbull was evident from his speech of 17 March 1959 to LegCo in which, while outlining future steps in constitutional development, he also introduced proposals for increased expenditure on the police force, included rhetoric warning of a deteriorating security situation, especially in Lake Province, and talked of the long and difficult task ahead of the country.

However the position continued to evolve. In particular the Tanganyika Elected Members Organisation (TEMO), consisting of the unofficials of LegCo, had formed themselves into an effective lobby group in league with TANU; and the chiefs decided to transfer their support to TANU also. Thus TANU could present a united front to the British government, though Nyerere evidently realized that Tanganyika's 'nationalism' was beginning to get out of hand. However, TANU now also began to worry publicly about finance and the possibility of seeking financing elsewhere. Turnbull toyed with the idea of introducing 'Dyarchy', as done in India, with a few subjects, including the budget, reserved for decision by the governor in ExCo, the rest to be settled by LegCo. He went back to the Colonial Office pressing for the next elections to be held in 1960 instead of 1961, despite the outcome of the Chequers meeting, even though the new unofficial ministers would have been in office for only a few months.[62] The Colonial Office was aghast at being faced with proposals for revising decisions recently taken at the Chequers conference and endorsed by the cabinet's Colonial Policy Committee. Turnbull was beginning to be distrusted.

Sir Frederick Crawford, governor of Uganda, who had also attended the Chequers conference, wrote a seven-page letter to Turnbull on 25 June 1959 in which he made clear his opposition to the timetable and approach proposed by Turnbull:

What disturbs me about your proposals ... is that they seem to represent an entirely political solution, unrelated to the availability of a sufficient number of

Africans of experience, ability and integrity to fill posts in the Public Service and in commerce and industry. Surely we ought to coordinate the rate of political progress with the rate of economic development and of Africanisation ... it seems folly to me to produce an arithmetical solution if one cannot find suitable men from local resources to carry the executive burden ... there is nothing like the number of Africans of education and character to take over the running of the Government services. Is it right because of purely political considerations and a doubtful security situation to move towards responsible government and hand over a country before it is anywhere near ready?[63]

An official of the Colonial Office – Max Webber – was given the job of studying all the implications of Turnbull's new proposals and putting forward suggestions as to how the secretary of state should respond. In a detailed minute containing many insights he essentially concluded that (a) the governor was on his own as there was no other part of the body politic in a position to resist TANU/ TEMA; (b) the governor should be careful not to allow himself to be bounced into making further proposals because they would be given detailed analysis in London and he could not rely on getting his way; (c) the governor should press ahead with strengthening the police; (d) there should be a toughening up of government responses to the more outrageous statements made by TANU; and (e) the governor should give careful attention to the morale of the Civil Service. However, Webber also wondered whether it was worth having a tussle over the timing of an elected unofficial majority – in 1961–2 or five years later – because in neither case would the country be ready to run itself, and a peaceful outcome with a degree of multiracial cooperation was worth something. On the other hand he doubted whether Nyerere was a 'moderate' and thought that once in power, non-Africans would probably have a tough time. He also drew attention to the fact that Nyerere did not in fact take one of the unofficial seats in ExCo and therefore had declined to join the government and showed no sign of doing so. He probably wanted to be chief minister and nothing else. Webber advised that the Colonial Office should not hurry to respond to submissions from Turnbull or the government.[64] Lennox-Boyd commented on Webber's minute that 'he had been greatly helped by his minute and was ready to discuss'.

At that point, events were overtaken by the results of the October 1959 General Election in Britain, which was followed by some ministerial changes. Iain McLeod took over from Alan Lennox-Boyd as colonial secretary who left the government for personal reasons. It is fair to say that Lennox-Boyd, while keen to see gradual constitutional change and predisposed to defer to the man on the spot, was sceptical about the speed at which this could be carried out responsibly, especially in East and Central Africa. He did not believe the implicit timetable ought to be speeded up. By contrast, on becoming colonial secretary, McLeod said that he 'was going to take a thoroughly radical line in winding up the residue of the imperial system and that it was his intention to be the last Colonial Secretary'.[65]

However, even Iain McLeod was uneasy about Turnbull's proposals following the September elections, writing to cabinet in November 1959,

The risks in adopting the Governor's proposals are obvious. In the first place Tanganyika and its people are, generally speaking, by far the most backward in the East African Region, and in particular the financial position looks like being extremely difficult over the next few years. Secondly, ... there are wild elements in TANU who might press for an early advance to self-government (whatever Nyerere might do). Thirdly, any such advance would inevitably have repercussions in Kenya and Uganda, where further prudent constitutional advance is under consideration, and the proposed widening of the franchise would have repercussions in Central Africa where a higher set of qualifications had been adopted for access to the franchise.

The cabinet decided to postpone a decision to allow study of the potential impact of the Tanganyika proposals on the work of the Monckton Commission in Central Africa, to seek the views of the governors of the other East and Central African territories, to carefully consider the reserve powers to be retained by the governor and to ask the governor to attend the next set of discussions.[66]

Following receipt of comments from other East and Central African administrations, the electoral qualifications proposed for Tanganyika were modified by the Colonial Office to include more stringent educational and tax qualifications, producing an electoral roll of about one million. After further negotiations, HMG agreed to allow the governor's proposals to come into effect after further elections in September 1960[67,68]. These elections produced a complete victory for TANU, so a new administration assumed office with Nyerere as chief minister. The council of ministers was to continue to be presided over by the governor until independence. In reporting this to the cabinet on 4 October 1960, McLeod made no mention at all of the lack of progress in 'Africanizing' the Public Service. Neither did Turnbull in his public announcement in Dar es Salaam. A cabinet meeting held in London in March 1961 reluctantly agreed to the independence of Tanganyika on this basis 'no later than March 1962', mainly on account of the risk of losing the cooperative relationship Turnbull had established with Nyerere and TANU.[69]

Why did Turnbull push through self-government so much earlier than previously envisaged? He knew how ill-equipped Tanganyika was to administer itself, as we show in the following chapter. It is evident that he felt tied by policies adopted and speeches made by his predecessor, Twining. The reasons given in Iain McLeod's memorandum to the cabinet (mentioned previously) were 'the unexpectedly united front shown by the elected members of all three races in

LegCo' and the report of yet another UN mission which assumed 'that HM Government might be expected to receive with sympathy any resolution from the Legislative Council seeking the termination of the Trustee Agreement and the introduction of independence'. However. Nyerere had already previously indicated his acceptance of 1969 as a target date for self-government. Why then did Turnbull and McLeod (and indeed Lennox-Boyd before him) not negotiate from that 1969 date rather than accept the much tighter timetable?

In retrospect, proceeding so rapidly in Tanganyika was a major mistake. Tanganyika had the weakest administration in East Africa – and in fact in the whole of the British African territories, except possibly Nyasaland. In retrospect, Turnbull and McLeod should have worked harder to postpone independence, as Arden-Clarke and Lyttelton had done in Ghana, and insisted on a longer period of self-government and at least one more round of elections, as previously envisaged up to 1969, to enable young, inexperienced officers and ministers to acquire greater experience in running their country. By then there was no reason for Nyerere to doubt Britain's intention of bringing Tanganyika to independence within the Commonwealth and there was no domestic alternative to challenge TANU. There would have been no significant change in policy, only one of timing. This would also have made it easier to give Kenya and Uganda the time they needed to sort out a number of difficult questions, and possibly eased the time pressure on the Central African Federation. It is evident that Turnbull, like Twining before him, had private, unrecorded meetings with Nyerere. Thus he had the venues for arguing the case for a slower pace in the advance to independence. If he tried, he was unsuccessful and the impression is, as the Colonial Office concluded at the time, that he conceded too much too quickly.

The independence of Tanganyika required a resolution in the General Assembly of the United Nations terminating the Trusteeship Agreement. Nyerere expressed himself keen that the proposed Federation of East Africa should come into effect before then but if that proved impossible for Kenya and Uganda, Tanganyika would anyway wish to maintain the Common Market represented by the East Africa High Commission. This presented difficulties as the commission was a colonial-era institution with a role for HMG, but ways around this were worked out.

In 1971, a decade after Tanganyika's independence, Sir Charles Phillips, who had lived in East Africa from 1908 until the 1960s while working for a tobacco company, was formally interviewed by Rhodes House. He had participated as a representative of the private sector in many official studies and commissions, for example, as chairman of the wartime Tanganyika Economic Control Board, as a representative of Tanganyika in negotiations on the UN Trusteeship Agreement with Britain, in negotiations leading to the Central Legislature of the East African High Commission, as an unofficial member of the Tanganyika Executive Council, and as a member of the Tanganyika Unofficial Members

Organisation (TEMO). Though he lived part of the time in Mombasa, he took a great interest in Tanganyika and had an unrivalled knowledge of the country. His testimony is of such interest that a synopsis of the interview record is incorporated at Annex 8.

Kenya

The Kenya Executive and Legislative Councils were established by Order in Council in 1906. Membership was initially of expatriate officials and representatives of the European settlers. Elections of un-officials to LegCo were introduced in 1919, limited to Europeans again. After considerable controversy Asians were enabled to elect five members in 1927; the first nominated African members were added in 1944 and 1946. Thus the principle of separate communal rolls, which was to bedevil the Kenya electoral law and the franchise system until independence, was built into the system of representation at an early stage.

In 1934 the Kenya government appointed a Kenya Land Commission under Carter which sought to adjudicate various claims to land. This was a painstaking piece of work which provided detailed particulars of land ownership of all kinds. In retrospect, however, the commission made a fundamental error in its approach which was to look at the issue from a tribal/communal standpoint – excessive weight was given to the previous undertakings given about tribal reservations, communal land, the 'White' Highlands and so on. The result was that the country became increasingly locked into a pattern of tribal/communal land distribution which created water-tight compartments, none of which could ever be economically self-sufficient.

Detailed research in the British and Kenyan official archives has shed much light on the way in which land rights were adjudicated and implemented leading to severe social and economic dislocation, which became acute after the Second World War.[70] The following paragraphs which summarize some of the findings are important in understanding the tensions in rural Kenya and some of the factors contributing to the emergence and growth of the Mau Mau movement. British settlers began to move into Kenya at the end of the nineteenth century. From then until about 1920 they were struggling to create farms and needed much African labour to assist them. Thus the farmers were happy for African squatters to move onto their farms. There was sufficient land for everyone. But as the farmers prospered and sought more land, and with a rising African population, they were less willing to allow the squatters to remain there. A Resident Native Labour Ordinance was enacted in 1918 to enable the settler farmers to evict and otherwise constrain the activities of the squatters. But, with the collapse of commodity prices in the late 1920s, the farmers had to reduce the area under cultivation/grazing and some abandoned their farms. Thus the pressure on the squatters eased and indeed there was official encouragement for peasant agriculture in order to maintain supplies and tax revenues. Figures published in the East African Standard in 1931 showed the following picture of the White Highlands (land alienated to the settlers):

White Highlands

Total area	6,857,000
Area under settlers' crops or grazing	2,828,000
Area occupied by squatters	1,850,000
Unoccupied	2,179,000

However in 1937, reflecting the settlers' concerns at the potentially permanent loss of land occupied by the squatters, the Kenya government enacted a new Resident Native Labour Ordinance transferring responsibility for administering the labour law and the squatters to the district councils, which in the White Highlands were dominated by the settlers. The Colonial Office was quite evidently concerned about the delegation of such a critical matter to district councils and it was not until 1940 that they approved the legislation, perhaps under pressure to ensure the colony could make a substantial contribution to the war effort. HMG's approval of this legislation was a major error with long-term malign consequences. There were in fact divisions among the settlers, between those engaged in crop production requiring much labour and those engaged in meat and milk production which required less, which could by themselves have justified reconsideration of the ordinance.

By 1945, the Kenya commissioner for labour, Wyn Harris, had realized the problems being created on the land and among the squatters and warned the chief secretary of the Kenya government that 'the problem of the squatters is going to be one of the most serious problems of this country'.[71] The chief secretary and Governor Mitchell ignored these warnings. However, during Mitchell's absence on leave, his deputy appointed an interim committee under Cavendish-Bentinck, the member for agriculture, who was also a farmer himself, to study the subject again. This committee eventually accepted the Labour Department argument that the squatter problem was essentially an agricultural problem and that it was politically impossible to evict large numbers of squatters to the reserves.

In another part of Kenya, the Mau escarpment, 4,000 Kikuyu squatters had been moved in 1941 from land they had occupied unofficially in Masai country to Olenguruone where the land was steep, covered with thick bamboo scrub and at an altitude which ensured it was cold at certain seasons. By the late 1930s it had become evident to agricultural officers that overcrowding on the reserves especially was leading to severe erosion of the soil, especially where there was a steep gradient. At Olenguruone much squatter labour was required by the agricultural officers to create anti-erosion terraces on the steep slopes. For a variety of local reasons, opposition to the policies on land allocation and management became intense in Olenguruone. Faced with this, the government reacted by evicting those squatters who continued non-cooperation with the government officers. However, the spirit of this resistance spread to other settlements and areas with them.

The tribal chiefs inevitably became involved in all these disputes. The system of indirect rule introduced into East Africa from Nigeria was based on assumptions about the role and status of the tribal chiefs and about access to land which were probably realistic when first adopted but became less so as both the tribal structure and Kenya society evolved. The recognized chiefs had obligations to perform, including those connected with the Local Native Councils and Native Tribunals, and received a stipend to compensate them. Thus they tended to become more and more identified as agents of the government which tended to place them in opposition to Kenyans who had left their tribal homeland for the cities or who had acquired more aspirations with education – what David Throup refers to as 'proto-capitalists'; and to isolate them from the members of their tribe. Furthermore, there was an imperceptible change over the years in the attitude of the tribesmen to land, with a progressive move away from the former usufructural systems in the direction of individual ownership and entrepreneurship. This change over time in the status of the chiefs vis-a-vis the members of their tribe and the dilemma it created for local government had already been identified as a new issue in Nigeria in the 1930s. The Kenya government under Governor Mitchell was slow to come to terms with these changes. In consequence, a barrier emerged between the people and the government, as represented by the chiefs, which tended to conceal the depth and nature of the antagonisms caused by overcrowding in the reserves and cities, the conflict with the settlers over access to land and the demands placed upon peasant farmers by the agricultural and soil protection policies.

Further resistance to government policies emerged in Murang'a in 1947 arising from increasing social differentiation between both the tribal authorities linked into the state and the more successful native traders and farmers on the one hand; and the landless, unemployed, vagrants and the poor living in the reserves, especially in and around the towns and cities on the other. The population increase in Nairobi, which rose above 100,000 in the early 1950s, also created acute social and economic distress among essentially de-tribalized Africans which the city council and police were unable to control. Street gangs, consisting mainly of Kikuyu, became very powerful and dangerous, though members of other tribes were often opposed to them. The housing situation was desperate. The Municipal African Affairs Officer, T. G. Askwith, warned that the gangs were on the brink of a violent confrontation with the government.[72] He feared that the lawlessness was part of a plan to confront the government, reaching out to the nearby Kikuyu districts where there was also much discontent.

The Municipal Council and its African Advisory Council was uncertain how to deal with this threat – through the tribal associations or by a modern system of local government. The situation boiled over in May 1950 over strikes in essential industries and services.

It is evident that the conflict over land between the settlers and the Kikuyu, exacerbated by the delegation of powers to district councils, taken together with the changing status of the tribal chiefs who in essence had become agents of government; the onerous imposition of labour requirements by the agricultural department to implement erosion control measures; and the dire state of living and social conditions in the Nairobi slums contributed to a determination among the Kikuyu to resist and force a change in their situation. The tragedy is that the dangers were recognized and reported to government before the Mau Mau uprising began, by various members of the public and government in close touch with the people. Michael Blundell mentions several of them in his book.[73] However an out-of-touch Secretariat and governor did not give these reports enough credence and failed to address the issue. Once the revolt began, the secret oath taking and the violence perpetrated among the Kikuyu themselves made it very difficult to understand and defeat.

The best source on the Mau Mau rebellion is Sessional Paper No 5 of 1959/60 which is a detailed study titled 'The Origins and Growth of Mau Mau'[74] written by Mr F. D. Corfield, an experienced member of the Sudan Political Service and former governor of Upper Nile Province. This report clearly traces the origin and growth of Mau Mau; it shows conclusively (a) that the allocation to the attorney general, the senior law officer, in 1946 of executive responsibility for supervision of the police and internal security of the country, and for Prisons and Immigration, was a grave mistake, which was not fully corrected until 1953; (b) the creation of the post of Secretary for Law and Order in 1949 was a step in the right direction, but there was no organized body to direct and control the organization of intelligence, or to assess its importance. Furthermore, Special Branch had no operation outside Nairobi and Mombassa, and the dissemination of intelligence upwards and downwards did not occur. There was in fact much known about Mau Mau before the declaration of the emergency by the new governor in 1952, but it was not collated or distributed or acted upon.

Oliver Lyttleton, newly appointed as colonial secretary in 1952, met the retiring governor of Kenya, Sir Philip Mitchell, who claimed that Kenya was both peaceful and prosperous. He soon realized that Mitchell had actually lost touch with the situation and did not know what was happening. The new governor (Sir Evelyn Baring) immediately recognized the deficiencies, obtained advice from the director of the Security Service in Britain and set up the requisite organization for this purpose. But by then Mau Mau was in full swing. One of Baring's first steps on arrival in Nairobi was to declare a State of Emergency giving the government exceptional powers. Though there was concern about Mau Mau spreading to other tribes, it was in fact limited mainly to the Kikuyu, who numbered about a million, roughly 20 per cent of the African population of Kenya at that time.

Mau Mau had grown up out of worries about the loss of land to the European settlers since the beginning of settlement in the late nineteenth century. Some tribes were not concerned, but the Kikuyu from the beginning set up political bodies to organize resistance. In 1902, Colonel Meinertzhagen, serving in the King's African Rifles, wrote 'the Kikuyu are ripe for trouble and when they get educated and their medicine men are replaced by political agitators, there will be a general rising'.

The first significant organization was the Young Kikuyu Association led by Harry Thuku. This was modified into the Kikuyu Central Association (KCA), whose main objective was to 'get back the land'. In 1928 Jomo Kenyatta joined KCA. There were several other Kikuyu-focussed organizations, some of which established private schools, some were church-related, where female circumcision became an issue. Kenyatta persuaded the KCA to take a delegation to England to argue their case, which happened in 1929. Dissatisfied with his discussions at the Colonial Office, Kenyatta then went to Russia and attended meetings of communists in Berlin.

Meanwhile in Kenya another organization came into being, also led by Harry Thuku, named the Kenya Provincial Association (KPA) which enjoined its members to remain loyal to the government and the King. Both organizations gave evidence to the Carter Land Commission. After the war, the KCA was reformulated as the Kenya African Union (KAU), with Harry Thuku as chairman. A number of Kikuyu who had served in the armed services, which tended to loosen their tribal linkages, were also members of the KAU. Jomo Kenyatta returned from England in 1945 and was elected president of the KAU in June 1947, using this position to advocate elimination of European and Indian influences in Kenya and the setting up of an all-African state. He over-played this argument with non-Kikuyu members, some of whom resigned their membership. However, the KAU continued to expand and gradually emerged as Mau Mau, The participants came under the influence and thrall of people who had reverted to the practice of increasingly terrible forms of oath taking. Lyttelton, who had experienced the horrors of the First World War trenches for four years, wrote in his autobiography 'I can recall no instance when I have felt the forces of evil to be so near and so strong ... the restoration of law and order posed some of the same problems as those we are grappling with in Malaya. In Kenya, as in Malaya, the enemy, for that is what they are, were difficult to find. They swooped suddenly upon isolated homesteads or tribal villages or police posts, and then vanished into the forests. Many, perhaps most of their passive supporters had been intimidated by threats and murder into giving unwilling succour to the militant Mau Mau ... thirty two Europeans were murdered between 1952 and 1959. ... In this period more than 1,800 African civilians were murdered, ... the overwhelming weight of the Mau Mau attack fell on their fellow Africans ... after reinforcing the police and the military with a brigade-strength British army unit ... it was imperative to put down the rebellion ... at long term however neither the institutions, political, economic and educational, nor the lives, property and land of the settlers could be secure unless the confidence of the Africans was regained by giving them a share in government ... the alternative of force was impossible ... we did not believe in government by force.'[75]

(NB: Later discoveries of mass graves suggest much larger numbers of Africans were killed – Lennox-Boyd thought as many as 18,000–20,000 [see Annex 4]).

Lyttelton met the settlers and, as described in his autobiography, spoke to them with brutal frankness:[76]

Sixty thousand Europeans cannot expect to hold all the political power and exclude the Africans from the legislature and from Government. ... When, as the result of over-conservative or traditional policies you provoke an explosion, you are not slow to ask the British Government and the Colonial Office, which at other times you attack, for troops, aeroplanes and money to suppress a rebellion; I warn you that one day you will be let down, and therefore besides force, which must now be used and which we will furnish, you must turn your minds to political reform, and to measures which will gradually engage the consent and help of the governed ... the security of the money, hard work and skill which you have lavished on your farms and your industries cannot rest upon battalions of British troops; it can only rest upon the building of a multi-racial society.

He concluded that 'the settlers had few political responsibilities except as critics of government and that the constitution was no longer adapted to Kenya's needs.'[77]

Lyttleton was urged by some settlers to employ summary justice to Mau Mau suspects; that too many safeguards watched over the accused. But he refused. He said 'the impartial administration of justice must be insulated and separated from the executive ... it is the very pillar, the very ark of the covenant of democracy.' He did however, with success urge the speeding up of the administration of justice by practical measures. Lyttleton believed that Mau Mau received support from the Soviet Union through their embassy in Addis Ababa and also from the Congress Party in India – he believed that the activities of the Indian High Commission went far beyond the bounds of diplomatic propriety.[78]

The Mau Mau insurrection required stern measures to defeat it, including the detention of as many as 90,000 members of the Kikuyu tribe and the screening of over 35,000 members of the tribe who were resident in Nairobi. In the detention camps efforts were made to segregate those who had been intimidated into support for Mau Mau from the active participants; and all of them from the leaders of the movement and 'irreconcilables'. In due course most of those in detention were released back to their communities. Undoubtedly there was considerable brutality in the camps, often on the part of members of other tribes or Kikuyu who had stayed loyal to the government; in some cases tolerated by officials. Oath taking evidently continued within some of the camps. In the operations to catch the members of Mau Mau an estimated 11,500 were killed, of whom about 1,000 were executed after being captured and tried. The death penalty was enforced for anyone found carrying arms. The severity of the measures taken reflected the horrific nature of the oaths which bound the members of Mau Mau and the violence they wreaked on the people.

Lennox-Boyd said later[79] (Annex 4) that there was a feeling among Kikuyu chiefs who were cooperating with the government that this was the only way to bring the nation round to a state of tranquillity. He also revealed that while the report of a Parliamentary mission of Members of the House of Commons to investigate Mau Mau was published, the cabinet of Winston Churchill, which included a number of men who had experienced the horrors of both world wars, decided that the findings in the Confidential Annex to the report were so shocking and revolting that they should not be published, though copies were placed in the libraries of the House of Commons and the House of Lords (see Annex 4). Lennox-Boyd also said that he did not think he ever came under pressure to commute a sentence of death. He believed the vast majority of the country and of the Kikuyu wanted peace and order restored and members of Mau Mau were only linked to it as a result of intimidation. He concluded, 'In their interest the only thing was to stiffen one's resolve and to back them up.' Michael Blundell concluded that critical to the defeat of the revolt was the courage and tenacity of members of the Kikuyu tribe, including many who had become Christians, who despite terrible torture and death defied the Mau Mau gangs.

The Emergency did however also provide a situation in which the field administration and agriculturalists were able to push through social and economic reconstruction which had been contemplated earlier but found impractical. The appointment of Swynnerton as director of agriculture gave added encouragement to agricultural officers seeking to expand peasant agriculture, including the growing of more valuable crops such as tea and coffee. The need to recover from the emergency made funding available on a larger scale and gave energy to innovative interventions directed at achieving higher incomes and larger production.

Much has been written about colonial Kenya but the book which is perhaps most helpful in understanding the complexity of the situation, and the acute strains and stresses caused for those directly involved by Mau Mau and the approaching self-government, was that of Michael Blundell. Blundell was a Kenya settler and farmer, who became first an unelected and eventually an elected member of the government, and participated in many of the pre-independence negotiations. Some of those among the European settlers who could not come to terms with the changing situation of the country reviled him. But he helped to bridge the chasm between the extremists of both kinds.

Following the Lidbury Commission and with the ending of the Mau Mau rebellion, Kenya was ripe for reform both of the constitution and through further steps in localizing the civil service. However, given the strong attachment to tribe and communal group in Kenya this was always going to be very difficult. Rebecca Fane writing on nationalism in Kenya in 1956 pointed out,

> in Nairobi, members of different tribes live, if they can, in different districts and in their work prefer to be together. If a contractor employs a gang the members of it are normally of one tribe; on the farms members of different tribes do not live with members of another tribe; inter-tribal marriages are very rare – the majority of African tribesmen are 'foreigners' to each other. The new politicians are conscious that if 'Africanism' is to succeed, 'tribalism' must take a back seat. Yet nationwide political organisations could threaten again the peace and security of the country … before Kenya can make a success of being a primarily African state, two conditions must be fulfilled. First there must be a breaking down of tribal barriers … in the society as a whole; and second, there will have to be a far greater number of educated men and women with the training, experience and judgement which are the necessary equipment for taking part in the affairs of a modern state.[80]

Looking back on the issue now, fifty years later, this proved to be a prescient analysis. Today, tribalism still protrudes into Kenyan national political life. Michela Wrong's vivid description of John Githongo's experiences as the official charged to combat corruption in Kenyan public life attests to that.[81]

An interesting light on the state of the country in 1957 is cast by a telegram sent to the secretary of state in London by Sir Evelyn Baring on his re-appointment as governor of Kenya in October 1957.[82]

> Returning to Kenya after three years, I find immense changes for the better. As a military problem Mau Mau has virtually ceased to exist in the last three years, some 50,000 detainees have been released and reabsorbed in their home areas and none have been re-arrested. This process continues at the rate of 2,000 per month. This represents for the policy and practice of rehabilitation, a success almost beyond belief. … Meanwhile … the policy of land consolidation is bringing increased prosperity and increased opportunities to thousands of African farmers. … From the beginning I have had a feeling that there is a general desire for a settlement. … I am sure that it is right to associate people of the country of all races with its government … it is our

task to do all we can to increase the number of responsible Kenyans and to give them all possible encouragement to work in harmony.

Given the mixed population and the recent history of conflict, writing the new constitution in 1957 was bound to be fraught with difficulty. The objective was to secure a legislature representative of the three main racial groups, which was necessary to obtain the degree of cooperation between them required to advance the country, economically as well as politically. In particular the franchise qualifications and the form of representation in LegCo became incredibly difficult and complicated. Candidates had to meet eligibility criteria (age, nationality, literacy etc.). There were three main racial groups which would elect members. Some of the seats were to be 'inter-communal' which required a system of nomination for them and arrangements for them to be elected by the remaining members of LegCo sitting as an electoral college. In addition, these inter-communal seats were to be divided equally between the three racial groups. Further, the rules were to be such as to prevent two of the three main racial groups combining to elect persons unacceptable to the third group. In addition there was to be a council of state among whose powers would be the power to approve or disapprove any increase in the number of inter-communal seats and any change in the way they are filled. Clearly, such complexity could not last and indeed before independence the constitution was revised again, twice.[83]

Writing in *African Affairs* in 1959, Michael Blundell, then leader of the New Kenya Party, wrote,

Africa today is in a hurry and measured in terms of human needs and happiness we can't afford to hurry – there is still so much to build from the human material which is so ignorant and immature. Yet I believe the general acceptance of the intention to build a self-governing country within the Commonwealth might well help us in reducing the urge of speed and remove the fear of being left behind in comparison with neighbouring territories, which acts as a spur to racial emotions and ambitions.[84]

A useful short description of the major economic role played at that time by the European settlers in Kenya is provided by M. F. Hill's Foreign Affairs article of 1959.[85]

By the time of the 1960 constitutional negotiations, conducted by Iain McLeod as colonial secretary, the atmospherics had changed. The Hola Camp incident in which eleven Mau Mau detainees had been killed put both the Kenya government and the British government on the defensive. The Devlin Report into the Nyasaland disturbances, which was highly critical of the Nyasaland administration, had also been submitted. Some assert that British policy in regard to the colonies changed after Prime Minister Macmillan's tour of Africa in early 1960, though to me the evidence for this is not convincing. I have seen no evidence, despite the rhetoric, that there was a decision in principle to speed up decolonization of colonies following his visit to Africa, though that was the result of McLeod's period of office. It would anyway have been out of character for a pragmatic Conservative administration. The impact of the Macmillan tour was discussed in an earlier chapter. Meanwhile, it was events on the ground which continued to determine the pace and direction of constitutional and political change in Kenya.

The 1960 negotiations provided for an election in early 1961 under a new constitution, and a still complex franchise, but the latter had been modified to enfranchise far more Africans. This represented a decisive increase in the African share in political power – it had taken that long since Lyttleton's speech to the settlers in late 1952. However, though the 1961 election produced a majority for the Kenya African National Union (KANU), they refused to form a government until Jomo Kenyatta was released from detention (he had been convicted under the Mau Mau prosecutions). The deadlock was resolved when the Kenya African Democratic Union (KADU), led by Ronald Ngala, agreed to form a government with support from Michael Blundell's New Kenya Party. A principal difference between KANU and KADU lay in the fear on the part of the minority tribes of being dominated by the larger Kikuyu and Luo tribes. As a result, KADU proposed the decentralization of power into provincial governments which could more effectively protect the interests of the smaller tribes. In announcing this policy KADU emphasized, 'By regional government we hope to develop a constitution which will prevent the emergence of tyranny or authoritarianism and absolute rule in Kenya' (statement by Peter Okondo MP in October 1961). KANU rejected this proposal completely. By then Kenyatta had been released from detention and following further negotiations a KANU-KADU coalition government was formed in April 1962.

KANU had by then commissioned an agricultural and educational survey, led by Arthur Gaitskell, a member of the 1953 East Africa Royal Commission and former director of the Gezira irrigation scheme in Sudan. This survey produced a report which KANU used to frame its policies for government. Despite the evident personal authority and political strength of Kenyatta, HMG continued to pursue KADU's decentralization agenda. This policy was strongly criticized by some Colonial Officers who considered that the creation of a series of regional administrations – each requiring civil servants – in a country with little money and few trained administrators could not make sense (see the arguments of T. Neil in Annex 5). However, there was also interest in official circles in diffusing more national authority to provincial levels in order to limit the subjects on which politicians at the national level could make a direct impact. There was by then growing apprehension at the possibility of articulate and ambitious politicians seizing control at independence and brushing aside the checks and balances the Colonial Office sought to create.

In a letter to *The Times* in March 1962, Kenyatta showed that KANU, representing ten tribes, had won 67 per cent of the votes at the last election, while KADU, representing nine tribes, had won only 16 per cent of the votes. The underlying reason for HMG's hesitation was the continuing distrust of Kenyatta among some administrators in Kenya, many settlers and some Colonial Office officials; his high standing among the Kikuyu was discounted. However the results of the election could not be ignored; Tom Mboya, then minister of justice and constitutional affairs, clearly indicated that KANU intended to modify the constitution, either constitutionally or unconstitutionally, and they had the votes to insist on this. He argued that it was wrong that an elected government, manifestly enjoying majority support, should be hampered at every turn by the minority. In the end HMG changed its position and incorporated in the independence constitution provisions for referenda to be held to address possible future amendments to the constitution.

In his article on the Party System and Democracy in Africa, which appeared in Foreign Affairs in 1963,[86] Tom Mboya expressed the confidence African political leaders felt in their ability to run an independent country effectively with a single political party created out of the pre-independence nationalist movement. He discounted the need for an opposition and the danger of a single party becoming oppressive and dictatorial. He was assassinated before he could learn respect for Lord Acton's notable dictum that 'power corrupts and absolute power corrupts absolutely'.

A new colonial secretary, Reginald Maudling, visiting Kenya in 1962, just as negotiations were beginning for the new, independence constitution wrote to the cabinet.[87]

It is widely believed that the date we have in mind for independence is some time in the first half of 1963. ... The people who most impressed me during my visit to Nairobi were the Provincial Commissioners. They gave me their unanimous advice:

(i) The rate of advance to independence, which they assumed would come in the Spring of 1963, was too rapid:

(ii) They could think of no way in which it could now be slowed down.

He asked,

must we accept this advice or is there some way either of taking some of the dangers out of independence, or of retarding the date, or of doing both? ... The dangers are not difficult to see. In political maturity the indigenous people of Kenya are far behind West Africans. The number of trained administrators, and the number of officers and senior non-commissioned officers available are still very small. There are strong tribal antagonisms that can easily be fanned by irresponsible leaders and they are based on fears, which have much substance, of Kikuyu domination. There is a large, articulate European population with a great and long-established stake in the country. Land-hungry Africans are casting jealous eyes on the European lands, but it is European agriculture that provides the foundation of Kenya's economy. Over everything still broods the threat of Mau Mau, the influence of ex-detainees in the KANU, and the persistence of personal violence. Small wonder in these circumstances that confidence is rapidly disappearing and the economy of the country is running rapidly downhill. The European farmers and the European administrators upon whom the country depends have little incentive to stay.

Referring to the two main political parties (KANU and the KADU) Maudling wrote, 'though their views are at present wide apart, I believe, myself, that underneath it all there may be more potential agreement than appears at first sight. If we can sweep away the verbiage about federalism and unitary states, and so on, and come down to the hard facts of powers and safeguards, we may be able to reach some agreement.' He proved to be correct. Kenya achieved self-government and independence in 1963,[88] though it would not be long before the fears articulated by KADU became a reality.

The Somaliland protectorate

British Somaliland came into being as British protectorate in 1905. The people are Hamitic and they had no written language until Osmania was adopted in 1945. Until its brief occupation by Italians in the Second World War, it was subject to a similar administration to other British protectorates. The country was very poor, the land being dry and prone to drought. The people lived mainly by grazing on land and by fishing around the Horn of Africa at sea. Inter-tribal feuds caused by the shortage of water and grazing lands often resulted in inter-tribal fighting, which sometimes strayed across the boundaries of Ethiopia and other territories.

As a consequence of its defeat in the Second World War, Italy lost its colonies of Eritrea and Somaliland and for a few years they were governed by a British Military Administration. In 1949 the territory of Italian Somaliland became a United Nations Trust territory, with Italy as the administrator. There were also Somalis living in Ethiopia, French Somaliland and Kenya. Immediately after the Second World War, some consideration was given to trying to create a single Somali nation (the British foreign secretary; Ernest Bevin, was interested in this solution, but it was vetoed by the Russians). At the UN it was decided that Italian Somaliland should become independent in 1960 as Somalia, despite its rudimentary state of economic and social development. The British territory was offered the chance to become part of this larger territory also in 1960. By normal British colonial standards, this was far too soon and much earlier than in more developed colonies. Britain's first response to this option was that, while it was supportive in principle, HMG did not wish to make any definite commitment as to dates. Meanwhile HMG would press ahead with economic, social and especially educational programmes in the country, with a view to self-determination in due course.[89]

The protectorate Somalis were keen not to lose British support until their relations with Somalia and Ethiopia were on a firmer footing. Under the Anglo-Ethiopian Treaty of 1897, nomadic Somali inhabitants of the Protectorate had rights of access with their animals to parts of Ethiopia (including the Haud) for grazing, and to withdraw water. Indeed the Somalis contended the land did not belong to Ethiopia anyway. A Protectorate Advisory Council was established in 1947 and statutory provision was made for the establishment of a legislative council to consist of the governor, three ex officio members, not more than five official members and not more than six unofficial members; and an Executive Council to consist at first entirely of official members. There was no single Somali chief or authority, though the people acknowledged two tribal groups, the Isaak and Darod. The Protectorate was mainly Isaak, who tended to support the Somali National League. A National United Front sought to unite all Somalis and favoured the British connection. British Somaliland was well behind such countries as Sudan, where many of its officials received training, in education, economic and social development, and was well behind in progress towards self-government.

In 1954, following signature of the Anglo-Ethiopian Agreement of that year, the British Military Administration of the Haud and certain 'Reserved Areas' was withdrawn in exchange for an Ethiopian guarantee of Somali access to the grazing areas. This disappointed the Somalis and the British cabinet felt at that time that Somalia was of sufficient potential strategic importance to warrant a serious attempt to persuade Ethiopia to cede the grazing areas to Somaliland.[90] As Egyptian and Russian interest in the area increased in the mid-1950s, HMG became concerned about the defence implications and seemed inclined to take a more active interest in the area. In May 1956, Lord Lloyd, a junior minister at the Colonial Office, visited British Somaliland and announced a programme of constitutional, social and economic development. A Legislative Assembly was to be established within twelve months; educational expansion and a scholarship scheme for study in other countries was outlined; water resources would be developed for towns and for irrigation and agriculture by means of soil and water conservation measures; Berbera port was to be developed; HMG committed itself to annual Grants-in-Aid of about £700,000 (2017 £16.5 million) comprising CD&W funds of about £500,000 per annum for development expenditure; and a grant to pay for the Somaliland Scouts, the armed militia. HMG also stated it was open to consider with the government and people the possibilities of some form of association with Somalia after 1960.[91]

In February 1959, secretary of state Lennox-Boyd visited the country. In a speech he confirmed that elections to LegCo would take place in March 1959, with an official majority remaining at that stage; this election would be followed by a commission to establish a revised constitution and a second election would be held later in 1960. After the second election there would be a majority of elected members of LegCo and a majority of Somali ministers in the Executive Council,[92] though certain powers would be reserved to the governor for a while. The governor would be able to attend ExCo by agreement with the members. Meanwhile advice would be provided for discussion with Somali ministers on the form of the constitution to be adopted before the Protectorate commenced negotiations with Somalia. This would have to determine the electoral system for the longer term, the role of ministers, department directors and financial control mechanisms. Terms of reference for the adviser are dated 1 February 1959.[93]

Quite obviously, all this came in a great hurry and very late in the day leaving no time for the Somalis to learn how to operate the proposed constitution. It was most unfortunate that the UN pressed ahead so rapidly in respect of Somalia in clear disregard of the complexities of the situation and the well-understood difficulties of creating and learning to govern a self-governing state. The UN also seemed disinclined to seek an agreement regarding the border between Ethiopia and the new Somalia, despite the long-standing Ethiopian claim to the area and for access to the Indian Ocean. Conflict was to follow in this area.

Central Africa

The two Rhodesias, Northern and Southern, came into being through the influence of the mining companies created by Cecil Rhodes and others, which negotiated treaties with the main tribal leaders in Central Africa or defeated them when they clashed. Particularly influential was the British South Africa Company which received its charter from HMG in 1889. Though the company's charter was due to expire in 1914, it was extended until 1922. Southern Rhodesia had a constitution under a British Order in Council of 1898 which provided for a Legislature, but control over 'Native Affairs' was reserved to the British government. Until 1923 in Southern Rhodesia and 1924 in Northern Rhodesia, the two territories were under the effective control of the company in accordance with its charter. Thus effective Colonial Office input into Northern Rhodesia was for the exceptionally short time of forty years. Southern Rhodesia came to be viewed by Africans as having been acquired by conquest during the Matabele campaign of 1893, making the native Africans 'slaves'; Northern Rhodesia became a British Protectorate from the beginning and the Africans there viewed themselves as being 'Protected Persons'. This perceived difference of status, though arguable technically, tended to colour the relations between the two Protectorates of Northern Rhodesia and Nyasaland on the one hand and Southern Rhodesia on the other.[94]

When Southern Rhodesia became a 'self-governing Crown colony' in 1923, its constitution incorporated provisions originally found in the Charter of the company whereby Africans who possessed the general electoral qualifications had the same right of franchise as Europeans. This reflected Cecil Rhodes dictum 'equal rights for all civilised men'. Other clauses also sought to safeguard the interests of the African population by requiring HMG's assent to changes in specific provisions of the constitution. Despite these provisions, there was strong pressure from Europeans living within the territory to delimit separate European and African areas along lines similar to those employed in South Africa, which gave rise to the Land Apportionment Act of 1930. Had the 1923 Devonshire Declaration of African 'paramountcy' in respect of Eastern Africa been extended to Southern Rhodesia, history might have been different. This omission permitted the 1930 Act, which was clearly detrimental to African interests and reinforced the social barriers between the races. Also detrimental was the Industrial Conciliation Act, which in effect, created a formal colour bar, which had no place in the British colonies (though it did on the railway serving the Copper Belt in Northern Rhodesia). The links between South Africa and Rhodesia were close at that time, though the mainly British settlers in Rhodesia were already becoming concerned about the drift of policy in South Africa under its increasingly Afrikaner governments. Furthermore, Rhodesia did evolve a concept of relations between the communities described as 'parallel development'. It was not long before this in turn was modified, stimulated partly by revisions made in 1941 to the Land Apportionment Act and partly by a general relaxation of the rigid differentiation of the communities which had come into being, which was analogous to, though less rigid than, the South African apartheid.

When Northern Rhodesia (Zambia) became a Crown Protectorate in 1924, its constitution provided for a legislative council and an executive council in the usual way. LegCo had an official majority until 1945, when the membership was changed to nine officials and thirteen unofficials, of whom eight were elected. The franchise favoured the Europeans on the Copper Belt, which provided most of the revenues, though when Northern Rhodesia entered the Federation steps were taken to open up the franchise to more Africans. Native Authorities and Native Court Ordinances were enacted in 1929, though these laws were replaced in 1936 by enactments modelled more closely on the Tanganyika pattern, including establishment of Native Treasuries. There was a special agreement with Barotseland, comparable with the Buganda Agreement in Uganda. Additional councils and courts were set up to administer the urban population growing up on the Copper Belt and along the railway line. These councils became subject to election in 1946. Regional Councils were created as the population rose and in 1945 these became Provincial Councils, presided over by provincial commissioners.

Meanwhile, Nyasaland (Malawi) was being governed at the local level by various native authorities whose constituencies were very much less clear or well founded than elsewhere. The principal reason for this was the muddle left by inter-tribal warfare and the upheaval left by the slave trade, which gave rise to less homogeneity within the communal groups. It was not until 1933 that, under the Nyasaland Native Authority and Courts Ordinance of that year, modelled very much on the Tanganyika ordinance, a more solid system was created. Provincial Authorities presided over by provincial commissioners were created in 1945. In 1953 District Councils were set up to reinvigorate the native authorities with the intention of taking over the local government functions of those authorities. By 1955, five of the District Councils had been established.[95]

It is appropriate to point to the tension created in Central and Eastern Africa by the increasing influence of the Union of South Africa as a result of the Second World War. Under Field Marshall Smuts, South Africa was a strong supporter of the Allied cause and its contribution of men and money was very apparent in both Central and Eastern Africa. However, in a note of 20 March 1941, Lord Harlech, formerly secretary of state, wrote:

> The root of the problem lies in the possibility that South African Nationalism may ... at some future time, take a strongly anti-British course ... it would be dangerous to fashion our plans (in Africa) on the assumption (that this may prove to be wrong) ... in our own interests we must keep clearly in mind the possibility of unfavourable developments. The dissident forces in South Africa are inherent and powerful. History and blood will tell; and it may be that the fusion of such peoples as Briton and Boer will not be an easy thing.[96]

The populations of the three Central African territories at the time of federation, according to the most recent census data and/or estimates used by Hailey in the 1956 African Survey, and that used by the Devlin Report[97] in 1959 in respect of Nyasaland, were as follows:

Populations of the three Central African territories

	African Survey		Devlin Report
	Population	Density per sq.mile	
Southern Rhodesia	2,146,000 (1951)	14.3	
Northern Rhodesia	1,816,000 (1950)	6.3	
Nyasaland (Malawi)	2,049,914 (1945)	54.8	2,740,000 (1958)

The population density and limited employment possibilities in Nyasaland led many Nyasas to go and work in other countries, particularly Southern Rhodesia and the Union of South Africa, and as we have seen the education system was modified to improve the skills required by men for such work. In the 1930s it was estimated that as many as a third of all adult Nyasa males were in employment abroad. Recruiting agencies functioned throughout the country. The Central African Council, established in 1944 and based in Salisbury, had a Standing Committee on African Labour which met periodically. At the committee's meeting of April 1950, attended by a Colonial Office welfare officer, it was noted that there were an estimated 30,000 Southern Rhodesian Africans, 11,000 Northern Rhodesian Africans and 45,000 Nyasas working in the Union of South Africa. There were an estimated 100,000 further Nyasas working elsewhere in Central Africa. The meeting was concerned to negotiate an agreement with the Union government designed to manage the flow of labour to the Union, which would both help meet the Union's need for labour, ensure that it be adequately paid and be provided with adequate living conditions. There was also concern at the impact the withdrawal of all this labour might have on the domestic economy and social stability of the three territories. A Colonial Office welfare officer had spent several months in the Union to work up a draft agreement and he was asked to finalize this.[98]

The migration of labour had ramifications for HMG in the International Labour Organization, on account of its obvious and malign social consequences. At the 34th Session of the International Labour Conference held in Geneva in June 1951, for example, the British delegate, Alfred Robens, minister of labour and national service, made a report to the conference and responded to criticism from a delegate of the South African employers about the lack of migrant labour and government interference in the flow of such labour to his country. Robens drew attention to 'the effects of the withdrawal of adult males on the social organisation of the population concerned' and defended the role of the Nyasaland government in placing limits on such migration.[99] It is quite clear that the experiences of migrant labour in South Africa (especially) and Southern Rhodesia were to become an important factor in the opposition of many Nyasas and other Africans to the Federation, and in the disturbances which came later (see the following text).

The Federation of Rhodesia and Nyasaland

The notion of 'amalgamation' of the two Rhodesias had been discussed informally for many years. Formal official consideration was given to the matter in 1938 when a Royal Commission on Central Africa was appointed under Lord Bledisloe, which discussed and studied the idea of 'amalgamation' of the two Rhodesias and Nyasaland. This notion was strongly pursued by

Sir Godfrey Huggins, the leader for many years of the European settlers in Southern Rhodesia and eventually the first federal prime minister. A principal reason for his enthusiasm for 'amalgamation' was economic and financial, related to the growth of the copper industry in Northern Rhodesia. But there was also a keen wish to exercise some control over the future of the 'big territory on the other side of the Zambesi'. Bledisloe himself considered the notion premature and 'amalgamation' was resisted by HMG, though it remained potentially interested in federation. In practice the idea had to be shelved when the Second World War broke out. The general view at that time, which was also the view of the Royal Commission, was that the Africans in Northern Rhodesia and Nyasaland were strongly opposed to 'amalgamation' on account of a fear of losing control of their countries to the Europeans in Southern Rhodesia.

The idea of 'amalgamation' rumbled on during the Second World War and what was seen as a possible interim measure was the creation in October 1944 of a Central African Council to facilitate relations between the three territories.[100] The idea suffered a setback when Huggins's United Party lost its overall majority in the Southern Rhodesian election of 1946, which it did not regain until 1948. This was also the year when the National Party won a majority in South Africa, marking a sharp turn towards 'apartheid' and strengthening in some quarters the argument for 'amalgamation' in Central Africa. Concern within HMG in this connection focussed partly on the threat of 'amalgamation' to perceived African interests, partly the fear of the settlers taking the matter into their own hands with a 'Boston Tea Party', and partly on the rising number of Afrikaner workers in both Northern and Southern Rhodesia.

African opposition to the idea of federation was stirred up further when it became known that a secret meeting of European settlers had been held at Victoria Falls in February 1949 to discuss federation. This meeting was implicitly encouraged by the colonial secretary, Creech Jones, as HMG was not willing itself to suggest a political solution of this nature. However, the fact that no African representatives were invited and reports that the proposed federal constitution discussed expressly excluded any form of African representation in the federal legislature was disastrous and politically inept. (The report on the proposed representation in the federal legislature was in fact incorrect, but it would undoubtedly have been highly discriminatory against Africans. The proposals for revenue sharing were also skewed in favour of Southern Rhodesia.) Additional evidence of African opinion in Northern Rhodesia on the idea of federation is found in a submission made to a Commonwealth Parliamentary delegation at Lusaka on 4 August 1951. This is a detailed and cogent explanation for the African fears based on their experience of the way Southern Rhodesia was governed.

The visit to Southern Africa in 1949 of Patrick Gordon Walker, Labour minister for Commonwealth Relations, proved to be influential within HMG. He returned from his visit viewing South Africa as a threat to Central Africa and emphasizing the need for some measures to strengthen relations between the three territories of Central Africa. An outline for a federation was produced jointly by the Colonial Office and the Commonwealth Relations Office (CRO) at a conference on the subject held in March 1951.[101] As the prospect of ministerial decisions on federation approached Gorell Barnes at the Colonial Office argued in February 1952 that the opportunity of the final negotiations should be taken to extract additional benefits for Northern Rhodesia and Nyasaland, from Southern Rhodesia, before HMG signified its support for federation.[102] In March 1952, Sir Geoffrey Colby, the governor of Nyasaland, wrote a long and well-argued letter to the new colonial secretary (Lyttleton) laying out the reasons why he thought federation was not in the interest of Nyasaland, and suggesting that Nyasaland be allowed not to participate in the federation.[103] Ministers in London considered Nyasaland's withdrawal would unbalance the concept.

In taking the decision to create the Federation in 1953, the colonial secretary of the day, Oliver Lyttleton, stated that 'the British Government was convinced the Federation was needed, though it recognised that African opinion in Northern Rhodesia and Nyasaland was opposed to it'. In his memoirs, and indeed in practice in different contexts, Lyttleton several times made it abundantly clear that he believed that if peace and stability were to be achieved, the consent of the governed must in some measure be gained. However, he was also clear that the governed referred to all the governed, not just some of them. He pointed out that in negotiating the constitution of the federation

> we had to strive for the right balance between state and federal powers, always a delicate subject, but in some degree we had to preserve the protectorate status of two of the three territories conferred on them by Queen Victoria at their request. ... Secondly, we had to devise a system by which Africans were assured of larger representation in the legislature than either a qualification of standards of education or property could have conferred ... we also set up an African Affairs Board with an absolute veto, to be followed by reference to the Secretary of State, upon any legislation which was discriminatory against any of the races in the federation.

Lyttleton sought to maintain the rapid economic advance occurring in some parts of the federation – Southern Rhodesian agriculture and industry, Northern Rhodesian mining and the creation of major hydroelectric power plants. He went on:

> Our policy was one of partnership. The skill and experience – economic, social, political of Great Britain – must be the foundation if a free, law-abiding, well-administered and prosperous society is to be built ... all these will be

useless unless the African is brought increasingly into the control of affairs …
his labour, his goodwill and his consent must be engaged … only partnership
will achieve the common aim.[104]

It is legitimate to ask why, in the face of so much evidence of the opposition of
the people of Nyasaland to participation in the federation, the British government
persisted in its inclusion when it came into being. The Bledisloe Commission
in 1938 accepted the evidence that the Africans in both Northern Rhodesia
and Nyasaland were strongly opposed to 'amalgamation' as it was referred
to then. This opposition did not change. The case of Northern Rhodesia was
different because it enjoyed substantial benefits from mining on the Copper Belt.
Nyasaland had to export men to work in other countries to gain a living. Were
they just obtuse to refuse federation? The 1949 Victoria Falls meeting confirmed
their fears. In March 1952 Sir Geoffrey Colby, the governor of Nyasaland, wrote
his letter to the secretary of state laying out why he thought federation was not
in the interest of Nyasaland and suggesting it be allowed not to participate in
the federation. One of Sir Burke Trend's findings in 1959 was that opposition
to federation was still universal among the Africans. Against all this evidence
of opposition, HMG persisted in Nyasaland's inclusion. Arguably it was HMG
which was being obtuse. We cannot therefore be surprised that the opposition
to federation eventually took a violent form; and when they got the chance to
leave the federation, they did not hesitate.

When it came to the vote in the House of Commons, Gordon Walker abstained
rather than voting against with his party.

Contemplating the state of the federation in his memoirs twenty years later,
Lyttelton agreed with 'those who allege that the Europeans in the federation
sat still during a period of seven years and made no progressive, or at least
too hesitant, moves to engage Africans in a further share of the Government'.
Lyttelton also described another reason for favouring the federation when he
was in office, referred to earlier, but which is now largely forgotten. 'Afrikaaner
elements had begun to penetrate deeply into Southern and to a lesser extent
into Northern Rhodesia. The Broederbond was the active instrument of this
invasion. It was projected by some that Afrikaaners would hold political power in
Southern Rhodesia within a decade and might within that time force a federation
of Southern Rhodesia with the Union'.

These various concerns were reflected in the outcome of the negotiations
leading to the creation of the Federation of Rhodesia and Nyasaland in 1953
– the federal constitution provided for the two protectorates to retain their own
governments for as long as their people wanted them; the powers of the federal
government and the protectorate governments were strictly delimited and the
powers of the territories were not subordinated to the federation. Representatives
of Southern Rhodesia in the federal assembly were chosen by election, those of

the two protectorates by electoral colleges. The Crown was represented in the Federation by a governor general.

Devlin later wrote (in 1959), 'the fundamental postulate of all opposition then and now to the Federation is that the African in Southern Rhodesia is much worse off than he is in either of the Protectorates because, it is maintained, in the Protectorates he is treated as a human being and in Southern Rhodesia he is not.'[105] Though Devlin probably reflected the majority view of Africans in Nyasaland, there were notable exceptions elsewhere, including L. C. Vambe, an African journalist from Southern Rhodesia whose address to the July 1959 meeting of the Royal Africa and Royal Commonwealth Societies appeared in African Affairs.[106]

Vambe explained why he was strongly in favour of the Federation on account of what it was doing for Africans and in light of the trend of opinion and policy in the federal government. In respect of Nyasaland he argued:

> Nyasaland is a poor country ... a reservoir of cheap labour ... now Nyasaland benefits from the growing strength of the federal economy. ... Southern Rhodesia has become the Mecca of the African from all neighbouring territories ... 40 % of the labour force come from outside, 100,000 from Nyasaland, who come of their own free will and not by compulsion ... they find conditions so much better than in their own country that most do not want to return to their home countries ... they find employment and wages which are twice or three times what they get in Nyasaland ... they are better housed, fed, clothed ... there are better educational facilities and a better health service. ... Why malign a country which is doing so much for so many Africans? Southern Rhodesia is dismantling the colour bar and allowing mixed trade unions ... it is creating an apprenticeship scheme for school-leavers ... these things should not be belittled ... it is from these measures that other progress will flow – economic, political and social ... the speed of change is even alarming reactionary forces within the country. ... Nyasaland should get internal self-government; Northern Rhodesia should aim for parity ... we will also need a constitution containing a Bill of Rights and a Court to interpret the constitution ... but destroy the values and institutions which all Africans of good sense cherish and you destroy the hope and spirit of the current generation ... I cannot see what on God's earth is going to prevent the African's emancipation.

Another interesting reflection on the federation from the perspective of Northern Rhodesia was cast by Godwin Lewanika, president of the Northern Rhodesia Mines African Staff Association, when he also spoke at a joint meeting of the Royal African Society and the Royal Commonwealth Society in 1958.[107] His view was a highly practical one but informed by notions of fairness and a positive vision for the future of the federation. His talk ranged over electoral politics, the drastic need for more bursaries and scholarships to train young people for professional-level jobs, the extent of racial 'partnership', the nature and approaches of the African Congress, the need for everyone to pursue the federation to make it work for all, the Dominion status option, trade unionism and the need to make 'partnership' a reality.

Before leaving consideration of the Central African Federation, we should note the deep concerns expressed by both Governor Benson of Northern Rhodesia and Governor Colby of Nyasaland, following creation of the federation. They articulated many concerns but especially the dispute over the hydroelectric schemes, the way in which the federal government was simply seizing increasing control by administrative actions, the citizenship rules under federation and the distribution of benefits from federal expenditure.

There were three alternatives under consideration for hydroelectric plants – the run-of-river scheme on the Shire river in Nyasaland, the Kafue storage dam in Northern Rhodesia and the Kariba high dam scheme on the Zambezi River, which provided the boundary between Northern and Southern Rhodesia. They had different characteristics and the Shire scheme by itself, though the least costly and offering the highest economic rate of return, would not have satisfied power demand from the two Rhodesias. Kafue was probably the least cost solution of the two storage schemes and was favoured by the mining companies, but Kariba was selected for a mixture of reasons. The result was that on completion, the operation of the dam was controlled from Southern Rhodesia despite the fact that the main load centre, and the main justification for the scheme, was in Northern Rhodesia, on the Copper Belt. Thus Northern Rhodesia's mining schemes helped to meet the cost of a high level of investment in Southern Rhodesia. None of this need have mattered had the relationship between the two Rhodesias been harmonious, but that was far from the case.

Benson, the governor of Northern Rhodesia, was also critical of the outcome of the federal fiscal commission in his letter to Secretary of State Lennox-Boyd of 17 September 1955[108] and in a later letter to the Colonial Office of February 1956.[109] In a detailed, nine-page letter, informed by his years spent as chief secretary of the Central African Council, Benson explained how Northern Rhodesia was now having to contribute towards the service of debt incurred by Southern Rhodesia before federation, while Northern Rhodesia had not incurred such debt but had paid its way and built up reserves. Copper prices were now high and Northern Rhodesia was not enjoying the full benefit due to the system of federal taxation, and if prices fell, Northern Rhodesia would have to take its place in the queue if it wished to borrow abroad. Benson also raised many concerns about the way in which federation was being implemented, but especially the way in which the federal government was seizing control by administrative action of powers which, under the federal agreement, had been allocated to the territories. He listed eighteen of these powers in his letter of 6 June 1956 to the secretary of state, Lennox-Boyd.[110]

Equally interesting was a communication, also of September 1955, from the governor of Nyasaland, Sir Geoffrey Colby to Gorell Barnes at the Colonial Office proposing that Nyasaland withhold approval of the financing of the Kariba Dam (a federal project) until adequate provision for federal development expenditure in Nyasaland was agreed, an argument reiterated in his valedictory despatch of January 1956 to the secretary of state.[111] Evidently, there were cogent fears in the two protectorates that the distribution of benefits of federal revenue and expenditure decisions was weighted in favour Southern Rhodesia and, in particular, was being distorted by the financing needs of the Kariba Dam.

In March 1956, Lord Malvern (formerly Sir Godfrey Huggins) demanded full self-government for the Federation though he understood that this would require an Act of Independence to be passed by the British Parliament. Following initial discussions in April 1957 when British ministers accepted in principle proposals for an enlarged federal assembly, the assembly passed the Constitutional Amendment Act which provided for such enlargement. This was challenged by the African Affairs Board under the then existing constitution. One feature of the Act was revised franchise rules.

The franchise problem was multifaceted. Access to the franchise depended on citizenship, but the nationality status of most Africans in Northern Rhodesia and Nyasaland was British Protected Person (BPP), while Southern Rhodesia already had its own citizenship law which carried with it the status of British subject throughout the Commonwealth. So long as this remained the case, creation of a common electoral roll would be very difficult. Federal ministers, quite reasonably, considered it strange that HMG should be pressing for enfranchisement of BPPs in federal elections when they still did not have the vote in either Northern Rhodesia or Nyasaland. The root of the problem was that BPPs were extremely reluctant to give up their protected status, by becoming federal citizens, because they had not been reconciled to the Federation. This possibility was foreseen when the federal constitution was drafted – the Federation could go forward to full membership of the Commonwealth only when the inhabitants of the three territories so desired it. This implied that the federal government must first win the allegiance of the Africans of Northern Rhodesia and Nyasaland. This in turn required acts by the federal government which were simply not forthcoming. Ideally, the franchise rules should have been identical for both territorial and federal elections, but this required an identity of political interest and citizenship which was simply not there. Lord Malvern, Welensky and others seeking Dominion status for the Federation seemed not to accept this point, or to be seeking a way around it. It is difficult not to conclude that the leaders of the federal government simply lacked the discernment, imagination and sheer political nous required to lead Southern Rhodesia into real and effective partnership with Northern Rhodesia and Nyasaland, without which the Federation was doomed.

Seeking to understand the complexity of the problems of the Federation of Central Africa, we can take account of comments made by Sir Burke Trend, a former British cabinet secretary, when he visited the Federation in September/October 1959.[112] His visit occurred while he chaired a commission of officials from Britain and the Federation established to prepare the ground for the pending Federal Review Commission (The Monckton Commission). He found:

(i)   The machinery of government was extremely complicated, divided as it was between federal and three territorial governments, with both concurrent and separate functions.

(ii)   The atmosphere in Southern Rhodesia was not a happy one; the colony's selfish preoccupation with the maintenance of the white man's complete social dominance was one of the greatest obstacles in the way of Sir Roy Welensky's more enlightened policy. Though the students at the new multiracial university live and work side by side within its boundaries, they must travel in separate buses outside its gates.

(iii)   The Northern Rhodesian administration was staffed by gentle, kind and firm men, desperately anxious to do the best for the Africans; very few resources; not very conscious of the federal government; barely concealed resentment that the largest and richest territory (of the Federation) should be controlled (however ineffectively) from Salisbury, the capital of Southern Rhodesia.

(iv)   The ultimate outcome was clearer in Nyasaland than in Northern Rhodesia – the disparity of whites and blacks is so marked that no reasonable person doubts that Nysaland must become a 'black' state.

(v)   All three territories were largely *unaware* of federation as an effective principle in their daily lives; there was little sense of 'belonging' or of 'sharing' a common burden of responsibility.

(vi)   The African opposition to federation was still, to all appearances, absolute and universal. There had been an absence of any attempt to 'sell' federation to the African.

(vii)   Federation in Central Africa was not federation as it exists elsewhere. There was no voluntary surrender, or merging, of separate powers and authorities by states which had much in common. It was imposed.

(viii)   The parliamentary system at the federal level was incompatible with the direct administration in the two northern protectorates, where the existing arrangements are the only ones which enable Britain to discharge its responsibilities to the Africans as BPPs.

(ix)   Many of those we met prayed that the Monckton Commission could propose both a sound and workable political solution and propose a symbolic act to convince the Africans that federation is as much in their interest as anyone else. For it does have much in its favour; time would serve to demonstrate this and some recent steps had been favourable.

The fact is that as a result of racial segregation and in the absence of closer communications between the different races, especially in Southern Rhodesia, the federal government is out of touch with and indifferent to African opinion and decision-makers in the other two territories, which is at the very least politically inept. Their decisions reflected this ignorance.

Finally, just a short note about Roy Welensky, a controversial figure in Rhodesia. Lyttelton recalled how when he met Welensky for the first time, the latter said he was '50% Polish, 50% Jewish and 100% British'! He entered politics as an unofficial member of the Northern Rhodesia LegCo. But in due course he became the federal prime minister, and a very assertive one. His approach to the notion of 'partnership' was very much that of Cecil Rhodes – he expected people to work their passage before being given responsibilities of a political nature. While admirable in concept, this approach could not work within the timetable of political reform which he advocated and was becoming a necessity, both in the territories and at the federal level. It is unfortunate that such a vigorous and persuasive politician could not find a way to gain the confidence of Africans in the creation of the federation. Instead, he became the feared opponent of the Africans of Northern Rhodesia and Nyasaland. It is still astonishing that such a vigorous politician did not meet either Banda or Kaunda until they met in London in 1960 for negotiations on the federation.

British policy-making and the federation

As Philip Murphy noted in his introduction to the BDEE Volumes on Central Africa, in the years before the creation of a Central Africa Office in 1962, just before the dissolution of the federation, the British Government's policy-making structure was a recipe for conflict and confusion.[113] Southern Rhodesia conducted its relations with London through the Commonwealth Relations Office (CRO), which also had overall responsibility for relations with the federal government. At the same time, Britain remained directly responsible for the administration of the Federation's two northern territories, which came under the authority of the Colonial Office. Over time, this geographical division of responsibility gave rise to a distinct ideological cleavage between the two departments ... with the CRO displaying a marked sympathy for the concerns of the European settlers while the Colonial Office tended to show a far greater sensitivity towards African political aspirations ... this led to the CRO and

CO defending sets of principles which were virtually incompatible. ... The problem was recognized by ministers and officials at the time ... the sense of working at cross-purposes led to inhibitions about the sharing of information ... these divisions were reflected in the structures of British administration and representation within Central Africa ... thus widely divergent advice was submitted by officials on the ground.

In February 1957, Welensky proposed a single ministry be created within HMG to handle Central African Affairs.[114] Probably the objective situation and local facts were the main factors leading to dissolution of the federation, but the attempts to solve the various problems were obstructed by the differences between the ministries in London.

The following section summarizes the steps taken by the three countries prior to the eventual collapse of the federation, and to their own independence. The negotiations proved to be very contentious partly because Northern Rhodesia and Nyasaland were faced with existing structures and policies designed for the federation and not solely for their own government.

Southern Rhodesia (Zimbabwe)

At the time of federation in 1953, the franchise for the Southern Rhodesia Legislature required electors to have property of no less than £500 or an income of £240 a year, in addition to a speaking and writing knowledge of English. Of the 49,000 qualifying electors, only 1,500 were African. Thus it was not to be expected that the Africans would support such a franchise. There was apathy among the Africans who did meet the franchise qualifications – very few registered or voted. There were legally enforced social barriers between African and non-African. As late as 1960 there were still no African members of the Legislature, whose membership therefore did not reflect the nature of the country. Nevertheless, speaking at the Royal Africa Society in 1960, Richard Gould-Adams, a well-respected journalist, said, 'I found moderate African leaders accepting in principle a qualification to vote. And I found ... European leaders were much more ready to accept that ... the qualification must not on any account be raised once Africans begin to qualify in reasonable numbers'.[115] Elsewhere in this speech he pointed out the higher standard of education found in Southern Rhodesia – 'A higher proportion of Africans has been educated in Southern Rhodesia than in most African countries ... because the country is better organised and rather richer'. (See previous chapter where it is recorded that Southern Rhodesia committed itself to universal primary education by 1960.)

In the event, a conference held in London and Salisbury negotiated a new, somewhat more liberal constitution, supported by Joshua Nkomo's National

Democratic Party, which however still retained a controlling settler majority. It was approved by referendum in 1961 by a majority of two-thirds.

Northern Rhodesia (Zambia)

It is of interest that a non-statutory African Representative Council was created in Northern Rhodesia in the early 1950s. This had twenty-nine members drawn from all parts of the country who were elected by the delegates at meetings of African Provincial Councils, except in Barotseland, where the paramount chief would nominate members. Meetings of the Council were scheduled by the governor, who also attended. The secretary for native affairs, an official of the government, would also attend. Meetings were open to the public. It seems that Northern Rhodesia was the only territory which created such a body, which acted as a sounding board for discussion of public policy and other issues in a more informal way than was possible within LegCo.[116]

As indicated earlier, the constitution of 1924 provided for an Executive Council and a Legislative Council. By 1945 LegCo had an unofficial majority, with three members representing African interests. By 1953 when the Federation came into being, LegCo consisted of ten European elected members, two European unofficials representing African interests, two African unofficials nominated by the governor and nine officials. This was modified again so that there were then eighteen unofficial members, six of whom were African. ExCo had five officials and four unofficials, all of whom held portfolios in government. The low level of African representation in both councils up to this stage was a result partly of the franchise rules which limited the franchise to British subjects, excluding BPPs (which was the status of most of the Africans); and partly to the importance of the European miners to the economy. However, a step forward was taken on 9 September 1959 when Northern Rhodesia merged the then existing separate European and African Civil Services into a single non-racial Northern Rhodesia Civil Service.[117]

Public and Police Service commissions were inaugurated in January 1961 with an advisory status, appointments still being made by the governor. The intention was that the creation of the two commissions by Gazette Notice would in due course be followed by Orders in Council on the Uganda pattern, with the commissions then becoming fully executive in nature.[118] A judicial Services Commission was envisaged for the time of self-government.

Meetings of the African Congress Party in the country gave rise to suggestions that federation should be opposed by such means as a general strike, weekly paralysis strikes, mass exodus from towns, non-payment of taxes and so on. The attorney general of the day drew the attention of the leaders of Congress, through two African members of LegCo, to the legal position and warned them that political strikes would be illegal. He did not threaten force and made it clear that the government wished Africans to have the fullest freedom of speech. The contrast between this emollient approach and that described next in Nyasaland is striking.[119]

Events and the atmosphere in Northern Rhodesia deteriorated however during the course of the Monckton Commission with some disturbances in the Copperbelt especially, involving some violence and somewhat reckless moves by African politicians. In September 1960 HMG and the Governor, Sir Evelyn Hone, felt that some holding statement was required to assure people that discussions on the future constitution of Northern Rhodesia would resume soon after the Monckton Commission's report had been issued. There was also increasing pressure for a solution from private persons, including Sir Ronald Prain a leading mining executive, who feared that Kenneth Kaunda might be replaced as leader of UNIP if there was no progress. New momentum was generated by the publication of the Monckton Report in October 1960. The negotiations on the constitution of Northern Rhodesia proved to be very delicate, contentious and protracted. The Prime Minister of Southern Rhodesia, Sir Edgar Whitehead, as well as Sir Roy Welensky, both said that if HMG conceded parity of representation between Africans and others in LegCo, Southern Rhodesia might leave the Federation. The Africans were aiming for a clear majority. The Colonial Secretary felt the least he could agree to and keep the Africans engaged was 16:15.[120] McLeod threatened to resign if he was not allowed to handle the negotiations as he felt fit.[121] The offer finally made at the constitutional conference in May 1961 was that there would be 15 members elected on an upper roll, 15 on a lower roll and 15 by electors selected by both groups, which meant that both sets of voters would have to seek support of electors of both rolls. Discussions on this proposal continued but disturbances in the territory increased pressure on the participants not to concede too much to the federal representatives. There were also considerable disagreements within the British Cabinet, between HMG and Welensky and between the Colonial Office and the Governor of Northern Rhodesia. In October 1961 Macmillan replaced McLeod with Reginald Maudling who experienced similar difficulties. He argued the matter through in a minute to the Prime Minister of January 1962[122] and in February 1962 announced that a variant of the May 1961 proposals would be adopted. An election on the basis of the new constitution in late 1962 produced a legislature opposed to the Federation.

Nyasaland (Malawi)

The status of the administration in Nyasaland up until the mid-1950s was summarized earlier. As the administration evolved, so did LegCo and ExCo. Up until 1956, the members of LegCo were either officials or nominated unofficials, among whom were only three Africans out of the twenty-one members. In 1956, the unofficials were made subject to election. In 1957 a Speaker took the place of the governor in chairing the council. There was still an official majority with twelve officials, and eleven unofficials, of whom five were African. The non-Africans were elected by constituencies on a high franchise; the Africans by the three African provincial councils sitting as electoral colleges. ExCo remained unchanged from 1951 to 1959 with eight members, chaired by the governor, including two nominated unofficials, neither or whom was African. The lack of Africans in ExCo was criticized in the British Parliament at the time. Changes in 1959 added two unofficial Africans to ExCo. In LegCo, the total membership in 1959, excluding the Speaker, was twenty-seven, namely fourteen officials, six non-Africans (elected), seven Africans, of which four were elected by African Provincial Councils sitting as electoral colleges and three were nominated. By any measure, the membership of the councils still retained to the government exceptional control and gave the Africans only limited opportunities to effect changes in legislation or acquire experience in the arts of government.

Civil disturbances and the Devlin Commission

In 1959 there were serious disturbances in Nyasaland which entailed deployment of the police and armed forces to keep control. Fifty-one persons were killed and seventy-nine wounded. These events were examined by a commission appointed by HMG and sitting under Justice Devlin.[123] Since similar disturbances on this scale were not common and because of the consequences for the Federation, I summarize here the commission's main findings:

(i)   The Nyasaland African Congress (Congress) was formed in 1944 as a convention of a number of African associations concerned with African welfare. By 1959 it had branches not only in Nyasaland but also in the Rhodesias. It was affiliated with Congress parties in the Rhodesias. In 1951, while Dr Banda was still living in England, and while careful examination was taking place between HMG and the three Central African governments of the case for federation, Banda issued a booklet explaining why he was opposed to federation. Inside Nyasaland, opposition to the Federation was being led by Congress. There had been disturbances before (1954) in connection with the nature of the federation during which eleven Africans were killed and seventy-two injured.

(ii) The announcement that the federal constitution would be reviewed in 1960 stimulated a demand within Congress for further constitutional reform in Nyasaland, especially for there to be an African majority in LegCo. They argued that it was essential that such a majority be in place before the delegation for the negotiations on the revisions to the constitution was selected. Governor Armitage responded that he had not yet prepared recommendations on the future of Nyasaland in the Federation for HMG but indicated that he felt an African majority government was premature. Congress then took their demand directly to the colonial secretary in London, who said he had yet to receive proposals from the governor. As Devlin wrote,

> Already a clash between the Government and Congress was highly probable; already the differences between them had got almost beyond discussion. ... The election of a few Africans to LegCo had not altered the fact that the Government was a benevolent despotism; about its benevolence there should be no mistake; the despotism was that of a kindly father, not of a tyrant.

(iii) To make sense of the 1959 disturbances, the Devlin Commission studied events since 7 July 1958, the date when Dr Hastings Banda returned to Nyasaland. There had been disputes between the government and Congress about (a) assembly, which required permission; (b) about the application of rules designed to prevent soil erosion; and (c) about intimidation by opponents of federation, concerning which Devlin concluded 'the Government exaggerated the extent and effect of intimidation'. On 21 October 1958, force was used to disperse African crowds. On 20 February 1959, firearms were used for the first time. On the 3 March 1959 a State of Emergency was declared and the Congress Party proscribed. In the course of four days, the leaders of Congress were arrested and the resulting disturbances put down. This is when most of the casualties occurred. From 9 March an operation began to restore law and order in the entire country. From 13 April a campaign took place to 'stamp out Congress' and return to normal administration.

(iv) In paragraphs 42, 44 and 45 of his report, Devlin wrote:

> This conflict of thought and feeling between a Government that is still paternal in outlook and an opposition that is not yet as mature as it believes itself to be, is no doubt a common feature in the emerging of democracy all over the world. What is peculiar to Nyasaland is that the feelings of anger and bitterness and frustration which this sort of conflict commonly engenders were largely concentrated on one point, namely the controversy over federation ... on this issue there is a deep and bitter division of opinion separating the Government from the people. ... The Government says that it cannot and will not go back upon federation; it treats the question

as one which is no longer open. Congress on the other hand believes that in its opposition to federation it is supported by the whole of African opinion.

In advance of the debate in the British Parliament on the Devlin Report, Sir Norman Brook, the cabinet secretary, wrote to the prime minister, twice, providing succinct opinions on the report's findings[124]:

- The governor's action in declaring the Emergency was firmly vindicated. The government had ample ground for apprehending violence.

- The governor was not influenced in taking this action by the Government of the Federation.

- The government was not unduly influenced by intelligence reports of a murder plot, whereas Colonial Office ministers took them seriously.

- The report is much more critical of the action taken by police and military after the declaration of the Emergency. Unnecessary violence was used in the initial round-up of Congress leaders.

- The use of firearms to control crowds was probably justified by the circumstances as a means of preventing matters getting out of control.

- Individual officers in the riots 'did what they did because they honestly felt they could not discharge their duty in any other way'.

- The report argued that 'the suppression of the Congress movement and the assertion of Government authority were undertaken in a tough and punitive spirit' and this approach was authorized by the Government of Nyasaland.

There is other evidence on this matter from people well informed about Nyasaland e.g. Guy Clutton-Brock[125] and the writer of a Leader in The Spectator of 27 February 1959.[126]

In a sense, Governor Armitage was right – federation was the settled policy of HMG and the colonial government was bound to implement it, subject to the review scheduled for 1960. But the government knew the policy to be against the widely expressed preference of the Nyasaland people and would require imagination and hard work to persuade them of federation's advantages. It should have been possible to implement the policy with more imagination and a more open exchange. Instead, even criticism of the notion of federation became sedition. In the light of the Devlin Report it became clear to HMG, as laid out in a memorandum from the colonial secretary to the cabinet, that it could not go on with this policy blindly and it was necessary to find a way out of the federal imbroglio and unwind the State of Emergency in Nyasaland. One aspect of this was constitutional reform in Nyasaland; another was consideration of the implications for Northern Rhodesia; the third aspect concerned the implications for the Federation to be considered through the Central Africa Advisory Commission under Lord Monckton.[127]

In cabinet, HMG decided:

(i)   To publish the Devlin Report, together with the governor's comments on it.

(ii)   That the governor had been justified in declaring a State of Emergency and taking the measures required to keep control.

(iii)   To encourage the governor to consider with the colonial secretary measures required to advance the constitutional arrangements for the territory.[128]

It is now clear that the lack of well-educated and experienced African officers in the civil service and police contributed to the disturbances in Nyasaland in 1959 – the leaders of Congress prior to Banda's arrival were not capable of persuading a sceptical government of the need for constitutional reform. However, also contributing to the breakdown of law and order was a governor and administration which failed to engage adequately with the Nyasas on the issue of federation. The neighbouring government of Northern Rhodesia faced the same opposition to federation but approached and handled the issue differently and more effectively. HMG acted upon the findings of the Devlin Commission, but did not publicly endorse its report.

In regard to reform of the Nyasaland constitution, McLeod announced in January 1960 that the governor had agreed that this would have to be done in advance of the review of the federal constitution to be carried out by Lord Monckton. In regard to LegCo, McLeod felt the unofficial members should be decisively shifted in favour of Africans, and he also considered that among those still in custody after the March disturbances were sufficient talented and educated men to fill these seats effectively. However, the governor still felt that for the time being he needed an official majority in LegCo so that he could be sure to get his bills through. In regard to ExCo, the governor accepted the need to get more Africans onto the Council and that they should either be given ministerial responsibility for certain departments or at least be 'associated' with an official with that responsibility. In regard to the franchise, it was recognized that the qualifications would have to be reduced to get sufficient African participation, and consideration was given to the then current Tanganyika model which provide for an income threshold of £75. However, this was below the Northern Rhodesia qualification of £150 with simple literacy or £120 with two years secondary education. In the end the federal government accepted a £100 income test but was very concerned about the appointment of African ministers.[129]

Both the Commonwealth secretary, Lord Home, and the colonial secretary, Iain McLeod visited the region and in February 1960 the cabinet in London agreed in principle to the release of Dr Banda and some other Nyasas.[130] Both the federal government and the Southern Rhodesian government were adamantly opposed to the release of Banda from detention; they felt HMG had misread his personality and capacity for creating trouble and evil. They were particularly concerned about the likely impact on African opinion in Southern Rhodesia. Nevertheless, HMG decided to release Banda in March 1960 so that he could meet McLeod during a planned visit to the country and meet Lord Monckton, who was carrying out the review of the federal constitution, and who was due to visit the country in April. McLeod argued that the negotiations could not prosper so long as Banda was still in detention.

Parenthetically, it is worth noting that the Southern Rhodesian government was at that time (early 1960) facing a threat from the Dominion Party which favoured Southern Rhodesian secession from the Federation with a view to some association with South Africa.

The advisory commission on the Constitution of the Federation of Rhodesia and Nyasaland (Monckton)

Lord Monckton was appointed to chair the commission on the federal constitution in 1960. It is not necessary for purposes of this book to go into all the arguments made and conclusions arrived at by Monckton. I have summarized the commission's findings in Annex 5. But the effective outcome was that both Northern Rhodesia and Nyasaland withdrew from the Federation in 1963 and Southern Rhodesia then attempted to carve out its own future. All three countries lost much from the failure of a brave attempt to create a large, multiracial state in Central Africa. This disappointing outcome resulted mainly from the failure of the Rhodesian settlers, the federal government and the Colonial Office to give adequate weight to the fears of the Africans and their failure to address those fears and demonstrate how the federation would benefit all residents; good long-term intentions were not sufficient to draw the majority of Africans into the scheme with any enthusiasm.

As The Economist wrote at the time:

If the settlers cannot govern by consent, the settlers will not be able to go on governing. Fitness or unfitness to govern is ceasing to be relevant. Either the Africans are going to be set on the road to power, or they are going to reach for power by themselves. The white man has no real choices but to accept this and, having done so, to bargain for the best deal he can get.[131]

The High Commission Territories

Bechuanaland (Botswana), Basutoland (Lesotho) and Swaziland

These three territories became British dependencies in the nineteenth century in recognition of their fear of being incorporated into the expanding Transvaal and Orange Free States of South Africa. Their forms of government initially reflected very much the traditional tribal forms. The British government exercised authority in these countries through a High Commissioner, resident in South Africa; hence the nomenclature used. In due course the traditional forms of government were modified at the initiative of the British authorities by the creation of native authorities to facilitate improved administration in the interests of the people as a whole. This had implications for the status and role of the chiefs and lengthy deliberations were required to arrive at a mutually agreeable division of authority.

In Bechuanaland, national bodies eventually came into existence, specifically the African Advisory Council and the European Advisory Council. In 1951 these were joined together into a Joint Advisory Council (JAC). Initially the JAC focussed mainly on issues of policy but in time it began to look into detailed provisions of new draft legislation – it became a de facto legislative and executive body. In due course the JAC appointed a Constitutional Committee to consider the best form of representation for the country in the long term. Interestingly, it favoured a communal system rather than a common roll, on grounds that this could help avoid sectional conflict. It also included a means for individuals of knowledge and ability, who did not stand for election, to be nominated to the Legislative Council. Two European and two Africans could be nominated to the Council by the local Resident Commissioner (a position introduced in all three territories in 1964 to replace the role played by the High Commissioner). The same communal balance was retained in the Executive Council.

In his book Peter Fawcus, one-time resident commissioner in Bechuanaland, wrote:[132]

In the light of subsequent events in both Swaziland and Bechuanaland, it may be of interest to record that the 50:50 black-white composition of the LegCo condemned so forcefully by Cowan for Swaziland in 1961, was introduced in Bechuanaland in the same year. It helped to foster racial harmony there throughout the lifetime of the four-year transitional constitution and paved the way for internal self-government in 1965, with the full agreement of all racial groups, on a simple franchise of one person one vote on a common roll … parity of the two main races was unusual in British colonial territories in which the African population greatly outnumbered the European. Its successful introduction was due to relationships established during the previous three years in the JAC, to the respect which the Council earned in the territory, to the well-argued recommendations of the Constitutional Committee and, fortuitously, to the weakness of the opposing political parties (the Federal Party and the People's Party) during the years 1959-61. ...The final constitutional organisation retained a House of Chiefs parallel to LegCo, in view of the importance which many people gave to the traditional institutions. The House of Chiefs was to consider and discuss bills referred to it concerning tribal affairs, including customary law, tribal organisation and property and other tribal matters, before LegCo enacted legislation. Members of the House of Chiefs could not also be members of LegCo. This was fundamental – probably nowhere else in Africa did the role of the tribal chiefs survive at the national level in a manner in which they were able to operate independently; elsewhere they survived by joining political parties and thus tended to become partisan advocates of their tribe or interest.

Undoubtedly, Botswana also owes much to the emollient and public-spirited character of Seretse Khama and his family, who led the country from 1956 when Seretse returned from exile in London until his death in 1980, while these institutions were bedding down. In parallel, a successful decentralization policy was implemented over a fifteen-year period, devolving power to local, district and town councils.

In Basutoland there was a complex system of chiefs at various levels, all with a very limited jurisdiction, which in 1948 was reformed by the creation of district councils, presided over by district commissioners. A constitutional commission made proposals for the achievement of self-government by Basutoland in 1964. However the British government was concerned that the constitution left Britain with responsibility for some functions without the authority to discharge them, altered the headship of the state prematurely and gave the public service commission authority to proceed to terminate the role of colonial officials too quickly. There were considerable differences of view in the National Council about these proposals and it took time to work out a solution.[133]

In Swaziland a native authority ordinance was enacted in 1950, with the paramount chief in council as the sole native authority. By the end of the 1950s, further reforms were needed. The Swazi people could not agree on the terms of a new constitution during the course of three years of negotiations and a conference in London so in the end the colonial secretary decided to go ahead and promulgate by Order in Council the version of the constitution which he thought had most support and which also reserved some powers to the Ngenyama, the traditional ruler of the country. This constitution provided for elections to a legislative council with representation from all the interest groups, which it was planned to hold in June 1964.[134]

In May/June 1965 a Joint UN/UK mission visited the three territories to look at the needs for future economic and technical assistance. This was followed by a further economic mission later in the year.[135] The report described the substantial remaining needs for assistance especially to stimulate the economies and in education (see earlier chapter). In all three countries there was an urgent need to stimulate localization of the Public Service, which had far to go (see the following chapter). Emphasis was given to various subsectors of the rural economy – raising the productivity of peasant farming in Swaziland and Basutoland, expansion of dryland crop production and the improvement of cattle marketing in Bechuanaland in particular. At that time Britain was the principle source of financial and technical assistance.

Malaya

Malaya and Singapore had been relatively prosperous before the Second World War with the Malaysian economy based on tin, rubber, palm oil and rice production. However, much of the country remained dominated by tropical rain forest so the population was sparse and physical infrastructure limited. Malaya's economy, based as it was on commodity production, had been affected by the low prices of the Depression years. Singapore's economy was very different based as it was on shipping, trade and commercial relationships. It could not avoid the impact of the Depression but was more diverse. Both countries had made social progress, especially Singapore, and education was making substantial progress.

There was however an important social issue which preoccupied the Malay rulers in the 1920s and 1930s. This concerned the immigrants and their place in Malay society. The issue was addressed in a minute by the High Commissioner, Sir S. Thomas, in August 1941, just before the Japanese invasion.[136] He had set up a Committee in 1939 to consider the question of the appointment of non-Malay Asiatics to higher posts. The Sultan of Selangor quoted Ormsby-Gore's Report of 1928 in which he had said 'British influence became established in the Malay States not as the result of conquest or aggression, but at the invitation of the Rulers … . Our position in every State rests upon solemn treaty obligations … . They were, they are and they must remain Malay States'. The Rulers on the Committee further stated 'on no account would they agree to any public pronouncement of policy, but as a working measure they would not oppose the appointment of non-Malay Asiatics to higher posts if no suitable Malay was available, provided that their own consent was sought and unanimously obtained, that the proposed candidate had been born and had lived all his life in the Federated Malay States (excluding periods of absence for education), and that his father had done meritorious work here'. Thomas pointed out that the posts referred to were in the technical departments, not in the administrative service which was restricted to British or native Malay persons, and the Rulers would never agree to any departure from this. He further commented that Malaya was fortunate to have this policy as the intensive development of Malaya could otherwise have threatened the Malay people. A special fund of $1 million was set up to meet the cost of training Asiatics (especially Malays) for higher posts.

This issue of the relationship and place in Malay society of the immigrant people, principally Chinese and Indians, manifested itself through all the subsequent policy decisions and pronouncements and was not made easier by the activities of the Malaya Communist Party, consisting mainly of Chinese, during the period of the Emergency (discussed in the following text).

During the period of the Japanese occupation in 1942–5, there was considerable forward thinking done in London about the approach to take when Japan was defeated. A Malayan planning unit was created in 1943 composed of colonial officials of military rank. Malaya consisted of the Colony of the Straits Settlements, comprising Singapore, Penang and Malacca, and nine Malay States ruled by Muslim Sultans in treaty relationship with Britain, four of which were joined in a federation – effectively a Protectorate. It was concluded in London that this loose arrangement of separate states would have to be changed post-war if the country was to be able to move forward. In addition, North Borneo and Sarawak, which were governed by a Chartered company and the Brooke family respectively, were to come under more direct rule. A 'Malayan Union' was to be created, though Singapore was to be governed separately by a governor. The shock of the Japanese invasion no doubt prompted this new policy approach on the part of HMG and the proposed departure from the relationships referred to in Ormsby-Gore's statement. Several people knowledgeable of Malaya argued during the pre-cabinet consultations that this proposal would be resisted by the sultans and by many of their people who exhibited a considerable loyalty to their rulers. They proved to be right.

The war cabinet in January 1944 created a ministerial committee on Malaya, chaired by Clement Attlee, the future Labour prime minister, to prepare formal proposals for the post-war period. On 18 May 1944, the War Cabinet decided to commence confidential preparation for the reoccupation of the territories involved and the preparation of the necessary directives to the military commanders who would command the reoccupying forces, whatever the nationality of those forces. It was expected that Britain would negotiate fresh treaties with all the rulers as soon as possible. The intention was to create a single united authority representing the States and Settlements, subject to the jurisdiction of HMG under statutory powers. There would be a Legislative and Executive Council based in Kuala Lumpur.[137] In May 1945, HMG authorized a statement to be issued to official agencies about the future policy towards Malaya.[138]

Meanwhile, with the creation of the Southeast Asia Command (SEAC) with Admiral Mountbatten as Commander, a wider political coordination was required focussed on all countries and areas allocated by the United Nations to his command, which included Burma, Siam (Thailand), the Dutch East Indies (Indonesia) and Vietnam (except for the North), in addition to Malaya. At this time, before the atomic bombing and capitulation of Japan, it was still expected that all these countries would have to be re-occupied by the Allies by force. The reoccupation of Malaya by British forces was preceded by SOE operations which made contact with the leaders of the Malayan Communist Party (MCP) and other resisters, grouped as the Anti-Japanese United Front (AJUF), most of whom were ethnic Chinese, and negotiated a temporary arrangement for the supply of weapons and warlike goods in return for Malay acceptance of British military orders during the rest of the war and in the subsequent period of military occupation. Despite this, excesses on the part of the AJUF caused bloody Sino-Malay exchanges and clashes in the month following the reoccupation. On 3 September 1945, the cabinet formally decided HMG's policy in regard to Malaya and Borneo.[139] The military administration was established in Kuala Lumpur on 12 September 1945 under Brigadier Willan in accordance with the terms of a proclamation issued by Mountbatten. Willan was to take the surrender of the Japanese units and he met each ruler to assess his relationship with the Japanese during the occupation. In effect he prepared the way for Sir Harold MacMichael who was appointed HMG's representative in the area. Between 10 October 1945 and the end of the year, MacMichael concluded new agreements with the Malay rulers under which they surrendered sovereignty of their states to the Crown. A White Paper describing HMG's policy was issued on 22 January 1946 (Cmnd 6724). However these measures and MacMichael's manner alienated the rulers and many others, Malay and non-Malay. As early as mid-November 1945, great concern was being expressed by those knowledgeable of the country about the MacMichael agreements on grounds that they represented a breach of faith with the country and its rulers and were likely to lead to unrest.

As elsewhere, the period of the military administration was a strain on everyone due to shortages of food and goods, high prices, profiteering, the disruption of the administration, overworked functionaries, a degree of score-settling, lack of jobs and anxiety about the future. The occupation had caused some Malays and Chinese to become much more politically conscious than they had been pre-war. A Foreign Office assessment made the point that 'while the Japanese did their utmost to destroy what had been, they put nothing in its place. ... By its very nature the spirit of resistance encouraged a law-breaking as opposed to a law-abiding temperament, so what was born of duress had to some extent become a habit difficult to eradicate'.[140] The occupation deeply upset the whole social structure of the occupied countries and released a surge of nationalist movements. Against this background, the War Office and the Colonial Office adopted a firm set of targets and dates to govern the conversion of the military administration into a civil one.[141] In Singapore, where there were many troops, resentment was also caused by the occupation of buildings, black-markets in stolen goods, ill-discipline in some cases and delays in reopening institutions such as schools.

Mountbatten pressed the colonial secretary for early announcements in Parliament on the creation of the Malayan Union and the institutions which would comprise it. He was already concerned that unless the Union and its institutions were presented as a temporary expedient, they would be viewed as autocratically imposed from London with virtually no local input. As he said, 'I am convinced that it is only in this way that the Malayan Union proposals have a chance of being welcomed by Malaya and the world in general, as a progressive measure'.[142]

A prominent Malayan figure, Dato Onn bin Jaafar, called for a Pan Malayan/ Malay Congress in early March 1946 to debate the White Paper issued by HMG on the subject. Bourdillon in the Colonial Office evaluated the nature of the opposition to the White Paper. He wrote,

> To sum up, I think we must admit a genuine and fairly widespread Malayan revulsion against the White Paper. ... In almost all the reactions from popular bodies, as opposed to Sultans, it is citizenship which is attacked ... my impression is that the popular reaction amongst Malays is based almost entirely on fears, exaggerated, but real, of the citizenship proposals.[143]

General Hone, head of the Malaya Planning Unit, by then located at Mountbatten's HQ, argued against issuance of the necessary Order in Council on citizenship on the eve of the resumption of civil government in the country. Prime Minister Attlee agreed to this until local consultations had taken place.[144] At the end of March, the Malay rulers decided to boycott the swearing-in ceremony of the new high commissioner, Sir Edward Gent. The Sultan of Kedah, on behalf of the group, said that he had cabled the secretary of state saying that no disrespect was intended but while the Sultans would accept Federation, they would not accept Union. In response, the secretary of state, George Hall, reiterated that the transfer of jurisdiction which underlay the MacMichael treaties could not be undone and that the maintenance of a strong central authority in Malaya was fundamental.[145] On 22 May 1946, when Malcolm MacDonald was sworn-in as commissioner-general of the British territories in South-East Asia, the Malays again boycotted the occasion. On 25 May he cabled Hall to say, inter alia, we must face the fact that Malay opinion is, in effect, solid.

> At the same time, Malayan opinion is friendly to Britain and HMG and wishes for complete restoration of understanding and goodwill ... both conservative and progressive opinion charge the Sultans with having completely surrendered their position as leaders with the MacMichael agreements. ... The Sultans are by no means free agents ... they are in every case instructed as to their attitude by the United Malays National Organisation (UMNO) which is headed by Dato Onn.[146]

These representations began to shift opinion in London. On 3 December 1946, the cabinet considered and approved proposals satisfactory to both Malaya and HMG.[147] It would in fact take the next year to work out and implement the details of the federal constitution and for it to be formally inaugurated. Thus it was two and half years after the end of the war before the Federation of Malaya came into being following major disagreements between HMG and Malaya, not the most auspicious start to the post-war relationship. It is of interest in view of later events that at this time Singapore was very keen to join the Malayan Federation.

The citizenship issue emerged strongly post-war. Previously, the Chinese community in Malaya had not been subject to Malay rule to any significant extent as their settlement in Malaya was consequent upon the British control of Penang, Singapore and Malacca where the tin-mining was concentrated. In these areas they were twice as numerous as the Malays. British control was direct control – indirect rule as adopted in Africa did not emerge here. The Chinese moved from Triad rule to British rule. To create an independent Malaya would require a nationalist movement comprising both communities, but post-war the Malays feared the Chinese, who in turn were stimulated by the events in China itself. Some Chinese, especially the communists, began to threaten security in Malaya. Some Indians were associated with this insecurity. Initially it was felt that the insecurity was related to a trade dispute, but by mid-1948 it was realized that things were more serious than that; it had become political. Following some murders a State of Emergency was declared in mid-June 1948. This coincided with the recall of the high commissioner, Sir Edward Gent, who in fact was killed in a mid-air collision on his way back to Britain. Within a month of the State of Emergency being declared, thirty persons were murdered. On 17 July, the MCP was proscribed.[148] The cabinet's Defence Committee considered the situation and decided to send a British brigade to Malaya by the end of August 1948 and invite Australia to consider supporting this action. Additionally, measures were taken to expand and strengthen the police, the first line of civil defence. In September, Sir Henry Gurney was appointed as the new high commissioner.

Gurney devoted considerable time to working out ways to enlist greater support from the Chinese community for public policy. He concluded that the 'bandits', as he referred to them, could not be described as 'popular'; their support depended on intimidation. The security forces would have to gain the initiative before the people generally would be able to resist this. He also pointed out the difficulty that many Chinese, especially the better-educated ones, looked to China where they saw that the communists were in occupation of vast tracts of the country and the Kuomintang were in retreat. By 1949 they were in power. HMG recognized the communist government of China in January 1950, much to US displeasure. Gurney concluded among other things that immediate steps had to be taken to isolate the Chinese squatters, who were in some cases in illegal occupation of land, and who were providing food and other support to the 'bandits'. He planned to use more actively the power of banishment of Chinese to China. It was also pointed out that the 'bandits' were not representative of all the Chinese in Malaya, many of whom had come to appreciate over a century of British rule in Penang, Malacca and Singapore and were proud of their British nationality. Gurney also engaged in discussions with Chinese members of LegCo and other prominent figures with a view to obtaining help from the Chinese against the 'bandits', in particular for them to cease the payment of protection money. He discussed with the State administrations ways for them to get closer to the Chinese community in their areas. He urged HMG to make public pronouncements to the effect that in due course Singapore could be constitutionally linked with the Federation and that Britain had no intention of leaving Malaya in the foreseeable future. The Malayan Chinese Association in due course came out openly with appeals to all Chinese to cooperate with the government, to give information and to stop giving help to the 'bandits'.

The security costs of the Emergency were a preoccupation in both Malaya and London. Gurney estimated the costs facing the Federation, which he calculated to be St$109 million in 1949, St$68 million in 1950 and St$67 million in 1951. HMG approved a Grant-in-Aid of £4.5 million (St$38 million) for 1949 and £3 million in 1950. In February 1950, the Chiefs of Staff Committee in London reviewed progress in the Malay Emergency and recommended the despatch of a Gurkha Infantry Brigade, together with additional air force resources and the strengthening of British battalions already in Malaya. They also supported appointment to a new civil post of director of Anti-Bandit Operations, recommended by Gurney, of Lt General Briggs. In April 1950, Prime Minister Attlee established a special cabinet committee 'to keep the situation in Malaya under review and report as required to the Defence Committee, to authorise such measures as they may think necessary to preserve law and order in the Colony'.[149] Emmanuel Shimwell was appointed chairman.

At the end of 1949, Gurney had proposed to the Colonial Office that it was time to move towards a Member system in the federal government, whereby un-officials would be given responsibility for portfolios such as education or health, in place of the British departmental directors. This was an important step in all colonies moving towards self-government, and Gurney saw this step in Malaya as being desirable 'to lead into the federal executive and legislative councils, in positions of responsibility, Malay and non-Malay leaders who show themselves as competent and available'.[150] In his despatch of 9 April 1950, Gurney conveyed a memorandum outlining his proposals, which had been considered by ExCo and by a Conference of Rulers at which the latter agreed to consult their Executive Councils on the issue of elections for State Councils. They had accepted proposals for a member system on the understanding that any Asian members appointed would be in a proportion of not less than three

Malays to one Asian non-Malay. In practice, Gurney did not expect to appoint more than three/four Malays as members initially and thought it possible that no Chinese would be willing to take on such a responsibility. He did not propose to make any constitutional changes to enable this innovation.[151] The Colonial Office reaction was favourable though it pointed out that in due course constitutional changes would be required to place the proposal on a formal basis. They were also concerned to prevent the racial ratio becoming sacrosanct.

Simultaneously, the Colonial Office was preparing economic and social plans for Malaya. By 1950, the economy and basic services were back to pre-war standards but measures were needed to broaden the economy from tin, rubber and rice and to expand and improve the physical infrastructure and educational and health services. In April 1950, the Commonwealth Conference in Colombo, led by Australia, Ceylon and India, agreed in principle to promote economic development of SE Asia to guard against the menace of communism. Out of this initiative emerged the Colombo Plan, from which Malaya was to benefit substantially.

Lt General Briggs drafted in May 1950 and obtained approval of the local chiefs of staff and HMG's Malaya Committee of a 'Federation plan for the elimination of the communist organisation and for armed forces in Malaya'. With additional forces deployed (by November 1951 they exceeded twenty-three battalions, with supporting units) and the improving economy, this offered the prospect of extending effective administration and control to all populated areas, entailing a large measure of squatter resettlement in compact groups (the Briggs villages), a strengthening of local administration, improved road communications and the setting up of more police posts in these areas. By November 1951, 350,000 squatters had been resettled in protected villages, a considerable achievement.

An important meeting took place in June 1950 in Malaya which focussed on the tempo of transition to self-government, which it was now thought might occur within 15 years. A new generation of Malayan leaders would come to the fore whose influence would tend to speed up the pace. The British role, after the Emergency, would be to retain the support of politically conscious people, but slow things down where possible so that they may have time to fit themselves for their responsibilities. There was also concern to see that the pace of events in Singapore and Malaya was synchronized as best possible so that Singapore could in due time slot into the Federation, and that informally steps should be taken towards that goal. The High Commissioner said at the meeting that Malaya was so preoccupied with the Emergency that it would be some years before it could take initiatives in this connection.

By early 1951 the stress of the Emergency was evident in the meetings and exchanges among HMG, the army and the civil administration. Both Gurney and Briggs talked of resignation at different times, though their difficulties were worked out and eventually the Federal War Council seemed to work quite well.

The British cabinet held several meetings on the military situation in Malaya, at a time when the Korean War was stretching British forces on a worldwide basis. In April 1951, Gurney wrote to the Colonial Office giving an encouraging report on the effectiveness of the new Members in ExCo and LegCo, an innovation which had been very well received by Malay opinion.

In early October 1951 Sir Henry Gurney was assassinated by 'bandits' in Selangor, his position being taken over ad interim by the chief secretary, Del Tufo, pending a new appointment.

This event coincided with the election of a Conservative government in Britain with Winston Churchill as prime minister. Oliver Lyttelton became colonial secretary and he concluded that the most immediate problem he faced was the situation in Malaya. His predecessor in the Labour administration, James Griffiths, told him that they had been baffled by Malaya, 'At this stage it has become a military problem to which we have not been able to find the answer'. Lyttelton decided to go there immediately (December). He knew the country from pre-war days and was reluctant to accept Griffiths' conclusion. He found the situation worse than he imagined – the last high commissioner had been murdered three months previously; no replacement had been appointed; civil affairs were in the hands of the acting high commissioner, the military and paramilitary in the hands of General Briggs. These authorities were co-equal and neither could overrule the other outside their own spheres – which were not properly defined. The commissioner of police and the head of special branch were not cooperating adequately; the constitutional position was a tangle of treaties; departments were being run by Malay appointees nominated by the Rulers. The only bright spot he found was the creation of the protected 'Briggs' villages to which some vulnerable squatter/farmers had been moved.[152]

Lyttelton's solutions entailed appointment of a senior general as high commissioner in charge of both military and civil affairs; appointment of a civilian deputy high commissioner to handle much of the political and administrative work and a military Deputy Director of Operations; retention of the Federal War Council despite its excessive size, but creation of a small 'war cabinet' within it, consisting of the high commissioner, his civil and military deputies, the chief secretary and four prominent Asians; and putting the police firmly under one man so that operations and application of the law were consistent and responsive to a rapidly changing situation. Lyttelton had to get the agreement of the Malay rulers to these appointments, which he did after difficult negotiations. General Sir Gerald Templer was appointed High Commissioner, Sir Donald MacGillivray was appointed deputy High Commissioner, on transfer from Jamaica; Colonel Arthur Young was appointed Commissioner of Police, on secondment from London. This combination of appointments worked well. Templer gained the respect and confidence of all the different communities and interests in the country – in Lyttelton's words 'he recast the military plan, knit the police into it, made some wide constitutional changes, re-organised the intelligence, travelled tirelessly and eventually dominated the country'. Within a few years Malaya was well on the way to independence, achieved in 1958.[153]

Lyttleton was accompanied to Malaya by his parliamentary private secretary, Hugh Fraser, who stayed there after Lyttleton returned to London to study in greater depth the organization of the government of Malaya. Among other things he wrote:

> In practice the Federation is cursed with a written Federal Constitution, primarily devised not as an instrument of administration, but as a political compromise, with the Central Government safeguarding the non-Malay and the States the Malay interests. ... Whatever the future may hold, the immediate necessity is to gear more closely the central and provincial administrations ... there is a need for a two-way traffic of ideas to be established between the British Residents and the High Commissioner.[154]

At his swearing-in ceremony on 7 February 1952, General Templer released the text of his Directive from Lyttleton, which had been authorized by the prime minister. This directive placed the defeat of communist terrorism in the context of the longer-term objective of a peaceful, fully self-governing nation.[155] It sought to pull together the people of Malaya in support of a single, united objective. By the end of the month Templer had decided to merge the functions of the Federal War Council with those of the Federal Executive Council, which would then become the sole instrument of the federal government. In December 1952, discussions between General Templer and the Colonial Office focussed on the General's view that the federal legislature should be reconstituted with a better geographical balance of representation. He also felt there was a need for some definite constitutional goal at which to aim. He outlined a tentative timetable for self-government with town and local government elections beginning in 1953, elections for one state council (Johore) and one Settlement Council in 1954 and the remaining states and settlements in 1955; federal elections in 1956–8 and self-government by 1960. However, he also said that he did not feel there was any real desire for independence among any of the Malayan communities. The country lacked political leaders and there were no political parties. He felt the current need was for a strong Malayan centre party with a non-communal platform. It was agreed that the Malayan Attorney General should be asked to commence discussions with constitutional specialists when next he was in Britain.[156] Professor Wheare of Oxford participated in these discussions.

In order to broaden the level of experience in government, Templer and MacGillivray in March 1953 sought comments from London on the creation of more Members of ExCo with portfolio responsibilities and the appointment of deputies to all the members, who would sit in LegCo and who would be comparable to parliamentary under-secretaries in Britain. Lyttleton approved this proposal. In May 1953, Templer felt that he could no longer postpone action in respect of future federal elections. Initiatives were being taken by the political parties in the matter and he argued that in the absence of an initiative on the part of HMG, this jockeying for position would continue to confuse the electorate. Templer had the support of the Rulers in taking the matter to ExCo prior to an announcement in LegCo. The Colonial Office concurred and MacGillivray announced in LegCo the creation of a working party of forty-six members 'to examine the question of elections to the Federal Legislative Council and constitutional changes in the Federal Government arising therefrom; and to make recommendations'.[157]

A meeting was held in the Colonial Office in November 1953 to consider the progress in the working party. Templer and MacGillivray attended. This focussed on the eligibility of civil servants to stand for election, since most of the better-educated Malays were in the public service (accepted, for the period of one parliament); on literacy qualifications for voters (rejected); the system of voting (three member constituencies, with two votes per voter, to prevent the suppression of minorities); ex officio members (chief secretary, attorney general and financial secretary, and during the Emergency, the secretary for defence); a neutral and experienced person to define constituency boundaries. In December Templer sent a further report on the working party deliberations to the Secretary of State.[158] He was encouraged by the desire to moderate the hitherto accepted principle of communal representation; the recommendation was to allow a limited number of nominated seats for small minorities; the number of elected members was agreed to be between 42 and 57 in a total membership of 88 or 93. The differences here were still to be narrowed down. The interim report of the Constituency Delineation Commission had been submitted to the Committee. The Rulers reviewed the recommendations of the Committee in March 1954 as an amendment of the Federation Agreement was involved, and decided to accept 52 elected members out of 99, a small majority, with the rest to be ex officio or nominated. Minority members of the Committee, essentially the UMNO-MCA Alliance, who sought a fully elected LegCo, or at least a minimum of a three-fifths majority, sought to lobby the Secretary of State. Thus began a period of four months of intensive negotiations, lobbying, boycotts, demonstrations and politics over the matter of the size of the elected element in LegCo, which ended in July when agreement was reached on the method for appointing nominated members.[159] It was all extremely tiresome for everyone involved. Out of this also came a proposal for a review of the Federation Agreement of 1948, which the changed circumstances seemed to require.

In late 1953 the succession in senior posts in the administration was settled. Templer was to stay on as High Commissioner for another six months and then be succeeded by MacGillivray. There would then be no replacement of the deputy high commissioner and the G.O.C Malaya (Lt General Bourne) would become director of operations. It was hoped and expected that the military task would lessen as the political and constitutional activity intensified. At the same time, consideration was being given to ways to foster closer relations between Singapore and Malaya. A Joint Federation/Singapore Coordination Committee was established under the chairmanship of the commissioner-general, Malcolm MacDonald, and the existence of constitutional commissions in both Singapore and the Federation created an opportunity for discussions of the issue. However, Lennox-Boyd, Colonial Secretary, cautioned that this should be handled slowly and carefully and in view of the wider South-East Asian context, the issue could not be taken much further by Malaya and Singapore alone, certainly not before the federal elections.

In mid-1953 Templer lifted some of the Emergency restrictions on movement of goods and people in a limited area around the city of Malacca, creating what he called a WHITE AREA. The purpose was to demonstrate that areas where 'bandit' activity had fallen away and where the population was cooperating with the government, things would improve. Within the area, all curfews were lifted; there would be no food controls; restrictions on shopkeepers would be lifted. He wanted to show that there would be life after the Emergency if the people played their part in defeating the 'bandits'.

While visiting Britain in May 1953, Templer gave a speech regarding the state of affairs in Malaya. He considered that the armed forces now had the initiative over the 'bandits' and he was spending much more time on economic and social development and on the administration. He referred to the election of seventy local councils and the prospect of a further fifty more in the State of Johore. He mentioned that participation in the elections was at 79 per cent. Progress was also being made in the election of town councils and State and Settlement Councils had also been authorized by those councils. He mentioned that schools in Malaya were packed to capacity, forcing two shifts per school in many cases and the sacrifice of amenities. Bursaries were made available to children who could not afford to go to secondary schools. He emphasized the need for Malays to participate more in the country's commercial and industrial life, then dominated by the Chinese. It was an upbeat assessment after a tough and worrying period since the Emergency was declared.[160]

The first elections to the federal legislature actually took place in July 1955, somewhat earlier than Templer had expected, and resulted in a Council with a small majority of elected members. The political parties which participated all committed themselves to appointment of a commission of some sort to consider future constitutional advancement. The first contact with the leaders of the MCP regarding the ending of the war and the Emergency occurred in late December 1955, six and half years after the declaration of the Emergency and two months after the offer of an Amnesty made by Tunku Abdul Rahman, the leader of the federal government after the elections. These talks were carefully handled by the Tunku, Marshall, the first minister of Singapore, and Sir Cheng Lock Tan, but in the end were not successful. The elected leaders of the two states could afford to bide their time while the pressure on the 'bandits' increased, though the hard core of communists in Singapore were a worry to Marshall. The Secretary of State, at MacGillivray's request, had previously clarified that HMG saw no reason to regard the continuance of the Emergency as an obstacle in the way of self-government, an assurance which was very well received in Malaya and removed a potential stumbling block.

Lennox-Boyd also sought and received cabinet approval to negotiate a set of understandings with the Rulers and the federal government regarding HMG's responsibilities for defence of the Federation, the continued maintenance of internal security, financial and general relationships with HMG, Malayan nationality, and the composition and terms of reference for a constitutional commission. The cabinet was keen to ensure that Australia, New Zealand and Singapore should be kept informed and consulted as required.

Negotiations along these lines took place in London in February 1956, with Lord Reid being appointed as chairman of the constitutional commission, with representatives from Australia, Canada, India and Pakistan. In his report to the cabinet on the negotiations, Lennox-Boyd wrote "The conference was undoubtedly successful. ... Agreement was reached on all points ... the agreements are far-reaching, but we had all recognized beforehand that it was right to go a long way in order to obtain an amicable settlement, and they include satisfactory safeguards for all our vital interests ... the business of the conference was throughout conducted in an atmosphere of goodwill ... and the Malayan delegation has returned to the Federation with feelings of genuine cordiality towards HMG and the British people."[161]

Malaya became independent on 31 August 1957.

In the following April, negotiations also took place on the future constitution of Singapore. These were prospectively more difficult on account of the rivalry between the then current chief minister, Marshall and his political opponents, and the degree of influence on internal security sought by the Commonwealth governments providing armed forces during the Malayan emergency. Marshall failed to win the concessions he sought and resigned in June 1956. He was in due course succeeded as chief minister by Lee Kuan Yew, who was prime minister when Singapore became independent in 1963.[162]

The West Indies

In Chapter 2, reference was made to the Royal Commission on the West Indies of 1938–9.[163] The commission described a troubling situation in colonies which had been British for centuries. The impact of slavery, though by then over a century in the past, and the plantation economies, cast a baleful shadow forward so that the islands seemed almost calcified by it. The Royal Commission gave everyone involved a shake-up and stimulated a series of actions – constitutional, economic and social – to address deeply entrenched and unsatisfactory conditions.

In 1921, following pressure from the West Indies for reforms, including extensions of the franchise, constitutional changes, amelioration of racial barriers and possible steps towards federation, the Colonial Office had sent Wood, Parliamentary under-secretary of state for the colonies to visit the colonies and report. In 1924 measures were taken to introduce elections to LegCo in several of the islands but they failed to satisfy the demands for better conditions and more direct representative government. Sparked partly by the collapse of commodity prices during the Depression years but also by generally low incomes and poor working and living conditions, disturbances became widespread in the sugar estates and agricultural areas, and even in the oilfields of Trinidad.[164] Out of work emigrants to the United States, Cuba and other places were forced to return to the islands. The disturbed conditions, which grew in 1937/8, led directly to the appointment of the Royal Commission, whose findings both alarmed the British government and gave rise to measures, especially the Colonial Development & Welfare Act, which for the first time committed Britain to large-scale financial support of colonies which had previously been expected to be financially self-sufficient. In the West Indies themselves, the disturbances led to considerable strengthening of trade unions and political parties allied to them.

The enhanced political exchanges also facilitated further consideration of federation as a means of creating political, constitutional and social institutions with greater scale and potential. There had been a limited experience of federation in the Leeward Islands from 1871 and in the mid-1930s a 'Closer Union Commission' had looked at the possibility again and found some support in the small islands, Barbados and Trinidad, but not elsewhere. The Royal Commission expressed support for the notion of federation and in 1945, the colonial secretary, Oliver Stanley put federation forward again as a way to achieve internal self-government. He said:

> I consider that the aim of British policy should be the development of federation in the Caribbean at such time as the balance of opinion in the various colonies is in favour of a change and when the development of communications makes it administratively practicable. The ultimate aim of any

federation which may be established would be full internal self-government within the Commonwealth.

In 1947 a well-attended conference was convened at Montego Bay attended both by West Indian politicians, colonial officials and the Colonial Office, including the Secretary of State, Arthur Creech Jones. The Colonial Office generally thought federation was the only way to achieve self-government for such small, isolated communities and economies. The conference established a Standing Closer Association Committee (SCAC) composed of delegates of the legislatures under an independent chairman, Sir Hubert Rance, to formulate specific proposals. It published its report in March 1950.[165] Parallel studies were also made of the possibility of creating a Customs Union and unifying the Public Services.[166]

The result was an acceptance in principle of federation on the part of Trinidad, the Leeward and Windward Islands. Barbados and Jamaica wanted to amend the proposals somewhat. British Guiana had accepted the Customs Union in principle but rejected federation. British Honduras reserved its position. Barbados was generally lukewarm to the proposals and thought there ought to be another round of discussions in the Caribbean before the proposed meeting in London. HMG was generally supportive of the SCAC proposals but had no intention of imposing them. The decision had to rest with the potential members of the federation.

In April 1953 a further conference was held in London to draw up specific proposals for a West Indian Federation, attended by all the British Caribbean territories but with Honduras and Guiana there as observers only. This conference would also address relations with Britain, in particular the powers to be reserved to the Governor General and to Her Majesty-in-Council; and the level of financial support. Finally, the colonial secretary, Lennox-Boyd, decided to use the occasion of his opening speech to the conference to say that it would be for the Federation, when established, to determine, in light of the obligations of membership, when it would apply for full membership of the Commonwealth, a decision which cannot be made by HMG alone, but only by its full membership.[167] He wanted to do this to clarify to the delegates and the electors in the islands the ultimate destiny which HMG envisaged for the federation. The Federation was established in 1957 under Statutory Instrument 1364 of that year. An Annex to this document contained the constitution of the West Indies.

Subsequently, some steps were taken towards its realization. For example, on 10 July 1958, the Colonial Office wrote to the governors suggesting creation of a consultative group to consider how to create a federal civil service, determine its relationship with the territorial civil services and the public service commission, and define the rules and establishment procedures to govern appointments, transfers and remuneration.[168] However, the Federation did not in the end survive and was dissolved in 1962.

Several factors contributed to the decision to dissolve the federation. At its first session, the federal government decided to review its own constitution which by then was less advanced than those of some of the individual islands which constituted the federation – there was a move towards a greater degree of self-government within the federation. Second was the rapidly changing economic condition of the islands themselves since the original decision in 1948 to move towards federation. Manufacturing, tourism and the extractive industries prospered, though they did not generate much employment. Emigration to Britain and other countries, especially the United States, increased. Thirdly, Jamaica in particular developed an increasingly independent economic approach under Norman Manley which tended to militate against the economic structure emerging within the federation. When Jamaica left the federation, Trinidad did not wish to be left to bear financial responsibility for the small islands by itself. Finally, the notion that the small islands could not be independent countries by themselves was invalidated by the independence of Gambia, Seychelles and Malta.

Overall standing of government at independence

If one asks the question what was the standing of their governments as the colonies achieved independence, is it possible to give an overall answer? I don't think it is. I have emphasized the pragmatic way in which Britain, the Colonial Office and the colonial service went about bringing these countries to self-government and independence. If the problems were similar from one territory to another, the circumstances in them were very different from each other. Some countries were conspicuously unprepared for independence, such as British Somaliland where the timing was determined by international negotiations under the United Nations, Sudan where the timing was a result of diplomatic and strategic exchanges between Britain and Egypt and Tanganyika and Nyasaland due to the limitations of their education systems and the lack of trained manpower. Others such as the Gold Coast and Malaya were ostensibly ready for self-government and independence. But these were all matters of degree reflecting local factors and histories. In general however it can be said that the whole process was very rushed in some countries, compressed into a few years and independence was arguably premature in several countries.

In the attachment to the previous chapter on the status of tertiary-level education at independence and in Attachment 4 I have sought to present summary data on the timing of the creation of a public service commission and major local staff plans in each territory, in relation to the date of independence.

The tables have numerous limitations and not all events are strictly comparable. However, they do demonstrate:

(i)   That tertiary-level educational institutions in the countries which had them were only in the early years of their creation and development when these countries became independent. Thus the flow of well-educated men and women coming into the Public Service and the country at large was insufficient to fill the vacancies arising in the various departments and agencies of government, let alone the requirements of the professions, business and commerce.

(ii)   Everywhere there were serious measures taken to bring local people into the Public Service through creation of a Public Service Commission and serious staff planning. But these do not disguise how far these measures had still to go before it could be said that staffing would be adequate, and especially before those involved had had time to acquire the necessary experience for the major responsibilities of governing a country.

See   Attachment 1 Nigerianization 1948–52.
        Attachment 2 Tanganyika, Africanization, 1961.
        Attachment 3 Training Posts in Kenya, 1962.
        Attachment 4 Timing of Creation of Public Service Commissions.

Chapter 5

The localization of the Public Service in the British colonial territories

All the British dependencies, from India at one end of the scale to Gambia at the other, when approaching self-government and independence, went through a process, parallel to the process of constitutional change, of phasing out British and other expatriate staff and phasing in local staff as they acquired the necessary training and experience. To begin with this process was not really a process at all, merely the application of normal selection criteria, bearing in mind the limited availability of qualified men and women, the nature and functions of the posts to be filled, budgetary constraints and the locus of responsibility. But over time the process became more deliberate and policies were adopted to bring about localization of the public service. At no time were British officials in the administration of the dependencies more than a few in number – at independence in 1947, there were a mere 1200 members of the Indian Civil Service (ICS), of whom more than half were by then Indian. In 1949, out of a total colonial public service of 300,000, only 12,000 or 4 per cent had been recruited outside the colonies; and of them only about 1,250 were engaged in the administration of the colonies.[1] Partly for that reason it was essential from the British perspective for the key positions to be occupied by British staff until the moment when responsibility was actually transferred to the independent state. In general, the British government, acting pragmatically, avoided fixing a date for independence if it could possibly do so mainly because once a date was fixed a scramble ensued to determine who would assume power at independence – who would be the 'residuary legatees'. By and large such timetables were avoided, though informally officials and ministers had some idea what might be achievable. In general, all such implicit timetables were in the event speeded up. It is important to the purpose of this book to examine why they were accelerated and the consequences.

It is instructive to look at the process followed in India in a little detail because this set the pattern for the process followed elsewhere and serves as a valuable comparator for the experience in the colonies.[2] In the case of India, it was evident from an early stage that the adoption by the East India Company in about 1795 of a rule forbidding the employment of Indians in the higher ranks of the Company's service was neither viable nor justifiable, and there was much criticism of the rule among members of the ICS. Governor General Bentinck's view was that the policy should be to bring forward Indians as 'responsible advisers and partners in the Administration'. It was during his period of office that by the Charter Act of 1833 the administration was thrown open to appointment of Indians. This measure was followed by Queen Victoria's proclamation of 1858, marking the end of the Indian Mutiny, which included the intention that all Indians, of whatever race or creed should be 'freely and impartially admitted to offices in our service, the duties of which they may be qualified by their education, ability and integrity to discharge'. While these measures were important statements of policy, they were not very successful in attaining their objective and were followed in 1870 by another Act which gave the Government of India power to appoint natives of India to any office in the civil service, subject to certain rules. There was concern about the dangers of throwing open to Indians the competitive examination for the ICS at that time as the Bengalis had had the longest exposure to English and English norms and it was thought they would come to dominate the cadre of Indians in the ICS in a manner which would create problems of representation among the different peoples of India. As a result, Lord Lytton created a 'statutory civil service' open to nominees from the provinces but limited to 20 per cent of the annual intake into the ICS.

Municipal Councils had existed in India since the early 1850s but after the Mutiny the number was considerably increased with the encouragement of Lawrence and Mayo. However, in 1882 Lord Ripon issued his Resolution of the Governor General in Council describing the general lines upon which local self-government was to be extended. To quote Penderall Moon, 'while large discretion was left to Provincial Governments, it was indicated that municipal, district and local boards should be established wherever possible; that they should have a large preponderance of non-official members, that they should be elected rather than nominated; that there should be no insistence on having official chairmen; that they would be subject to some government control, but from without, not from within.' It is clear that Ripon had it in mind that in due course these measures should lead to elected legislative councils.

The creation in 1888 by Lord Dufferin of an Indian Public Service Commission (PSC), six of whose fifteen members were Indian, was another important step. The PSC was given the task of advising on the means of appointment to the public service. It rejected simultaneous competitive examinations in Britain and India for the reason given above, but abolished Lytton's statutory civil service and created a threefold division between imperial, provincial and subordinate services, the first recruited by the Secretary of State in England, the other two recruited in India from persons of Indian domicile. Additionally, one-sixth of the positions theoretically open only to the imperial service would be held open for Indians, giving the prospect of promotion of those in the provincial service to the rank of district magistrate or sessions judge, or higher still.

Other measures followed including the creation of a police service commission by Curzon in 1904, the addition by Minto of Indians to the Viceroy's Executive Council and to the Executive Councils of Bombay and Madras. Most importantly, in 1917, Secretary of State Montagu stated in Parliament that HMG's policy 'is that of increasing association of Indians in every branch of the administration and the gradual development of self-governing institutions with a view to the progressive realisation of responsible government in India as an integral part of the British Empire'.

This policy statement gave rise to the Government of India Act of 1919 which established 'dyarchy' as the system of government in eight Indian provinces. Under this measure, responsibility at the provincial level was divided between reserved subjects (justice, police, prisons and land revenue) entrusted to the governor and his Executive Council and all other subjects which were allocated to the governor acting with Indian ministers drawn from the Provincial executive councils. These councils were enlarged and at least 70 per cent of their members were to be elected. At the central level, the number of Indians on the Viceroy's Executive Council was increased and the former Legislative Council was divided into a Council of State and a Legislative Assembly, both of which would have an elected majority.

In 1912, a commission was appointed under Lord Islington to look again into the organization of the Indian public services. The commission took evidence over a period of two years and produced a report containing much information and analysis. However, with the outbreak of the First World War in 1914, it was not published until 1917, by which time fresh constitutional changes were in prospect. Following these changes and with a crisis of recruitment into the ICS due to insufficient salaries and emoluments, Islington's work was carried forward in 1923 by a commission under Lord Lee of Fareham, consisting of four Indians and four Britons. The Lee commission was also to look into the rate of Indianization of the public service. The effect was to slow to a trickle new British appointments except to the ICS and the Indian police. For these, the commission proposed that recruitment should be so adjusted that the ICS would be half

Indian after fifteen years and the police after twenty-five years. This objective was largely accomplished by the time of independence. In the army the deficiency was greater as Indians were not declared eligible for King's commissions until 1918. In 1922, the Indian government proposed Indianization of the Indian army over a period of forty-two years. The proposal was not accepted in full by HMG, but a modified scheme was adopted providing for the progressive Indianization of entire military units, followed in 1934 by the creation of an Indian Military Academy. Meanwhile twenty candidates were sent to Sandhurst each year and others to Woolwich (artillery) and Cranwell (airforce).

This process of localization of the public service in India was followed in all the colonies with variations from place to place and with different periodicities reflecting the availability of suitably educated and experienced men and women, the progress achieved in constitutional reform, but also the time expected to be available prior to the time of independence and the external factors bearing on the timing of the programme. The following sections describe the process followed in many of the major colonies.

Another case in Asia was Ceylon (Sri Lanka) which was administered until independence in 1948, not by the ICS, but by the Colonial Service. For this reason the experience of events in Ceylon became influential in other colonies, especially in West Africa, due to the service there or expert advice provided by men previously in the Ceylon service such as Sir Sydney Phillipson who advised on civil service questions in the Gold Coast and Nigeria and J. A. Mulhall who became the first chairman of the Gold Coast PSC. Ceylon achieved representative government in 1923 but the Parliamentary commission on the Constitution of 1927 under Lord Donoughmore criticized the situation 'as having shifted power from a responsible executive to an irresponsible legislature' – the exercise of power without responsibility. Furthermore, in view of the several different communities within Ceylon (and anticipating the problems which would arise in East and Central Africa),

> a condition precedent to the grant of full responsible government must be the growth of a public opinion which will make that grant acceptable not only to one section, but to all sections of the people; such a development will only be possible if under a new constitution the members of the larger communities so conduct themselves in the reformed council so as to inspire confidence. … 'It seems hardly necessary to observe that HMG is the trustee not merely of the wealthier and highly educated elements in Ceylon, but quite as much of the peasant and the coolie, and of all those poorer classes which form the bulk of the population. To hand over the interest of the latter to the unfettered control of the former would be a betrayal of its trust'.

This sentiment and dilemma was to appear in all colonies – was it reasonable, fair and sensible in the long run to hand over power at independence to the small, vociferous and ambitious minority who happened to have been the first people in the country to have had a full education and who in the majority of cases had had little experience of government? In some cases there was only one political party with any claim to be representative, nationally or regionally, and the result of handing over power to the party was sometimes to create a small oligarchy of men who as often as not were as concerned to advance their own interest as the public interest, a perversion of the objective of self-government. The role and functions of the traditional authorities, widely encouraged in British colonies under the system of indirect rule, was generally brushed aside by the nationalist politicians, though there were a few notable exceptions. It is difficult to see how this outcome could have been avoided, though the existence of a strong and independent public service and Judiciary would have served to mitigate the malign consequences.

In the case of Ceylon, Donoughmore proposed the transformation of LegCo into a State Council which would in turn divide into committees, the elected chairmen of which would become the heads of the executive departments, thus forcing politicians to accept responsibility for the implementation of policy. This would give authority to the members of the committees and enable them to gain experience of government. The commission also proposed to do away with 'communal representation', a system which was designed to ensure that all significant communities were represented in the institutions of state, but which had already been done away with in India in 1919 in favour of a common roll. This issue was also to become important in many colonies including for example Cyprus, Malaya, Kenya and the Rhodesias. In addition, the franchise was significantly widened to permit both men and women to vote at the age of twenty-one (in fact, earlier than in Britain in the case of women). Donoughmore's proposed constitution was approved by Britain and came into being in 1931.[3] A PSC was created in Ceylon under this constitution, though advisory only, appointments, promotions and discipline still being retained by the governor. In practice, it was found that due to certain peculiarities of the new constitution, executive bodies had too much influence on the civil service and this became something to avoid in other colonies. Modifications were made in Ceylon subsequent to Governor Caldecott's review of 1938.[4]

The main difference between Ceylon (and India) and the African colonies was that the process of localization of the public service was well advanced in many departments before any fundamental political changes took place. Thus by 1941, for example, seven years before independence, all posts in the Ceylonese Medical Department, all posts of accountant and many posts in the provincial administration and technical departments were held by Ceylonese. It was later perceived that the creation of largely self-governing states at a time when the senior civil service positions were often still filled by expatriate officers was a new experience and that the empirical character of the enterprise required from all concerned an exceptional effort of understanding. Experience was gained by the Colonial Office from events in Ceylon about the best way to introduce the electoral process into government, the different forms of franchise, how to select ministers and the relationships between and the roles of the Legislative and Executive Councils.[5] I shall address below for each country in turn the roles and powers of the PSCs to make appointments and promotions within the civil service, which became critical to the localization process in most colonies.

Before leaving the Indian comparator behind, it should be noted that from the time of the creation of the Indian PSC by Lord Dufferin in 1888 until independence in 1947 was a period of sixty years. In only one African colony (Gold Coast) was there more than thirty years to accomplish localization and even then with relatively few well-educated men and women. In the remainder of African colonies there was generally less than fifteen years and in some colonies less than that. The whole process was so compressed that nowhere was there sufficient time to create and establish a well-staffed public service with the necessary experience and detachment to run the countries satisfactorily after independence.

In July 1950, the Colonial Secretary of the day sent a memorandum to the British Cabinet describing the extent to which native-born administrators in the higher grades of the colonial civil services had been appointed and the measures being taken to facilitate more of such appointments.[6] The memorandum recorded that progress had been rapid since the end of the Second World War, particularly in the West Indies, Malaya and some countries in West Africa, which reflected the progress in higher and technical education. In the West Indies, more than 50 per cent of higher-level positions were by then filled by local staff; in Malaya 15 per cent, in Hong Kong 20 per cent; in Mauritius 75 per cent and Seychelles 40 per cent. However by 1950 none of the new universities being created were yet able to graduate more than a handful of students. There were in addition at that time 1,713 colonial students at British universities and 2,480 at non-university institutions. The situation in East and Central Africa was less favourable as the countries were in a very simple state when they became British dependencies and the level of education attained was still much lower than in West Africa. There were still no Africans in higher administrative or technical posts in that region.

Sudan

The formal localization process in Sudan had begun at the time of Newbold's initiative of 1944[7] when he required that every department of the government should prepare an agreed programme of Sudanization, to be carried out over the twenty-year period from 1945 to 1964. The programme involved a progressive limitation of the number of non-Sudanese posts, and accordingly of the recruitment of non-Sudanese staff on pensionable terms. No expatriate could be recruited without the approval of the Establishments Committee. Such recruitment was actually stopped in 1947, though a note in Foreign Office files of May 1948 records that there was concern that the level of British staff in the administration would decline too rapidly, 'as in India'.[8]

In March 1946, by which time a number of departmental localization programmes had been prepared, the Governor General approved formation of a committee to examine departments' proposals for Sudanization, to advise the Establishments committee upon them and to suggest means of improving or accelerating them. The Sudanization committee also posed the following three questions which were to arise in every colony sooner or later:

1. Which of these posts can be filled by Sudanese, and at what date?

2. How fast, and in what numbers, can Sudanese be produced capable of adequately filling the posts now held by non-Sudanese?

3. Are standards of qualification to be laid down, and the timetable of Sudanization adapted to them, or is a time-limit to be fixed and the level of acceptable standards adapted to reflect it?

All colonies found that in some measure they had to respond to the third question with a compromise. Though determined not to reduce selection standards, they found that until the regular output of those with full post-secondary educational qualifications was large enough to meet the needs, it was necessary for acquired experience to replace academic qualifications to a greater extent than had been acceptable previously, or would be acceptable later.

Parallel with this question was the question of performance and promotion. The principle adopted in Sudan in 1944 was 'A Sudanese may be promoted to a higher post if it is believed that he can maintain the standard of efficiency likely to be required by a Sudanese administration ... though he may require more support than a British holder of the post would require'. All departments were to apply these rules. However, Sudanization of the Judiciary caused an exchange between Khartoum and London on the grounds that the matter was ultra vires the powers of the Sudanization committee.

By 1947, the staffing of the Sudan service by origin and division was as follows[9]:

Staffing of the Sudan service by origin and division

	Division 1	Divisions 2 and 3	Total
Sudanese	110	6,608	6,718
British	606	263	869
Egyptian	12	280	292
Other	8	19	27
Total	736	7,170	7,906

As independence approached, a higher-level Sudanization committee was appointed under the terms of the Anglo-Egyptian Agreement of 1953 to handle the early localization of senior staff. The proceedings of this committee became tense and difficult as the only British member was from outside the Sudan administration and an already precipitate schedule of localization was being pressed beyond reason by some members of the committee. Progress was very rapid and by mid-January 1955, 427 posts held by British officials had been declared to be 'influential' and need not be localized immediately, but 253 British officials had resigned of their own accord. Still the Sudan government was faced with filling about 750 senior posts with Sudanese during the course of 1955.[10]

Sudan acquired independence in 1954, only ten years after the government adopted its 'Sudanization' policy and ten years before that policy was to have been fully accomplished. The numbers of British and Egyptian division 1 staff members did gradually fall away, but quite slowly. In practice, by 1962, six years after independence, none of the main departments of government had attained 100 per cent Sudanization of either division 1 or 2 posts, except in the case of division 2 staff of the Ministry of Finance, the Customs Department, the Veterinary Department and the police. However, this analysis misses out some important details. According to the Sudanization committee, by the date of independence, 307 British officials had been terminated, a further 346 had resigned and 388 had left on normal retirement. Of the 160 remaining, most were technicians or teachers. From 1956, the number of British officials began to rise again and by 1958 had risen to 375. But the composition had changed – the older more experienced officials had gone and those being recruited (on contract terms) were less experienced and less knowledgeable about the country. What the above table also shows is that only 110 Sudanese officers (15 per cent of the division 1 posts) had seven or more years' experience in division 1 posts prior to independence, a very shallow level of experience for running the largest country in Africa, and, with just one exception, in no way comparable with the level of experience found in the Indian or Ceylonese administrations at independence. A vigorous in-service training programme was developed, but this was not an adequate substitute for actual experience.

The exception to this was irrigation expertise, which had been acquired over the years of the creation of the Gezira, Managil and other large irrigation schemes between the 1920s and the 1960s. In the mid-1970s the author of this book was involved in the negotiations for financing of the large-scale Rahad Irrigation project when it was agreed that construction would be carried out by Sudanese personnel and contractors, supervised by the Ministry of Irrigation, with consultant engineering oversight limited mainly to the three major water control structures and some specialized agronomic techniques and innovations.

The situation in Southern Sudan in respect of experience in the public service was even worse than in the rest of the country. In February 1952, the Government of Sudan instituted an enquiry into the capabilities of Southern Sudanese to play their part in the country on equal terms. The number of well-trained and experienced Southerners was still few, despite the expanding educational opportunities. Nevertheless, experience from 1949 of the southern participation in the Legislative Assembly and the three southern Provincial Councils established in 1948, and the steady expansion of local government indicated a growing ability to run the provinces. The growth of the southern economy was slow, despite some bright spots. The remoteness and the still primitive level of infrastructure development contributed to the low level of economic development. Undoubtedly the sudden departure of British officials and their replacement by Sudanese who were less familiar with the region and did not know the local languages, contributed to the serious revolt which occurred in August 1955 (See Chapter 4).

The Gold Coast (Ghana)

Appointment of Africans to the public service in the Gold Coast and Nigeria began some years prior to independence and in the case of the Gold Coast, which we shall look at first, there were appointments of citizens to senior positions in the public service as long ago as 1887. An Africanization policy as such was first adopted in 1925, when Governor Sir Gordon Guggisberg adopted a policy of increasing the number of Africans in what he described as 'European Appointments' to 231. There was progress thereafter, with twenty-seven Africans appointed to senior positions, but progress was rather sedate until the Second World War, when in 1941 Captain Lynch, Assistant Colonial Secretary, was given the task of:

> making an intensive study … of the scope for Africanisation in each department …; making recommendations as to the number of appointments it should aim at filling with Africans in each grade or each department in each of the next 15 or 20 years …; preparing a statement of the qualifications for appointment to each of the grades.[11] Captain Lynch could not complete his task but his report did quantify the inadequate supply of qualified Africans for the senior civil service positions, which in turn gave rise to a substantial expansion of the scholarship scheme for the training of suitable candidates in Britain, to be implemented by a Scholarship Selection Board created in February 1945. This was followed in September 1946 by the creation of departmental committees to search among existing officers, not excluding those still in the 'Junior Service', for men and women likely to benefit from further education or training. This in turn was followed in early 1948 by a statement by the governor to the effect that it was the government's policy 'to appoint Africans to superior appointments in preference to Europeans whenever suitable Africans could be

found and further, to take all practical measures ... to augment the number of Africans suitable for such appointments'. In December 1948, an interim PSC was appointed to oversee appointments to the public service. The principles to be followed included the necessity of maintaining standards of entry to the public service, the need to ensure that promotions within the service should be on merit alone, and not take national origin into account; and acceptance that pensionable appointment of expatriates was to be permitted only if suitable staff could not be found on contract terms.

The report of the Watson Commission into the causes of the 1948 disturbances gave rise to recommendations for constitutional reform, including the placing of the PSC on a statutory basis, to insulate it from interference by members of the legislature; clarification of the relationship between the Scholarship Board and the PSC in regard to serving officers; and the advertising for the first time of vacancies arising in senior posts in the public service. In addition a Select Committee on the Africanization of the public service of the Gold Coast was appointed in 12 April 1949. The purpose was similar to the committee created in Sudan in 1944, namely:

To draw up a comprehensive scheme for the progressive Africanisation of each department of the Public Service during the next ten years, and for the education and training necessary to provide suitably qualified African officers in adequate numbers to take up senior appointments in the Civil Service and further, to make recommendations for its implementation.

The Select committee's report, The Africanization of the Public Service,[12] was published in 1950, just before important constitutional changes in early 1951. By then the number of locally recruited senior officers had risen to 221. This report was examined by the Gbedemeh Select Committee of the Legislative Assembly, along with the report of the Lidbury Commission on the structure, grading and salaries of the civil service.

In a letter dated May 1951 to Andrew Cohen of the Colonial Office,[13] mainly on constitutional matters and the tensions within the CPP in regard to the speed of achieving full self-government, the governor, Sir Charles Arden-Clarke, commented on the state of the civil service as follows:

Another question which will no doubt have to be considered in any discussions on the prospective demand for constitutional advance is the position of the Civil Service. It is unnecessary for me to state the problem here; it is one which is obviously occupying your minds in the context of many territories. At this stage, however, I think I should emphasise that *the progress which has been made towards recognition that the Civil Service must be treated by politicians in a responsible manner is slight and there is little likelihood of any appreciable change for the better, at any rate among back-benchers, as long as the majority of the higher posts are held by expatriates* (emphasis added). For this reason, as well as for others which are known to you, we must do our best to accelerate the speed of Africanisation, and accept if necessary a reduced standard of efficiency. As you are aware, an assurance has been given in the Assembly that expatriate recruitment to the Administrative Service will now be discontinued.

On 17 March 1953, a minute of a meeting between the governor and Colonial Office officials to discuss an interim report on the progress of Africanization, recorded:

It had become clear ... that pressure for acceleration of the Africanisation of the Public Service was reaching a point at which the safeguards for the Service contained in the constitution might be brought into question. This possibility must affect the Secretary of State's approach to the Cabinet about the next stage of constitutional development in the Gold Coast. ... Arden-Clarke said he had never left Dr Nkrumah in any doubt that if Africanisation were to be pressed to the point at which the safeguards of the Public Service contained in the constitution were affected, the Gold Coast must be prepared forthwith to provide all overseas officers concerned with adequate compensation for loss of career. Mr Nkrumah had recognised this. ... He felt therefore that there was good hope that the pressure for Africanisation could for the time being be kept in reasonable bounds and that the safeguards for the Public Service could be retained in the next series of constitutional instruments.

The note recorded further that the views of the Northern Territories Council on constitutional reform might have a sobering effect in Accra; the Northern Territories (of the Gold Coast) might agree to the abolition of the posts of ex officio ministers, but they would want to keep their (British) administrative officers for some years. (In 1956, a year before independence, the provincial commissioner for the Northern territories, Macdonald-Smith was to write that 'he had fifteen European and seven African Administrative Officers on his staff ... even the most senior of the Africans still had very little experience, though they were doing well and were well liked by the people'.)

Arden-Clarke's position on the need for continued service by expatriates was reiterated in a statement made in July 1953 to the Legislative Assembly by the prime minister, Dr Nkrumah, as follows:

(i) Although the Africanisation of the Public Service has made great strides in recent times, and in spite of the fact that the Government is doing everything possible compatible with efficiency to accelerate the pace of Africanisation, there will still be an urgent need for the experience of overseas officers in a fully self-governing Gold Coast.

(ii)   The Government does not propose to accelerate the pace of
Africanization at the expense of efficiency.

(iii)   Promotion will therefore continue to be on merit alone and there will be
no super-cession of serving officers on grounds of race.

(iv)   Pensions and reasonable terms of service will be guaranteed.

Another view of the issue is contained in an article which appeared in *The London
Times* titled 'Towards Self-Government in the Gold Coast'.[14] After referring to 'the
increasing discontent with what is considered the slow pace of Africanisation',
the Special Correspondent continued:

> This discontent is to be found principally among Back-bench and Opposition
> members (of the Legislative Assembly), but it is making itself felt. The work
> of an administrator, it is believed, because it is not technical, can be done
> just as well by an African, and in any case it is suspected that European
> administrators indulge in 'back-seat driving' of their ministers. The fact is
> that the administration is already seriously depleted. European recruitment to
> it has been stopped. The greatest difficulty is being experienced in retaining
> present members owing to the uncertainties of the situation. Recruitment of
> Africans in any numbers is only possible at this stage by the promotion of
> senior clerks, of whom there are a limited number. They in turn are doing jobs
> requiring immense training and experience so that they cannot themselves be
> easily replaced. Some departments are already verging on breakdown and the
> accountancy departments seem to have reached it, since there are delays in
> the payment of salaries. Africans who believe in speedier Africanisation talk
> of a moratorium on development and of a temporary acceptance of lower
> standards as a price that must be paid for self-government. But history seems
> to teach that the building up of a Civil Service with high standards is one of the
> hardest and longest tasks for a state to achieve. ... It seems at least short-
> sighted that Gold Coast Africans should want to throw away in advance a
> precious heritage, which, with a little patience, they will be bequeathed ...
> they carry on their shoulders the responsibility for showing that Africans can
> govern themselves in the generation now beginning in a manner consonant
> with certain standards. They will be judged by the world; and their success or
> failure will affect the political future of millions of their fellow Africans.

A Colonial Office minute of about the same date made the same point in a
different way:

> While Britain had fully accepted the need for constitutional development
> leading to full self-government, the speed of this constitutional advance has
> far outstripped the rate of Africanisation, which depends on the attainment

by many individuals of knowledge and experience which can be gained only over a comparatively long period of time. ... Public Service standards can be lowered at the stroke of a pen; they can be raised only with great difficulty over a long period, for public servants of poor quality, accepted when standards are lowered, cannot be ejected when it is sought to raise the standards ... no European would claim that an inexperienced European junior officer, however distinguished his academic career, could in a year or two accumulate the experience and judgment required of the holder of a very senior post ... yet it is on the belief in the fitness of Africans for promotion as rapidly as this that at least part of the case for accelerated Africanisation rests.[15]

The focus here has been on the public service, and in some disciplines the progress had been encouraging. But as Barbara Ward Jackson wrote in her Foreign Affairs article of 1953 on the Gold Coast: 'Yet today the educated community is still very small. ... Technical competence, outside the popular fields of medicine and law, is rare. The plain truth is that the skills and techniques of the community do not yet match either its aspirations or its present and potential wealth.'[16]

These passages encapsulate well the difficult balancing act and control of events required of governors, the Colonial Office and the politicians coming to power in all the colonies approaching independence. The difficulty was how to get from a situation in which procedures and norms were exercised under British control by largely British officials to a situation in which hopefully similarly experienced public officials of similar integrity, most of whom would be African, could be accepted by the public and be respected by African politicians. It was clearly understood among British officials and colonial secretaries that, despite all the political pressures to move fast, the longer the process of decolonization could be spun out, the greater the chance that the colony, when independent, would be tolerably well run. As Andrew Cohen, who was deeply involved in policy formulation in the Colonial Office and especially on the Gold Coast and Uganda, wrote in June 1951:

It is clear ... that the Gold Coast Ministers, even the best of them, still have a great deal to learn. ... Ideally, therefore, in my view the next step forward ... ought to be delayed for three or four years. The quicker such a step is taken, the shorter the transitional period before responsible government is attained will be and ... it would not be in the interest of the Gold Coast or the Commonwealth that the transitional period should be too short.[17]

The result of all these deliberations was a *Statement on the Programme of Africanisation of the Public Service in the Gold Coast* published by the government in 1954.[18] The statement can be summarized as follows:

- No expatriate recruitment unless the PSC considers it necessary to fill a vacancy;

- Contract terms only for expatriates, the term of appointment to be related to the expected availability of a suitably qualified African;
- If contract terms were not sufficient to attract an expatriate, pensionable terms could be offered;
- No lowering of standards of recruitment; promotion on merit alone;
- Retrenchment of serving expatriate officers in favour of Africans not to be contemplated.

The statement was accompanied by detailed recruitment targets by department and sector, recruitment criteria for different types of post, much material on training, scholarships and discussion of the budgetary impact.

The following table is of interest as it shows that even as Africanization received high-level and strong support from both the government and the African leadership prior to independence, and the number of Africans in the administration was increasing sharply, the number of expatriate staff in the administration increased also. There were several reasons for this. First, the 'etatist' view of the role of government prevailing at that time in governments in Britain and elsewhere, giving rise to a substantial expansion in the role of the state, which was viewed as the principal agent of development and change. Second, left-wing teaching at some universities in Britain, notably the London School of Economics, which influenced some of the politicians coming to power in the colonies. Third, the growing complexity of colonial government as the nature of the country changed through education and the growth of the economy.

Gold Coast: Africanization Figures 1949–54

1 Year (as at April)	2 Total Establish- ment	3 No. of Africans	4 No. of Overseas Officers	5 Percentage of (3) to (3+4)	6 Percentage of (3) to (2)
1949	1,663	171	1,068	13.8	10.3
1950	1,990	268	1,043	20.4	13.5
1951	2,176	351	1,200	22.6	16.1
1952	2,548	520	1,325	28.2	20.4
1953	2,560	751	1,388	35.1	29.3
1954	2,569	916	1,490	38.1	35.7

Source: Statement on the Programme of Africanization of the Public Service[19]

Treaty Series No. 47 (1953)

Agreement

between the Government of the
United Kingdom of Great Britain and Northern Ireland
and the Egyptian Government
concerning

Self-Government and Self-Determination
for the Sudan

Cairo, February 12, 1953

[with Agreed Minutes, Exchanges of Notes and Statute]

*Presented by the Secretary of State for Foreign Affairs to Parliament
by Command of Her Majesty
July 1953*

LONDON
HER MAJESTY'S STATIONERY OFFICE
PRICE 1s. 6d. NET

Cmd. 8904

Plate 1 Treaty Series No. 47, Sudan.

SUDAN: ELECTIONS FOR SELF-GOVERNMENT, 1953

INTRODUCTION

As a result of the Cairo Agreement of 12th February, 1953, between the United Kingdom and Egypt, the Sudanese are now holding their first General Elections. The Elections are being held under the new Constitution, which provides for immediate internal self-government, and for a decision by the Sudanese upon the future of their country within a year or two.

The Elections last from early November to mid-December.

This first general election in the Sudan has the advantage of supervision, provided for by the Cairo Agreement, by a Mixed Electoral Commission. The Commission have approved the issue of these photographs, in the hope that they may help to arouse the interest and sympathy of all democratic people, for the undertaking of a general election for self-government cannot but form a turning point of far-reaching importance for the future of the Sudanese.

These photographs have been taken in typical conditions. Actuality photographs taken as polling is proceeding can, owing to the size of the Sudan and the scattered nature of the population, only be very few and far between. Reproduction of these prints is quite unrestricted; and users may rest assured that they faithfully represent the scenes which are taking place during the elections.

Acknowledgment of the source of the photographs when used will form a gratifying tribute to the Sudanese and others who have been good enough to make it possible to prepare them, and to the immense labours of the Mixed Electoral Commission in their formidable task.

Khartoum, Sudan   November, 1953

Plate 2 Sudan Election.

THE ELECTORAL COMMISSION IN SESSION

The Cairo Agreement provided, so far as the elections are concerned, that
"there shall be a Mixed Electoral Commission of seven members. These shall be three Sudanese appointed by the Governor-General with the approval of his Commission, one Egyptian citizen, one citizen of the United Kingdom, one citizen of the United States of America, and one Indian citizen."

The Election Commission in session:

Left to right—

Mr. J. C. Penney, C.M.G.	United Kingdom member
Mr. Gordon Bulli	Sudanese member
El Sayed Khalafalla Khalid	Sudanese member
El Sayed Hassan Ali Abdallah	Secretary of the Commission
H.E. Mr. Sukumar Sen	Indian member and Chairman of the Commission
El Sayed Abd Es Salaam el Khalifa Abdullahi, O.B.E.	Sudanese member
Col. Abd el Fattah	Egyptian member
Mr. Warwick Perkins	United States member

Plate 3 List of names, Electoral Commission, Sudan.

Plate 4 Gold Coast Legislative Assembly.

Plate 5 His Excellency, the Governor opening the Budget Meeting of the Legislative Assembly, Gold Coast.

Plate 6 The Gold Coast Cabinet.

The Governor greets Chiefs of the Northern
Territories at the Coronation Durbar at Tamale.

Plate 7 The Governor greets chiefs of the Northern Territories at the Coronation Durbar at Tamale, Gold Coast.

Plate 8 Mobile Library, Gold Coast.

Plate 9 Entomologist at Work, Nigeria river blindness control.

Plate 10 Veterinary Centre and School, Vom, Nigeria.

Plate 11 Govt. House Dar es Salaam, Tanganyika.

Plate 12 Sir Edward Twining, Governor of Tanganyika.

Plate 13 District Commissioner on Tour Kerfue, Northern Rhodesia.

Plate 14 Gov. House, Lusaka.

Plate 15 Visit of Alan Lennox-Boyd, Secretary of State to Barotseland.

Plate 16 Members of the East Africa Royal Commission, 1953–5. Rowland Hudson, Sir Frederick Seaford, Sir Hugh Dow (Chairman) and Frank Sykes.

Plate 17 Members of the East Africa Royal Commission, 1953–5. Frank Sykes, Sir Frederick Seaford, Arthur Gaitskill, Daniel Jack, Rowland Hudson and Chief Makwaaia.

Plate 18 Colonial Secretary, Iain McLeod, addressing the Tanganyika Council; Governor Sir Richard Turnbull, centre left.

Plate 19 Makerere Medical School, Uganda.

Plate 20 University of Basutoland, Bechuanaland and Swaziland.

Plate 21 Faculty of Agriculture, Trinidad.

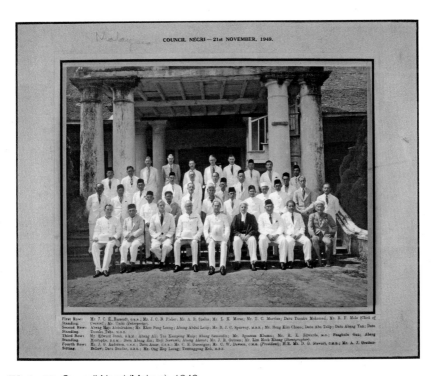

Plate 22 Council Negri (Malaya), 1949.

K.13735.
The autonomous University of Malaya was founded in 1949 by the amalgamation
of Raffles College and King Edward VII College of Medicine.

Plate 23 University of Malaya.

Plate 24 Hong Kong Uni Chemical Lab.

The armed forces in Ghana had very few senior and experienced officers at the time of independence, though many of them had had experience of conflict during the Second World War and there was a steady flow of young officers attending courses in Britain. There were plans to increase the armed services by 50 per cent over five years, yet two years after independence, the most senior rank held by a Ghanaian officer was still that of Major.

A related issue, already referred to above, was the impact the accelerated promotion of Africans would have on the morale of the expatriate staff, a very serious issue as self-government approached. This issue was well articulated by the acting governor of Sierra Leone in a despatch to the secretary of state for the Colonies in London on 18 March 1953[20]:

> Implications of Gold Coast telegram addressed to the secretary of state and repeated to West African governors have caused me and my official advisers considerable alarm. The position has long been accepted by the service that while rules of appointment may have to be varied to suit individual needs and aspirations of particular colonies, rules governing the promotion of officers, whether African or European, once they become established members of the permanent service, are sacred, and any attempt to vary them in favour of a particular race would be expected to meet vigorous resistance from governor and secretary of state, to whom the services look for protection. While accepting that exclusion of permanent officials from Executive Council may be inevitable, we view with grave misgivings the certain deterioration in public service morale which would follow any relaxation of this principle in respect of all other posts to which permanent officials may hope for promotion. I do not think it was at any time abandoned in Ceylon where the majority of highest paid official posts, that is, Permanent secretary, were on creation filled by Europeans at the request of ministers themselves. Relaxation in the Gold Coast will probably have immediate reactions here where at present there is considerable unofficial pressure to appoint an African as number two in the Education Department, over-riding the claims of several Europeans.

This issue required measures both at the level of the Colonial Office for the service as a whole, where the prospect of large numbers of expatriate colonial officials leaving prior to independence was alarming and had to be taken seriously; and at the level of individual colonies where arrangements had to be made to compensate officers for loss of office or promotion prospects, but not so early as to stimulate the early departure of experienced officers. The issue was taken to the British Cabinet by Iain McLeod in July 1960, when he was secretary of state, in a revealing memorandum.

> The richer and better developed territories – Ceylon, Ghana, Malaya and Singapore – have become independent or self-governing with a decline, but

not so far a catastrophic decline, in standards of administration. In the next few months, Nigeria and Sierra Leone will join them. ... The Civil Service of Ceylon was mainly staffed by local officers before independence. In Ghana nearly 60% of senior posts were staffed before independence by local officers and in Malaya, nearly 50% ... lump sum compensation for loss of career was made available at about the stage of self-government to members of Her Majesty's Overseas Civil Service; about a third of them left within a year of self-government and the drain has continued. But enough remained to be able, with local officers, to maintain the framework of government ... the first years of Nigerian independence will however be critical as both the Northern Region and the Federation rely more than the Eastern and Western Regions on overseas officers and we do not know how many of them will stay ... the bulk of the rest of the Service are concentrated in East and Central Africa where in the next few years our policy will be put to its most serious test ... more must be done if we are to be able to rely on the support of the Service in pursuing our policies in the remaining Colonial territories ... overseas officers become subject to the strains of approaching self-government years before the event ... as power passes to local politicians ... the present arrangements protect officers' existing rights rather than encouraging them to continue to serve.[21]

Nigeria

The notion of Africanization of the public service had become current in Nigeria before the Second World War, though there was no programme to press forward with this policy at that time. Further, during the War it was felt there had been an upsurge of corruption related to the rationing controls and there was concern to see this stamped out to the extent possible. It was even argued that the speed of Africanization would be to some extent dependent on the success in doing so.

In 1948, prior to Robertson's time, the governor of Nigeria of the day had appointed a large and widely representative commission under the chief secretary, Sir Hugh Foot (later Lord Caradon), 'to make recommendations as to the steps to be taken for the execution of the declared policy of the Government of Nigeria to appoint Nigerians to posts in the Government Senior Service as fast as suitable candidates with the necessary qualifications come forward, with special reference to scholarships and training schemes'. The commission's recommendations in August 1948 were unanimous, which is remarkable in such a diverse country as Nigeria. Implementation followed with some energy under a civil service commission and Central and Regional public service boards, but gradually some issues arose related to implementation and a new issue arose, not addressed by the Foot commission, which concerned the acceptability of officers from southern Nigeria in the civil service of the Northern Region. Further, it was felt by the governor, Sir J Macpherson, that the British staff needed some reassurance to ensure that enough of them stayed on long enough after self-government to support the new ministers and officials.

Thus in March 1952, Sir Sydney Phillipson, who had served in Ceylon, and S. O. Adebo, a Nigerian officer, were appointed as a two-man review group 'to conduct an enquiry into the policy of Nigerianisation of the Civil Service and the machinery for its implementation'.[22] Making heavy use of the earlier report and the work of the civil service commission, they submitted their report in April 1953, with publication in 1954. Using the figures contained in this report, we can summarize the progress achieved in Nigerianization between 1948 and 1952, as follows:

(a) The authorized establishment of the 'senior service' grades had increased in the period by about 24 per cent from 3,786 to 4,679.

(b) While the number of vacancies had been reduced by some 200, there still remained over 1,000 vacancies.

(c) The number of Nigerians filling 'senior service' posts had increased from 245 to 685, an increase of 180 per cent, though they still filled only 19 per cent of the available positions.

(d) The number of expatriates had also increased from 2296 to 2984, an increase of 30 per cent. Thus expatriates still filled 64 per cent of the senior service positions.

(e) The 'Junior service' had so far been very much the major source of recruitment into the 'senior service', not graduate recruitment.

The review team felt that as much progress had been achieved as was possible in the time available and that the adoption of different policies would not have yielded better results. In particular, breaking down the distinction between the 'Senior and Junior Services' removed an artificial barrier to promotion from the Junior service, whose original purpose had long been superseded. Thus promotion from what was formerly the Junior Service became significant, as was found to be necessary in both Sudan and the Gold Coast. While acknowledging the need for promotion to the senior service, the report, and the widespread view at the time, was adamant that the lowering of standards of admission to the professional groups and the Administrative Service would be against the public interest. 'Nigeria in its onward march will need a first-class Civil Service.' The report pointed out that the time was fast approaching, if it had not already been reached, when the recruitment of expatriates to many service groups would be unnecessary, especially at the entry level. However, the replacement in a wholesale manner of experienced by inexperienced officers would gravely impair and might destroy the efficiency of the civil service. On the other hand, a bolder policy of trying out promising officers in responsible positions was essential.

The Phillipson/Adebo report, also concluded the following:

- That the central or unitary character of the public service had in actuality been much modified by delegation of certain powers of appointment, promotion, postings and discipline to governors of the Regions and to Heads of departments whereby … the various services, though all-Nigerian in theory, tended in practice to become Regional services, particularly below the superscale level. Nevertheless, in spite of these practical modifications, the unitary character of the service remains a fact of great importance.

- As the unity of the civil service of Nigeria was not, under their proposals, to be broken, and as it was important that there should be a Nigeria-wide view and oversight of the process of Nigerianization, they held that a national PSC should be the authority competent to handle all those subjects on which common action in the interests of Nigerianization was necessary.

- The upgrading of the civil service commission to become a greatly enlarged PSC with full executive powers, as well as advisory functions, and a Nigerian majority, was an urgent requirement.

- No non-Nigerian staff should be appointed on pensionable terms except with the approval of the PSC.

- The arrangements for serving officers selected by the secretary of state and all new appointments of expatriates should be those adopted in the Gold Coast following the Lidbury report, viz the former to continue to be the responsibility of the secretary of state and all new appointments to be subject to the governor general as members of the local civil service, unless the PSC decides that there is no-one suitably qualified available locally.

One issue which came up strongly in Nigeria under the new constitution was the fact that elected Nigerians could become ministers without reference to their age and academic accomplishments. They asked why they could not, therefore, be appointed as Heads or Deputy Heads of Departments in the Civil Service? Nigerians still had to learn that those elected are there as representatives, and by the will of the people, whereas the civil servant is there by virtue of his qualifications and experience, and is appointed on merit. It was of the essence of the parliamentary and ministerial system of government then being built up in Nigeria that the popular representatives in the Assembly and the officials in the public service, though complementary, should remain distinct in character and function. Another issue which came up everywhere, but perhaps especially in Nigeria, was the issue of 'upward thrust' to the highest levels of the service more rapidly than might be expected by, for example, early retirement terms for expatriates or by appointment of Nigerian understudies to superscale posts. For some talented young officers their own interest here came into conflict with the public interest, which required a system of appointment and promotion in the public service which would retain public confidence over the long term. To avoid conflict between senior expatriate officials and Nigerian officers on these issues, the report argued strongly that the PSC in Nigeria had to be predominantly Nigerian in composition.

Despite the conclusions indicated above, a delegation of Northern leaders argued to Phillipson/Adebo (a) that there should be a Northern Regional PSC to handle all matters of staffing in that government; (b) that their indents for expatriate staff should be made directly to the Colonial Office or Crown Agents in London; and (c) that the Northern PSC should be consulted before any transfers to the Northern Region of senior staff of the central departments. This was a difficult issue and arose partly out of the increasing awareness of the Northern leaders of the retarded state of education in Northern Nigeria and the relative in-experience of Northern members of the public service by comparison with Southerners; and partly out of the societal differences between the predominantly Muslim North and the predominantly Christian South. In the event, this Northern concern to avoid being swamped by Southerners was to lead to the postponement of the independence of Nigeria by several years.

A very good indication of the pressures which accompanied Africanization comes in two letters, the first from Williamson of the Colonial Office to the chief secretary of the government of Sierra Leone, dated April 1953.[23] The latter had written to comment on the impact of developments in Nigeria and the Gold Coast on the process of creating a new PSC and appointments to and promotion within the public service in Sierra Leone. He had mentioned that the governor had found it expedient to consult the Executive Council, whose functions were partly political, on appointments to the PSC. Williamson made it clear that he found this unacceptable and likely to expose the public service to greater political interference. He passed on the detailed regulations on discipline being used in the public service in the Gold Coast, with an expression of hope that Sierra Leone would emulate them. He also reiterated the determination of Arden-Clarke in the Gold Coast to safeguard the conditions of service of the expatriate officers, to ensure they stayed on rather than finding reasons for leaving the service. He felt this to be most important in handing over to a reasonably experienced and impartial civil service at independence.

The second letter is from a Mr Grey in the Federal Department of Education in Nigeria to Alan Pifer of the Carnegie Foundation, copied to Sir Christopher Cox, Education Adviser to the Secretary of State, written less than a year before Nigeria became independent in 1960.[24] The context was the Higher Educational commission of 1959 under Ashby and the related Manpower Survey of Nigeria which the Carnegie Foundation was to undertake. Grey wrote:

> There are indeed advantages in securing from an eminent international commission a report based on a most careful and competent survey to be presented to an independent Nigeria some twelve months after independence … few states would then have such authoritative guidance on which to base plans for the social services. … However, throughout its history, Nigeria has had the services of surprisingly small numbers of overseas administrators and professional and technical men. There can be few countries, if any, that have come to independence in little more than half a century from the first beginnings of organised government on the western pattern with total outside help so small in proportion to area and population; and I doubt if any country has come to independence with so few of its own people (in proportion to total population) trained in the various techniques required for the operation of a modern government. The proportion of local men and women able to fill posts requiring higher education qualifications is not so bad in the Western and Eastern Regions, but it is startlingly low in the Northern Region – and in the north are more than half the population and two fifths of the land area of the Federation. …I agree with you that you have cause to worry lest our Ministry of Education cannot do justice to the importance of the Commission … if our chosen instruments fail, we have no-one else to put on the job save at the cost of a breakdown in some other task of equal importance. … We are very short of high-quality Permanent Secretaries … Professor Harbison is quite clear that a real manpower survey could only be done by the Nigerian Government itself … but there is the additional complication that there are five different governments in Nigeria, the Federal, three Regional Governments and that of the Southern Cameroons which wishes to join us … the point I have been labouring to make is that each of the five governments and all the professional, technical, industrial and commercial ventures in Nigeria … have a great need for skills obtainable only by higher education. Those needs cannot presently be met from local resources.

The situation of the Nigerian army was complicated by the fact that the Royal West African Frontier Force recruited men from five countries and remained under British War Office control until 1956. Officer training for this force had commenced at a site near Accra in the Gold Coast but the number of officers going on for training in Britain was small for a country the size of Nigeria and the senior ranking Nigerian officers at independence held the rank of Major, as in Ghana, for a force of five battalions of infantry and some special sections.

Attachment 1 summarizes the situation of the senior ranks of the Nigeria public service in 1959, the year before independence. What this shows is that in the

Western and Eastern regional governments, between 50 per cent and 65 per cent of executive, technical and administrative staff were by then held by Nigerians, together with 25–30 per cent of superscale posts. Data are lacking for the Northern Region except for the superscale posts, where the situation was similar. At the federal level, the proportion of posts still held by expatriates was somewhat larger. The table also shows that vacancies in the regional governments were between 20 per cent and 40 per cent; at the federal level they were very similar. These data say nothing about years of experience but, as elsewhere, the rapid promotion of Nigerian officers in the years before independence meant that the level of experience of senior staff was still very limited and, taken together with the high level of vacancies and the still high proportion of superscale posts held by expatriates, the prospects of independent Nigeria having a strong and efficient civil service at the time of independence were not good. This is not to say there were no outstanding Nigerian civil servants at that time; some of the best were still remembered and active as recently as the late 1980s (locally referred to as 'the Super Perm-Secs'). Nevertheless, it is clear that postponement of independence by ten to fifteen years would have transformed the situation. Robertson himself considered that Nigeria became independent at least five years too early (see report of his discussion with Prime Minister Macmillan in January 1960) (Chapter 2).

East Africa

In 1947–8 a commission was appointed under Holmes to review the structure, remuneration and superannuation arrangements of the Civil Services of East Africa.[25] It concluded that 'the time was not yet ripe for the introduction of common scales of salary for all those in the Civil Services. It recommended that scales should be set for those recruited from abroad, including those recruited by the Secretary of State, and then scales should be worked out for those engaged locally'. Out of this emerged the so-called Three-Fifths-Rule, whereby those recruited locally were paid three-fifths of the pay accorded to those recruited abroad for similar work. The reasoning was that increasingly appointments would be of Africans and salaries for them should be in proportion to other African salaries, not expatriate ones. The higher salaries for expatriates were partly a consequence of an expatriation element. However, the commission stated that there could be 'no finality in the relativity of the salaries for Africans vis-à-vis other races'.

A further commission on The Civil Services of the East African Territories and the East African High Commission[26] was appointed in 1953 under Lidbury (a separate exercise from the study under Lidbury of the Gold Coast civil service) and reported the following year. Lidbury demonstrated that the number of Europeans in the public service in Kenya was strikingly higher than it was in the other two countries:

Europeans in the Administrative and Professional Grades

Kenya	2,040
Tanganyika	1,100
Uganda	600

The commission found no such differences in standards of administration as would justify this much preponderance of Europeans in the Kenya administration, the effect of which was to limit opportunities for Kenya Africans leaving secondary school and to slow down the rate at which they gained experience in more senior positions. It was by then apparent that policy-makers both in Britain and East Africa were not happy with the 'Three-Fifths-Rule', which they saw as a barrier to progress, and wanted to

see a unified structure for the civil service which would effectively abolish the rule. (Uganda had already taken a decision to abandon the three-fifths rule – see below). The commission found a nightmare of different terms and conditions of service, of different grades and sources of recruitment in the four countries and the High commission, with some racial criteria still in use, and decided to propose a unified structure based on the level of responsibility and the qualifications for appointment.

The commission found the following situation in 1953 in terms of sizes of the Civil Services, annual intake and output of the local schools (Division I, limited to expatriates, omitted):

Size of civil service

	Kenya	Tanganyika	Uganda	Zanzibar
Division II	2,875	3,000	1,700	530
Division III	2,200	1,950	1,400	205
Subtotal	5,075	4,950	3,100	735
Divisions IV and V	2,040	1,100	600	72
Total	7,115	6,050	3,700	807

Annual Intake

	Kenya	Tanganyika	Uganda	Zanzibar
Division II	144	150	85	27
Division III	110	100	70	10
Subtotal	254	250	155	37
Divs. IV and V	102	55	30	4
Total	356	305	185	41

School Output (Cambridge School Certificate and Higher School Certificate)

	Kenya		Tanganyika		Uganda		Zanzibar	
	Boys	Girls	Boys	Girls	Boys	Girls	Boys	Girls
School Cert								
African	139	5	94	3	186	6	1	-
Asian	217	69	87	18	40	13	29	13
Arab	7	-	-	-	-	-	2	1
European	157	131	1	-	-	-	-	-
Higher Cert								
Asian	9	-	-	-	-	-	-	-
European	21	23	-	-	-	-	-	-

The figures in the top part of the table are for the civil service alone and do not include any positions outside the public service. For example, the data do not include the staff of the High Commission, which extended over all three mainland countries, and which were almost as numerous in their grades as the total of the three countries, nor any of the professions.

It is evident from these numbers that the East African countries were not yet in sight of being able to staff their public services from native Africans alone; the output of those with the School Certificate was still far from meeting the needs of East Africa as a whole; and a large proportion of the recruitment for the administrative and professional services would have to continue to be from external resources for some years to come. The commission concluded that the avenues of entry and advancement must be so arranged as to give full scope to the qualities and aptitudes of all applicants, whatever their background. This was not going to be easy to implement – the work of the service had to continue – yet at the same time the doors had to be thrown open to people of all backgrounds without encouraging a loss of experienced or well-qualified staff. There remained an intention at the working level, which was emphasized in all official statements, that appointments and promotions should be on merit and that race should not be a selection criterion. Though admirable in concept, this objective came into conflict with the policy of Africanization and led to accusations of bad faith and discrimination. Within ten years, all four countries were to be independent, but they were to remain dependent upon expatriate staff in key places for another decade.

Periodically, the governors of the East African territories would meet with the secretary of state and other London officials to consider the state of affairs in their territories, the influences bearing on them and other relevant matters. The meeting held in Entebbe in October 1957 was of particular interest and timeliness in view of the concurrent independence of Ghana, the progressive steps being taken in Nigeria, Tanganyika and Uganda and the emergence of Kenya from the Mau Mau conflict. The exchange among the governors and the secretary of state anticipated many of the negotiations and decisions which would be necessary in the Eastern African territories before they became independent.[27]

The King's African Rifles

Before looking at the Africanization issue in East Africa by country, it is timely to say something about the localization of the King's African Rifles (KAR), which posed generic issues and was presented with a severe test soon after the East African countries became independent. As elsewhere, some promising officers were selected for training in the military academies in Britain and there was the normal training in all the specialized aspects of military operations. However, all the senior officers were still on secondment from the British Army. In 1957, following a review in 1955 by Sir Gerald Templar of colonial security, the administrative and financial responsibility for East African Land Forces (EALF) was transferred from the War Office in London to the three East African Governments. Operational control remained with GOC East Africa Command. Thus the whole cost of the EALF (except a small garrison in Mauritius) was met by the colonial legislatures. In 1960, the colonial secretary and the governors of the three countries (the Nyasaland battalion of the KAR was not considered at that time) concluded that this arrangement posed dangers in the approach to independence, and recommended that the financial responsibility and overall control be returned to HMG. The main reason was that as Africans began to take ministerial responsibility prior to independence, they would begin to regard defence as being within their scope of responsibility and this might prejudice the central operational control and strategic mobility at a time of anticipated tension and possible insecurity. The governors put this matter to the leading politicians in the three countries, who concurred. The British Cabinet considered the matter in January 1960 and accepted the Colonial Secretary's recommendation to concur with the local recommendations.[28] At that time, and indeed until after independence, all the battalion commanders were British, as were a number of more junior officers. Very few Africans had reached the rank of major, one of them being Major Amin, who subsequently became president of Uganda. All NCOs were however African.

In January 1964, just after Kenya became independent but a year or more after Tanganyika and Uganda became independent, elements of the battalions in all three countries mutinied and had to be disarmed. The trigger for the mutiny in Tanganyika on 20 January 1964 was the revolt in Zanzibar on 12 January, which ousted the Sultan. The mutiny of the Jinja garrison in Uganda occurred on 23 January; that of the Kenya garrison at Lanet was on 24 January. British forces were used to disarm unreliable troops. Royal Marines based in Aden landed in Tanganyika, off HMS *Centaur*; a battalion-strength force was flown into Uganda from Kenya and other such troops put down the mutiny in Kenya.[29] (Note that the different battalions of the KAR became at independence the Kenya Rifles, the Uganda Rifles and the Tanganyika Rifles, respectively).

Ex post facto analysis of the reasons for the mutinies included a variety of causes:

- The violent coup d'etat in Zanzibar, which was easily accomplished by a small number of poorly armed men, which probably set the ring-leaders in Tanganyika thinking;
- Lack of material improvement for the men since independence;
- Contacts between industrial malcontents and malcontents in the armies;
- Some political manoeuvres by politicians in Tanganyika and Kenya;
- Failure among politicians and junior officers to abide by military rules, which led to slackened discipline;
- The relatively slow pace of Africanization, especially in Tanganyika.

The slow pace of Africanization of the KAR is attested to by both officers of all three units where there were mutinies and by diplomats who reviewed the events. A minute of a meeting of the East Africa Defence committee as late as July 1963[30] had noted:

'The General Officer Commanding said that the crash programme of training African officers … was proving generally successful … training continues to proceed well, though in general the new African officers were weak in administration. He hoped that this year regular commissions would be granted to fifteen short-service commissioned officers, as a start to providing a regular officer career structure. … At present only three local officers hold regular commissions in the KAR. There were also three Kenya cadets at the Royal Military Academy, Sandhurst'. As late as October 1963, a Major Troughton in the War Office in London was writing 'I have been waiting to see if more definite proposals were forthcoming concerning the expansion of the KAR … the only information we have had so far from the GOC East Africa Command

... is an outline organisation of an expanded KAR ... so far as I know, no agreement has been given to effect this expansion'.[31]

This was written when Tanganyika and Uganda were already independent states and in the year of Kenya's independence. We have to conclude that the pace and energy of Africanization of the KAR prior to independence was well behind that in the public service. This is surprising because the army is normally well organized and motivated to provide for the training and commissioning of new officers and men, and gives it high priority.

Uganda

Uganda had the advantage that Makerere University College was situated in Entebbe, which constituted a singular attraction to Africans of ambition to achieve professional-level qualifications of the kind required for the higher levels of the public service. Nevertheless, to ensure that adequate funds existed to pay for such education, whether in Uganda or elsewhere, a decision was taken in early 1952 by the administrators of the Uganda Cotton Fund, a government marketing organization, to establish a fund from the profits of cotton sales for this purpose.[32] Uganda was ahead of the other two countries in regard to civil service reform and Africanization. In October 1952, the Uganda Government took the decision to establish a single unified Uganda civil service and appointed a Standing Committee on the Recruitment, Training and Promotion of Africans for Admission to Higher Posts in the civil service. The committee was to look into the implications of establishing a single unified Uganda service with basic pay for all and overseas pensionable allowances for those recruited in Britain, and to study the implications and the means of ending the three-fifths rule and other impedimenta, which would otherwise get in the way of a unified service. They were encouraged in ending the three-fifths rule by a statement made by the colonial secretary, Oliver Lyttleton, in the House of Commons, in December 1951, in which he said, 'This system was introduced under the auspices of the party opposite (Labour) as a result of the Holmes Report. I dislike the system and I hope to see it abolished.'[33]

The Standing committee considered the prospects for African appointments sector by sector – Administration, Medical, Agriculture, Veterinary, Cooperation and so forth. The expectation was that the Medical Department would be fully Africanized first. They also came face-to-face with the dilemma of how to appoint professionally well-qualified, but inexperienced, African applicants, in preference to more experienced (European or Asian) expatriates, without lowering the standards of entry. The committee posed the question but did not provide the answer, which would only be addressed later. Uganda was also the first of the three countries to create a PSC, which it did in 1957. In an attempt to limit political interference in its work it gave the PSC a high status in the constitution, establishing it by Order in Council.

In the period 1954–6, Sir Andrew Cohen, then governor of Uganda, worked hard to get a School of Public Administration established at Makerere with a view to giving a more local emphasis to the training provided to young entrants to the administration. In addition, some of the other departments expected to send trainees to the school. Cohen's idea was to begin with training for Assistant District Officers and their equivalent in the other departments and to establish training grades within the public service for such trainees. The school was to be opened to trainees from all four East African countries. Funding was eventually obtained from the Carnegie Corporation for creation of the school.[34]

Tanganyika

A Standing committee on Training was established in 1955 to give close attention to the training and recruitment of qualified men and women for the public service. In July 1957, the government created a 'Training Grade' within the civil service salary structure for serving officers being given on-the-job training in various posts, generally by understudying experienced officers.[35] Those in the Training Grade were also required to take further formal examinations. In November 1957, the Standing Committee was replaced by a committee on Local recruitment and Training, with the chief secretary of the government as its chairman, to advise government on all aspects in the implementation of the recommendations of the Lidbury report. This was followed by a Staff Circular on training of local staff for higher posts.[36] In 1960 a comprehensive Five-Year Plan for Africanization of the civil service was adopted by government.[37] This showed that by the end of the 1950s, there had been progress. The number of local officers in senior posts, including those in the Training Grade, had risen from 112 in 1956 to 810 by 1961, of which 616 were Africans. However, this still only amounted to 17 per cent of the total establishment in those grades. The plan at that time was that by 1965/66, the number of Africans expected to be holding senior posts in the public service would rise to 3,196, or 60 per cent of such posts. In February 1957, the secretary of state answered a question on the number of African District Officers, of which there were thirty, all of whom were then actually Assistant District Officers in training posts.[38] See Table at Attachment 2.

Tanganyika became independent in March 1962. At that time the large majority of senior positions in the public service was still held by Europeans or Asians, and most Africans in the senior service were very inexperienced. The result of this acceleration of the timetable for Tanganyika's self-government and independence was that its public service at independence was woefully deficient both in staff with a full education and even more so in experienced administrators, judges and technical staff, deficiencies which were to handicap the country for many years. This outcome was foreseen at the time and given publicity by members of the United Tanganyika Party (UTP), which, though a minority party, had a diverse membership. As early as August 1957, Brian Willis, a member of the UTP, in a letter to *The Times* noted that 'in Tanganyika, the appeal of multiracialism meets with a spontaneous response from Africans … the membership of our party is 61% African, 30% Asian and 9% European. No other political party in Africa (including TANU) can produce such numbers'; the point being that UTP sought membership of all those who could contribute to Tanganyika's future. In October 1957, Hussain Juma, chairman of the UTP, made similar arguments, also in a letter to *The Times*; he was given support by Graham Page who wrote arguing that

> any independent observer could only conclude … that TANU … and the Africans cannot now find or, I believe will in a generation, more than a fraction of the qualified persons required to take over government and development, trade and the professions; that it would be a breach of the trust under which we administer the territory to abandon the Africans and non-Africans to the wilder politicians.

An interesting situation arose in early 1960, only two years before independence, when a new appointment had to be made to Chairmanship of the Tanganyika PSC, with a term of office of four years. Although this was formally an appointment to be made by the governor, in practice Sir Richard Turnbull took the view that he would endorse a selection made by Julius Nyerere, the chief minister, unless the person selected was manifestly unsuited. Initially Nyerere looked to West Africa for a suitable person. Turnbull considered it would be a mistake to go for a European so close to independence, but was conscious of the need to keep the confidence of the European officers in the service as this would have a considerable bearing on the number of officers who would be willing to stay on in Tanganyika after independence. Turnbull and Nyerere eventually agreed that the best candidate would be John Keto, a Tanganyikan graduate of Makerere University and Chairman of the Tanganyika Broadcasting Board. He had recently led a delegation to a UNESCO conference. He was already a member of the PSC.[39]

Kenya

The civil service commission in Kenya had been established by local legislation in 1954. As indicated above, in 1957, the Uganda government created a PSC by Order in Council, which gave it a status above the political level. In 1959, Kenya proposed to the Colonial Office that it follow Uganda in creating its PSC by Order in Council, which meant that its status constitutionally was such that it would hopefully not be subject to interference by elected ministers. Disciplinary matters had been retained by the chief secretary under the prior legislation and in the aftermath of the Mau Mau revolt the government did not want to change that arrangement too quickly, but in 1959, it agreed that disciplinary matters should be made a function of the PSC also.[40] The Colonial Office eventually decided that both the PSC and the simultaneously proposed police service commission should be created as components of the new Kenya constitution then being negotiated. Before independence, a separate Judicial Services Commission was also created under the constitution. The constitutional objective of these commissions was of course to limit the extent of possible political or other interference in the civil service, the police and the Judiciary.

Annual Reports were published by the Kenya PSC and it is worth dwelling on the report for the year 1962 which gives a flavour of its activities two years before independence.[41] It summarized the government's localization policy as follows:

- Preference to be given to qualified Africans in all appointments from outside the service;

- A vacancy normally filled by promotion to be filled by a qualified local officer, in which case retirement on compensation to be offered to expatriate officers who might otherwise fill the post;

- Creation of vacancies for qualified local people by the retirement of expatriate officers, where necessary.

The Commission directly recruited new staff from the university of Makerere, the Royal College in Nairobi and from Kenyans studying in Britain and the United States. It also created training posts, as in Tanganyika, and the table at Attachment 3 gives an idea of the variety of such posts created in 1962. Only 58 posts were actually filled by expatriate recruitment during that year (down from 250 in 1955), of which 30 were Nursing Sisters. Only 128 positions were identified for future expatriate recruitment, of which 60 were for teachers. The number of Africans in senior posts had increased to 1564, an increase of 42 per cent in one year. The Commission Report went on:

Administrative and executive posts can usually be filled at a reasonable standard; professional posts still present considerable difficulty as the number of men with full professional qualifications is low, but having regard to the many students taking professional subjects in East Africa and abroad, future prospects seem reasonably good. Accounting posts are difficult to fill; few Africans take readily to accountancy though special courses in this subject have been started in the Treasury, the Ministry of

Works as well as the Kenya Institute of Administration. But serious concern is felt at the total inadequacy of candidates qualified to fill technical posts – the type of post that requires a full apprenticeship training, a City & Guilds or equivalent qualification and a reasonable standard of English to enable a man to improve his craftsmanship by study. ... The Ministry of Works has training schemes which can improve skills and enable work to be done up to a certain standard. But it has not been possible to find locally the instructors required by the Polytechnic and other technical schools.

Commission staff visited the universities regularly and in 1962 they visited universities in the United States attended by Kenyans, the trip being funded by USAID.

A useful innovation was the creation of the Kenya Institute of Administration, similar to that in Uganda. A small start was made with the recruitment of African Assistant administrative officers into the provincial administrations in the early 1950s. Though the numbers may have been small, some of them found their way into senior positions in the independence era. There was a great expansion of the service during the Emergency as District Assistants or as officers engaged in the Land Consolidation and electoral registration exercises. There were other opportunities for those who managed to participate in the 'Mboya Airlift' of young officers to training institutes in the United States. But it was to be the early 1960s before Africans began to be appointed as district commissioners. Another way into the administration was of capable and senior officers in the Education Department.

A comprehensive and very interesting light is shone on the prospects for Kenya as it approached independence in a note prepared for the Economic Commission of 1962 by T. Neil who was then Permanent Secretary of the Ministry of State for Constitutional Affairs and Administration. The note also discusses the implications of the proposals to regionalize important functions of government, in terms of cost and staffing. The note is of such interest that I have included a summary of it in Annex 5.

East Africa Common Services Organization (EACSO)

When Tanganyika became independent, it was necessary to reform the East Africa High Commission, which was responsible for Post and Telecommunications, Railways and Harbours, Revenue and Customs and other technical functions in East Africa, as the commission was a colonial-era institution created under the Crown. The EACSO was the result. Responsibility for the new organization rested with a group consisting of the principal elected minister responsible to the legislature in each of the three East African territories. Special arrangements were made for the Directorate of Civil Aviation and the Desert Locus Survey. The PSCs responsible for advising on staffing matters became executive. This had implications for the staff, many of whom were expatriates. The management of the old commission initiated an expanded localization scheme in September 1961, before Tanganyikan independence, though it was to prove difficult to settle eligibility criteria for appointments under EACSO until the rules of citizenship had been settled for all three states.[42] In practice, the new arrangements worked quite well until the Organization was wound up and transferred to the individual countries in the 1970s.

British Somaliland

The localization of the Somali public service was a specific objective from the time of the 1950–1 Annual Report of the Education Department. Initially there was no PSC per se, but the Education Department carried out staff planning of the kind a PSC would normally do, so as to get young entrants to the service into positions with individual training plans for them. During his visit in 1956, Lord Lloyd had re-emphasized HMG's support for a programme of localization. In the late 1950s, a Public Service Board was created to assist in staff planning and quite extensive use was made of supernumerary positions to give young officers exposure to the ongoing activities of their departments. To facilitate entry to the service of promising Somalis, no new permanent and pensionable staff were being recruited from overseas from the mid-1950s. Appointments of foreign staff was by contract appointment only.

Tables prepared in 1959 show that output from the intermediate schools was expected to increase by 400 per cent by 1967, and output from the secondary school by 500 per cent, though these percentage increases were from a very low base. Most of these school leavers were expected to go into some branch of the public service and were expected to be the principal source of recruits for the service as the existing staff in the lower levels of the service did not have the education or skills required for much promotion. There were no tertiary-level education facilities in the country, so necessarily such training had to be taken abroad, especially in Sudan. At that time (1959) the number of Somalis taking courses abroad in various fields included teacher training, administration, public works, natural resource use and so on, and the number of such students expected to return were as follows:

Students Overseas < June 1960	Students Returned by June 1960	Total
164	97	261

An average of eleven students were due to return to the country each year up to 1964. These young men (nearly all men at that stage) would of course be totally inexperienced, but the candidates for training would be there. The available tables therefore show that most positions in the public service could in principle be localized by 1964.[43]

From the time in 1959 that HMG became committed to support of the government in its quest for British Somaliland to merge with Somalia, the question of localization ('Somalization') became a matter of urgency. A commission led by a Mr Howes was appointed to prepare a report on the matter. His report became available in January 1959, when it was reviewed in the Colonial Office. Howes calculated that out of 412 senior and junior posts then held by expatriate staff, 241 could be localized in the course of 1959 without disturbing the permanent expatriate staff, provided suitably qualified Somalis could be found (not assured at that time). That would leave 171 posts to be filled by Somalis over the next 7 years. He also proposed that expatriate staff remaining would be retained as required and only be released when Somali replacements were available. This report as amended was submitted to the Somali Legislative Council in July 1959.

The government was keen to follow this up with a White Paper describing the way in which this plan would be implemented. It produced a draft for Colonial Office review by September 1959. This draft made certain assumptions about a compensation scheme in respect of expatriates. However, the Colonial Office considered that the course and timing of the negotiations with Somalia was very uncertain and that they could not at that time commit themselves to such a scheme, even if the Treasury were willing to accept it.[44] The amended White Paper was published in October 1959, together with a list of senior supernumerary (under-study) posts to be created to be filled by existing Somali officers to be selected by the public service board. These included two judges, three police officers, twenty-five departmental specialists and four accountants. There were also thirty-nine Indian or Pakistani staff in the Somali public service and HMG was committed to ensuring that their interests were not overlooked.

The state of the Somali public service at independence was notably weak and we have to wonder why HMG could not have insisted on a slower timetable to allow more time to appoint and train staff. Once a decision in principle was taken to the merger of the British territory with Somalia, it would have served the country better for the merger to be delayed for a few years until the administration was stronger and able to hold its own within the larger Somalia.

The Central African Federation

The year 1956 was the year when the issue of parity in the federal civil service became an important public issue, with Lord Malvern's announcement that there would be one federal public service open to anyone in the country, irrespective of race or creed. The issue was covered in some depth by the Rhodesian Herald of 17 November 1956. There was support for a measured move towards parity, but all African doctors had achieved that status through the influence of the federal minister of Health. The Herald's Special Correspondent asked why this was permitted:

> the opposition (to immediate parity) springs from the fact that they want to make a reality of partnership on merit, rather than on a doctrinaire basis ... where a man not only proves that he can do the job, but that you can trust him to do it without supervision ... experience not only in the Federation, but in other parts of Africa also, strongly suggests that the granting of responsibility without supervision is often the green light to corruption and graft.[45]

The federation also intended to promote Africans to a commissioned rank in the armed forces; the Southern Rhodesian government modified the Land Apportionment Act, partly under pressure exerted from Britain on the creation of the University College of Rhodesian and Nyasaland (Chapter 3); the Industrial Conciliation Act was made applicable to all miners, and the mining companies opened up various grades of miner to all races.

A Public Service Board had been created in Southern Rhodesia in 1927 modelled on the South African PSC, but at that stage it was advisory only. It gained powers of decision when the Board was upgraded to a commission in 1944. For various reasons the PSC had difficulty recruiting enough suitable candidates to the public service. In 1954 there were 157 vacancies in an establishment of 779 posts. Southern Rhodesia had a considerable number of well-qualified officers of European descent in the civil service and, given the temper of the times and the extent of autonomy allowed to the territory since 1923, perhaps there was less pressure to push ahead with African appointments in the 1950s. This was not because there was a particular shortage of suitably educated Africans, for the reason given above, rather that they were expected to serve the same term and type of apprenticeship in working up through the ranks of the civil service as was expected of European officers. Furthermore, with the creation of the Central African Federation centred on the Southern Rhodesian capital of Salisbury, there was both a greater choice of appointment and more opportunities for well-educated and experienced civil servants of both European and African origin.

Northern Rhodesia used the Uganda precedents and forms for creation of a PSC and police service commission, which were set up in 1960. This was done by administrative instructions in anticipation of the drafting of a new independence constitution. It had the usual functions and powers, with the actual power of appointment, discipline and so on remaining with the governor. The PSC was required to favour suitably qualified Africans for appointment, if necessary in training posts. It was not expected that a Judicial Services Commission would be created until it was included in the final constitution before independence.[46]

The mining companies in Northern Rhodesia had commercial reasons for thinking long term and establishment of attractive terms of employment, including social provisions for the miners, was a must. Initially there were separate trade unions for European and African miners, and strikingly different terms of employment. At the staff level, there were separate Staff Associations also. However this began to give way as African miners assumed more responsible positions and as social contacts broadened. By 1958, they were moving towards joint meetings of both unions and Staff Associations. In regard to training, the companies sponsored apprentices through training schemes and colleges and in due course the employment rigidities began to break down so that appointments could be made largely on merit.

Nyasaland

A PSC was finally created in Nyasaland by administrative instructions in early 1960 and the decision taken to combine this appointment with that of Speaker of the legislature (an approach also taken in South Arabia). Both posts were considered to be non-political and combining them would tend to reinforce the status and independence of both positions. The PSC was then constituted legally in the constitution to confirm its status. The PSC had three members, initially two Africans and a European. The commission was to advise on recruitment, appointment, promotion, training and other matters concerned with the civil service, though the decision on such matters remained with the governor. The chairman had a right of direct access to the Governor.[47]

In Chapter 3, attention was drawn to the deficiencies of the Nyasaland education system, especially the lack of progress with secondary and higher education. This became glaringly apparent again in the Devlin Report. As a result, a Committee on Africanization of the Nyasaland civil service was proposed in 1959. This was established in 1960, very late in the day, initially under the chairmanship of A. L. Adu, a senior Ghanaian civil servant. His informal report of October 1960 to Sir Hylton Poynton at the Colonial Office drew attention to

the very great urgency in producing within the next few years a sufficient number of trained Nyasalanders in senior positions to ensure the stability of the administration in Government service. Unless this is done, the territory will be ill-prepared to meet the problems which arise out of political and constitutional developments and of the inevitable loss of the service of the expatriate officers if, and when, self-government does come.[48]

The country became independent in 1963, only three years after this letter was written. At that time there were only a handful of Africans in administrative grade posts. The Mpemba Institute near Blantyre was running nine-month courses for junior administrative staff, but this was no substitute for well-educated and experienced staff, who were simply not available.

The High Commission Territories (Swaziland, Basutoland and Bechuanaland)

The 1965 UN/UK mission looked at the state of localization of the public service in some detail.[49] It found that in 1963/5, a central training school was giving courses in administration, local government, law and language; and for postal, telephone and telegraph technicians; and providing clerical training for the private sector. At the higher levels of the public service, localization had far to go. In Swaziland for example, out of 229 university graduates in the service, 148 were European, 46 were non-Swazi Africans and only 35 were Swazi. The only 'A'-level stage teaching facilities in the three countries at that time were at the new University of Bechuanaland, Basutoland and Swaziland (UBBS). The mission recommended that this be upgraded to a separate 'A'-level teaching college, separate from but located at UBBS, as such teaching facilities could not at that time be justified in each country. Graduates from this college could then either enrol at UBBS or go to other universities elsewhere in the world.

The following 1 April 1964 figures for the higher levels of the public service in Swaziland were emblematic:

Grade	Authorized Establishment	Total No. in Post	No. of Locals in Post
Superscale, administrative, professional and scientific	123	108	8
Technical	230	160	16
Executive, secretarial	164	144	32
Police and Prisons – top ranks	22	19	3
Teachers	144	114	4
Total – key posts	653	545	63

Bechuanaland

The constitution provided for creation of a PSC, initially with advisory powers only, to control appointments to, and the promotion, transfer, disciplinary control and dismissal of members of the public service. In due course the PSC became a fully independent body. However, at the time of independence, Botswana's education system was still not producing enough trained people to staff the public service effectively, delaying considerably localization of the service. In fact, the first study for a localization policy was produced only six months before independence. The striking thing was that faced with this situation, the first president, Seretse Khama, declared that 'we should never sacrifice efficiency on the altar of localisation'. He implemented a cautious localization policy with the implication of continued reliance on expatriate personnel in many posts. The contrast with most other African countries is striking. Fawcus concluded,

> Botswana's continued success and tranquillity has not been due solely or even mainly to the wealth it has acquired as a result of considerable mineral discoveries. It has been due in large measure to the political stability it has achieved as a result of the attachment of its leaders to multi-party democracy, to the rule of law, to the protection of human rights and the holding of free and fair elections at regular five-year intervals.[50]

Malaya and Singapore

The approach of Malaya and Singapore to self-government and independence was disrupted by the attempt by communists to take over Malaya by means of an insurrection. This began after the end of the Second World War and it took until the mid-1950s to defeat. Nevertheless, progress in strengthening the public service was good, despite the emergency.

Singapore set up a PSC several years before Malaya, mainly because the emergency in Malaya delayed progress. The first two Chairmen of the PSC in Singapore were both retired Malayan civil service judges. Though discussion about creation of a PSC in Malaya commenced in 1949, it was not until 1953 that the Conference of Malayan Rulers approved the creation of an interim public service Appointment and Promotions Board. Initially the Board was chaired by the chief secretary to the government. This cautious approach was appropriate for two reasons. First, in view of the continuing emergency in the country, there were special considerations to take into account. Second, the support of the state rulers was required and they had to be brought to acceptance of the concept of a PSC, which would put senior appointments beyond their traditional control. A committee of Inquiry was established by ExCo in early 1953 to study the localization issue in depth and make recommendations. These addressed the need for and scale of the scholarship and training programmes, the maintenance of standards, the speed of Malayanization and expatriate recruitment. The committee was particularly concerned to avoid a lowering of standards of the administration and to be realistic about the speed at which Malayanization could occur. Later in 1953, with the encouragement of the Colonial Secretary, the Board was formally initiated with a retired European member of the Malaya Civil Service as the first chairman and a Malay deputy chairman. This was important in retaining the confidence of the British members of the civil service as independence approached. The responsibilities of the PSC were initially limited to the top three civil service grades, the Police Force and the Judges of the Supreme Court who belonged to the Malaya Civil Service.

With the federal elections of 1955 and the emergence of an elected Federal Government, the localization issue was raised at an early stage by Tunku Abdul Rahman, the chief Minister, and discussed with the Secretary of State in both Malaya and London. In 1956 the Federal Government published its plan for the Malayanization of the Public Service, under which the minimum time in which each department could be localized had been worked out. The Federal Government set its face against the wholesale replacement of qualified overseas officers by unqualified Malays, both because of the inefficiencies which would result and in order to avoid having all the senior posts held in a few years time by Malays with considerable experience but less than adequate formal education. Fully qualified younger Malays served under experienced officers in junior grades to acquire experience. Each expatriate officer was informed how long his services could be retained if he were to opt to stay in the service.

The terminal date for such options was fixed at either July 1960, 1962 or 1965. Officers who were thus guaranteed employment for a fixed term could however give six months' notice of retirement at any time. In practice, the exodus of expatriates was somewhat faster than this timetable implied and there was a considerable loss of senior officials, especially in the administration, whose function was most closely affected by the change in political control. Though this did open positions for promotion of Malays, there was some loss of experience. However, recruitment of expatriates for service in Malaya on contract terms continued upto and beyond independence in 1957. In 1956, twenty-nine officers were appointed of whom twelve were teachers and eight civil engineers. This emphasis on technical staff was understandable and acceptable even after independence. Following independence, it was not appropriate to use the machinery of the Colonial Office for recruitment, but the Crown Agents continued to provide these services on an agency basis. (NB. It is of interest that even as late as the mid-1990s, when the former republics of the Soviet Union became independent states, the Crown Agents continued to provide similar services on an agency basis to the new Central Asian states.)

The procedure adopted by Malaya and Singapore was reasonably successful in retaining British officers after independence, partly due to the attractive salaries they could afford to pay. The following table provides the data for 1957–59 for both countries.

Malaya and Singapore, 1957–59

Date of Commencement of Compensation Scheme	No. of Entitled Officers	No of Expatriate Officers Remaining in Post on:		
		1 Jan 1958	Oct 1958	30 April 1959
Singapore Jan 1957	416	254	157	151
Malaya 1 July 1957	1,579	1,059	809	722

West Indies

As indicated in Chapter 4, the level of education in the West Indies was relatively high before independence and the number of local appointments to the senior ranks of the public service also relatively high. But there were problems on account of the number of individual territories. Even after the creation of the West Indies Federation in 1957, there were five territorial governments (Barbados, Jamaica, Leeward Islands, Trinidad and Windward Islands). In addition there was the nascent Federal Government, which did not survive for long, and potentially British Guiana (Guyana) and British Honduras (Belize). In July 1958, the Colonial Office encouraged the Governor General and officers administering the territorial governments to rationalize the salary scales and to set up consultation machinery among the federal and the Territorial PSCs.

Country comparisons

A recent and ongoing study by Dr Valentin Seidler and others of the impact of overseas officers on the quality of administration of the former colonies since independence is producing some revealing new analysis of the subject. The October 2016 edition of the Overseas Pensioner contained some preliminary findings of interest. One graph compares the percentage of overseas officers in the civil services of Sudan, Sierra Leone and Botswana over the years prior to and following independence. The data show that the overseas officers in Sudan were largely phased out within four years, in Sierra Leone within eight years and in Botswana within twelve years after independence. Teasing out the conclusions of these findings will take time, but they seem to likely reinforce the conclusions reached elsewhere in this book that localization of senior civil service positions came too soon in some colonies; that more time would have been beneficial in producing more well-qualified and experienced officials and specialists.[51]

The Colonial Service in Transition

It is evident from Chapter 3 (Education) and Chapter 4 that the British government accepted in full its obligations to the colonial territories in preparing them for self-government. However, in his book 'The Public Service in New States'[52] Kenneth Younger, a former Labour minister, made the point that the Colonial territories were surprised at the speed of approach of self-government. Most colonial officers agreed. Colonial Governments found it necessary to compromise on the standards of appointments to the senior ranks of the Public Service under the pressure of the evolving timetable for self-determination. In the interest of a smooth transfer of authority and administration, HMG sought to facilitate the continued service of experienced officers both before and after independence. In 1954, HMG issued a paper titled 'Reorganization of the Colonial Service (Cmnd Colonial 306)'.[53] This paper stated that the political developments taking place in many territories as a result of the government's declared policy of furthering advance towards self-government made it necessary to review the situation of the Colonial Service. In particular, members of the service were entitled to ask what their position would be if, as a result of constitutional changes, the government could no longer exercise effective control over their tenure and conditions of service. The paper went on to say that the work of the Colonial Service was by no means over and that the responsible leaders in the colonial territories recognized the continuing need for the skilled and experienced assistance of British staff. Thus the serving members of the Colonial Service, and all those appointed subsequently, became members of Her Majesty's Overseas Civil Service (HMOCS). The problem of retaining these men and women was one which could only be solved by the governments of Britain and the territories, acting in partnership. This required a formal agreement with each colony becoming independent on the terms of service of British personnel staying on after independence.

The categories of staff to whom membership of HMOCS applied were members of the existing unified colonial services, including Administrative, Agricultural, Audit, Chemical, Civil Aviation, Customs, Education, Engineering, Forestry, Geological Survey, Legal, Medical, Mines, Police, Postal, Prisons,

Research, Survey, Veterinary and Queen Elizabeth's Colonial Nursing Service. Members were to receive no emoluments in this capacity except the pay and conditions applicable to the post they held. They were however to be eligible for consideration by the Secretary of State for postings anywhere in the Commonwealth or in foreign countries.

The creation of HMOCS however failed to stop, though it may have slowed down, the loss of Colonial Officers. This was due in part to political difficulties, actual or apprehended, resulting from the transfer of power to local governments, partly to the wish of younger officers, especially those with families, to get to work in a new career as soon as practicable, partly as a result of dissatisfaction with present emoluments and partly to the attractions of the lump sum compensation scheme available to those who did leave the service. Nevertheless, some members of HMOCS and other specialized staff continued to serve in the independent former colonies for many years after independence, and in some surprising fields. As recently as the mid-1970s there were still British staff serving in the Kenya public service. HMOCS continued to provide expertise and support to those governments, and similarly to other independent former colonies in the Commonwealth for many years. Other arrangements were made later by various British government departments to supply expertise to former colonies in various fields on an ad hoc basis.

Nevertheless we have to wonder if something could have been done to create a framework, acceptable to both the newly independent countries and to HMG, which would have enabled former Colonial Officers to go on working longer in the new states. As described in Chapter 2, Colonel David Sterling and Lord Home both pursued the idea for a while. The nub of the difficulty was that authority cannot be shared or divided. Once a country became independent, its relationship with HMG changed fundamentally. Only by postponing independence could officers continue in post with full authority. Thus any cadre of men and women going on working in the new states after independence could only be advisory, or contracted with limited terms of reference, and this is not always a satisfactory position to be in. We should also take note of the talk given by William Clark on February 1, 1962 to a joint meeting of the Royal African Society and the Royal Commonwealth Society, in which he argued that 'once the fact of political independence had been accepted, the next problem was to prevent a disastrous dip in standards of life during the next three or four years after independence'.[54] He accepted that 'European skills are likely to be withdrawn at a rate faster than they can be immediately replaced by African skills'. Clark went on 'in talking to a rather discouraged (Colonial) Civil Service I felt that most of them really believed that their mission had been ended, perhaps prematurely, but certainly ended. They felt that the Africans did not want them and that the British Government, in conjunction with the new African governments, was paying them off through a pretty generous compensation scheme. They felt they would feel out of place in the new African state and the sooner they got back to Britain, the better their chance of starting some sort of new career. Yet almost everyone admitted that he would be sorry to leave, disappointed at the break in career.'

Clark argued that the British government should think again about the possibility of establishing some sort of Commonwealth service which would continue after the imminent end of the colonial empire. He was particularly concerned about the technical services: 'so far as possible we should try to slow down the exodus of existing experts and when that is not possible we should try to provide stop-gaps from among our professional people and young graduates'. He was in fact about a decade too late. As we know, no such service was created. Britain and several other countries have supplied technical knowledge and experience to the former colonies by various means, in particular by seconding staff on advisory terms, by the supply of contracted specialists for specific purposes and by supplying volunteers under such schemes as Voluntary Service Overseas, though the effectiveness of this support has often been limited by exogenous conditions, political changes or insecurity.

Reference was made in Chapter 3 to the World Bank's review of 'Free-standing Technical Assistance for Institutional Development in Sub-Saharan Africa' carried out in 1988–90, more than 25 years after most colonies became independent. The review concluded 'development efforts in many countries are still severely handicapped by the poor performance of institutions at all levels' the limited capacity of government ministries to determine appropriate policies and allocate resources economically, the poor management of public sector enterprises or the undeveloped potential of the private sector. Many African countries also face chronic shortages of qualified personnel. They still depend on foreign personnel even to maintain existing levels of performance. The need to strengthen indigenous capacity of African institutions is urgent. Broad-based programmes of institutional development must be seen as central to any strategy for African development.

See Attachment 1 Nigeria Public Service senior staff, 1959.
    Attachment 2 Africanization of the Public Service in Tanganyika.
    Attachment 3 Kenya Public Service Commission, 1962.
    Attachment 4 Decolonization – Timing of creation of Public Service
        Commission and major staff plans.

Chapter 6

Other influences – other countries and the United Nations

Following the Second World War, the international context of Britain's colonial policy changed markedly. The expansion of American power and influence meant that Britain had to take American views into account in formulating its policies. On the other hand, Britain was the principal ally of the United States in the Cold War, which served to temper the US attitude to the colonies. The creation of the United Nations enabled Britain to demonstrate a responsible approach to the colonial issue. Britain was also interested in the way France, especially, was handling its colonies. After 1947, newly independent states which had been British territories, especially India, began to influence Britain. After 1955 the so-called non-aligned group of countries which sought to remain neutral in the 'Cold War' between the Western world and the communist bloc – including Indonesia, Yugoslavia and Egypt – became a factor. This chapter will look at these other influences bearing on the British government in respect of decolonization and assess the extent and nature of the impact they had on policy and practice.

The British Empire at its apogee was the largest and most influential international political phenomenon in recent times, or perhaps at any time. A quarter of the world's land surface was within the British domain and large parts of the oceans were effectively British. A combination of an instinct for trade and commerce, the propensity of British people to settle overseas, naval supremacy for a century and a half, victory in most of its wars for over 200 years, the adoption of free trade and the Gold standard for its currency, leadership in the industrial revolution, a flexible, yet principled, form of government, produced an empire which was confident, not to say complacent, about its business and the way to run itself. Setbacks, follies and worse were there, but up until 1914, there was little inclination on the part of those who ran the empire to consult anybody else.

However, if you examine the statements and formal reports of the government over the period – see for example George Bennett's 'The Concept of Empire' which in a small book illustrates the thoughts and principles animating British statesmen and administrators in regard to the empire during this period; or run down the list of commission reports and policy papers on imperial matters produced over the years – you see the remarkable breadth and depth of thinking, analysis and consideration given to public policy and practice in regard to the colonies, yet relatively little central control or prescription. Room was allowed for colonial governments and enterprising or energetic men and women to pursue their interests and aspirations within a structure of law and political practice which was set eventually in London – policy by policy – debated in public and in Parliament. Only the South African war of 1899–1902 gave pointers to the changing international context bearing on British policy-makers.[1]

Thus until the shattering experience of the First World War, the British Empire carried on by itself. Even after that war, the inertia and impetus of what went before carried it further forward in large areas of the earth – especially the Middle East and parts of Africa – so that arguably it over-reached itself. However, as we have seen in the earlier chapters, in the 1920s and 1930s, significant steps were taken in colonial policy reflecting the ongoing debates about the clearly anticipated future independence of India and the emergence of the notion of 'Trust' in regard to colonies, which also underlay the principles set at Versailles for the League of Nations. After the Second World War the severe financial and economic constraints facing Britain certainly acted upon policy-makers, but the direction of policy had been set before the war and firm and imaginative policy directions, largely shared by the two major political parties, gave colonial administrators all the lead they required.

Among the other colonial powers, Spain had few territories and did not offer much relevance to British territories. Portugal had large territories in Africa, but its approach to them was very different from Britain's, reflecting the prevailing authoritarian form of government at home. 'The Portuguese are in Africa to stay', said its spokesmen, 'we are not disposed to pack up and leave the states we have built.'[2] Belgium had large territories in Africa, especially the Congo. However, Britain considered that while orderly and productive the approach taken by Belgium to the future evolution of its territories was short-sighted and in fact alien to the evolving policies in its own colonies. Pierre Ryckmans's Foreign Affairs article of 1955[3] was honest about Belgium's role in the Congo but also asked his readers to be realistic as to what the Congo would be like without Belgium. As he put it, 'If it is right to say good government is no substitute for self-government,' it is equally true to say 'Self-government is no substitute for good-government'. 'We do not believe that the extension of the right to vote is an end in itself; we consider political progress to be a means to an end, the end being cultural and economic progress.'

The Netherlands/Indonesia

The Netherlands had had a large territory in the former Dutch East Indies, now Indonesia, which had been occupied by Japan during the Second World War. Pre-war, this had been a most productive and largely peaceful territory following 300 years of Dutch rule. The territory had achieved an effective administration, good transport linkages and a wide range of productive assets; its people were broadly well fed and prospects were favourable. Exports from the Dutch East Indies had been nearly twice the combined exports of China and India prior to the Second World War, and its credit was good. There was a well-developed and efficient system of taxation providing resources for public purposes. Social relations between the Dutch and the inhabitants were on the whole good, though not everywhere. The Dutch East Indies had much to be proud of. There were no doubt exchanges with other colonial governments in Asia, including India, Singapore and Malaya among British territories.

Following the end of the Japanese war, and reflecting the new perspective on empire, the Dutch were keen to transfer this inheritance to the Indonesian people in good working order with some guarantees for its maintenance and further development. They naturally felt that with their knowledge of the country they could do this better than any other agency.

At the surrender of the Japanese in August 1945, Admiral Mountbatten's South-East Asia Command (SEAC) advanced its headquarters from Ceylon (Sri Lanka) to Singapore. SEAC's major tasks were to effect the surrender and repatriation of over 700,000 Japanese personnel, evacuate allied prisoners of war and establish law and order in preparation for the resumption of civil government in Burma, Thailand, Malaya, Singapore, Southern Indochina and most of Indonesia, all of which had been much damaged by the war. The military and other resources available to SEAC were grossly insufficient to carry out these tasks. There was everywhere an outbreak of ethnic conflict, nationalist demands, political uncertainty, food shortages, currency problems, profiteering, and plain banditry. SEAC was given initial responsibility for occupying the key places in the former Dutch colony pending establishment of a civilian government. Initially SEAC had only 1,000 British men and officers to take the surrender of 155,000 Japanese prisoners of war in the former Dutch East Indies and arrange for their repatriation. The Netherlands had even fewer resources, as it was just itself seeking to recover from occupation by Germany. Thus it was unable to reassert its sovereignty promptly and large quantities of arms abandoned by the Japanese fell into the hands of a mixed band of nationalists, communists, Japanese-trained auxiliaries, Muslim groups and individuals seeking political office. Some were merely stolen.

When the Netherlands was eventually able to mobilize itself to resume government, it faced a very difficult and confused situation. It did not help that in the hope of stabilizing the situation the local British commander, on the basis of little local knowledge and in breach of an Anglo-Dutch agreement of August 1945, had recognized a Republic declared by nationalists with Japanese connivance. Though the idea of the republic excited local support, it lacked almost all the attributes of government and tended to take a totalitarian form. The United States was too preoccupied with many other matters in the Far East to produce a coherent policy. Thus with anti-colonial rhetoric from the United States, the UN and other quarters and a mixed assortment of Indonesians opposed to the re-establishment of Dutch control, the Netherlands government's Proclamation of 10 February 1946, which asserted its intention to assist the Indonesians towards nationhood and independence with material and administrative assistance, fell on many unreceptive or deaf ears.

In mid-1947, the country was still in a disturbed state with the so-called Republic unable to produce a coherent government. The Netherlands' authorities resolved to carry out a police action to restore law and order. Though this went well, it was interrupted by a decision of the Security Council of the United Nations and appointment of a three-man UN Commission for Indonesia, which tended to condone the misdeeds of the Republic and not acknowledge the legal position and objectives of the Netherlands government. Nevertheless, by the end of 1949 the country was more or less restored to order, the 'Republic' overcome and negotiations then ensued for elections and self-government.[4,5]

In the event, the independence of India in 1947 may have been more influential on events in the Dutch East Indies and the creation of Indonesia, than the reverse. These were the two largest colonial dependencies for two centuries or more and perhaps we should not be surprised that they both became independent within two years of each other.

France

Writing in Prosser Gifford's collection of essays on 'The Transfer of Power in Africa',[6] Tony Smith's comparative study of French and British Decolonization identified four respects in which Britain was favoured:

'First, there was the legacy of the past in terms of ideas and procedures on imperial matters, precedents built up over the centuries and decades before the Second World War ... the British proved temperamentally and institutionally more fit than the French to cope with the overseas challenges to their rule.'

Second, there was the much closer relationship between the United States and Britain which persisted from the war years into peace-time and the Cold War period.

Third, the French multi-party system with its weak governing consensus during the Fourth Republic was not the equivalent of the strong two-party system in Britain. The "collective conscience" of the political elite in France was significantly different from that in Britain.

Fourth, the nationalist groups in some French colonies after 1945 presented France with acute dilemmas, especially in Indochina and Algeria where major revolts broke out, which were by and large absent in the British colonies'.

Smith pointed out that since the eighteenth century, Britain had been following 'Burke's sage counsel' to reform in order to preserve, characterized in colonial policy by the evolution of the Dominion system from the time of the Durham Report of 1839 in regard to Canada and by the series of reforms in India coming at intervals of ten to fifteen years up until independence in 1947. By contrast, he argued, even when a group of French colonial civil servants met in Brazzaville in 1944 to draw up proposals for imperial reorganization post-war, they failed to address the central issue, namely the possibility of colonial evolution towards independence – even to consider the possibility of eventual separation as a viable political option. He quotes the preamble of the conference report:

'The ends of the civilising work accomplished by France in the colonies exclude any idea of autonomy, all possibility of evolution outside the French bloc of the Empire: the eventual achievement, even in the future, of self-government in the colonies is denied'. By 1947, this had been made clear on successive occasions to the Indochinese, the Tunisians and Moroccans, to the Malagasies, to the Africans and to the Algerians. Indeed the matter had been fixed by the Fourth Republic's constitution in the terms providing for the 'French Union' in its Title 8. 'The authority of France over the Union was beyond dispute … in legislative matters the Union was totally subordinate to the National Assembly.' What the Union assured, in essence, was that the peoples of the empire would be neither French nor free.'

In his note on Anglo-French Relations in West Africa of November 1951[7] addressed to the Foreign Office, Andrew Cohen also noted the differences between the British and French colonial systems and described the practical steps being taken to facilitate exchange between them in West Africa; but decried the fact that such cooperation at the metropolitan level had atrophied.

Seeking an explanation for the strikingly different approaches taken by Britain and France in addressing the colonial issue, Smith concluded that it is to be found in the different historical experiences of empire:

The British were practitioners of 'informal empire', that is supporting dependable local leaders in order to assure a stable environment for trade and investment free of direct political control. For the French on the contrary direct rule alone permitted domination … to be imperialists, the French were perforce Protectionists. … Britain had adopted Free Trade, which by itself reduced control of colonial policy, and had been experimenting with an approach to institutionalising the transfer of power from London to the various colonial governments since 1839. No similar tried means existed with the French for them to draw upon after 1945.

Smith also considered that the differences between Britain and France in regard to colonial affairs reflected the impact of the Second World War. Britain had entered into a close alliance with the United States, fortified by the remarkable and influential relationship between Roosevelt and Churchill. As indicated in Chapter 2, Roosevelt was by and large prepared to set aside colonial issues in his negotiations with Churchill to avoid difficulties in regard to the conduct of the war. By contrast, relations between Roosevelt and de Gaulle were dire and prejudicial to French interests. It was not until de Gaulle had established a provisional government of liberated France that the United States in October 1944 recognized de Gaulle's position.

When asked in 1948 how he would 'significantly modify the foreign policy of France' should he return to power, de Gaulle responded,

I will not have to change the foreign policy of France since at present France has no foreign policy. Her regime does not permit it any more than it permits her to have an economic policy worthy of the name, a social policy, or a financial policy, etc. The truth is there is nothing. Thus I will not change this policy which does not exist, but I will make the policy of France.[8]

Smith continued,

Time and again throughout the history of the Fourth Republic ... one finds a shared anguish at the passing of national greatness, a shared humiliation at three generations of defeat, a shared nationalistic determination that France retain her independence in a hostile world – all brought to rest on the conviction that in the empire they would 'maintenir'. ... The one national body where a realistic colonial policy was held was ... the French Communist Party which alone of the major parties in France respected the historical limits of the moment and recognised very early the kind of flexibility a successful post-war imperial policy must possess.

Smith added further,

It is important to emphasise that French policy was essentially the same throughout the empire; political reforms were granted only so long as they could be seen to be tending to preserve French rule. Demands for change which might ultimately destroy the French presence were immediately to be squelched. De Gaulle was the chief architect of this plan and he made its terms clear to the Vietnamese by his declaration of March 25, 1945, which his successors in power re-affirmed in their negotiations with Ho Chi Minh in the summer of 1946. ... The French subsequently demonstrated the seriousness of their resolve. In November 1946 they shelled the port of Haiphong ... to rid the city of the Vietminh; in March/April 1947 they responded to a nationalist raid on an army base in Madagascar with repression. Following the Setif repression of May 1945 the Algerians were momentarily cowed ... but a revolution offering no quarter finally broke out in 1954.

The situation in Tunisia was more positive. On 18 May 1955, *The Times* featured a leader titled 'French Settlers' Rearguard Action' which addressed the negotiations taking place regarding the future of the country.

> The agreement was the result of many months of hard bargaining. It reserves to France the control of Tunisia's foreign relations and defence, including policing the frontiers. The administration of justice and control of the internal police – two subjects which caused prolonged argument – are to be transferred from French to Tunisian hands gradually over periods of fifteen and twenty years. There are conventions affecting economics, finance, education, technical cooperation and so on, all of which emphasises the inevitably close relations which must persist between a self-governing Tunisia and metropolitan France. ... In a world of exacting nationalisms this political advance is distinguished by its spirit of compromise and reason. ... But the majority of French settlers, of whom there are today about 150,000, against four million Muslims, do not see things in this light. They are conscious that, whatever constitutional forms are eventually decided, power is shifting away from them. Within their lifetime they will become a political minority.[9]

In April 1957, just as the Gold Coast (Ghana) became independent, eight territories of French West Africa went to the polls under an 'outline law' of June 1956 to elect territorial assemblies from which their own prime ministers and governments would be chosen for the first time, an important and irrevocable step which placed the future of French West Africa in African hands. This gave them nearly as much control of their internal affairs as the regions of Nigeria had at that time. They spent much of the next year setting up a federal executive as a logical follow up. There was some thought that this might emerge as a form of 'French Commonwealth'. However this notion was opposed by Houphouet-Boigny, a member of the French assembly, whose Parti Democratique de Cote d'Ivoire (PDCI) emerged as the principal nationalist party in the most prosperous of these countries, and whose assembly rejected the idea of federation in favour of independence within the French Community. Houphouet-Boigny had earlier become France's principal ally; instead of starting a guerrilla movement against them, which some advocated, he realized that his personal commercial interests, and those of men like him, lay with France. PDCI entered into an alliance with the French Communist Party; and following the revival of the inter-territorial Rassemblement Democratique Africain (RDA) was feeling its way to a new relationship with France. However this all came to a halt when the Fourth Republic fell in 1958 and de Gaulle resumed power as first president of the Fifth Republic.

By the terms of the Fifth Republic's Constitution, the African territories were given two options: either 'federation' in subordination to France, or independence. In the referendum of September 1958, only Guinea chose independence. France had pulled out of Indochina after Dien Bien Phu and de Gaulle made a similar break with Algeria in the late 1950s at the cost of acute political and social antagonisms within France. But why did eleven of the twelve French territories in Africa choose to remain within the French Community? For by so doing they accepted that foreign affairs, common economic policy, higher education, justice and communications would be handled for the French Community as a whole. General de Gaulle had offered them independence at any time they wanted it, so there was no political pressure to remain. There were economic and commercial attractions, and as Leopold Senghor of Senegal argued the spirit of the Constitution was liberal and egalitarian. Senghor went further; in his Foreign Affairs article of 1961[10] he wrote,

> The French Community, created by General de Gaulle in full agreement with Africa's true representatives, is one of the greatest achievements of our time. Besides being a masterly concept to which I and with me the majority of the leaders of Senegal are deeply committed, it also is one of those ideas capable of catching the imagination of the masses. Sweeping away the contradictions of the colonial system, it enables the former mother country and its erstwhile colonies to form a friendly cultural and economic union and thus forge a lasting link between Western Europe and Africa.

The Investment Fund for the Economic and Social Development of the Overseas Territories (FIDES) was created to facilitate the flow of funds from France to the members of the Community. Universal adult suffrage was granted simultaneously and the democratic institutions of France were gradually established in the overseas territories. The author of this book recalls sitting in the assembly in Djibouti in 1962 listening to the debate as the members considered President de Gaulle's bid for re-election.

However in his African Affairs article of January 1959,[11] J. H. Huizinga argued that the explanation for the attraction of the eleven former French colonies to join the French community is to be found in the different political philosophies of Britain and France. British policies led in the direction of nationalistic solutions, the rights of peoples and collectives to dispose of themselves; French policies by contrast reflected their belief in more universal, supra-national, revolutionary traditions. In practical terms the French government went on paying for large numbers of French technical staff to go on working in the former colonies under the direction of the African governments. Perhaps they were thereby less independent, but they were also able to benefit from much French expertise and financial support.

In summary, the constitutional concept of the French overseas territories was so different from Britain's that in many ways it offered nothing of interest to those formulating policy for Britain's colonies. However, we should note a few significant events or approaches which proved to be influential on British policy. First, France's war against the communist insurgency in Viet Nam offered some parallels with that being waged by Britain in Malaya. The difference between them was mainly the policy for the future of the two territories. Malays had the prospect of self-government and eventual independence. Viet Nam had the prospect of a sharply constrained autonomy within the French Union. Secondly, in North Africa, where there were large numbers of French settlers and where religion was also a factor, a way had to be found to break out of a violent and futile war. The impact of this conflict on British policy was significant – policy-makers were determined to avoid such a war in the African territories in which there were British settlers – that is Kenya and Rhodesia. Thirdly, the return to power of Charles de Gaulle as president in 1958, and his decisive actions in regard to the French colonies, highlighted the determination of France, like Britain, to shape the future of its colonies in a manner which responded to current realities, rather than to abandon them as Belgium did the Congo or seek to avoid the issue as did Portugal in its territories.

In his African Affairs article of July 1963, 'French-Speaking Africa Since Independence' J. H. A. Watson, formerly British ambassador in Dakar, drew out the distinctive features of French colonial policy and the attitudes of the Africans in French colonies.[12] He emphasized that the French really did intend to assimilate the African countries into Overseas France; to make them ultimately into a part of the great worldwide French cultural, political and economic heritage. He admired the political skill demonstrated by the West Africans, with their single political party (the RDA). Despite this, the parties and the leaders were already organized on the basis of the separate states, which really only came into existence with the demise of French West and Equatorial Africa and the creation of the French Community in 1958. Watson pointed out that it was Houphouet-Boigny who in 1960 persuaded General de Gaulle to allow the states of the Community to become genuinely independent, with French representation taking the form of ambassadors. Despite this, economically and in other ways they remained very closely dependent on France. French assistance to the area was very large and influential – in 1963 there were some 1,400 serving experts in both Senegal and Ivory Coast making a major contribution to the governance and effectiveness of the states. The CFA franc facilitated financial transactions, though eventually it became an encumbrance to exports from the area due to its valuation. In due course, the Africans began to worry about how they could wean themselves, without loss, off this close embrace by France.

Representatives of the British and French governments met from time to time to discuss colonial matters. An example was the meeting of December 1954, at which the British delegation emphasized that there had been no change in British policy since the last ministerial discussions in 1951, and that no change was contemplated. That policy was 'helping the Colonial territories to attain self-government within the British Commonwealth. To that end we are seeking as rapidly as possible to build up in each territory the institutions which its circumstances require; and to pursue the economic and social development of the territories so that it keeps pace with their political development'. The British delegation was instructed to emphasize to the French delegation that responsibility for policy and administration had passed very largely into the hands of elected ministers in the territories and the responsibility of British ministers was to that extent circumscribed.

Another example was the meeting of 12 November 1959 at which both the French minister of foreign affairs, M. Couve de Murville, and the British foreign secretary, Selwyn Lloyd, were present.[13] M. Couve de Murville opened the meeting by saying that he was strongly in favour of the habit of consultation which had grown up between officials and he was anxious to see this developed as far as possible. He was anxious that the two states did not oppose each other in Africa; he thought this cooperation should be extended to the United States and he considered the three states should seek to arrive at common views. He thought all the French colonies would in due course become independent and things were going fast within the French community. He said there were no serious problems of race between France and Black Africa. However, France was somewhat concerned at the prospect of all these new states become members of the United Nations. Most of the more detailed discussions addressed particular country questions:

- Nkrumah's apparent desire to absorb French Togoland, which was expected to become independent in April 1960;

- Issues to do with the future of the British Cameroons where plebiscites were being held in the two zones to decide whether they would go into Nigeria or join the French Cameroons;

- Guinea and the policies of M. Sekou Toure. M. Couve de Murville said relations between France and Guinea were very difficult and he considered Sekou Toure a communist who was receiving arms and support from the communist countries. Lloyd said this issue might come up at the Summit Meeting with Khrushchev;

- Somaliland and the Horn of Africa, where relations with Ethiopia may well be the key.

The United States of America

Undoubtedly, the most pervasive and influential external influence on British colonial policy after the Second World War was the United States. Up until the Second World War, the United States had little official contact or interest in Africa. American missionaries were to be found all over Africa, but there were very few US consuls or embassies and in Washington Africa made little impact. Some African students found their way to the United States, where they encountered the segregation which persisted in large parts of the country until the late 1960s. Reference has been made earlier to the Atlantic Charter and it is clear that President Roosevelt came away from his meeting with Winston Churchill with a very different view of the references in the charter to 'self-determination', which he thought ought to apply to colonial peoples also. He envisaged European colonial empires being placed under some sort of international administration, which did not go down at all well in Britain.

Roosevelt first discussed Indian affairs with Churchill in December 1941. Churchill recorded that he had reacted so strongly and at such length that the president never raised the subject verbally again. As the Japanese army approached India, the issue simmered between them with Churchill sending the president copies of Indian state papers he had received from Dr Jinnah, president of the Muslim League; Sir Firoz Khan Noon, a Muslim member of the Viceroy's Executive Council; the Military Adviser to the secretary of state for India, pointing out the communal diversity of the Indian Army, which was critical to the defence of India; the governor of Punjab on the dangers of an immediate statement on the future of India; and in April 1942 Pandit Nehru's statement regarding the defence of India. Churchill's aim was evidently to demonstrate to the president the complexity of the country and the need for very detailed and careful negotiations with the various parties regarding India's future, which was out of the question at such a critical moment in the war. This debate with Roosevelt over the condition and future of India and the Colonies worried Churchill deeply, 'Anything like a serious difference between you and me would break my heart and would surely deeply injure both our countries at the height of this terrible struggle.'[14] Commenting on this exchange, Max Hastings wrote, 'He (Churchill) deemed it rank cant for a nation which had itself colonized a continent, dispossessing and largely exterminating its indigenous population, and which still practised racial segregation, to harangue others about the treatment of native peoples.'[15]

The following draws on the essay by Wm. Roger Louis and Ronald Robinson in Prosser Gifford's compendium.[16]

In their Open Letter ... to the People of England in October 1942, the editors of *Life* magazine wrote, the American people might disagree among themselves about war aims, but they were unanimous on one point: 'we are not fighting to hold the British Empire together. ... If your strategists are planning a war to hold the British Empire together they will sooner or later find themselves strategising all alone'.

However, there were different views within the US government. The State Department emphasized 'international trusteeship'; in a document titled 'Declaration on National Independence for Colonies' the State Department wrote, 'It is accordingly the duty and the purpose of each nation having political ties with colonial peoples ... to fix at the earliest practicable moment, dates upon which the colonial peoples shall be accorded the status of full independence within a system of general security.' There would have to be 'an international executive authority in the West Indies, Africa and South-east Asia to enforce timetables to advance colonies to independence ... there would have to be international accountability'. By contrast, the Navy Department was concerned about security in the Atlantic and Pacific, and was much more cautious about the United States making commitments with uncertain ramifications.

In due course, other realities began to temper the position taken by the State Department. First, the CD&W Act of 1945, which increased the resources of this scheme from £5 million per annum to £120 million (2017 £4,923 million) was an emphatic statement of intent by the British government, and may well have been designed partly to influence US views of its colonial policy. Second, the Colonial Office in London strongly rejected the US proposals for 'international executives' and pointed to the steady progress being made in the direction of self-government. Third the US Navy's security concerns came to dominate policy-making in Washington. Though acknowledging that British power would be much reduced after the war, the Navy's concern was to be realistic about the post-war world and be prepared to acknowledge and accept their British ally and her empire as contributions to international security for as long as possible. At Yalta, Roosevelt and the State Department settled for a trusteeship formula that was limited to former mandated territories under the Versailles Treaty and the dependent territories of the defeated Italy (Libya, Eritrea and Somalia).

As Roger Louis noted,

'The general policy of the US government had shifted gradually from one of dismantling the British Empire to one of giving it tacit support. The watchword "security" had begun to eclipse that of "independence"' ... It is generally true that after 1945 the fire of anti-colonialism burned much less brightly within the US Government. By the time of the San Francisco conference the American military had prevailed over those who sought to liquidate colonial empires by placing them under international supervision. In 1945 the US had acquiesced in the return to their former rulers of several colonies which had been occupied by the common enemies ... equally there were no conditions for the European Recovery Programme, supported by the Marshall Plan, to liquidate the colonial empires except that they should be more accessible to American trade and investment. During the early years of the Cold War there was very little question of American pressure to decolonise, though the dilemmas of orderly imperial liquidation persisted[17]

The Cold War now became a major factor influencing policy in both Britain and the United States. In the Far East, the United States, which was involved in the Philippines, Korea and generally speaking China became involved in the future of Indochina and Indonesia. The conflict between America's frequently emphasized anti-colonial sentiments and its concern about the spread of communism left all parties confused, including both the French and Dutch governments. In Malaya, Britain was fighting the communist-inspired insurgency and was able gradually to assert sufficient support for the rising Malayan state to defeat the insurgents and bring Malaya to self-government and independence in 1958. In the Near East Britain, which had been gravely over-extended, was happy to hand over its defensive role in Greece in the face of the communist insurgency to the United States, and its mandate in Palestine to the United Nations.

British perceptions of the US government's policy on the colonies and its increasing interest in Africa can be followed in the official correspondence and decisions, summarized in the following extracts, which follow a chronological sequence:

In January 1949, in his inaugural presidential address President Truman stated in his 'Fourth Point' that the United States 'must embark on a bold new programme' for the improvement and growth of under-developed areas and invited other countries to pool their resources in this undertaking. In its edition of 12 February 1949 *The Daily Telegraph* welcomed this potential extension of the US-financed European Recovery Programme to the colonial territories.

In his despatch of 14 January 1950 to Ernest Bevin, the Foreign Secretary, the British Ambassador in Washington, Oliver Franks, wrote, 'like you, Sir, I have been much concerned to observe that the views expressed by British and United States representatives at the United Nations were so often in conflict on matters affecting colonial and trust territories'.[18] This eight-page despatch reviewed in some detail the embassy's position:

'We for our part should make a much greater effort to make our case known to the world in general and to US opinion in particular ... anti-colonialism in the US today is a traditional attitude rather than an active crusading force ... there is a willingness ... to assume, without enquiring into the facts, that the policies of the colonial powers have not really changed much in the last two centuries. ... US officials are moreover apt to overlook their own racial problem when dealing with colonial questions since, fortunately for them, it does not fall so readily within the purview of the United Nations ... it is gratifying to find that in the Africa section of the State Department ... the officials who know best what we are doing are for the most part prepared to recognise that the UK now runs its colonies primarily for the benefit of their inhabitants. ... I have mentioned the growing influence in the State Department of the Bureau of UN Affairs ... praise for the UN has become a good in itself in which criticism, however well-meaning, is often badly misunderstood ... we have the long-term task of educating American public opinion about the realities of present-day colonial administration ... we should have a frank exchange of views with the State Department. ... We shall have to be prepared to expose without reticence the principles on which our colonial policy is founded and to explain ... what we are trying to achieve and what are the difficulties to be overcome ... we shall then be entitled to ask for their assistance in achieving our aims, not only in the UN but elsewhere. ... I cannot stress too emphatically ... that US spokesmen will not risk falling seriously out of line with US public opinion on these issues however unrealistic and sentimental it may sometimes be ... it is important to note that almost everywhere in the State Department a clear distinction is drawn in our favour between British and French colonial administration.'

In October 1951 Anglo-American discussions were held in London concerning the handling of colonial questions at the United Nations.[19] Britain had modified its approach and was seeking to use the debates and voting on resolutions to gain maximum publicity for the achievements of British policy in the colonies. This had been successful in 1950. But the UK representatives took the opportunity to state that there were basic principles on which the UK could not compromise:

(i)   The UN could not be allowed to interfere in the day-to-day administration of Trust or non-self-governing territories;

(ii) The UK could not give any formal undertaking to consult the Trusteeship Council before effecting changes in the political structure of a Trust territory, although in practice such consultation would be held when possible.

(iii) The UK could not report on the implementation in non-self-governing territories of an assembly resolution if it did not apply also to independent states.

(iv) In no circumstances could the UK permit discussions of the political or constitutional affairs of a non-self-governing territory.

The need for time to enable the African territories to acquire knowledge and experience of government was emphasized by Cornelis de Kiewit in his Foreign Affairs article of 1954.[20]

British colonial policy for more than a hundred years has shown an almost instinctive ability to recognise the moment when it was no longer wise to defer grants of self-government. When the colony had adequately consolidated its territory, established enough stability in its finances, acquired enough political experience and developed a sufficiently diversified economic and social pattern to carry the burden of autonomy, then autonomy was almost always granted. In much of Africa the demands for political change are arising ahead of the implicit time schedule which British colonial experience has followed. This is another way of saying that the territorial arrangements and the sum of available skills, experience and modern social virtues are still markedly less adequate than was considered safe and reliable in earlier grants of autonomy. … There is so much unfinished business in Africa that the trained and experienced observer shudders at the thought that the temper of the times may precipitate major political decisions which the continent is unprepared for or able to make … outside the few industrialised centres, Africa generates new capital in utterly insignificant amounts … as former Governor Sir Philip Mitchell said of Kenya 'the ignorance, inexpertness and low productivity of native agriculture provide a totally inadequate foundation for an enlightened state of society, a high standard of living and elaborate social services'.

In a note of 29 June 1955, the UK representative at the UN reported on the visit to Africa by Adlai Stevenson, who had been the Democratic candidate in the American presidential election of 1952.[21] He had been to the Gold Coast, Kenya, the Rhodesias and Uganda, as well as the Congo and the Union.

He was profoundly impressed by the manifest affection and respect in which the local peoples hold their British colonial officials. The native leaders' desire for independence was, he said, only equalled by their determination to hold on to their British civil servants … he had come back with a deep admiration for our colonial administrators. He said that their devotion to an often thankless and always underpaid task, frequently performed in lonely and primitive conditions, thousands of miles from home and civilisation, was one of the most impressive things he had ever witnessed. It was an inspiration to see honest and intelligent men thus absorbed in an utterly selfless and disinterested service.

In preparation for the Bermuda Conference between Prime Minister Macmillan and President Eisenhower in May 1957, the Cabinet Secretary, Norman Brook, minuted to the prime minster in regard to the discussion of colonial affairs

I should imagine that the best way of broaching this subject would be to introduce it under the cover of your general thesis about the future handling of the United Nations. The President is in a fair way to sacrificing all possibility of independent action by the way in which he has exalted the position and authority of the United Nations; and you will wish to try to get him to realise the danger of this policy, not only for us, but conceivably also for the United States themselves.[22]

On 28 June 1957 the colonial secretary, Lennox-Boyd, wrote to the governors of all African colonies and Aden to convey the substance of an assessment of communist influences in Tropical Africa agreed between the British foreign secretary and the US secretary of state Foster Dulles at the Bermuda Conference,[23] and the conclusions of the conference. The British objective had been to invite the US government to overhaul their traditional attitude towards 'colonialism' and to recognize that the objectives of British colonial policy are the antithesis of 'colonialism' as commonly represented and that on their own merits they are valuable objectives to support and pursue in the interests of human advancement, and for this very reason they provide the best hope of erecting a strong barrier against communism in under-developed Africa. He reported that the following propositions were accepted at the conference:

- The governments of the United States and the United Kingdom have a common purpose in combating Soviet objectives in Tropical Africa.
- The best counter to Soviet aims is to pursue resolutely and systematically the constructive policy of leading dependencies *as rapidly as practicable* towards stable self-government or independence.
- The problems of different territories differ widely … a most difficult and important problem exists of striking a balance between moving too fast, which may lead to anarchy or oppression and open the way to communist influence; and moving too slowly, thus driving the potential leadership into communist collaboration.

Vice President Richard Nixon visited Africa in 1957 while attending the Ghana Independence celebrations and concluded, according to Assistant Secretary Joseph Palmer,[24] that 'the emergence of a free and independent Africa is as important to us in the long run as it is to the people of that continent'. Elsewhere in his speech, Palmer also said, inter alia

The concept of a nation has not hitherto existed in the historical experience of much of Africa south of the Sahara. The national vision, in fact, often materialises only in the course of – and almost as a means of – acquiring governmental autonomy. In this respect the national movement often has the explicit or implicit understanding of the administering authorities, and in such cases the construction of the nation becomes a cooperative venture of indigenous and external forces. The United States favours the orderly transition from colonial to self-governing status in African territories. We emphasize in this connection that self-government and independence carry with them grave responsibilities to the world community and that therefore neither status should be conferred or acquired lightly … racialism in Africa takes many forms, all of them divisive to a regrettable degree but most of them presently under what is a remarkable control, considering the stresses involved.

An indication of increasing US interest in Africa was the sanction of Congress at this time to the setting up of a separate division in the State Department to deal with African affairs. Dulles emphasized that 'HMG should not feel that the United States were exercising pressure for premature independence of colonies – there was an evolutionary trend towards self-government and the right to self-government must be qualified by the obligation to act responsibly'.[25]

On 15 July 1958, Lord Hood wrote from the British Embassy in Washington to the foreign secretary, Selwyn Lloyd, under the title 'The Attitude of the United States to Tropical Africa'.[26] He emphasized the greatly increased interest on the part of the United States in African affairs, and reiterated that Nixon's visit and the recommendations he made on his return to Washington did much to stimulate and publicize the growth of interest both inside the administration and outside it. He referred to the division of the Office of African Affairs into two, with the creation of the Bureau of African Affairs, supported by a large research staff. He wrote:

There are several lines of thought and emotion within the US … that people should be free to choose their own government and enjoy the benefits of the Declaration of Independence of 1776 ever more widely … qualified by the realisation that many African peoples are simply not ready to manage their own affairs and that the concepts of personal liberty and national independence have little immediate application to them … they recognise the benefits that enlightened Colonial administration has brought and can still bring to many territories and fear that in many parts of Africa progress towards independence has outrun or is outrunning the capacity to make it work … in most British territories progress towards independence is as fast as it safely can be, if not too fast … since the enactment of the Loi Cadre, much the same can be said for the French West and Equatorial African territories, though there is uncertainty over the readiness of the French to accept the final loosening … the Belgian Congo is widely accepted in this country as a pattern of enlightened Colonialism with a prosperous and expanding economy … the Portuguese territories are regarded as serious liabilities for the Colonial powers.

In November 1959 a British delegation including representatives of the foreign office, the Colonial Office and the Commonwealth Relations Office visited Ottawa and Washington to discuss the report titled 'Africa: The Next Ten Years'.[27] The delegation reported the talks could not have been more friendly and that they found the Americans extremely well informed about Africa and taking great trouble to be so.

An acute test for the United States in Africa came with the collapse of the Belgian Congo amid its concern about the 'leftward drift' they feared in Africa. As Rupert Emerson wrote in his Foreign Affairs article of 1962,[28]

> The United States has already experienced a not inconsiderable loss of standing with many Africans, a disillusionment deriving often from the ambivalence of the American position. The unhappy affairs of the Congo contributed markedly to this, and in particular the assassination of Lumumba for which many held the United States responsible. In the eyes of most Africans, Lumumba was the chosen national leader of the Congo and the defender of its unity, but the United States was clearly on the record as opposing him and backing Kasavubu; it was accused of collaborating with Belgium and condoning Katangan separatism.

Thus there had been a remarkable change in the US government's approach to the colonial issue. From an inclination by President Roosevelt to intervene by setting target dates and creating institutions of international control, US policy had arrived at a well-informed acceptance of the need for time for colonies to acquire the knowledge, skills and experience required to govern effectively.

The United Nations

Chapter XI of the Charter of the United Nations contains a general declaration of colonial policy and under Article 73(e) a specific obligation (on colonial powers) to transmit regularly to the secretary-general, for information purposes, statistical and other information of a technical nature relating to economic, social and educational conditions in the territories for which members of the UN are responsible. Chapters XII and XIII deal with the International Trusteeship System, which is the UN successor to the League of Nations mandates system.

Under Article 77 of the Charter, an International Trusteeship System was established and made applicable to territories held under a mandate of the former League of Nations, territories which might be detached from enemy States as a result of the Second World War and territories voluntarily placed under the system by States responsible for their administration.

During the First Session of the United Nations in January 1946 the United Kingdom declared its intention to put all three African territories for which it had a mandate (Tanganyika, parts of Togoland and of Cameroon) under the trusteeship system, and to establish Trans-Jordan as an independent state. No statement could be made about Palestine at that time. The other mandatory States made similar declarations. Thus the United Nations was given a direct role in regard to the administration of Trust territories. An official of the Colonial Office noted in a minute of 16 January 1947.[29]

> Throughout the discussion [of these Resolutions] there was evidence that many delegations which have no colonial responsibilities desired to go far beyond the provisions of the Charter in conferring upon the UN a power of supervision over all colonial territories. ... I take the view that it would be unfortunate if at this stage in the UN any encouragement were given to the Assembly to contravene the provisions of the Charter.

A later example of this problem at the UN occurred in October 1956; Britain was meeting with Belgium and France, in advance of a meeting of the Trusteeship Council. Its representative, Bourdillon, said that the UK 'resolutely opposed the Council's recommendation that the administering powers should indicate intermediate target dates for political progress in the Trust Territories, and that we had made representations in Washington protesting against the American initiative in this matter'.[30]

The writer of the minute added,

> I may add that perhaps the most significant development was the realisation by the United States that their interests in this matter lay with the other Colonial Powers rather than with the irresponsible critics ...

> that there was a serious risk of the General Assembly adopting a Resolution which would have the effect of summoning a Conference of United States nationals from United States territories such as Alaska, Puerto Rica and Hawaii behind the back of the United States Government – probably on United States soil. ... It will clearly be necessary to try to follow a common line, especially as the Member States which have responsibilities in this field are in a minority of eight against perhaps forty, and that in the present atmosphere of the UN political prejudice and racial emotion count for very much more than reason and experience.

In his Foreign Affairs article of 1952 titled 'Excesses of Self-Determination'[31] Clyde Eagleton discussed the abuse as he saw it of the term 'self-determination' which he said had always been abused, in the sense that nationalism tends to run to extremes, but which, he thought, 'is being torn to pieces in the United Nations today'. He went on, the term 'self-determination' was crowded into Article 1 of the Charter without relevance and without explanation the speeches go far beyond anything hitherto thought of in connection with self-determination; it is not merely independence which the speakers demand, but perfect satisfaction of all human desires. Furthermore they would limit the claims to self-determination to colonial people only the trouble is that the movement thus far has no standards, no common sense, indeed, no clear objectives. It seems chiefly to be an urge, born of resentment the textbooks of international law do not recognize any legal right to self-determination, nor do they know any standards for determining which groups are entitled to independence further, Article 2, paragraph 7 reaffirming the rule of international law forbids the United Nations to intervene in the domestic affairs of any Member. He referred to the Indonesia case in which the UN, riding rough-shod over the provisions of the Charter regarding domestic questions, decided to tear Indonesia away from the Netherlands and give it the independence it sought. Thus it is no longer self-determination which is being discussed but determination by any group able to get a Resolution through the General Assembly. The General Assembly instructed the Human Rights Commission to insert into the proposed Covenant on Human Rights the words 'All peoples shall have the right of self-determination.' Eagleton argued that the United Nations must provide some criteria for its own judgement of questions of self-determination, so that it may act fairly and consistently.

Oliver Franks mentioned in his letter quoted earlier that within the United States, 'the UN has become a good in and of itself'. But the limitations of that 'good' were well described by Vernon MacKay in his Foreign Affairs article of 1956.[32]

The speed of this political transformation (of African countries) provides a new perspective on a wide range of problems, and it raises anew the question of whether Africa is going too slow or too fast. Too slow or too fast for what? Too slow to satisfy African aspirations? Or too fast to create economically viable and politically stable states? How can the principle of self-determination be effectively applied in a continent so varied that its people speak 800 languages? ... Questions like these reveal the need for a United States policy that looks ahead and beyond the end of colonialism in Africa. ... Although the political excitement in the trust territories is a part of the general awakening of post-war Africa, the United Nations is responsible for intensifying this agitation ... six of the African trust territories have been toured three times by Visiting Missions of the Trusteeship Council. ... These visits are great events in Africa. ... The United Nations has also stirred up political activity by granting a growing number of African requests for oral hearings before the Trusteeship Council and General Assembly. ... A decade of trusteeship has highlighted many problems of both Africa and the United Nations ... it has jolted the anti-colonial Members with the discovery that universal suffrage can produce unexpected results in non-literate societies ... with a franchise limited to 8000, the anti-French party dominated French Togoland; when universal suffrage was accepted, the pro-French party rose to power. ... The depth of these conflicting emotions on the colonial issue is partly responsible for the dilemma that confronts the US in shaping a policy towards Africa. ... As the social anthropologists are continually pointing out, African society is in a state of transition in which the restraints and disciplines of the old social order are breaking down. What is needed now in much of Africa is not faster political advance but a still greater effort to build economic and educational foundations for the social cohesion necessary to make freedom meaningful.

In his 1962 article referred to earlier[33] Rupert Emerson expressed

the hope that the United States can abstain from being drawn into every African issue and every dispute between African states and the European powers. If anything, the United Nations already forces too large an intermixing of everybody in the affairs of everybody else, but it is certain that the United States cannot be disinterested in any major aspect of the fate of Africa even if it can avoid entanglement in more local issues.

In 1961, the General Assembly of the United Nations established the Committee of Twenty-four to examine the implementation of the assembly's 'Declaration on Colonial Territories and Peoples' which called for an end to colonialism. In a despatch to a number of ambassadors in February 1964, the British foreign office described its attitude as follows:

Our attitude to the competence of the United Nations and its subordinate bodies in relation to dependent territories continues to be based on the provisions of the United Nations Charter. This, in our view, does not authorise United Nations intervention in the affairs of individual territories, other than Trust territories. We do not consider that the General Assembly or the Committee of Twenty-four can create obligations binding on us by passing resolutions which we do not support. With these reservations we shall continue to serve on the committee and to play a full part in its work ... at the December 1963 session of the General Assembly, the United Kingdom came in for fierce criticism, particularly in the 4th Committee. ... One significant new feature of the resolution passed at the end of the debate was the specific request to administering Governments to facilitate the tasks of the sub-committees instructed by the committee to visit territories. This is an issue on which we clashed with the committee in 1963 and we shall continue to refuse to accept intervention by visiting missions from the committee … we are likely to be as heavily engaged in 1964 on the committee's activities as in previous years … especially on Aden, Southern Rhodesia and Gibraltar … but also many other of the 38 territories on the preliminary list, most of which are British.[34]

India

The British government had regular exchanges with India in the context of Commonwealth and other gatherings, on account of its own experiences as a dependent state prior to 1947 and the continuing close links between Britain and India. HMG evidently hoped that India could help to reassure African leaders about British intentions for Africa, despite often inflammatory remarks appearing in the Indian press and in some statements made, for example, at the UN. An opportunity for informal exchanges occurred at the time of the Coronation of Queen Elizabeth in 1953. The Indian Premier, Pandit Nehru arranged to meet Prime Minister Winston Churchill on 11 June. At Churchill's suggestion, Nehru wrote to him beforehand to outline the matters which might come up.[35] He wrote on exchanges taking place to bring about a truce in the Korean War and the military coup which brought a new government in Egypt. But he also wrote:

> Perhaps I might draw your attention to the extraordinary changes which have come about in Asia and even Africa during the last few years. I am not referring to the political changes, which are great, but rather to the changes in psychology of masses of men. There is an upsurge of the human spirit in these great continents, a dawning political consciousness, a demand for economic betterment and an intense nationalism. Much is said about communism and an attempt is made to divide the world into the communist group and the non-communist group. For some purposes that might be helpful. But this ignores certain other vital factors, in particular the revolutionary upsurge in Asia and Africa. I think this is one of the dominant factors of our age and many of our difficulties are caused by a lack of awareness of this dynamic situation. … This upsurge has not always worked for good and it has sometimes resulted in evil consequences. But the fact to recognise is that Asia, and to some extent, even Africa are changing rapidly, in so far as men's minds are concerned. The situation is not only dynamic but, to some extent, explosive ….

> I am gravely disturbed at events in the whole of the continent of Africa. … From the larger point of view, masses of people in Africa are becoming exceedingly bitter and frustrated and they will naturally look to others and more undesirable people for help. … In East Africa, more especially Kenya, horrible things have occurred and everyone must condemn the murders

and other outrages that have occurred there. But if I may venture to say so, the situation is progressively deteriorating and affecting the rest of Africa. I have been in a way connected for the last twenty years or so with important leaders of the Africans in East Africa as well as the leaders of the nationalist movements in Morocco and Tunisia. I am therefore in some position to judge of what is happening there. Practically everyone I have known is in prison. The Africans are obviously not very mature or developed people. When well treated, they respond in a very friendly way. Otherwise they are apt to go astray ... But there can be no solution of this problem by merely law and order methods which are of course necessary. ... Quite apart from the immediate situation there, the land question is of paramount importance. All over Asia it is the land question which is first – in China, Japan, in India. Apart from this, there is the question of racial discrimination and the openly avowed object of racial domination – you will appreciate that much that was tolerated in the past is not tolerated today.

The Colonial Secretary, Oliver Lyttelton also met with Nehru on this occasion[36] when the discussion was less philosophical. Nehru was interested to hear of progress in Malaya and of the 'Operations Service' designed to increase the confidence of the public in the police. In regard to Kenya, Nehru emphasized that you could achieve little by force but had to win the confidence of the people. Lyttleton mentioned that this was the objective of the Kikuyu Home Guard. Nehru again emphasized the importance of the land issue.

Another instance of consultation with India occurred over the preparation of the paper titled 'Africa – The Next Ten Years' in 1959. Staff of the British High Commission in Delhi held a series of meetings to discuss the draft of the paper with Indian officials of the ministry of external affairs, specifically Y. K. Puri the joint secretary of the ministry and the deputy secretary responsible for African affairs. They also met with the finance minister, Morarji Desai, and with Krishna Menon, who was well known for his left wing and anti-colonial views. The exchanges are recorded in a letter of 8 December 1959 from the High Commission to the Commonwealth Relations Office.[37] They emphasized:

- The bitterness caused all over Africa by the Algerian war and the racial policies of South Africa.

- A change in the temper of Africans in the direction of direct action rather than negotiation.

- The growing xenophobia in many parts of Africa against all people of non-African origin – Asians as well as Europeans – a negative consequence of 'pan-Africanism'. The attempt at multiracial cooperation in the Federation and East Africa could well become a casualty of this phenomenon. They wondered if it would not be better for Southern Rhodesia to leave the federation and join South Africa.

- Nehru had very much welcomed Prime Minister Macmillan's assurance that the British government would not permit the federation to achieve Dominion status unless the position of the Africans was adequately guarded.

- The malign consequences for Britain of its voting with Portugal and France against resolutions on apartheid in South Africa.

- Their concern at the boycott of Asians businesses in Uganda, especially. (Four years later all Asians were expelled from Uganda.)

The Asian-African conference at Bandung

This conference occurred in Bandung, Indonesia, in 1955 under the leadership of Nehru of India, Sukarno of Indonesia and Nasser of Egypt. Jugoslavia, though at that time a communist country under Tito, associated itself with the conference as a means of putting distance between itself and Soviet Russia. Non-alignment in the Cold War became the leitmotif of the conference.

Conference of Independent African States

This conference took place in Accra on 22 April 1958 at the invitation of the newly independent Ghana government and was the first gathering of its kind limited to independent African states – the Organization of African states still lay in the future. This summary draws on the report of the British high commissioner in Ghana to the Commonwealth relations office and Liberia was represented by its president; Ethiopia by the emperor's youngest son; the other states (Libya, Morocco, Sudan, Tunisia and the United Arab Republic) by their foreign ministers or lesser dignitaries. The discussions were held in camera and the public record is contained in a declaration. This reaffirmed the States' loyalty to the Charter of the United Nations, the Universal Declaration of Human Rights and the Declaration of the Asian-African Conference held at Bandung. It proclaimed solidarity with the dependent people of Africa and pledged itself to forging a distinctive African Personality in the international sphere; sought to persuade the Great Powers to discontinue the production and testing of nuclear and thermo-nuclear weapons; to encourage trade and economic planning among the states; encouraged exchange visits and training and so on; and charged the Permanent Representatives of the States at the United Nations to be the permanent machinery for coordinating all matters of common concern.

The Communist States

As a principal member of the Western Alliance established to resist the influences of the Soviet Union and communist China, Britain inevitably was concerned to see that the communist states made as little impact in its colonies and former colonies as possible. As indicated earlier the general view was that communism would make little progress in Africa so long as there was discernible and, from the African point of view, acceptable progress towards self-government. In Africa there were few large urban centres which was where in the past communism had made most progress, and the rather arid arguments for proletarian rule had little appeal to most Africans. However, Britain took measures to assist the colonial police and security personnel to identify threats from communist sources and these are described in some detail in Professor Andrews' official history of the British Security Service,[38] which describes the role of the security liaison officers appointed by MI5 to India and numerous colonial territories, many of whom were retained until the 1970s, twenty or more years after independence. Undoubtedly, these officers played a significant role in countering communist influence and infiltration in these countries.

Chapter 7

Press coverage of colonial questions

This chapter contains a review of the contemporary coverage of colonial matters by the British newspapers. It is not the same as a survey of public opinion, but its coverage is varied enough to be a surrogate for one. It provides a vivid and evolving picture of the diverse issues and policy dilemmas facing those in authority during a period of rapid change in the colonial territories themselves and at home. It provides a picture of the domestic context in Britain within which policy was being formulated and the reception given by the press to events in the colonies. In many cases, the writers of the articles are known; in other cases of articles by unidentified correspondents, or editorials, and the anonymous articles in *The Economist*, the writers are not publicly known.

The Times especially maintained a steady coverage of colonial matters from the 1930s onwards and from the end of the Second World War the coverage in the other papers increased. I have not felt it necessary to go back beyond the mid-1930s because many of the most important pre-Second World War events in colonial administration occurred after 1936 – the Royal Commission on the West Indies (1938), the De La Warr Commission on Education in Eastern Africa (1936/7), The Bledisloe Commission on Central Africa (1938), the publication of Lord Hailey's African Survey (1938), the Commission on Higher Education in Malaya (1937) among them. I will, however, mention two significant events for the economies of the colonies which occurred before 1936, which were well covered in the press. The first was the creation in 1929 by the British government of the Colonial Development Fund, the purpose of which was to provide finance for exports of capital goods from Britain to colonies which required them. The second event was the adoption in 1932 by the British government and other members of the Commonwealth of Imperial Preference. This measure was viewed by those who favoured it as being a means for knitting together the economies of the entire Commonwealth through the reduction of tariffs on trade within the Commonwealth. Though this measure was therefore protectionist in nature, so far as the colonies were concerned it improved the marketability of many of their products and provided a measure of support to their economies at the time of the Great Depression.

In general the quality of reporting and writing in the press on colonial questions was high which is a tribute to the importance given by the press and the public to colonial affairs. There were some outstanding analysts and journalists writing on colonial affairs. In such a large archive, it was necessary to be selective. I have sought to show the way in which the press covered the evolution of policy, the trend of events and differences of opinion and perspective on colonial questions; and to indicate the importance given to the different issues, as well as the changing emphasis over time. There were numerous actors interested in colonial matters – the inhabitants of the territories, their governments, those who provided technical advice, scholars, politicians, the British government in its various manifestations, UN agencies, newspaper editors, in addition to journalists. The press coverage reflects the reports, comments and opinions of all these actors. The stance of the Beaverbrook Press and the *Daily Mail* was broadly predictable – keen to perpetuate and strengthen imperial ties – and did not change, so I have not felt it necessary to use their reporting.

The period during which decolonization occurred is now more than fifty years ago and the thinking and language used at that time may seem in some respects outdated. However, the arguments made and the rhetoric employed can be seen here on their merits. If readers come to these excerpts with an open mind, they will I think conclude that the press brought a varied, serious and informative approach to their reporting and editorials, entirely appropriate to the topic and their role. There have been different interpretations put subsequently on some of the events described or on the coverage by reporters and editors. However, these are necessarily ex post facto and not necessarily more accurate, well informed or objective.

After trying alternatives, I concluded that the best way to handle the reporting was chronologically rather than thematically, principally because some matters came up again and again over the period, and also because a chronological treatment gives a reader some feel for the evolution over time of policy and practice.

The 1930s

Many of the matters which became most difficult to handle in the approach to the future independence of the colonies were already identifiable in the 1930s. On 9 January 1936, there was a report in *The Times* by a correspondent attending the League of Nations mandates commission. The focus of the meetings was on so-called amalgamations of low-level tribal treasury units taking place in the British mandated territories to create more capable, larger units, with larger responsibilities and greater taxing powers. This report reflects an interest in upgrading the capacity of local government. On the same date, there appeared a trenchant letter from Daniel Hall, one-time Chairman of the Kenya Agricultural Commission, drawing attention to the increasing land hunger in Kenya and making the point that it is irresponsible to consider Africa capable of accommodating more European settlers. The East Africa Royal Commission of 1953–5 was to address this issue in detail twenty years later.

In the same edition of January 1936, there appeared an article by *The Times'* Colombo correspondent reviewing, at the end of the first parliament of the new constitution, the impact of the constitutional changes introduced in Ceylon (Sri Lanka) in 1930. These reforms provided for elections on a universal, not a communal franchise, which first occurred in June 1931, and which had a 60 per cent turnout, of which 62 per cent of the electors were male and 38 per cent female. The method of appointing ministers was considered to have weaknesses, but overall there had been a major step forward towards self-government. These elections became an exemplar for the first elections held in colonial Africa, which took place in West Africa in the late 1940s, though the franchise was not universal there until the elections held immediately before independence.

In February 1936, *The Times* featured a series of three articles by Margery Perham, who was already one of the best-informed and most perceptive observer writing on colonial Africa. The first of these described how the system of indirect rule introduced by Lord Lugard in Northern Nigeria had spread to most other British African colonies in a pragmatic manner and in their own time, and this approach had subsequently been endorsed by a Joint Committee of both Houses of Parliament in London. The second article pointed out that the way in which indirect rule was thus extended to other territories was very much in the tradition of the evolution of local government, both in Britain itself and the colonies over a period of 300 years, and that further evolution must be expected. The third article addressed the need for 'trusteeship on a broader basis' which could accommodate educated Africans and convince them that the present system leads towards, not away from, their ideal of national self-government. In its editorial on Perham's articles, *The Times* concluded that the essence of the system of indirect rule was the recognition by the British administrator that his function was not to dictate but to teach, and stressed that nothing must be done to cut across this slow, primary task of political development.

Self-government as an objective was no longer controversial.

In May 1936 *The Times* featured articles by a correspondent on the proposal adopted by the Legislative Assembly of Southern Rhodesia (Zimbabwe) for the amalgamation of the two Rhodesias as self-governing colonies. In an editorial, *The Times* pointed out that the differences between Northern and Southern

Rhodesia were greater than the similarities and the maintenance of Northern Rhodesia (Zambia) as a separate protectorate was still desirable. A letter from Frank Melland supported this argument but pointed out that Northern Rhodesia was not receiving adequate attention on the part of the Colonial Office. He wanted the secretary of state for the colonies to give the matter greater priority.

In 1937, *The Times* gave publicity to the address of the Secretary of State for the Colonies, Mr Ormsby-Gore, to the educational associations in Britain and to a debate in the House of Commons on Colonial Education. In August, the paper reported the appointment of a Commission on Higher Education in Malaya. In September the paper gave extensive coverage to the report of the Commission on Education in East Africa (the De La Warr Commission). In September 1938, the paper gave publicity to the appointment of the West Indies Royal Commission focussed on social and economic conditions. The publication in 1938 of Lord Hailey's African Survey was the subject of a first leader in *The Times* on 8 November 1938. In December 1938 the paper reported on a joint meeting of the Royal Empire and the Royal African Societies at which Lord Hailey had, among other things, raised the issue of the suitability of parliamentary forms for the government of the African colonies, a dilemma which was to vex colonial administrators right up until independence. Thus a year before the outbreak of the Second World War, a diverse range of matters was receiving high-level attention, especially the need and prerequisites for the commencement and expansion of higher-level education in the colonies.

The 1940s

In February 1940, as the European war deepened, Malcolm MacDonald, now Colonial Secretary, published his 'Statement of Policy on Colonial Development and Welfare' in the form of a White Paper. This statement was reviewed with acclaim by the editor of *The Times*:

> His simple matter-of-fact language does not conceal the greatness of the underlying conception of the trust exercised by the British people before the conscience of humanity, for the welfare and advancement of the many less advanced races they have undertaken to govern ... the principal of the isolated and self-supporting Colony is to be abandoned and replaced by the institution of a new Colonial Development and Welfare Fund, based on the idea that all the Colonies are integral parts of the body politic of the Empire, sharing the benefit of its economic resources in proportion to their needs, a practical response 'to the duty not only of the guardian to help the ward but also of the comparatively rich to help the comparatively poor'.

The Bill setting up the Colonial Development and Welfare Fund (CD&W Fund), which was to provide up to £5 million per annum (2017 £269 million) initially for development in the colonies, was passed by Parliament in May 1940 just as the British and French armies were retreating before the German Blitzkrieg towards Dunkirk and defeat, and Britain was girding itself up for total war. The act creating the Fund was described in the debate in the House of Lords using Portia's words in The Merchant of Venice as 'a good deed in a naughty world'. The first commitment under the CD&W Fund was to be to the West Indies in response to the findings of the Royal Commission (Cmnd 6174), a report received with intense satisfaction in the West Indian islands'.

As the war progressed, and people started to think about the prospects for the post-war world, the colonial issue began to resurface. *The Times* in November 1942 reported a vigorous defence by Mr Malcolm MacDonald of the British colonial record in a speech to the Economic Club of Detroit. This speech presaged much future debate with the Americans on this subject. It was followed in December 1942 by a robust defence of the British colonial record by Lord Cranborne, participating in a debate in the House of Lords, who said, inter alia, 'while self-government in the Colonies is our ultimate objective, the problem of making free institutions understood and operative in backward and primitive communities was not easy – even some European countries had failed to govern themselves, and preferred to be governed by others'. He enlarged on what had been done to advance education

A report in *The Times* by their East Africa correspondent in July 1943 of an article which appeared in the East African Standard anticipates the post-war debate about the mix of education required and the way to diversify employment opportunities. 'The higher education of eager youths who suffer early and bitter disillusionment because there is no place for them or their attainments amongst the squalor and ignorance of the masses of their own people ... must no longer be the outcome of our educational system.'

As the end of the war approached and the United States faced the question of the future of the Pacific islands they had occupied during the war, the way in which the proposed San Francisco Conference would address the issue of the colonies resurfaced. In its lead article on 31 March 1945, *The Economist* addressed the task facing Colonel Oliver Stanley, the Colonial Secretary, when he visited the United States. Quoting Colonel Stanley it wrote:

Responsibility for the colonies has devolved on this country more often by treaty and agreement than by conquest, and it is a responsibility we cannot share with others. We believe that any such division of responsibility is not only impractical, but wholly against the wishes of the colonial people themselves ... if the international discussions on the colonial question could concentrate on how to improve the mandate principle instead of taking the form of impractical proposals on the one side and flat refusal on the other, some concrete results might be achieved. As it is, it looks as if the colonial problem … which was not a factor in the outbreak of war, might well become a bone of contention at the Peace Conference.

On 14 May 1946, *The Times*' third editorial, commenting on an article on British colonial policy by a correspondent, noted that the system of indirect rule, with its policy of laissez-faire had led to 'some very serious consequences, in particular where the best-educated among the indigenous people were often outside the tribal system – an intelligentsia has grown up which has no part in the local government, often directed by illiterate and animist chieftains' (see report from EA Standard earlier). This emerging divide had been noted by perceptive observers in the 1930s, but was to become a driving force for reform of local government in the colonies, post-war stimulated by Lord Hailey's study in 1940/2. In July 1946, *The Times* reported Lord Hailey, speaking in South Africa, pointing out the need for 'adjustment of political relations between a settled European community and an African population, by which it is out-numbered'; he referred to native communities between whom 'there is no tie or any spirit of nationalism'; and again asked whether the parliamentary system is the best form for self-governing colonies'.

On 10 July 1947, *The Times* gave prominence to an article, by a special correspondent, about the status and future prospects for higher education in the Sudan.

In a fascinating letter to the editor of *The Times* of 17 January 1949, Margary Perham responded to a letter from Elspeth Huxley with a far-sighted comment. She wrote,

It has so happened that the colonial peoples least qualified by their past degree of civilisation and unity to conduct a modern State are likely to have the shortest apprenticeship in that art. We have to find ways of giving their leaders responsibilities that satisfy their need for self-expression and status without ourselves abandoning the tasks … including the scientific management of their imperilled natural resources … which the realities impose upon us.

In a different approach, Sir Harold MacMichael and Sir Armigel Wade, on the basis of long experience of colonial government, argued in letters to the Editor of *The Times* in April 1949 that government in the colonies should be based on local loyalties, which are meaningful to African tribal people, rather than national self-government, which lacks such meaning to them. However, Rita Hinden, Secretary of the Fabian Colonial Bureau, replying on 5 May, wrote 'What surprises me is that these views should still be expressed when practice in some African colonies has already left them years behind … I hope your correspondents will forgive me if I say that their attitude seems at least one generation behind what is being done and said by Africans and Europeans in Nigeria today'.

Also on 17 January 1949 *The Daily Telegraph* carried a report of a speech made by Malcolm MacDonald, then Commissioner-General in South-East Asia, in which he said,

> Britain looked forward to the day when Malaya would take her place beside other self-governing peoples of the British Commonwealth. ... That is a promise; we shall not break it. We shall support with all our hearts any movement seeking to associate Malays, Malayan Chinese and other communities owing their undivided loyalty to Malaya in a brotherhood of all peoples of this country inspired by common patriotism.

The Malayan emergency was then at its height and the speech was obviously intended to encourage Malays in their struggle and provide a clear objective for all the people of the country.

On 16 February 1949, *The Daily Telegraph* carried an editorial titled 'Capricorn Africa'.

> For over twenty years, there has been a movement to join the two Rhodesias, with or without Nyasaland (Malawi). Today, the possibilities of creating a new Dominion in what has been called 'Capricorn Africa' seem the more attractive because of the effort to develop the Continent as a new larder for the world. Moreover, it would be idle to deny that Dr Malan's policy in the Union of South Africa suggests to many minds the desirability of strengthening outside the Union influences more certain to adhere to the Commonwealth. Yet Northern and Southern Rhodesia – the one a Crown Colony, the other self-governing – differ widely from one another and still more definitely from the Protectorate of Nyasaland ... a federal Dominion in which different native policies prevail in the three states is a theoretical possibility, but any agreement that emerges at the Victoria Falls conference will certainly require further study.

The following day the paper reported that 'Delegates from the three countries achieved a large measure of agreement on the proposed federation of their countries ... a committee of technical experts was formed ... their recommendations will be discussed at a second meeting of delegates after which a referendum would be held and a third meeting would then decide how to approach Britain about the proposal.'

In the course of a debate in the House of Lords on Colonial Policy, reported in *The Times* of 14 April 1949, Lord Swinton, a senior Conservative politician and former Colonial Secretary, enunciated the five principles which in his view should govern Colonial Policy: First, we were trustees for all and not for a section or a minority and we must discharge our trust to all our beneficiaries. Second the greatest need of all the people for whom we are trustees was improved health and well-being and the true opportunity of the individual to enjoy those things. Third, economic and social progress depended upon cooperation between the European and native populations. Fourth, the ultimate goal was self-government, but the path towards it would be infinitely varied. Fifth, the prerequisite of self-government was a capacity to govern. Without security and law and order, a country could have so-called independence, but its citizens might have no real freedom. (Looking back over the last fifty years, the sagacity of this fifth remark is striking.)

The Times published another fine article by Margery Perham on 20 June 1949 about Parliamentary government in the Sudan. She felt it had made a good start under the new constitution, which provided for participation of both northerners and southerners, who had taken the opportunity to address their particular local needs and done so with moderation and dignity. She noted that one of the southerners had deprecated a demand for speedy self-government and pointed out the danger of an unready people passing under a minority government which – quoting Winston Churchill – 'would own the people instead of being owned by them'. She cautioned the government that this early parliamentary accomplishment is limited and precarious for the constitution was enacted in the face of its repudiation by Egypt, a co-dominus. As she said, the few senior British officials in Sudan found themselves 'squeezed between a hostile Egyptian Government and a British Foreign Office neither constituted nor qualified to direct the internal administration of the Sudan, and … therefore their chief loyalty was to the Sudanese, whose interests they must interpret as best they can'.

In the same month, *The Times'* second leader on 29 June reviewed the Colonial Secretary's Annual Report for 1949. When discussing the sections on political and constitutional development in the colonies, the paper cautions,

> The sections of the report on political and constitutional development give a picture of backward people being hurried forward at all stages to catch up with the more advanced. The report does not bring out the differences in quality between the various organs of government set up, and it is necessary to bear in mind that many of the local councils and boards brought into being have principally an educative value at this stage and are still of little importance administratively.

In December 1949 *The Times* carried several letters which reviewed the outcome of a meeting of the General Assembly of the United Nations, then still meeting at Lake Success. Concern was expressed, not least by Sir Hartley Shawcross, the British Attorney General, at the wish on the part of small and some large countries to 'meddle' in colonial matters. 'A great many small Powers were lamentably uninformed about the realities of the colonial situation and were irresponsible in their decisions. That is dangerous in its implications for the future of the United Nations'.

The 1950s

On 5 March 1950, *The Observer* featured an article by a Special Correspondent on the process by which the draft new constitution for Nigeria had been fashioned by the Nigerian Legislative Council (LegCo) under Governor Macpherson, by means of an elaborate consultation with many interest groups in the country. This consultation culminated in the decision in 1951 to adopt a constitution which provided for a Federal Council, with ministers, and three regional legislative and executive councils, in addition to district councils. Though ambitious, this constitution proved a success in the period prior to independence in 1960 and helped to enshrine the notion of federation, as a constitutional approach for the long term.

The following month *The Manchester Guardian* carried an editorial titled 'Dr Azikiwe' on the suppression of the 'Zikist' movement in Nigeria as a result of political violence in Eastern Nigeria. Commenting on the new constitution on 27 July, *The Daily Telegraph* said that though it would not satisfy the extreme nationalists, it might 'cut the ground from under their feet'.

On 21 May 1950 *The Observer* reported on discussions being held with the Colonial Office regarding the proposal of Sir Godfrey Huggins to create a Central African Dominion of the two Rhodesias, a proposal referred to previously on several occasions by *The Times*. The discussions foundered on the Colonial Office insistence that Africans had to be brought into more active involvement in the legislative and administrative functions of responsible government before increasing the political power of the European settlers who then dominated the Government of Southern Rhodesia in particular.

In its Comment column on 4 June 1950, *The Observer* wrote, 'By all modern standards the 80,000,000 people in the British colonies are better off today than they have ever been. They live longer and suffer from less disease; illiteracy is lower, national income is higher, and the opportunities for exercising personal and political appraisal of the nature of these problems should find a place in any serious report on the colonies'. On 10 June, *The Economist*, also commenting on the 1950 Annual Report of the Colonial Office, wrote,

The constitutional changes in the colonies are the most spectacular developments in the period under review. But the material progress is also remarkable. For the first time, the annual report is able to record that the development and welfare projects are no longer hampered by (wartime) shortages of materials and equipment – though more technicians are still badly needed. For the first time development and welfare is approaching the limits imposed by finance ... it may be that the improvement in the well-being of the colonial peoples, on whom the development and welfare policy depends, is at last beginning to make a mark; is helping to set the pace.

The Manchester Guardian of 13 July 1950 carried an extensive report of a debate in the House of Commons, opened by Mr James Griffiths, the new Labour Colonial Secretary, on the Colonial Office Annual Report referred to earlier. Matters touched on in the report included infrastructure investments in Africa, the striking progress made in combating such diseases as malaria and tuberculosis (malaria had been virtually eliminated in Cyprus and British Guiana), the impact of health improvements on the rate of increase of the population, the idea of a federation of the West Indies, progress in the fight against the communist insurgency in Malaya, the poor quality of the colonial press, the welfare of colonial students in Britain, the contribution of colonial exports to ameliorating the 'dollar gap' and the progress achieved by the Desert Locust Service in combating the devastation caused by locusts. In the same edition, the paper elaborated on remarks made by Anthony Eden, then Deputy Leader of the Opposition, in the debate on the quality of the colonial press – he offered warnings against the danger of yielding too much influence to 'clamant minorities' in the march towards self-government and deprecated 'the most poisonous misrepresentation of the British government and the Korean conflict in the press of West Africa'; he also offered the support of the Opposition for the Supplementary Estimates submitted for assistance to Malaya. The 29 July edition of the paper provided another example of mendacious reporting in the Nigerian press where totally unfounded attacks were being made on the University College of Ibadan, created with CD&W financing and then just in its second year. The paper's correspondent sought to justify this attack as 'natural and healthy'.

On 27 July 1950, *The Manchester Guardian* reported on the approval by the Colonial Secretary of the proposed new constitution of Nigeria. The paper commented that this greatly increased regional autonomy and gave Nigerians a full share in shaping government policy and the future of the country through the creation of a Central Council of Ministers and the Regional Legislative and Executive Councils.

Both *The Economist* and *The Observer* addressed the implications of the decision of the British government to amend its policy vis-à-vis the United Nations in respect of colonial affairs. Hitherto the government had stonewalled all attempts on the part of the UN and the Trusteeship Division to concern itself with British colonies, on the grounds that they were an internal matter. *The Economist* devoted a two-page article to the issue. After five years of the stone-walling approach, and the accompanying criticism, often by governments which would never welcome a similar focus on their own internal affairs, the

British government had changed tack and had decided to provide full information. As Nora Beloff commented in *The Observer* of 3 September 1950 'The British delegates have assembled all the facts available, met all criticism with analytical answers, and piled up irrefutable evidence that Britain is spending more money and using more skill, experience, and resources in developing the backward areas of the world than any other nation. ... British spokesmen have not only justified themselves but indicated a willingness to place their superior knowledge and experience at the disposal of their critics'.

On 25 September 1950, *The Manchester Guardian* reported on a speech by the Colonial Secretary, speaking at a meeting of the Labour Party and the Fabian colonial Bureau in London, in which he said, 'We have been criticised in some quarters for going too fast in West Africa ... it has been urged that more political experience is required and that economic development is not far enough advanced. ... I do not share these fears. I believe that political maturity is best achieved by giving people real responsibility.' The speed of constitutional and political change was to remain a critical issue until the independence of the colonies – and in retrospect remains at the centre of the debate on the subject by historians.

In October 1950, *The Daily Telegraph* published an article by two members of the British Parliament, one Labour, the second Conservative, titled 'Red Shadow over the Gold Coast' in which they articulated their fears, following a three-week visit, regarding the elections scheduled for early 1951 and their distaste for Dr Nkrumah's 'crude nationalism and anti-white economics'. There followed several letters over the following days, some urging greater understanding and others emphasizing 'the domination of African political opinion by a small group of self-seeking extremists, the scurrilous outpourings of a seditious and libellous press, incitement to riot and civil dis-obedience.'

The 5 November 1950 edition of *The Observer* featured an article by Patrick O'Donovan entitled 'Prosperity Comes to Swaziland'. This highlighted the large financial assistance provided by Britain in the agriculture and rural services of the country. The Commonwealth Development Corporation (CDC) was planting 74,000 acres with timber, developing a 50,000 acre irrigation scheme, and supporting a Native Land Settlement Scheme under which families were being settled on good land with seven acres each for plough land, grazing for fifteen head of cattle and a smaller area of irrigated land suitable for vegetable production. 'Yet political change is neither taking place nor sought in view of the fact that the country is bounded on three sides by the Union of South Africa.'

The election held in the Gold Coast in February 1951 under the Coussey constitution, which brought the Convention People's Party (CPP) to power, was well covered by all the major British papers. *The Manchester Guardian*'s correspondent described the result as a victory for nationalism. The scale of the

CPP's success was nevertheless intimidating for the opposition parties, which returned few members.

In April–May 1951, *The Observer* carried a three-part series of articles by Patrick O'Donovan titled 'The African Drama'. With an air of resignation he wrote, 'There is no sign that the inhabitants of Africa – white or black – have profited by their late arrival in the history books; that they have learnt anything from the failures and tragedies of other peoples in a similar position. They are going to suffer as other nations suffer; to a large extent the cause of their suffering will be of their own creation. Yet it is necessary to get one's despair into proportion. There is every reason to believe that they, like other nations, will survive, but it is not easy to foresee what shape their survival will take.'

The Economist featured a long article in its edition of 21 April 1951 titled 'Countering Dr Malan'. Reporting speeches made by Dr Malan, the Prime Minister of the Union of South Africa, and others by politicians in the Rhodesias, the paper wrote, 'In the Union and out of it, Dr Malan is exploiting a genuine dilemma. The whites fear black numbers. In South Africa they are outnumbered four to one, and elsewhere by ten to one. Policy must take cognisance of this terrible disparity, which is creating a white nationalism opposed by a new black nationalism. The Europeans outside of the Union do not want to repress anyone, but they do not want to be repressed either. In South Africa the United Party has temporarily been defeated by the Nationalists, but in Southern Rhodesia, Sir Godfrey Huggins is trying to work out a policy which will mean neither two separate racial communities (apartheid) nor one community sitting on top of the other (basskap). The ultimate aim he says is partnership. The trend is clearly towards putting everything on a racial basis'. It is a trend which Dr Malan supports. But this is the very trend that the Europeans in their own interests should oppose, if only because of their small numbers. This can best be done by reverting to the policy attributed to Cecil Rhodes of 'equal rights for all civilised men irrespective of colour'.

On 16 June 1951, *The Economist* reviewed the Colonial Office Annual Report for 1950/1 (Cmnd 8243). It wrote: The Secretary of State is still required, more or

less, to give his attention to all matters in all colonies simultaneously ... leaving the reader wondering that the system works no worse than it does. Indeed it is working today with considerable success. This is due largely to a fact, which no one is ready to believe – that the Colonies are no longer 'governed' by the Colonial Office at all. They are supervised in Whitehall and certain key decision are taken there, but their day-to-day administration is in the hands of the Colonial Governments and Legislatures on the spot. Increasingly, year-by-year, more powers are devolved from London; and within the Colonies powers are shifting, with unbelievable speed, away from the officials and on to the shoulders of the colonial peoples themselves. The essence of colonial policy in these last years has been the transfer of power. ... It must not be thought from this satisfying record of progress that all is now peace and contentment in the Colonies. There are many sore spots and threatening points of danger. The Secretary of State remains a harassed and all-too-busy man. ... But he and his departments have this merit; they do appear to know where they are going.

In the previous month *The Daily Telegraph* published a review by Martin Moore of Lord Hailey's recently published 'Native Administration in the British African Territories' (HMSO, in four volumes), which was as vast a marshalling of facts as his previous African Survey. This became an essential input into the reconsideration of the mechanisms of Indirect Rule and the creation of local government structures capable of supporting and facilitating change at the national level, in particular the creation of central government structures required for the rapidly evolving constitutional and political situation.

On 3 November 1951, *The Daily Telegraph* published a report by Douglas Brown on the uncertainty created in Sudan by Egypt's unilateral repudiation of the 1936 Anglo-Egyptian treaty and the two condominium agreements of 1899; and the lack of response by the British government. The Editor in a leader wrote 'these tendencies can only be arrested by a conviction that the British intend to carry out their declared intentions for the country ... we are not there to exploit the Sudan but to prevent it from being exploited. If the pretence that the condominium still exists is a hindrance to us in our task of preparing Sudan for eventual self-government, then it should be dropped'. Finally, on 16 November the paper reported the statement made by Eden, now the Foreign Secretary, who reaffirmed the British government's pledge to bring Sudan to self-government and regarded the Governor General as being fully responsible for continuing the administration of the Sudan. Having attained self-government, it would be for the Sudanese to choose their own future status and relationship with Britain and with Egypt.

On 8 November *The Daily Telegraph* reported on a press conference held by the new colonial secretary, Oliver Lyttelton. He said 'The Conservative Government had no intention of going back on constitutional changes already made in the colonies, or of retarding progress. ... We are very progressive people in the matter of constitutional changes ... we will not be committed with regard to what is pending or under consideration, but what is already done or promised will be carried through'. He mentioned work going on to prepare for increased production of raw materials in short supply (see the following text) and referring to an upcoming visit to Malaya said 'his main object was to be on the spot at a time when policy was in a fluid and formative state because of the recent and pending changes in higher positions. The need was to achieve a balance between the military and police forces on the one hand and political control on the other.'

On 15 November 1951, *The Manchester Guardian* carried a short report of the first speech by Lyttelton in Parliament, in which he said that 'certain broad lines of policy were accepted by all sections of the House (of Commons) as being above party politics … in particular that all aimed at helping the colonial territories to attain self-government within the British Commonwealth and to that end sought as rapidly as possible to build up in each territory the institutions which the circumstances required … the second was that they were all anxious to pursue the economic and social development of the colonial territories so that it could keep pace with political developments'.

On 21 November 1951, *The Daily Telegraph* featured a report of the Cabinet's approval of a scheme to stimulate the production of various commodities by colonial territories, specifically cotton in Uganda and the West Indies, copper in Northern Rhodesia, manganese in the Gold Coast, sugar in the West Indies, Fiji and Mauritius, timber in British Honduras, British Guiana and West Africa, petroleum in Trinidad and Brunei, and vegetable oils in Africa. Bottlenecks to increased production had been identified and a dollar credit to finance equipment purchases was under consideration.

The following day *The Daily Telegraph* featured a leader on the situation in Malaya in the context of mounting concern at the lack of progress in defeating the communist terrorists, despite the commitment of considerable armed forces. 'In the light of past experience in dealing with terrorist movements, the two essentials would seem to be a centralised authority and an efficient system of intelligence, both of which have been notably lacking in Malaya. The military authorities have been hampered by the civil administration and a frustrating attempt has been made to combine constitutional and social experimentation with the repression of terrorism.'

On 29th November 1951, following the introduction of the new constitution in Nigeria, *The Times*' Lagos Correspondent reviewed the progress achieved towards elections to LegCo, especially in the northern region which was to fill half the seats in the Federal Council. The correspondent pointed to the slow start made in modern education in the north, but also argued that 'they (the northerners) bring to the study of political problems a steadier mind and some would say a keener insight, than are always evident in the south'. He also expressed the latent fear (among southerners) 'that as the north progresses, the south may be deprived of its traditional leadership in the struggle for freedom'.

On 31 May 1952, the visit of Mr Lyttleton, the Colonial Secretary, to Nigeria and the Gold Coast was addressed by *The Manchester Guardian*, which reported that he had spent a week in Lagos studying the working of Nigeria's new constitution. As indicated earlier, this provided for three regional Legislative and Executive Councils and a Federal Council of Ministers, presided over by the governor. This constitution was more complex than any promulgated in a dependent territory since that adopted in India in the 1920s. Some of the ministers complained that as yet they were not much involved in government business, which was handled mainly by officials, but the council was still new and everyone was still learning to make the constitution work as intended.

On 6 September 1952, a leader in *The Manchester Guardian* drew attention to the difficulty teachers were having returning to work in Britain after a period of teaching in Africa. The Colonial and Education Secretaries were pressed to work out a way to ensure this happens smoothly, so that more teachers could, with confidence, devote a part of their teaching career to meeting the acute needs of the colonies for experienced teachers.

The Manchester Guardian on 23 October 1952 carried a report of a statement made by the new Minister of State for Colonial Affairs, Henry Hopkinson, in which he said:

> The growth of democratic institutions in the Colonies in modern times had generally followed a common pattern, developing from a central legislative body to a ministerial system whereby elected members were placed in charge of departments of Government and were answerable for their policies to the Assembly. ... The principle here is that power must be matched with responsibility ... this is perhaps the most delicate stage and is a prelude to complete self-government. At this stage the greatest forbearance must be observed on both sides, and indeed by the world at large, if the critical approach to the final transfer of power is to be smooth ... unless a Government was capable of preserving a sufficient degree of order and of economic and social stability, the premature achievement of self-government could only be damaging to the vast majority of its citizens.

In its Comment of 30 November 1952, *The Observer* compared and contrasted the drastic emergency regulations applied in Kenya to control and end the Mau Mau rebellion with the actions taken by the South African government to control the activities of the Passive Resistance campaign, which the South African authorities argued was a similar case. *The Observer* disagreed and considered the two cases to be different – while Mau Mau was predominantly committed to violence and was supported by a minority of Africans in one tribe, the Passive Resistance campaign in South Africa was non-violent in character and had the moral support, at least, of the mass of non-Europeans in the Union.

The Manchester Guardian of 1 January 1953 published a letter from a former member of the Colonial Service who said, inter alia,

> young, new Colonial administrators used to receive a letter from the Secretary of State telling them that they were expected to regard the territory they were assigned to as their home and that they must study closely the people among whom they would work; their manners and customs, views and

language ... most District Officers were then as conversant with the ideas and ideals of their African protégés as they were with those of their own country – and that can only be acquired by long residence in the regions concerned. ... They were not misled, as are many benevolent Europeans today, by the pseudo-democratic self-seeking propaganda of de-nationalised African political adventurers ... they stood for the whole people to whom they were attached and among whom they lived and worked.

[Undoubtedly, the essence of this critique was quite widely shared by members of the Colonial Service as political ambition and self-promotion by new politicians, under the cloak of nationalism, began to take control of affairs in the colonies.]

In its edition of 7 February 1953, *The Manchester Guardian* published a letter from Ted Leather, a Member of the House of Commons, arguing that not enough attention was being given to the benefits the Central African Federation could bring to Nyasaland in particular. He pointed out that expenditure on education in Nyasaland at £180,000 was less than half the expenditure in Northern Rhodesia, which had a smaller population. He argued that Nyasaland with 'its two-crop economy' would find it virtually impossible with its own resources to make any great improvement in the standard of living of its people. He concluded: 'Surely there is a moral obligation on the two Rhodesias with their stronger financial position to assist their less fortunate neighbours, both in their neighbours' interests and their own.'

The Economist of 21 February 1953 contained an extensive analysis by a correspondent of the twists and turns within the National Council of Nigeria and the Cameroons, which, despite its name, was the leading political party in Eastern Nigeria sometimes led by the talented, but mercurial, leader, Dr Azikiwe. It cautioned the Governor General and the Government of Nigeria not to allow itself to be dragged into these political manoeuvres, but to stand ready to take the initiative if they seemed to be leading up a blind alley.

The Times of 11 March 1953 gave extensive coverage to the two reports on African education (East and Central Africa, and West Africa, respectively) prepared by two study groups sponsored jointly by the Colonial Office and the Nuffield Foundation, funding being provided by the foundation; and to the subsequent conference held at Cambridge in 1952 attended by the two study groups and by African and British education specialists. The study arrangements were informal and not restricted to officials; everyone who had views on the subject could meet the study teams. Though the East/Central African group made numerous recommendations, the West Africa group did not, though it put forward numerous suggestions. Despite this difference in format, both groups came back convinced that much African primary and secondary education was alien to the life and traditions of the people and needed reform; they both emphasized the need for better teacher training.

In April 1953 *The Times* reported on the resignation of some members of the Nigerian Council of Ministers and on the statement of Mr Lyttelton, the Colonial Secretary, encouraging the continued search for a constitution which can receive the support of all Nigerians, within the federal principle. The resignations occurred over the issue whether any of the three regions of Nigeria should be able to attain self-government in advance of the others. The subsequent conference in London produced a somewhat revised constitution which provided for self-government in 1956 of those regions which wished it, within the Federation, but not without some stormy moments reported in *The Times* of 20 August 1953.

The Economist, trying in its 2 May edition to describe and make sense of the complex political manoeuvres going on outside the Nigerian conference room, summarized these through the eyes of university students: 'University opinion on the crisis is passionate but amorphous. Intelligent enough to discount the cruder forms of nationalist propaganda, undergraduates are nevertheless profoundly in sympathy with its purpose. "I don't know how I am not free", said one of them, "and yet I desire freedom with all my heart". Nigeria's next generation of politicians will not become anti-British unless Britain at the last minute withholds the consummation of all its previous colonial policy – independence'.

The Times of 5–6 May 1953 contained an important two-part article titled Africa Emergent, written after an extensive tour of Africa by the paper's Colonial Correspondent. He wrote that the situation in Africa has no precedent and there is a massive population among which the forces of nationalism are at work in all their classic and recognisable outlines. They are working fast among peoples who are still either primitive or so recently emerged from a primitive state that generally speaking they would today be unable to run an administration without European help and survive ... this irresistible force of African nationalism is beginning to beat about the immovable object of European settlement ... the British government pursues the progressive introduction of the somewhat ill-defined policy known as partnership ... the government however labours under a handicap in that it has already given away much of its power in the effort to train the peoples of Africa up to self-government by the progressive introduction of transitional constitutions ... employment of the powers reserved to the Governor under these constitutions is now almost unthinkable.

The correspondent noticed the rising role of the Asian communities in Africa and indicated that the Asians feared that their situation was closely tied to that of the Europeans in Africa.

African nationalism tended to oppose the chiefs, but this is changing ... imperilling the system of indirect rule which has depended on the close cooperation of the district officer with the chief ... one reason for the weakening of the colonial administration in so many places is ... the overloading of its officers ... indeed in many places the colonial police are in more direct contact with the African than is the district administration ... it would be wrong however to suppose that African nationalism is wholly anti-European. Among ambitious and political Africans this may be so. ... But among both educated and rural Africans there is a general demand for the European as arbiter; many are afraid of what Africans would do to each other. The deciding factors in the future will be whether African politicians quickly learn what is needed in the true interests of their countries; whether the European settlers can realise that it is to a large extent their reluctance to recognise realities which makes the extreme movements successful; and the final deciding factor is the extent to which administrators and technicians from Britain can establish a new relationship with semi-emancipated peoples and continue to work with them for the very long period required before they can effectively run their own countries.

(This article articulates many of the dilemmas facing both colonial administrators and the rising politicians in the colonies.)

On 17 May 1953, *The Observer* carried a report by Colin Legum on the policy changes being made in the focus and remit of the Colonial Development Corporation (CDC) and the Colonial Development and Welfare Fund (CD&W Fund), respectively the two major sources of financial assistance from the British government to British colonies. CDC was now to be required to meet normal commercial lending criteria, which was a departure from its original remit, which was to bridge the gap between projects funded by the colonial government and projects financed by commercial enterprises. CD&W was a source of official financing and was to satisfy economic and social criteria. It was considered that close collaboration between the two agencies in the field would serve to bridge the potential gap in the funding of projects.

The creation of the Central African University to which students of all races were to be admitted, recommended by Sir Alexander Carr-Saunders, was strongly supported by an editorial in *The Times* of 21 May 1953. The editor argued that 'the sphere of higher education is particularly suitable for making a beginning in partnership because it is here that the cultural gap, which is so grave a handicap to social relations, is at its narrowest'. The editor argued that there is nothing new or startling in the acceptance of academic achievement as being the criterion for admission, but saw the significance of this proposal as being that while in all probability the number of Africans and Europeans would be about the same initially, in the long term, the proportion of Africans would rise.

On 11 June 1953, *The Manchester Guardian* reviewed the report of the conference on West Indian Federation held in London in April. All the territories involved were represented, except British Honduras and British Guiana which are more sceptical of the proposal and which were represented by observers only. This conference was the third held on the subject, following detailed proposals for the federation prepared by the 'Standing Closer Association Committee'. The attraction of federation was that by creating a larger unit it offered a road to the achievement of dominion status; the governing consideration was the need to reconcile the interests of the three more influential territories – Barbados, Jamaica and Trinidad – which were concerned that they would have to subsidize the smaller islands. Trinidad was concerned that it would be flooded with immigrants seeking work in the oil fields. Jamaica wanted the capital to be situated on one of the smaller islands – Granada was proposed – and there were debates about the distribution of revenues between the individual territories and the federation. If the plan were to be approved by the territories, the British government was prepared to give effect to it legally and offered financial assistance for ten years. No final decisions were made at the conference.

On 25 July 1953 *The Observer* carried a report from its Colonial Correspondent, Colin Legum, which described the reaction in Uganda to the hint made by the colonial secretary Oliver Lyttelton, during a speech in London, that he was sympathetic to the idea of creating a federation on the Central African model in Eastern Africa. Reaction in Uganda had been swift and unequivocal; Africans, Asians and the small European settler community condemned the idea unanimously. Mass meetings were planned to object and demand a statement from the governor. The proposal was even floated of Uganda leaving the East African High Commission (which would have been reckless for the land-locked country).

The outcome of Nigerian constitutional negotiations was the subject of an important article in *The Times* on 20 August 1953. Significant features were the decision to make Lagos a federal territory, a declaration of policy that in 1956 the British government would grant to those of the three regions which desired it full self-government in respect of all matters lying within the competence of the regional governments. This latter would come with the proviso that the regional governments would not act in such a way as to frustrate the proper exercise of its responsibilities by the federal government. The principal party in the Western Region, the Action Group, withdrew from the conference over the question of whether the four federal ministers nominated by the Western Region, who had resigned, would be reinstated. The significance of this question turned on whether such ministers should continue to be nominated by the regional government, acting as an electoral college, or whether they should be appointed by the chief minister following direct elections.

On 25 August 1953, *The Manchester Guardian* reported the text of the surrender terms offered to Mau Mau by the Governor of Kenya:

We will not negotiate with any gang leader. We offer no general amnesty and in fact military operations will be intensified. The treatment of Mau Mau leaders now in detention will in no way be altered by the offer, which applies only to those who on their own initiative voluntarily surrender. It does not apply to those captured in action or those who surrender on the point of capture. Those who surrender are offered their life, not their liberty.

Each case will be examined and it is probable that the great majority will be detained. The offer does not apply to men against whom there is a prima-facie case of murder. Such a case would be brought against a man who voluntarily surrendered. But other capital charges, such as carrying firearms or consorting with Mau Mau gangs, would not be brought.

The paper commented that it was probable, now that the surrender terms were public knowledge, that the majority of the Kenya public would support them. It was also considered most unlikely that the Kenya government would offer any terms which might be construed as being inducements to the Kikuyu to cooperate to defeat the Mau Mau. The policy of the government was to press on with the far-reaching programme of economic development and social betterment in spite of the emergency, and which was begun before the emergency. The paper went on 'The real significance of the surrender offer is this ... now those not stained with murder or other atrocity have the assurance of life and the hope of eventual liberty'.

On 31 August 1953, *The Times* in an editorial welcomed the decision of Makerere University to institute its own medical qualification to take the place of the London M.B. which, it argued, was not entirely suited to African conditions and which would tend to reduce the numbers of those qualified to practice in East Africa. Registration for medical practice would now follow a seven-year course at Makerere and two years as an intern at an approved hospital.

On 21 November a special correspondent of *The Times* wrote on the situation in Uganda, in particular the total rejection of the notion of federation with other countries and the place of the Baganda tribe within the country. The article also noted that the Indian population was still increasing and the place of the Asians within the Uganda body politic had yet to be resolved.

With the approach of several colonies towards self-government, the issue arose as to whether at that stage such countries should become members of the British Commonwealth. The expectation had been that that bridge would be crossed at independence, not self-government. Writing in *The Observer* Colin Legum pointed out that the decision as to whether a country would become a member did not lie with the British government alone, but with all its members. It was not at all clear whether South Africa would say yes or whether, in the case of the Gold Coast, for example, Dr Malan would force a choice on the members – South Africa or Ghana. (In due course South Africa was expelled from the Commonwealth, but that decision still lay in the future.)

On the 6–9 October 1953, *The Daily Telegraph* gave prominence to the naval and military operations undertaken to forestall an insurrection in British Guiana (Guyana) led by communist sympathizers. In its first leader on 10 October, the Editor stressed that though the government of the People's Progressive Party, led by Dr Jagan, had been elected into office, following carefully prepared elections, it was in the process of subverting the constitution and bringing about a communist-controlled government. The government itself had sponsored strikes which had the inevitable effect of undermining confidence both within and without the territory. The governor, Sir Alfred Savage, revealed in a broadcast speech that some ministers had informed him privately that they were being intimidated to go along with policies with which they disagreed, though they had not felt able to say so in public.

On 23 October 1953, *The Manchester Guardian* provided an extensive report of the debate initiated in the House of Commons by Mr Lyttelton, on his decision to suspend the constitution of British Guiana and send British troops to take control of the country. The justification was to prevent the subversion of the local policies by communist politicians. In this act he had received the support of Mr Bustamente, the chief minister in Trinidad and Mr Manley, leader of the PMP in Jamaica.

On the 17 October, *The Economist* also addressed the issue under the heading 'colonies on Parole'. 'The general outline of the story is tolerably clear. The Guianese ministers were certainly subject to Communist influence and there is some evidence to show that they were using their position as ministers to gain control over the trade union movement and to exercise political influence over the police and the Civil Service. The Governor became convinced they were aiming at a proletarian dictatorship and that incidentally they were ruining the economy; he recommended that the constitution be suspended, and his advice was followed. … What are the implications of this action? … The question is empirical and the answer must depend on the circumstances … the suspension of the Guianese constitution does not mean that similar action elsewhere would be possible or effective … or if it could be done at all if the constitution has been in place for some years … especially if there is a democratically elected government in place.'

On 2 December 1953, *The Manchester Guardian* wondered about the causes of the 'colonial discontents' and concluded that each has its local explanations, which are not to be found in any general policy position of the British government, whichever party is in power, though some conservatives argued that Labour's forward policy on colonial matters in the period 1945–51 contributed to the current discontents. However, the paper looked carefully into the case of the deposition and banishment of Kabaka Mutesa of the Baganda by the Governor of Uganda and concluded:

"It looks as if the Kabaka had created a quite needless difficulty, and it is hard to see to what end his policy would have led. Buganda is only one of the four provinces of the Protectorate and the Baganda only one of many tribes, though the largest. The Uganda National Congress did not share his policy. His refusal to nominate any representatives to the new Legislative Council would seriously hamper and possibly cripple the progress of Uganda towards self-government. ... Much is obscure; Baganda politics are intricate; and conceivably both fear of federation and the call for (separate) independence of Buganda are largely symptoms of some underlying strain. It is especially regrettable that this squall should have blown up at a time when Uganda, under a vigorous and liberal-minded governor, is on the threshold of great advances."

On 9 December 1953, *The Manchester Guardian* carried a long article by Rita Hinden titled 'Insurgent Africa Today; Which Self Will Govern?' After summarizing a long list of colonial policy questions and problems she wrote:

Fear is the connecting thread running throughout ... fear makes men irrational, arrogant, uncompromising, at times plain stupid ... this fear has its origin in two violently crystallising consummations in British Africa, the triumph of African nationalism in the Gold Coast and the triumph of white nationalism in South Africa. ... What has happened in the Gold Coast fills the heart of European residents in Africa with fear ... this was something they had scarcely believed possible in their lifetime ... similarly what has happened in South Africa has struck terror into the heart of every African. The second reason for the fear is an extension of the first, namely the approach of self-government, which has raised in each region fear of the 'others'. Will the North be preponderant in a self-governing Nigeria? Or the Ibos or the Yorubas? And what then will be the fate of the minorities? This confusion as to purpose is heightened by a confusion as to institutions ... even when we are quite clear that what we want is democracy, we tend to identify democracy with a particular set of institutions ... but democracy is not just a matter of forms and institutions – it is a set of values ... which spring from a belief in the dignity of each individual, his right to be accorded equal respect ... from these follow the rights to freedom of speech, conscience and association.

The Economist of 19 December 1953 featured a two-page article titled 'colonial Bogeyman' which examined the position of the two main British parties on colonial policy. Their conclusion was that the Labour opposition party was doing a poor job of questioning government on colonial questions and that the colonial secretary, Oliver Lyttelton, was doing a much more proficient job than they were accusing him of. Furthermore, in substance the two parties were very close on policies as such and criticism was more merited by tactics and process than substance. The following week they commented on the motion of censure the

Labour opposition had moved on the government's colonial policy, which had redounded on them, when they failed to get support for the motion.

Following the same theme, on 17 December 1953, *The Manchester Guardian* published a report of the debate in Parliament on colonial affairs and the report by its Parliamentary Correspondent headed 'Mr Lyttelton Scores Another Triumph'. He wrote:

> Many think that the Labour party blundered in putting down the vote of censure on the Government's handling of African affairs, which was defeated in the House of Commons by 301 votes to 272. Mr Griffiths did nothing to repair the blunder, if blunder it was, by a speech which started from the initial proposition that the troubles in Africa began in 1951, that is with the Tory government … Mr Lyttelton's reply was based on the very different proposition that the origin of the troubles antedated both the present and the late Government; that, in short, the troubles resulted from 'the mighty ferment caused by the projection of Western ideas into the continent over a considerable period'.

The Daily Telegraph featured a leader in its edition of 5 January 1954 titled 'Colonialism and Communism'. The Cold War between the communist powers and the Western world had a tendency to distort realities when they came into conflict. This leader indicated that Pakistan was resolved to strengthen its defences and was considering the possibility of buying weapons from the United States. India had reacted somewhat hysterically by describing such action as 'a step not only towards war, even world war, but a step which will bring war right to our doorstep'. 'Mr Nehru's fundamental attitude is determined by his policy of neutralism and the idea that to have any truck with the Western powers (other than receiving their economic help) is to invite "colonialism."' The leader went on, 'If Mr Nehru could escape from the illusion of "colonialism" he might begin to realise that Communism throughout the world has a single purpose and that an equal solidarity among all those who oppose it is the only means of stemming its advance.'

On the 6 January 1954, Sudan's newly elected Parliament was inaugurated in Khartoum. The governor general, Sir Robert Howe, said, 'the whole procedure of democratic elections was new and strange to the Sudanese. Nevertheless, and despite the practical difficulties of distance and climatic conditions, the size of the poll in most constituencies showed that the electorate generally had a real sense of their duties as citizens'. He went on: 'A public service of high standard and integrity, free from political influence, such has been built up in the Sudan, is a priceless asset in any country, but particularly to one which is about to embark on full self-government. But self-determination is valueless in itself unless it exists in the context of freedom and neutrality, free from external influence'. This last comment was obviously directed at the future of Sudan's relations with Egypt.

On the 6–8 January 1954, *The Daily Telegraph* featured a set of three articles on Mau Mau and Kenya by the paper's Special Correspondent, H. D. Ziman. The correspondent first set out to persuade readers that this was not merely 'another independence movement'; neither was it a Marxist movement. He described it as

> an entirely African horror, more outrageously brutal in its methods than anything encountered in Malaya, but also less efficient and intelligent. ... Though the undoubted purpose of Mau Mau is to drive all Europeans out of Kenya, the murder of settlers and their families is sporadic, not an everyday event; by contrast, several large-scale massacres of Kikuyu had been carried out by Mau Mau. ... A recollection of the disembowelled children, sliced and mutilated women and burnt corpses of all ages and both sexes, which are the accomplishment of Mau Mau among their fellow-Kikuyu, corrects any impression that its addicts are just naughty children ... despite the loathsome oath-taking and murderous nature of the Mau Mau leaders, and the role often played by Kikuyu women in the oathtaking and massacres of loyalists, large groups of Kikuyu had sometimes come to a minor chief and demanded to be formed into an entirely unofficial Home Guard against Mau Mau; a number of Christian leaders had been brutally murdered for resisting Mau Mau. ... Only of course with the help of Kikuyu men and women can Mau Mau be eradicated for the long run ... and further attention be given to the issue of land availability.

On 11 January 1954, *The Manchester Guardian* featured an interesting editorial on 'African Franchise'. This was stimulated by the proposed visit of the colonial secretary to Northern Rhodesia to study the franchise question. The Editor asked the question:

> Is there any reason why a common roll and communal franchise should not exist side-by-side? It seems clear that the few Africans who could now qualify for the vote on the same terms as the Europeans cannot adequately carry the responsibility of speaking for the whole body of their countrymen, civilised and uncivilised, tribal or urban alike. On the other hand is it right that they should count no more than an illiterate peasant who never stirred from his village? Why should there not be two distinct forms of franchise? First, a common roll, confined to those with the present financial and educational qualification or something like them, of whatever race, and voting in fairly small constituencies; second a form of communal franchise for those Africans not enrolled, with a limited number of representatives, probably chosen by indirect election and representing very much larger numbers, so that communal members did not outweigh the common roll members. As the weight of Africans on the

common roll grew, the numbers chosen communally would decline. (So far as I can find out, this approach to the franchise was not tried anywhere, though it was seriously considered in the Central African Federation.)

On 12 January 1954, *The Daily Telegraph* featured an article by Colin Welch, titled 'Colonies on the March Towards Self-Rule'.

For good or ill, our whole Colonial policy is based on the procession towards self-rule. It cannot at this stage be arrested, still less reversed. ... Colonial Government is in essence based on a double subordination. ... The legislature is subordinate to the executive; and the Colonial Government is subordinate to the Imperial Government. As the Colony advances, the first subordination is weakened, and finally abolished, and then the second. ... This progress is sometimes interrupted by plural societies where complications arise in regard to representation – Chinese outnumber Malays in Malaya; Indians are almost as numerous as Fijians; and Europeans in Kenya fear they will be totally outvoted. ... Give education time to do its work and plural societies will cease to matter – one often hears it said – yet time and education are not always on the side of unity ... the other great problem is the obvious incapacity of some Colonial peoples to operate representative institutions ... which is not necessarily removed by time and education. ... Be that as it may, the future of representative institutions in those Colonies where it now flourishes cannot be regarded as entirely assured. Like liberty itself, such institutions tend to survive where they are disproportionately valued, where people are prepared to forego other things, indisputably good or advantageous, rather than see them perish. Whether they are so valued in our Colonies, time alone will show.

The first leader in *The Daily Telegraph* of 16 January 1954 commented on the visit to Kenya of a two-party delegation from the House of Commons.

In broad outline, one may predict what the delegation will find. They will find in Mau Mau a movement which, so far from being popular, is being heroically resisted by many of its own tribesmen and is regarded by the remainder with terror, hatred or indifference. They will find grievances among the Africans (particularly about land), which the Mau Mau has exploited and to which it has given an anti-European twist; they will also find that the present leaders of Mau Mau did all in their power to prevent these grievances being addressed. They will find an administration which even now, with every excuse, is far less negligent of African and Kikuyu welfare than it was of its own security. They will find settlers who, in the face of terrible provocation, have on the whole retained a refreshingly flexible and liberal outlook. They will find security forces trying to combat by civilised methods a movement which knows no law, and meeting with some success. ... They will find above all people like themselves differing not in the excellence of their intentions but solely in the angle from which they view the perplexing problems with which they are faced.

On 24 June 1954 *The Daily Telegraph*'s second leader again discussed the visit of the colonial secretary to Northern Rhodesia.

Two crises are quietly smouldering away ... the constitutional crisis burst into flame with Mr Lyttleton's announcement of increases in representation of both Europeans and Africans in LegCo and the indication he gave that in due course the Africans would be brought onto the common voter's role ... some Europeans argued that in this way Africans would acquire some of the rights of British subjects without any of the responsibilities. ... This type of friction is bound to arise so long as (Colonial Office) control is anything more than an illusion; the reality of this control, so often doubted by those who opposed the Central African Federation, is best proved by the fact that it is sometimes resented. ... Mr Lyttletlon will also visit the Copperbelt ... where the crisis is social and racial in its origin ... the African in the mines is steadily acquiring new skills, new responsibilities and new demands ... he is faced by the solidly-organised European miners' trade union which fears for the future of its members and their children. ... Their attitude is not shared by the mining companies, all of which are friendly to African advancement ... events elsewhere suggest that in the end the African workers' wishes will be fulfilled.

In August 1954 *The Times* carried two letters on women's education in Uganda, including an appeal by the wife of the governor for more qualified women in England to volunteer for teaching work in Uganda.

On 17 August 1954 *The Daily Telegraph* carried an article by Lord Altrincham, governor of Kenya from 1925 to 1931. He criticized the communal roles adopted under the Lyttelton constitution which he felt would lead to 'inter-racial jockeying for power in the Legislature ... which would freeze the races into permanently antagonistic groups'. He advocated a great extension of local self-government based on tribal groups 'so that Africans may prove and develop their title to it un-dominated by their more advanced compatriots'. In a letter to the editor, Philip Goodhart agreed with Lord Altrincham's warning but argued he had the wrong solution. 'Tribal separatism – the desire of many African peoples to throw off the laws and taxes of a modern state – is the curse of the newly-born countries in West Africa, Nigeria and the Gold Coast. Devolution on the scale proposed by Lord Altrincham might well cripple the Governments of Kenya, Uganda and Tanganyika who alone are capable of providing the health services and secondary education'. 'Meanwhile a substantial spread of local self-government is in fact taking place ... but it cannot be extended indefinitely with much danger'.

On 23 August 1954, *The Manchester Guardian* published an article by its London staff describing the 'Statement of Policy on Colonial Affairs' adopted by the British Labour Party, then in opposition. The most significant departure from the party's prior policies, and from the prevailing consensus between the two main parties, was the intention to set a timetable for self-government of each colonial territory. A week later, on 31 August 1954 *The Times* carried a letter from Sir Olaf Caroe, formerly Governor of the North-West Frontier Province of India, warning against the notion of setting of timetables for the transfer of power in each colony, as had been proposed by the Labour Party. He argued that such timetables force all those concerned immediately to take things into their own hands, as had happened in India and Palestine. The 'alternative, he argued, was to build in each territory a political system which had within it the seeds of organic growth, such as would produce a mature plant able to stand unsupported. For British territory this meant representative institutions, for all communities … and in plural societies … this meant that these institutions must be based on a qualitative not a quantitative franchise'. A follow-up letter critical of any 'irrelevant abstractions' argued that 'our traditional empiricism should guide us to an appraisal of each separate colonial situation'. In the event, Labour's proposed new policy was never implemented because by the time Labour were in office again, ten years later in 1964, most colonies were already independent.

On 21 November 1954, *The Observer* carried a Profile of the Governor of Uganda, Sir Andrew Cohen. This traced his ascent from junior official in the Colonial Office to Governor and described his accomplishments as under-secretary of state for the Colonies. But it also described how he fell out with the Kabaka, Mutesa II, through impatience and arrogance, leading to his expulsion of the Kabaka to England and how Cohen had been humiliated by the crowds when he went to the Assembly Hall in Kampala to make a speech in which he was going to announce that the Kabaka was to be restored to his position.

On 27 November 1954, *The Economist* carried an article which reviewed the findings of the report of a World Bank mission to Nigeria to review the prospects for economic growth over the next five years. The article was critical of the Nigeria government's marketing boards which, in its view, were not permitting enough raw materials to go to processors within Nigeria and were tending to use the profits of the boards as a source of government revenue. The journal thought the report, as technical paper, produced useful recommendations, but it criticized its insensitivity to the local political context, its recommendations to scale back the reforms of government within the federal format and especially the sharp increase in taxation it proposed.

In January 1955 *The Economist* carried a two-page review of the situation in Malaya. The communist insurgency continued, though the area affected was now getting smaller. However there still remained an estimated 5,000 insurgents in the jungle, though the number killed or captured had fallen to 713 in 1954. Talk of an amnesty was criticized as many of those still in the jungle had committed grievous crimes and 'Britain's first duty in Malaya was to provide a code of law and to see that it is observed'. However, lower commodity prices meant that Malayan revenues had fallen and the country was dependent on grants from Britain and a loan from the Colony of Singapore. Despite this still troubled background, the immediate political prospects looked reasonable and barring accidents the first general election in the country's history would take place in mid-1955, with the prospect of there being a small elected majority in the Legislative Assembly for the first time. The article concluded – Twenty years ago there was no such thing as public opinion in Malaya

> now, the problem is to see that it takes a responsible view of its own problems, and then to ease it into the saddle … meanwhile the Malay/Chinese Alliance, the party with the best prospects for the election, needs a social and economic platform, as currently it exists merely to work for a transfer of power.

On 19 January 1955, *The Daily Telegraph* contained a long leader which examined the rationale and effectiveness of the amnesties offered to Mau Mau members to induce them to submit to government. Both in Britain and Kenya there was much concern at the essential capriciousness of amnesties which are amended over time and whose terms for the same crimes are also amended.

The 5 February 1955 edition of *The Times* and the 14 March edition of *The Daily Telegraph* featured a letter from the Ministers of the Northern Region of Nigeria which sought to attract officers retiring from the Sudan civil service as that country became independent.

> We would welcome suitable British officers from the Sudan service … we look primarily overseas for our professional and technical staff and we wish it to be widely known that a welcome and a future awaits all suitably qualified overseas officials who are sincerely prepared to serve the needs of our people. We should particularly like to have here those with experience of Sudan which, as several of us know from personal experience, has so many features in common with our Northern region.

The Economist published an article entitled 'Revolt in Ashanti' in February 1955:

> Dr Kwame Nkrumah's troubles are growing. Somewhat belatedly he decided that he must take the Ashanti National Liberation Movement seriously, and offered to parley … on regional devolution. But now with the backing of the Muslim party of the North, the Ashanti leaders have refused … so far, fortunately, the challenge has not become a challenge to law and order. But it clearly has great attraction for Ashanti minds … its real protest is against the

transfer of power to Africans with a European outlook, whether politicians or officials. With this reaction, the Colonial Office has no sympathy ... it is leaving it to Dr Nkrumah and the Governor, Sir Charles Arden-Clarke, to settle the matter. The Gold Coast, a compact, prosperous, viable African territory is the key experiment in democratic African home rule. If tribal separation triumphs there it will be widely taken ... that Africa south of the Sahara is not yet ready for full responsibility to run their own affairs.

Two months later, Dr Azikiwe in Nigeria, commented on the article pointing out that federation is a way out of the difficulty in the Gold Coast, if there is the will; as it had been in Switzerland and Canada (he was uncharacteristically modest in not mentioning his own country, Nigeria).

On 22 February 1955, the second leader in *The Daily Telegraph* commented on the visit to Tanganyika of a team from the United Nations Trusteeship Council.

Tanganyika continues to offer the happiest picture of tranquil progress in East Africa ... it may seem strange therefore that Tanganyika should be subject to a surly report of the investigators ... it will seem even more strange that Britain, which administers Tanganyika, should be bluntly told to prepare the territory for self-government within 20 years and to fix a timetable ... that decision rests with HMG ... as it happens, constitutional advances have ... been the most notable feature of the past twelve months in Tanganyika ... but there is no question of the Africans at large being qualified on their own merits ... one remarkable young Tanganyika chief, a member of both LegCo and ExCo, recently offered to resign his hereditary tribal functions in order to enter the administrative Government service.

(In the event Tanganyika became independent seven years later.)

In March 1955, *The Times* featured another two-part article by Margery Perham titled 'Nigeria Prepares for Independence', with the subtitles 'The problem of Unity' and 'The problem of Staff'. She started by referring to the objective of the Colonial Office, namely seeking to

preserve a proper measure of unity ... yet today in Nigeria the will to unity seems weak. Political leaders in the past have found it easy to rouse the educated minority into united opposition to British tutelage. But with the removal of this useful overhanging surface against which to generate pressure, and with the introduction of almost universal suffrage, the leaders have had to look inwards and downwards and to create support out of such material as they could find. The most promising was tribal separatism. ... We therefore have an ironic situation in which Britain strives to unite and rule while the Africans try to divide and rule. But tribe is an inexact word and disunities of Nigeria are neither simple nor uniform … the Action Group Ministry, under the able and austere Mr Awolowo, is busy building up a strong (Western) region, fit almost for independent life and inclined to turn its back on the rest of Nigeria. Dr Azikiwe, with the National Council of Nigeria and the Cameroons, aims for a more unitary constitution. This is the natural ambition for a people mainly Ibo, crowded upon poor soil, with too little revenue … they knew nothing of chiefs, large states, cities and the pride of having a history … their gaze is wholly on the future … the Northern Peoples' Congress stands for the maintenance of a solid, separate North based upon its ancient traditions … and though their own tardy acceptance of Western ideas and techniques has left them humiliatingly dependent upon the southerners, and especially the Ibos … yet the long-robed Hausa and Yoruba may be thrown upon the defensive by the Ibo, as, naked only yesterday, they stream out of their forests in their shirts and shorts, energetic, ambitious, modern-minded, democratic and heading for a fully united Nigeria.

Miss Perham went on:

There is in Nigeria today … profound goodwill towards Britain … the feverish grasping of full power has ceased and the leaders seem to be pausing on the edge of independence … the senior British officials … are the last people to stop paying out the rope because the pull on it has slackened … as experienced agents of an experienced nation, they know too well that power cannot for long be held in suspense or in division … the time we have for making use of (the goodwill) is likely to be very short … we have here a most urgent problem upon the solution of which in the next five or ten years may depend the whole future of Nigeria and of Britain's association with it … there is abundant good will and an almost crushing sense of need, which of course, extends beyond the sphere of government to the deeper and more enduring levels of the Christian churches and the new university … special, if not desperate measures, are needed.

On 12 March 1955, *The Economist* featured a two-page article titled 'The Diamond Coast'. The article described the origin of the diamond trade in Sierra Leone, the post-war evolution of the diamond business in the country and its implications for the new African government in the process of taking over from colonial officials, under the leadership of Siaka Stevens, Minister of Mines and Commerce. A central buying agency was under consideration. 'But who, in the present state of the Sierra Leone administration … would operate and police such a scheme. The illicit dealer could still buy against the agency and have the competitive advantage of not paying income tax. Whether or not a private monopoly (for example, De Beers) is an adequate means of realizing Sierra

Leone's diamond wealth ... the long term interests of the African people are being prejudiced'.

On 4 March 1955, *The Daily Telegraph* commented in a leader on the settlement of a strike by African miners in Northern Rhodesia following recruitment of an additional 10,000 miners. 'The copper companies allowed them to capitulate on remarkably generous terms' but had demonstrated that it was easy to find additional labour for the mines. The European miners had also been persuaded to accept the use of African miners on semi-skilled work hitherto reserved for Europeans.

A leader in *The Daily Telegraph* of 4 June 1955 commented on the achievement by Tunisia of Home Rule

Time has seen the triumph of the forces of moderation on both sides. Tunisia regains her identity after more than seventy years; France retains her former protectorate in a new form of voluntary association within the Union. It marks a change in French policy after the experience of failure in South-East Asia ... limited but effective self-government is now granted to the Tunisians, to whom even moderate reform would have been refused three years ago. They are free to choose their own constitution and are assured of control of the police and judiciary in gradual stages ... risks are attendant on any transfer of power. But France has had to take a chance on the successful evolution of the new Tunisian state. In so doing she has chosen her ground well by coming to terms with the effective leaders of Tunisian nationalism.

On 9 June 1955 *The Daily Telegraph* reported the withdrawal of the offer of amnesty to Mau Mau in Kenya with effect from 10 July, nearly six months after the offer was made. Any terrorists who had not surrendered by then would forfeit all rights to land in Kenya. Blundell, the responsible minister, said that 650 terrorists, including twenty gang leaders, had given themselves up; many of them had given valuable information to the government in their fight against Mau Mau. The surrender talks had revealed a split among the terrorists and every effort was being made to make the date of the amnesty withdrawal known to Mau Mau in the jungle by overflying aircraft with loudspeakers and leaflets.

In its edition of 11 June, *The Daily Telegraph* welcomed the report of the East Africa Royal Commission; it sees the real issue in East Africa not as 'Who shall farm the land?' but as 'Who can farm it best?' – a finding inimical to the gross abuse of good land in the African reserves, where want is more due to bad farming than overcrowding, and to the still empty stretches of the White Highlands.

In its 16 June edition, *The Economist* ran a two-page article titled 'Adam Smith in East Africa'. The article was based on a review of the report of the East African Royal Commission.

The principal obstacles which the commission found to land being economically allotted and cultivated were the tribal organisation and the restrictions of land use based on it. The core of its recommendations, which are many and detailed, is that such restrictions should be finally swept away; that individual profit, enterprise and ambition should set the pace of change; that in an expanding economy based on market values, there would be room – and in fact need – for all races at any foreseeable rate of population growth; and that if this were to be so, race hatreds nourished on insecurity would disappear. ... The commission would also free crop prices from controls and abolish forced savings through marketing boards ... but it would place a ceiling on the size of holdings and prevent excessive sub-division of such holdings ... in summary, the Royal Commission is asserting that in East Africa (and the assertion could be made almost equally well of British Colonial policy as a whole) the balance has been tilted much too far away from economic change and progress, and that it needs to be corrected. ... On this fundamental issue ... there cannot be any doubt that the Royal Commission is abundantly right.

On 18 June, *The Daily Telegraph* reported a speech of the South African prime minister who had said that the British government had indicated this was not a suitable time for any further negotiations about the future of the three protectorates (Swaziland, Basutoland and Bechuanaland). British spokesmen had said they could not hand over the territories to South Africa without consultation with the native peoples – implying consent.

On 22 June 1955, *The Manchester Guardian* published a report of a wide-ranging debate in the House of Commons on colonial affairs, summarized by the paper's Parliamentary Correspondent. This occurred soon after the Bandung Conference of Non-Aligned states, as they were known, comprising former imperial possessions such as India and Indonesia, now independent, and countries such as Jugoslavia which sought to evade control from communist Russia, and whose discussions helped to set the international context for the situation in the colonies. During the debate, the Minister of State for the Colonies, Hopkinson said that negotiations on proposed new constitutions had taken place within the last year on all four West African countries, all three East African countries, Northern Rhodesia, Nyasaland, the Federation of Malaya and Singapore, the Leeward and Windward Islands, Cyprus and Aden. The secretary of state, Lennox-Boyd, gave prominence to the need to remain steadfast in resisting the communist insurgency in Malaya and Singapore on the one hand and continuing pressure on the remaining Mau Mau terrorists on the other hand. In both cases the majority of citizens were supporting the authorities but Britain could not relax in its support for the governments of those countries. Creech Jones, former Labour colonial secretary, 'expressed regret that, remembering the vast preponderance of Africans in Nyasaland, parity of representation had declined, and still more that no African had been admitted to the Governor's executive council'.

On 22nd June 1955, *The Daily Telegraph* reported the lifting of the ban in Kenya on the creation and operation of political associations, even though the State of Emergency still obtained ... emphasis in the plan is on building from rank and file membership, thus minimizing the risk of political agitators taking control of the associations.

The Times of 3 September 1955 featured the report of an observer of Southern Sudan soon after the departure of the British administrators. He was at pains to praise the dedication being shown by the Northern Sudanese Governors and officials he met to the cause of the southern region, and the grouping of the three governors (all northerners) into what they jocularly called 'the Anti-colonial Front', though pointed out the extent to which they were being handicapped 'by facile Cairo promises'.

Chatham House (The Royal Society for International Affairs) produced a short summary of the report of the Royal Commission on East Africa which was described by *The Manchester Guardian* in November 1955 as 'a classic among State papers'. However the paper considered its length and complexity had stood in the way of it being widely read and welcomed the initiative taken by Chatham House, which would make its findings more widely known.

In its 12 December 1955 edition, *The Manchester Guardian* reported on a meeting of the Liberal Party, which welcomed the 'bold and comprehensive report of the East Africa Royal Commission ... which had displayed revolutionary thinking on colonial policies'.

On 2 January 1956, *The Daily Telegraph* described the divisions among French political leaders over the issue of Algeria where 'political life has come to a standstill until the new Assembly and Government emerges'. Within France 'the Algerian issue has played a big part throughout the election campaign ... on account of its economic importance ... and because voters are concerned about the prospect of sons and husbands and brothers having to fight there'. It was followed on 7 January by a first leader in the paper titled 'Fiddling while Algeria burns'. 'The elections have at least established what must now be tacitly acknowledged common ground; it can no longer be pretended that Algeria is really "part of France". Public opinion in France is probably ready to accept a federal or other solution, short of total severance'.

On 3 January 1956, the editor of *The Times* wrote of Africa 'The two most important events in British Africa during 1955 were the mutiny in Southern Sudan and the breaking of the industrial colour bar in the Northern Rhodesian copper belt. The first is a warning, or rather a confirmation, of the deep fissional tendencies still present in African society. In this case the differences between north and south were great, since they involved blood and religion; but differences almost as great can be found elsewhere in Africa. The cultural and historical splits between tribes are as real as between European nations; in any attempt to set up self-governing national states in Africa, these differences will be ignored at peril.'

On 8 January 1956 *The Daily Telegraph* published an article by Patrick Morrah, titled 'Towards Malayan Independence', in which he described the complexities requiring attention during the discussions about to begin with Tungku Abdul Rahman, Malaya's chief minister, on the constitutional future of the country. The Tungku had recently met and negotiated with Chin Peng, the leader of the Malayan Communist Party, but had resisted the latter's call for recognition of his party; there was a grave danger of race conflict when British influence was withdrawn; the Malays, Chinese and Indians were now united in the independence movement but sooner or later their interests are bound to clash and the Malays, whose welfare the British are pledged to protect, may find themselves swamped by other races. These complications, coupled with the continuance of communist terrorism, tell in favour of a policy of caution; one obstacle had been removed by the recent declaration by the High Commissioner, Sir Donald MacGillivray, that the emergency would not be allowed to stand in the way of constitutional reform. Yet another question to be decided is the position of the Malay Rulers. This is a point of honour; British authority prevails in the states only by treaty with the Rulers, who accepted it as a protection against internal disorder. Any settlement which did not guarantee their personal position, which sacrificed them to expediency as the Indian princes were sacrificed, would be a gross breach of trust.

On 11 January 1956, *The Daily Telegraph* reported the proposals published by the Kenya government for direct elections by secret ballot of Africans to LegCo. Electors had to be at least twenty-one years of age and had to qualify in any one of seven categories reflecting education, income or property, service, seniority, higher education, legislative experience and meritorious service. A loyalty test would apply to members of tribal groups which had been behind Mau Mau. Creation of the electoral rolls would take time, but the objective was elections within fifteen months.

On 17 January 1956, *The Times* published an editorial titled 'Police in Africa'. It went on 'In Britain the police have the status of a "constable in Common Law" and were not the agents of the government; in the colonies statute law applies mainly in municipalities; the vast bulk of the native population is governed by native law and custom, supported by the district officer and "court messengers"; colonial police are in some measure an armed gendarmerie'. The article articulated clearly a fear for civil liberties in Africa.

On 23 January 1956, *The Daily Telegraph* carried a major article by Elspeth Huxley about Nigeria, timed to coincide with the visit of Queen Elizabeth to the country.

When the tumult and the shouting of the Royal visit to Nigeria have died, the constitution-makers will settle down to months of hard work to reconcile two contradictory elements – the desire of some people, but not of others, for immediate self-government, and the fact that Nigeria lacks the very basis of nationhood, national unity ... the Queen will not see one Nigeria with one language, one faith, one 'way of life'. On the contrary she will see a whole collection of races and peoples ... as alien to each other as Turks to Welshmen ... loosely grouped into three major regions. ... The situation that will face the constitution-makers is therefore complex. Self-rule for two regions but perhaps not for the third ... this is where personalities enter in ... the plain fact is that even regional-self rule, let alone the more distant federal prospect, is impossible without continuing outside help ... no amount of perfervid nationalism can telescope the span of human life, and it still takes 20 years for a man to grow up and another 20 to gain experience of managing the affairs of other men ... meanwhile the gap must be filled by British officers; many fewer recruits are coming forward than are needed ... the old jibe of 'Divide and Rule' is often thrust in British faces, but in Nigeria Britain has unquestionably ruled to unite ... already a demand to create new political units has arisen among the large minorities which exist in each region. Some Southern politicians support these demands from a desire to see their rivals weakened ... there is no unity at present, or only the slenderest threads of it ... until there is some accepted majority party at the centre capable of holding the reins of power, to hand these over would be to surrender to chaos.

On 2 April 1956, *The Manchester Guardian* published an article by Vernon Bartlett regarding the complex, acrimonious and potentially destabilizing local politics in Singapore as the country approached self-government. Additional complexity was added by the rivalry between the combative chief minister of Singapore, David Marshall, and his counterpart in Malaya, Tungku Abdul Rahamn. Later in the year, the paper covered the acrimonious process of finding more Asians to take on positions then still held by British personnel when they departed under the localization scheme.

On 26 April 1956, *The Manchester Guardian* reported a statement made by the Colonial Secretary to the effect that a second attempt was to be made to introduce democratic institutions in British Guiana. The original attempt had been subverted by communists and the constitution had had to be suspended in 1953. Initially both LegCo and ExCo would have equal numbers of elected and official/nominated members. Elections were planned for the following year.

The Mau Mau revolt was of such a violent and irrational nature that the Government of Kenya had to take large-scale measures to fight the terrorists and protect the majority of Kikuyu, other tribes and other residents who were being threatened and intimidated by the Mau Mau. This was bound to require detailed debate and attention in the House of Commons and an example was the debate on 6 June 1956, reported in *The Manchester Guardian* on the following day.

By then the insurrection was in decline and many of the insurgents who had been held in detention had been released either back to their villages or to land development schemes. This had proved successful and so far as was known, there had been no cases of released people rejoining the gangs in the jungle. The House was particularly concerned to understand the way in which the criminal code was being applied to those in detention or on trial, which still exceeded a thousand. There was also concern about the franchise for Africans. Elections to LegCo were scheduled for September for Europeans and Asians, under the communal franchise, and in the New Year for Africans.

The Daily Telegraph gave publicity to a meeting of the Capricorn Africa Society in a remote spot in Nyasaland in its editions of 29 and 30 June 1956. Created under the stimulus and energy of Colonel David Sterling, the Society sought to formulate a common multiracial plan for an area as large as the United States.

> Yesterday the delegates approved six precepts on which the 'Capricorn Contract', will be founded with hardly any amendment. But today, when they proceeded to land reform, education, labour relations and immigration, and returned to the discussion of electoral systems, progress slowed down … the common sense of the Capricorn idealists recognises the inevitability of gradualness. … But African nationalists are in a hurry. … Though political power seems nowhere near the grasp of these men of Capricorn, they already possess influence – and it is influence entirely for good. Unbridled racial nationalism, Black or White, can bring only disaster. … What the Capricorn contract now offers for debate is a plan to make this cooperation organic by building on it an inter-racial society.

On 21 June 1956, *The Times* featured a letter from a Mirza Ismail of Bangalore, India in which he wrote:

> As one who at no time in his long official career served directly under the British Government, and is not, therefore, under any special obligation to them, I feel that I am in a position to give expression to my feelings, without being misunderstood, on a matter which, I have no doubt, many will agree with me deserves the attention of all who have, until recently lived and flourished under British rule. It is time we expressed our genuine appreciation of the way in which Britain has actually brought our countries to their present hopeful position. One after another, territories long under British control are attaining independence. It is natural enough that their leaders should make vivid and picturesque contrast between the prospects of a glowing future and the past. Yet to blacken and misrepresent that past is in no sense helpful to that future. Unhappily, few of these leaders have emerged with credit and complete goodwill. I take as an extreme example certain observations made by the

prime minister of the Sudan on the inauguration of the republic. ... So spoke the leader and inspirer of a people who owe almost everything to Britain; their growing prosperity, through great schemes of development, law and order, and the human services; such capacity for administration as they have attained; such approach to unity as they have made. And in the very achievement of self-rule, they have been given, willingly, that help and guidance without which there could have been only failure – and danger. ... Britain's record not only in the Sudan, but also in other countries, now self-governing – India, Pakistan, Burma, Ceylon, Nigeria, Gold Coast and Malaya – is far from being a cause of shame. She has done for the peoples of these territories what no other country in human history has done for her subject peoples.

In June 1956, *The Manchester Guardian* published a report of the House of Commons debate on the British Caribbean Federation Bill, which provided the enabling legislation for the creation of the federation. This was to be on the Australian pattern, presided over by a governor general with a Council of State of eleven members, a legislature, Supreme Court and other statutory bodies. Prior to the establishment of the federation, talks would be held to agree the amount of British assistance which would be provided in the initial five years in the life of the federation.

On 18 July 1956, *The Times* published an editorial on the threat of Dr Azikiwe to resign from the premiership of Eastern Nigeria, together with trenchant comments on the increasing evidence of financial malfeasance and other corrupting influences. To quote the editorial:

With a libel suit due to be heard today in Calabar in which Dr Azikiwe has cited a member of the Opposition, it would be improper to comment on the rights and wrongs of this particular case. It is, however, distressing to observe how, on the very eve of their projected independence, a pattern is imposing itself in West African politics in which allegations and counter-allegations involving money play so prominent a part. Mr Lennox-Boyd, the new Colonial Secretary, should give the House of Commons the fullest possible information. It is vital that the truth in these matters should be fully established. No-one wishes to slow up the march of African independence, but the great mass of Africans themselves will want to be shown that those who are taking over from British rule have the same high standards.

On 12 August, 1956, *The Observer* published an exchange between a Mr John Hatch, who claimed in a letter that Labour had always been opposed to the creation of the Central African Federation, and Colin Legum, the paper's Colonial correspondent. This is interesting in that it reminds the readers that (a) it was the Labour Government which initiated the talks on a federal scheme, even though it soon became apparent that most Africans opposed the idea; (b) that Lord Attlee counselled the Labour Party to be loyal to the new State if the necessary parliamentary majority were obtained for its creation; that *The Observer* newspaper did not object to federation as such, though it opposed the particular form of it; and (d) that it was the Conservative government which chose the particular form of federation adopted.

In an article of 20 December 1956, titled 'Trying to Keep Up with Africa' *The Manchester Guardian*, in a review of Lord Hailey's 1956 Revision of his 1938 Africa Survey, wondered if it would ever again be possible to produce such a survey – the semi-static Africa which Lord Hailey surveyed twenty years ago has now broken up into a fast, moving kaleidoscope of political, social and economic change.

On January 23–25 *The Times* published a series of three articles by its Colonial Correspondent entitled 'a Continent in a Hurry'. The first of the series addressed the West Coast.

This was followed on 14 February 1957 by another *Times* editorial which argued, in respect of the Gold Coast, Nigeria and French territories approaching self-government that 'these new states will have many hard tests. The preservation of democracy will be one of the sternest. Democratic institutions are tender plants ... the leaders may face a choice of either allowing themselves to be stifled by anti-democratic influences or of themselves resorting to undemocratic means to maintain control'. Corruption ... will be dangerous for the credit of these countries when seeking loans for development, but may not necessarily be fatal to their survival as States. A third danger is that of communal strife. 'The tribe, not the nation, is still the unit which most induces in Africans a sense of belonging.'

Also appearing in this edition of *The Times* was a letter from a leading British construction engineer complaining that the World Bank's procurement requirement of international competitive bidding should be applied to the entire Kariba Dam project despite the fact that Britain guaranteed the Bank's loan for the project and that the rest of the financing was provided from British sources. [In the event, the largest share of the contracts went to Italian firms].

In January 1957, *The Times* became preoccupied with the means by which Britain would continue to supply technical assistance to colonies as they become independent. A whole range of such technical services would be required. Out of this agitation emerged the Department of Technical Cooperation, which later became a part of the Department for International Assistance in its various manifestations.

On 23–25 January 1957 *The Times* carried a series of three articles by its Colonial Correspondent titled 'A Continent in a Hurry'. The first of the series addressed the West Coast.

Visiting Africa year by year ... one has a sense of watching a film of history-in-the-making being run off in quick motion ... next time I visit the Gold Coast it will be Ghana; in the Belgian Congo I talked to young African intellectuals who are no longer afraid to draft and publish demands for total self-government for the Congo within 30 years (In fact the country was pitch-forked into independence three years later); in Central Africa I found a federation bursting and booming with energy which five years ago seemed nothing but a pipe-dream ... yet disturbing evidence is available of the increasingly authoritarian trends of African Party leaders, their efforts to weaken independent control of the civil service, the police and the judiciary; their habit of collecting personal bodyguards; and the exaggerated development of the cult of personality; an African government taking over from a colonial regime is faced with an electorate which is immature, mostly illiterate and ridden by fear and witchcraft; they are deeply divided tribally; violence is endemic ... Africa's boundaries are recent and sometimes artificial. ... Is it reasonable to suppose that any government will be able to control such a situation unless it is prepared to govern strongly? Along the southern edge of the Sahara desert most people are Muslim ... in a narrow sense they are backward, but they are nevertheless highly organised in a pervasive manner with spiritual and secular leaders accorded much respect and authority ... they may prove more capable in the long run of organising a stable society ... the Central African Federation is committed in theory to partnership ... it is not in fact installing apartheid ... the mind of Rhodesians is however ambivalent ... Africans find it inhibiting and many prefer the clear-cut situation in South Africa where the economic and educational opportunities are greater, even though it is impractical, as the Tomlinson Report found, and is degenerating into repression of the blacks.

On 1 February 1957, *The Manchester Guardian* featured an article titled 'Australia's colony'. In the combined territory of Papua and New Guinea, Australia was the administering power under the Trusteeship Council of the UN. The Australian authorities were struggling with the question whether to allow the country to evolve at its own pace or to allow private sector companies in to develop the considerable resources of the country, generating revenue for social and economic development. The war and the Japanese invasion of New Guinea had let in new influences and the paper commented 'The atmosphere today seems healthier; new and better educated men are replacing the traditional leaders; there is a remarkable development of cooperative societies; immigrant enterprises employ labour under less oppressive conditions'.

The Economist of 9 March 1957 featured an article about Tanganyika. 'Once again Britain has been prodded by the United Nations to set a time limit to its guardianship of Tanganyika, The General Assembly last month passed two resolutions: an umbrella demand for independence at an "early date" for all trust territories; and a specific call to Britain to explain the steps it is taking to guide Tanganyika towards democratic self-government. Britain has always dismissed these UN demands for a timetable as impracticable and trouble-making and in defence has said that it is impossible to judge in advance when a territory will be ripe for independence. The aloof self-satisfaction of British colonial policy in Tanganyika has, in the past, rankled more in the UN than in the politically placid territory itself. The arid and harsh character of much of the land, and the primitive life of most of the people, have encouraged a passive acceptance of an administration which is liberal by East African standards ... there are 31 official and 30 un-official members of Leg Co; and next year there is to be a cautious experiment in qualitative common roll elections, selected constituencies will elect three members, one of each race. But multi-racialism is being challenged by a growing and assertive band of African nationalists. ... Nyerere campaigns on the line that Tanganyika is ... "primarily African and must be regarded as such" ... he questions the qualitative common roll ... and suggests a period of 10–12 years for ending trusteeship. ... The Colonial Office may be forgetting the lessons of other territories in refusing to discuss a date. Tanganyika will not remain placid indefinitely.' (The country did in fact become independent within six years.)

The Times of 18 March 1957 contained an analytical piece by Margery Perham, this time on the prospects for Kenya after Mau Mau.

Mau Mau it seems is finished. But that terrible assertion of discontent, which, in its tenacity and beastliness, still seems to defy our understanding, has left a changed Kenya. The Africans can never again be seen as they were before this event; the settlers have proved their own tenacity. Yet today no absolute alienation divides the races. The danger was too grave to be met merely with hatred, and the Kikuyu reputation was saved by the amazing courage of the Christians and the loyalists, without whose help Mau Mau could not have been beaten. ... The economy has withstood the storm surprisingly well. ... In the administrative sphere what most surprises observers is the avalanche of reforms poured out both to regenerate the shattered Kikuyu and to satisfy the loyal tribes ... the new reforms have been the hopeless dreams of generations of administrators. Now the iron discipline, backed by the overwhelming military force needed for security, has been turned to social betterment and closer administration ... the recent African elections will send to the legislature men with the first chrism of democracy on their brows. They will almost certainly claim to by-pass the established structure of "native administration" and to act directly for, and upon, their constituents ... the Lyttleton constitution has a precariously balanced racial representation ... like a house of cards which stands so long as no one breathes, it works only because practical men make it work. ... British governments, uncertain how to apply the in-eradicable lesson of the Boston tea-party to multiracial Africa, prefer to give no answer, other than year-to-year adjustments to changing realities. Is this traditional empiricism any longer appropriate?

The Times of 24 May 1957 contained an editorial which addressed the situation in Tanganyika, the prospect of the first elections and the role of the two parties, the Tanganyika African National Union (TANU), avowedly African nationalist in orientation, and the United National Party (UTP), which advocated a multiracial government, but had lacked the leadership and cohesion to win support. The editorial makes an interesting and often overlooked point. 'To understand the trend of present day politics it is necessary to appreciate a fundamental change in orientation which has taken place since the Second World War. Previously, it was the assumption of the (British) administration that the interests of the indigenous African population were paramount. However, the terms of the United Nations trusteeship agreement, concluded after the war, made it clear that the British government should administer the territory on behalf of all the inhabitants and not merely the indigenous people. Thus multi-racialism became government policy'. (It was to become the de facto policy of the British government in several other territories too, where it was often opposed by the Africans and created severe and intractable political difficulties.)

The perspective of one rising Kenya politician, Tom Mboya, was apparent from his letter to *The Times* of 25 May 1957. 'He (Mboya) highlighted their (the African's) demand for increased representation, and decried the argument of the government that it was up to the Africans to negotiate with the Europeans and Asians'. This letter was in fact followed on 25 July 1957 by a report of a statement of Sir Alfred Vincent, leader of the European members of the Kenya LegCo, acceding to the proposal to increase African representation. (Formal negotiations on the constitution continued in Nairobi in October 1957, but they broke down over the level of African representation).

On 30 May 1957, *The Times* contained an editorial on the same issue, but on the way in which it manifested itself in Tanganyika. In that case Governor Twining had met the African member's objections halfway by agreeing to the holding of elections within the life of the new council in five constituencies in 1958, and the rest in 1959 – the limited administrative capability precluded doing so in all areas in the same year. The editorial went on 'In a multiracial society, it is seldom possible to please everyone at the same time. There are a number of Europeans in Tanganyika who have felt all along that political advance, so far from being too slow, was too rapid'.

The Times of 4 June 1957 contained another editorial addressing race relations, this time in the Central African Federation. 'In spite of some welcome statements to the contrary by individual African leaders, the aim of the few politically-minded Africans in the Federation is African governments on the Ghana model. ... The Europeans are divided, some seeking a reversion to the South African racial policy (apartheid) and some believers in a progressive racial policy' ... Sir Roy Welensky put the Federal Policy in a nutshell 'Wherever possible, the Federal Government has opened up channels of advancement to all qualified people. ... But it has not lowered the standards ordinarily required of a civilised community, nor will it do so while I am Prime Minister ... partnership does not mean we should accept lower standards; it means a man can have what he can earn'. Separately, *The Times* reported a speech in which Welensky criticized the Colonial Office 'for its ambivalence about the Federation and African politicians, encouraged by Labour members of the British Parliament, who are busy destroying any vestige of confidence Africans had in their local governments.' On 20 June *The Times* commented on the franchise proposals in the Federation and Southern Rhodesia and found them weighted excessively in favour of the Europeans, and in need of amendment.

In its edition of 8 June 1957, *The Economist* asked the question 'If British taxpayers' money, idealism, paper planning and dominion status for all would solve colonial problems, the Labour Party has the answer. But do they really get to the heart of the matter?' The article then went on to demonstrate just how unrealistic many of the Labour proposals were in terms both of public opinion in Britain and implementation capacity in the potential beneficiary countries.

A distinct perspective on the decolonization process was that of Sir Pierson Dixon, British Permanent Representative to the United Nations. His speech to a graduation day audience at William and Mary College, Virginia was reported in *The Times* on 11 June 1957. 'To grant independence to territories before they are ready would be to hand them over at best to corruption and anarchy and at worst to communism' one of his less pleasant duties in the United Nations was 'to hear crude and ill-informed attacks upon my country as a Colonial power .... So far from exploiting and oppressing the many millions of Africans and Asians who are the subjects of the British Crown, we are patiently and consistently bringing them forward into the twentieth century and equipping them with the political and economic resources which they will need if they are to stand on their own feet successfully'.

The lead editorial in *The Times* of 18 June 1957 addressed the speed of decolonization under the heading 'How Fast?'

Mr Lennox-Boyd (the Colonial Secretary) has this year had three notable successes – in the Central African Federation, where he laid the groundwork for the satisfactory agreement reached later with Sir Roy Welensky on the next steps forward; on his return journey he persuaded the Ghana leaders to accept a recipe for independence which was equitable to the Ashanti and other minorities; in discussions with Tunku Abdul Rahman, he made it possible for independence to be reached on time in Malaya ... To make a reasoned timetable for the creation of free States within the Commonwealth cannot be easy. In a world of growing nationalism and shifting powers Britain has somehow to present a balance between her obligations, her needs and her responsibilities ... for the colonial peoples ... their greatest need is for them to apply themselves to the practical problems of running a State in the modern world ... at present far too much of their energies is taken up with the anti-colonial struggle ... though in fact there is precious little opposition on the British side to struggle against. Far more important is to prepare themselves for the post-colonial period. ... Independence will bring no automatic solution to their social and financial difficulties. Colonial countries lead a sheltered existence ... they are walled off from the blizzards of the outside world by the administering power ... the emergent territories will be exposed to the full blast of a highly competitive outside world. Hence the necessity to concentrate on forging a sound governmental, administrative and economic structure. Without this, independence will prove an illusory benefit.

On 24 June 1957, *The Times* contained a report of a speech in Accra by Dr Busia, leader of the Opposition in Ghana, in which he expressed the fear of dictatorship and a 'personality cult' in Ghana, built around Dr Nkrumah, and said that this centralizing and personalizing tendency was not the wish of the people of Ghana. He went on: 'The Opposition strongly objected to these measures (to put the Prime Minister's head on the coins and stamps) and dissociate ourselves from statements made by the Prime Minister and reported in the press'. The Ghana Minister of the Interior, Edusei was reported as saying that the government would introduce a bill to make it possible to arrest and detain Opposition leaders who often criticize the government. Following him Dr Nkrumah said 'As for me, I am competent and calm. I have big eyes and ears and shall continue to do certain things in this country as Prime Minister because I see that as the only way by which I can put you on the path of parliamentary democracy.'

The Times of 15 July 1957 contained an editorial which examined political developments in Kenya following the African elections in January. 'The Africans continued to boycott the government appointed under the Lyttelton constitution, but the chairman of the elected Europeans, Sir Alfred Vincent, indicated they were ready to recommend an increase in the numbers of African members of Leg Co ... subject to safeguards for minorities. ... Additionally, Michael Blundell, the Minister of Agriculture, openly challenged the sanctity of the division of land into White Highlands and native reserves ... saying, "the people of this country will never get from their land the maximum productivity ... until they get over this senseless division of the land into separate and different partitions'." However, instead of welcoming these statements, the African leaders viewed them as intended only to appease public opinion abroad. The Editor went on:

> This reaction is in keeping with the negative and obstructive tactics adopted by Mr Mboya and his followers ever since they were returned to Leg Co after the elections in March. ... Kenya is once more at the crossroads.

In July, *The Times* also published the details of the new electoral system for the Central African Federation. These were complicated and involved two common rolls, with voters deciding on which they should register. The following month it publicized the results of the first elections to take place in Zanzibar, which it considered were a success, though the results posed serious issues for the Arab community.

The Times of 25 July 1957 discussed the nature of the franchise to be introduced for elections to the Uganda Legislative Assembly. After describing the qualifications for admission to the electoral roll, the editorial went on 'On the safeguards for the 60,000 Asians, there is the prospect of trouble ahead. The 1958 elections will continue to return representatives to the Legislative Council on a communal roll. In 1961 a common roll will be substituted. A minority report signed by the general secretary of the Uganda National Congress and others indicates that they are not in a mood to allow any political rights to minorities beyond that of "one man, one vote."' (This analysis proved to be correct. Soon after independence, all Asians were expelled from Uganda.)

The Manchester Guardian of 30 July 1957 contained a report of the House of Lords debate on the Federation of Malaya Independence Bill. Lord Reid, who presided over the Commission and visited Malaya and drafted the new constitution said,

> I have heard rumours, which I hope are not well-founded, that those who direct the investment of private capital are somewhat hesitant about the future of Malaya. I believe Malaya to be one of the minority of countries today where there is a clear prospect that foreign capital will receive proper treatment, I hope there will be an influx of such capital as is required for the development of the country. I believe it will be wisely used if it is forthcoming.

The Economist published a letter in its edition of 3 August 1957 from the General Director of the United Tanganyika Party (UTP), Brian Willis, in which he wrote:

> It may appear astonishing, but I believe in Tanganyika the appeal of multiracialism meets with a spontaneous response from the Africans. Of the membership of our party 60.9% are African, 30.5 % are Asian and 8.6 %

are European. No other political party in Africa can, I believe, produce such figures. ... Lack of confidence and a feeling of drifting towards extremism has been the dominant characteristic of Tanganyika until lately. ... There are signs that this been arrested by the political initiative taken inside the country. ... It would be a tragedy if the immigrant was forced to leave ... if the exploitation of Tanganyika's natural resources were to be taken out of the hands of immigrant hands, economic chaos would be inevitable. ... In such circumstances, many so-called friends of the Africans would in fact be pushing them back into the state of impoverishment and ignorance from which we are all attempting to help them to emerge. More than in any other country in Africa, the key to Tanganyika's development must lie in a genuine partnership between the races.

The Times of 15 August 1957 contained an editorial titled 'Racial Voting?' This commented on the recently concluded elections to LegCo in Zanzibar.

The Arabs find themselves in a difficult position as a result of the election; their hopes of finding a political modus vivendi have been dashed by the mass African vote; their fears of being isolated because of their aristocratic position on the island seem to have been justified ... the results of the election lend support to the view that Zanzibar is more properly linked with East Africa than with the Middle East. ... These were the first common roll elections held in East Africa.

It went on:

The comment of a prominent Arab in Mombasa is worth recording. In his view, the Zanzibar elections proved that the common roll principle was not possible in East Africa because any election would be fought on a racial basis. This is a somewhat categorical conclusion to draw from one election, but the question needs further study in the light of the British Government's acceptance of the principle for elections in Tanganyika next year (1958) and Uganda in 1961.

(Moving forward to 1964 for a moment, it is worth noting that in January 1964 a revolt by left-leaning and the majority Africans overthrew the Sultan of Zanzibar and the island's long-established Arab minority, with much loss of life, and established a republic. In April 1964, the presidents of Tanganyika and Zanzibar signed an act of union of their two countries, creating Tanzania).

On 26 August 1957, the lead editorial in *The Times* again discussed the issue as to whether the British government should set a timetable for the self-government of colonies in general and Kenya in particular, since Tom Mboya had again expressed a wish for such a timetable in respect of Kenya. The editor pointed out that the objective of policy, that is the achievement of self-government within the Commonwealth, had been expressed on many occasions and for many years, and by 1957 there could be no doubt on the evidence that the policy would be carried out. But in individual territories, the situations varied greatly and in some it was to be expected that this would take some years. It was the bringing about of conditions conducive to a successful self-governing state which ought to be the focus of attention, not the actual date of self-government. It would be unwise to set down all the factors and stages to be taken into account prior to self-government in the form of a blueprint, for it would almost certainly be impossible for either the nascent state or the British government to avoid departure from such a blueprint.

On 11 October 1957, *The Times* carried a letter from Graham Page, a British MP, agreeing with a letter published on 9 October from Hussein Juma, Chairman of the UTP, arguing that any independent observer of Tanganyika could only conclude:

> Anything approaching responsible government in Tanganyika would mean government by TANU, which has all the faults of the most immature of political parties and would be driven into intense pro-Africanism by the very pressures it generated in order to gain recognition; there would therefore be racial discrimination resulting in the collapse of commerce, the flight of capital and the breakdown of social services; that the Africans cannot find now or, I believe, in a generation, more than a fraction of the qualified persons required to take over government and development, trade and the professions; that it would be a breach of the trust under which we administer the territory to abandon the Africans and non-Africans to the wilder politicians.

(Given the record of Tanzania since independence in 1961, it is difficult to argue that Messrs Juma and Page were wrong.)

On 2 November 1957, *The Times* carried a letter from a reader which encapsulated many of the reasons why the European settlers in the Central African Federation simply could not understand why Africans were so opposed to the Federation:

> It is the reverse of the truth to suggest ... that the economic benefits of federation in Central Africa are inimical to political advancement of the Africans – if one has in mind not merely that votes should be cast but that they should be cast with some glimmering of their purport. Within living memory the whole population of the region was still existing in conditions of primitive savagery. They had no literature, no notion of science or industry ... they did not even understand the use of the wheel. ... All the

salutary features which were introduced such as hospitals, preventive medicine, education, justice were at first looked at askance by the Africans who now value them highly. Now African opinion is being led with no real understanding of what is involved to take a similarly unreasoning line about the process of federation ... such a population cannot be turned overnight into a mature body of citizens capable of working properly a democratic system in their country's interest ... much has been and is being done ... expenditure on African education in Nyasaland has tripled as a result of federation; Southern Rhodesia is engaged in a great drive to increase the number of trained African teachers by 1000 per annum ... it is the quickening flow of economic development brought about by federation which provides the revenue to make this possible. Very much remains to be done and will be done if those involved are allowed to get on with the job and still more if African politicians would play their part instead of seeking to lead their fellow Africans back into the squalor and stagnation of the jungle ... in Southern Rhodesia, no one is denied a Federal vote because he is black and no one gets it because he is white ... if the new Federal proposals are enacted this will be so throughout the Federation.

As the correspondent pointed out, in respect of the Central African Federation, 'many more Africans will become eligible to take part in the election of the African members than did so at that time ... the political situation will be totally altered in five or ten years time by economic factors alone, which will serve to enfranchise many who at that time did not meet the criteria.'

There is little doubt that the constitutional negotiations in these countries were complicated by the hope among some of the African political leaders that the Conservative Government, which was in power in London from 1951 to 1964, would be replaced by a Labour Government which they thought might be more sympathetic to their concerns, a hope which was sometimes encouraged by Labour politicians. This factor was brought out in a leader in *The Times* of 14 February 1958 which concluded its editorial review of the November 1957 constitutional proposals for Kenya that [the African boycott] would be strongly influenced by 'a clear statement by the British Labour Party advocating cooperation, for it seems that Mboya's intransigence is in part at any rate due to his belief that if the Conservative Government were to fall he will get all he wants (from Labour) on his own terms'..

On 8 April 1958, *The Times* published a letter from Professor Bauer stating what became his well-known (and broadly justified) critique of aspects of British colonial administration, especially their economic policies. Though British colonies had benefited greatly from British rule, as was to be seen by comparing colonies to neighbouring countries which were ruled by others, those accomplishments had been brought about under conditions of free trade. He quoted the Liberian spokesman in the General Assembly of the United Nations in March 1957, as asking the people of Ghana 'not to look down on the inferior economic achievements of Liberia, but to remember that Ghana's greater prosperity reflected the benefits of colonial rule'. As in Britain itself colonial administration, exacerbated by wartime pressures had also

> brought about a vast extension of government control and a resulting restriction of people's range of choice in the purchase of their requirements, the sale of their products and in their opportunities for employment ... tightly controlled economies, in which a few people exercise pervasive and extensive power are thus, with a few exceptions, a major legacy of recent British colonial rule ... political independence must not be mistaken for personal freedom ... the great increase in man's power over man ... much enriches the prizes (of office) and enhances the struggle for power.

A few days later, on 11 April 1958, *The Times* published a letter which discussed the notion of 'freedom' being used in connection with the movement towards independence of the colonies; 'our politicians and people will have to look at the word "freedom" practically and not emotionally. We must decide whether we regard the freedom of the individual or the freedom of the State as the more important. On the assumption that the object of government is the happiness and well-being of the individual, then "freedom" as applied to the individual is the paramount goal to be achieved ... the illiterate native imagines that the exit of the British means freedom to do anything he pleases. He naturally cannot be expected to understand that freedom is conditional on order. ... To exchange the impartial administration of the Colonial Office for the often corrupt and inefficient governments to which we hand over countless millions of backward peoples in the name of democracy is hypocritical, and a very retrograde step for the peace and happiness of the world. ... In America in particular, the meaning of "freedom" as applied to backward colonial peoples has been completely misconstrued by a welter of emotional hypocrisy'.

On 15 August 1958, *The Times* featured an editorial titled 'Getting Africans to the Poll'. It concluded, in respect of elections in East and Central Africa, that there were three reasons for low participation rates in the elections – 'lack of confidence, lack of knowledge and lack of interest'. The lack of confidence is brought about by suspicion of European motives and fear on the part of the Africans that they are obscurely, but effectively, being cheated. Lack of knowledge stemmed partly from the persuasion by the political parties of those eligible to vote, not to register or vote. In some areas there has been fear that registration would also be used to increase taxation. There was a need to counter these fears and ignorance by effective publicity by all available means.

The Economist of 16 August 1958 carried an article titled 'Safari in the South' which described General de Gaulle's planned visit to the French African territories. The article went on 'The general seems already to have made up his mind on the broad lines of his policy towards the French Union, and the verbal flexibility he showed before the consultative committee on the constitution in Paris last week did not extend to accepting the aspirations of Black Africa's advocates of independence within a French commonwealth. ... He is offering the federal relationship, with internal autonomy, which African moderates, in the person of his Senegalese Minister of State, M. Houphouet-Boigny, believe to be sufficient to guarantee African advance under French guidance and authority' ... and it is on French economic aid that the African states must rely in the years ahead. The Africans have been warned that to reject the constitutional project in the referendum in September will be to choose secession from the French Union '"at their own risk and peril."'

On 19 August 1958, *The Times* devoted a two-column article to a review of the report of the Nigerian Minorities Commission (the Willink report), appointed after the May 1957 constitutional conference, which concluded that the best form of protection for the minority tribes would be not to delegate any more powers to the regional level, but to strengthen the Federal government, where some degree of balance and compromise could be achieved. It was also essential that the police should not come under purely regional control; there should be one police force with a dual mandate to both the regional and Federal governments.

On 1 September 1958, *The Times* featured a further long editorial titled 'The General's Tour', commenting on the outcome of General de Gaulle's tour of Africa. His purpose was to explain the features of the new draft French constitution and the way in which this would impinge on 'l'Afrique Noir'; and the nature of the proposed relationship between metropolitan France and the African colonies. But he also listened to comments made. In particular, he explained in Brazzaville that 'within the Community, if some territory feels, at the end of a certain time, which I will not define, that it is ready to exercise all the charges and duties of independence, it will have the chance to decide on this'.

On 6 September 1958, *The Times* commented in an editorial on the outcome of the elections in Tanganyika, in which TANU, the nationalist party, achieved a sweeping majority. This election and the system of franchise used swept away any notion of a multiracial Tanganyika, which had been the UN policy for the country, and subsequently the aim of the British administration. The result was a government dedicated to nationalist solutions. 'On the debit side', wrote the Editor, 'any notion of a multi-racial state has been rejected; on the credit side, the Africans, unlike those of the Central African Federation, have taken an active part in multi-racial politics and the Europeans and Asians have shown themselves to be adaptable'.

On 22 September 1958, *The Times* published a full-page spread in which Obafemi Awolowo, the Premier of Western Nigeria, stated, 'This I believe … in which he laid out his views on freedom of Speech and Religion, freedom from Want, freedom from Fear, and also a section on foreign policy.'

On 6 October 1958, *The Times* published a letter from the Editor of the East Africa and Rhodesia journal in which he summarized the outcome of the Mwanza conference of African leaders from Kenya, Uganda, Tanganyika, Zanzibar and Nyasaland which ended in a decision 'to work for a Government of Africans by Africans for Africans on pan-African lines' and urged 'African nationalism, virile and unrelenting'.

The Times leader on 15 October 1958 titled 'A Courageous Step' pointed out that the order to French troops in Algeria not to belong to organizations of a political character, is the work of a disciplinarian, not a dictator. To be clear de Gaulle stressed 'I order them to withdraw without delay. … A report will be made to me of the measures taken for the execution of this instruction …

a door could be opened … for what General de Gaulle called 'an Algerian political elite'.

On 18 October 1958, *The Times* contained an editorial commenting on the timetable for the independence of British Somaliland. Neighbouring Somalia, which had been a UN Trust Territory since the end of the Second World War, was to become independent in 1960, by a decision of the United Nations. Quoting the paper's Special Correspondent in Hargeisa, the Editor wrote 'The choice in British Somaliland is therefore between continuing an orderly political advance by stages, thereby risking the country going sour through mistrust and frustration; and crash-changing into a higher political gear at once, thereby risking some form of political breakdown through lack of experience'. The underlying assumption was that the British colony would either way wish to join with Somalia in due course. (It is of interest that the former territory of British Somaliland in later years chose to take a different course from that taken by the part of Somalia previously administered by Italy and the UN.) In October–November 1958, James Thomson, a BBC reporter visited British Somaliland during the course of a Middle Eastern tour. Among his comments on the tour he wrote, 'It was only when I visited Somaliland and Somalia that I realized to what an extent British policy has been basically sound, but manages to seem unsound. When I left Hargeisa I was personally convinced that all the strictures against British "Somalization" policy as "too little and too late" were justified. After a week in Somalia I came to the conclusion that, whereas the British have Somalized very thoroughly from the bottom up to District Commissioner level, the Italians, under UN pressure, have Somalized from the top down to the District Commissioner level'.

The most traumatic event in the decolonization of Africa was the collapse of the Belgian Congo, an event which entered the lexicon as a term indicating chaos – 'like the Congo; as bad as the Congo'. The Belgian Congo had been run initially by King Leopold of Belgium as a private estate, which he expected to produce a profit. The means employed were rapacious and were widely criticized by other countries, including Britain. It was only when he died in 1908 that the country became a colonial possession of Belgium. From then on it was run by a triumvirate of the colonial administration, the mining and other businesses and the Roman Catholic Church, together with about 80,000 settlers (colons) who were mainly concerned with their own interests. As Colin Legum wrote in *The Observer* on 14 August 1960 'The Belgians have never been so aware of their empire as they are at the moment of losing it. They tried to repudiate it when the Congo fell into their lap. They largely ignored it when they had it, leaving its affairs in the hands of a small coterie of special interests. And they lost it in the end because there was no informed opinion other than that produced by Inforcongo, the public affairs agency of the Congo administration … it was reported that there were only twelve graduates in the entire country'.

When things began to unravel in 1959, with severe rioting, rigid racial segregation and the revelation by a Commission of a loss of control by the administration in the Lower Congo, the Belgian government and administration were divided as to what to do and while calling elections in the Congo, sought to determine the outcome. Some of the mining interests, seeking to protect their stake in the Congo, backed a Katanga secessionist movement under Tshombe, antagonizing Lumumba, the leader of the largest party in the Congo. The Force Publique mutinied and the Belgian government began to cut its losses in the Congo to save what it could in the Katanga. For years thereafter, Congo became a by-word for maladministration, insecurity and conflict. As Colin Legum wrote:

> The Congo was the 'blue chip' colony. Its disaster, so little expected and seldom foretold, has produced the incomprehension usually reserved for the news of the failure of an old and safe partnership in the City. It is impossible to believe that the solid burghers of Brussels have been guilty of a gigantic fraud. Nor indeed were they – unless it is a fraud to delude yourself.

In its edition of 17 January 1959, *The Economist*, in respect of the Belgian Congo, wrote,

> After a 'soul-searching' parliamentary debate, an openly penitent Belgian government has announced its plan for dealing with the suddenly agitated Congo. The first part is an undated cheque for independence, backed up by

a timetable of elections for local bodies, which are in turn to elect next year a skeleton assembly to which responsibility will be transferred in unspecific stages. ...The Belgians wisest course would be to grasp the nettle while the "soul searching" mood prevails and get down to discussion with African leaders about developing in the Congo the representative institutions which the Belgians have long condemned as premature in British and French Africa.

Two weeks later *The Economist* published a two-page article titled 'Fulcrum of Africa' on the Congo.

King Baudouin's promise that the Belgians will lead the Congo 'towards independence, without delay but also without inconsiderate haste, has been widely received as a decisive victory for African nationalism ... the timetable is vague; all that is clear is that racial discrimination is to go and by a series of indirect elections, the Congolese will elect some sort of national assembly, some time in 1960, to which responsibilities will be transferred by undefined stages thereafter. ... The significance of the statement lies in its timing and in the key position the Belgian Congo occupies in Africa ... for the first time the goal of independence under an African regime has been set for a territory in which there is a considerable European population (80,000 versus 50,000 in Kenya), without any by-your-leave from the settlers themselves. Deprived of any say in a paternalist government of the Congo in which the Africans were similarly vote-less, the Europeans are not even to be consulted about its future ... this is a tremendous shift in the balance of Africa, in a country in which economic advance was put before political advance for Africans ... it is suddenly revealed that this 'practical' colonial policy is bankrupt, striking most painfully the Europeans in East and Central Africa ... thus the hopes some white minorities had of waiting to see whether the West African states would really make a success of independence, behind a firebreak of Belgian and Portuguese paternalism, are growing slim ... there are now great dangers in this new impetus in the pace of change in Africa; which also implies big mental adjustments by the European minorities.

The Times reported on 26 January 1959 on the meeting of the East African Governors and the colonial secretary, at which the speeding up of African nationalism and Pan-Africanism was the principal focus of discussions.

On 22 May 1959, *The Manchester Guardian* carried a report from its correspondent in Ghana about the visit of Hugh Gaitskell, leader of the Opposition Labour Party in Britain. Speaking on democracy in Ghana Gaitskell said 'It is not possible for us in Britain to determine how you will develop your democracy. It is your own affair, but I think in every new country emerging into nationhood certain principles must be observed. They are national unity, a high degree of personal leadership and thirdly, and most important, the preservation of individual liberty at all costs.'

In July 1959, the report of the Nyasaland Commission of Inquiry (the Devlin Commission) was presented to Parliament and published. This received widespread and detailed examination in the press. A previous chapter gave a rather detailed description of the Commission's findings. What was highlighted in the press reports were Devlin's words 'Nyasaland is – no doubt only temporarily – a police state, where it is not safe for anyone to express approval of the policies of the Congress Party, to which, before 3 March 1959, the vast majority of politically-minded Africans belonged and where it is unwise to express any but the most restrained criticism of government policy'. (This finding came as a profound shock in Britain where the very idea of a police state is an anathema. Even in Malaya and Kenya, where armed insurrection was a major threat, such a description of the state would have been inaccurate and care was taken to observe the rule of law within the powers given to government by the declarations of a State of Emergency.)

In early 1960, the British prime minister, Harold Macmillan, visited four countries in Africa to study the situation, but also to indicate the lines of thinking of the British government on the major controversial issues. He spent three months on his trip. These visits were described in greater detail in Chapter 2, but inevitably the British press gave prominence to Macmillan's speeches. This chapter highlights the coverage by *The Economist*, which was extensive. 'Mr Macmillan must know that the things he himself says about Africa are now watched more closely and with a more critical eye than the things he says about almost anything else. This is not only because Africa represents modern Conservatism's crisis of conscience. It is because there is now an influential section of opinion in Britain which is profoundly concerned that this country should not appear in a bad light in Africa; it insists, no doubt in a rather muddled and imprecise way, that the right and moral thing shall be done somehow, and that there shall be some term to shifts and evasions. This strain of opinion may sometimes be irresponsible and even more often unrealistic – but what matters for Macmillan is that it runs right through national sentiment, from the left of Labour to the Tory Bow Group.'

On 13 February 1960, *The Economist* summed up the consequences of Macmillan's visit to Africa and the statements he made in four countries:

Wherever Mr Macmillan spoke in Africa he produced a rumpus, and his speech to the South African parliamentarians in Capetown produced in the end the biggest rumpus of all. The echoes will be long heard – not least in the House of Commons next week in London. Yet in every speech the Prime Minister stuck with consummate skill to statements of known British policy. Nowhere did he add anything substantial that was new; wherever possible he quoted what had already been propounded at Westminster or the United

Nations. Yet everywhere the impression exists that Mr Macmillan has boldly put a new and liberal face on British policy in Africa. ... But he would be wrong to think that he is returning with no more commitments than when he left. For it is the reaction to his words, not the words themselves, that is decisive – not what he said, or intended to say, but what he was thought by the African masses to have said with all the authority of the head of the British government. And the judgement is clear. Africans and the outside world have concluded that Mr Macmillan has come down firmly for coming to terms with African nationalism, and they have applauded; the white Africans have been horror-struck. This is the remarkable denouement when basic British colonial policy is simply restated with precision by the Prime Minister; it turns out to be devastatingly liberal.

There then occurred what became known as the 'Sharpeville massacre' when sixty Africans were killed in a police operation near Johannesburg. South Africa moved to ban the African National Congress and the Pan-African Congress. These events had a profound impact in the Central African Federation at the time of the visit of the Monckton Commission and the visit of the colonial secretary to Nyasaland and Northern Rhodesia.

On 5 March 1960, *The Observer* published a report from George Clay in Salisbury, Southern Rhodesia titled 'Rhodesian Whites Digging In – Fear of Macleod Sell-Out'. The report described the formation in Northern Rhodesia of an Association pledged to defend the status quo for the 70,000 whites in Northern Rhodesia, and of a similar association in Southern Rhodesia. There was talk of a 'State within a State' with 6 per cent of the land area of Northern Rhodesia being carved out as a self-governing state federated with Southern Rhodesia. A petition to this effect was to be submitted to the Monckton Commission and to the colonial secretary. In Southern Rhodesia, the opposition to British policy was centred in the Dominion Party which had thirteen out of thirty seats in the Southern Rhodesian Parliament, though no significant strength in the Federal Parliament. There was challenging talk of 'secession now', though this talk was deprecated by the business community which felt secession would ruin the economy.

On 16 January 1960, *The Economist* ran an article titled 'Africa's Rubicon' which discussed the main issues facing the Kenya constitutional conference due to start the following week. The paper felt the stakes were high for both Britain and Kenya and that this was the moment of truth for both the African politicians and the Kenya settlers. It urged McLeod, the colonial secretary, to present the issues bluntly to both parties and if necessary impose his own solution. The paper felt the settlers would have to negotiate a settlement in the end, as without some kind of settlement, political activism would become more vociferous and violent.

On 12 March 1960, *The Economist* commented on the new, republican Ghanaian constitution.

> It crystallises around a basic principle: that the Head of State and the chief executive should be the same man, whose powers should include all, perhaps more than all, those wielded by an American President and a British Prime Minister together – nearly as many as President de Gaulle has. The checks and balances of the American written constitution (the Montesquieu-derived division of executive, legislative and judicial powers) are omitted. The Ghanaian parliament's powers will be like the British, 'unlimited' in a unitary state; but the president, as automatically chosen leader of the majority party, will clearly be master of the parliament.

(Later, in 1964, Nkrumah declared Ghana to be a one-party state under his own life presidency. He was deposed two years later by the army.)

On 26 March 1960, *The Guardian* published a report from a correspondent in Kenya titled 'Not an Encouraging Prospect'. Following the Lancaster House conference on the colony's next constitution, the latter is regarded 'as something imposed by the colonial secretary, McLeod, impelled by the re-appraisal of Britain's colonial policy in the context of the so-called Wind of Change'. Though some Europeans are ready for an increased role for Africans in government, some are also beginning to send money abroad and instead of investing for the future are seeking high current returns. The African delegates were very disappointed by the outcome of the conference, which they thought would lead to self-government in 1961/2; the Asians were anxious due to a number of attacks by African thugs. There was debate among the Africans about the future of Jomo Kenyatta, still then in prison; there were irresponsible statements about the future of land in the White Highlands. Both the United Party and the New Kenya Party seemed to have lost ground.

On 2 April 1960, *The Economist* ran a five-page series of articles analysing the situation in South Africa, the impact of Macmillan's speech and Sharpeville on the South African markets, the impact of events in South Africa on the Central African Federation and Kenya and the rapid evolution taking place in the French Community since de Gaulle's visits, including the independence of Mali and Malagasy. This was a climactic time in the process of decolonization, when there was a tendency for the multiracial societies in Africa to polarize, a time of delicate negotiations by Iain McLeod and Lord Hume, under the leadership of the prime minister, Harold Macmillan, and by Lord Monckton's Commission on Central Africa, to find constitutional ways forward acceptable to the various parties. In French Africa, the direction had been set in a statesmanlike manner by General de Gaulle two years earlier, and by 1960, several countries were becoming independent.

On 9 April 1960, *The Economist* was reporting the release of Dr Banda 'in a manner which seemed to disarm everyone concerned'. However on 6 May 1960, only a month after his release, *The Guardian* ran a report from Nairobi titled 'Militancy of Dr Banda'. Banda was making statements about the future of Europeans and Asians in Nyasaland; his intention was to merge with Northern Mozambique and/or Tanganyika. He made antagonistic remarks about British civil servants and the British government.

On 25 June 1960, *The Economist* published a two-page article on the Congo and another report on Algeria. On the Congo it wrote:

The Congo's emergence as an independent state next Thursday is a capital event in African affairs. … If the Congo does survive as a recognisable entity in the coming months, black Africa will consider it has demonstrated beyond question its capability for self-government elsewhere. … The personal struggle between Mr Lumumba and Mr Kasavubu; the threats of secession from the Katanga province; the breakdown of local administration and health and sanitation systems; the mounting evidence of reversion to tribal division and conflict – all these serve to stimulate European expectations of disaster … the main legitimate criticism against Brussels is that, right up to the Leopoldville riots in January 1959, it failed to envisage any circumstances in which the Congolese should be prepared for responsible self-government. As a result, the Belgian record in the Congo, for all its labours and successes, is sadly destined to be written off in African history as the classic example of rapacious colonialism.

On 16 July, three weeks later, the journal published an article titled 'Congo Express Derailed', in which it described the rapid collapse of the state institutions:

The Congo, only a week after being put up for membership of the United Nations had fallen into such critical difficulties that the Secretary-General was impelled to summon the Security Council to an urgent night-time meeting. In the small hours of Thursday morning, the council agreed to his proposals to arrange for international military assistance to enable the teetering Congo government to get by until its own mutinous troops are in hand again. Belgium undertook to remove its paratroops as soon as a UN force could move in. … Anarchy in the new state not only raises knotty questions of world law … it also creates … a new position in the east-west struggle, now being switched so rapidly and perilously to Africa. Even before the mutiny, it was plain that the in-experienced government was in deep trouble and would have to seek international aid.

By 13 August 1960, the journal was writing:

> The Black Balkans exist: if there were any illusions about the predicament that Africa presents to the world, that it is in any way temporary, they had better be shed. The development of the Congo crisis leaves little expectation that the problems of Central Africa are likely to yield to an orderly, or pragmatic, series of adjustments and realignments. What is happening is neither unnatural nor unfamiliar. The powers are confronted with a region dominated by nationalism and its intellectual and physical excesses, with states claiming sovereignty yet unable to exert it throughout their own territories, and with nationalist leaders who, beset by the problems of underdevelopment and under-education, believe they can best maintain their political momentum by diplomatic adventure and excitement. Beneath this structure lurks an instinctive African primitivism; it is to tribalism itself, infinite and ageless, that social or economic failure speedily reduces the state. This is what Balkanisation means.

In regard to Algeria, the journal urged General de Gaulle to take risks in his negotiations with the Algerians; it is the only way if French influence in Africa is to survive.

On 13 October 1960, *The Guardian* published a report of a speech made by McLeod at the Conservative Party conference. He said 'I cannot promise you a popular colonial policy ... it is going to be expensive but it is our duty to do this, and it is our duty to put this burden on the taxpayers of this country so that we can carry out our duty to all the people in the British territories'. The report also recorded a speech in which the speaker said the debate was overshadowed by the Monckton Commission report 'a clear-cut case can be made for the federation on economic grounds but what was the value of that if it had no support from the people?' A speaker said that the Monckton Report contained one very dangerous recommendation. It appeared to suggest that the British government should initiate legislation which would break up the Federation under certain circumstances, in a given number of years. This could only result in political and economic disaster. Who would invest in a federation which was about to be wound up? There was concern expressed for the European settlers 'who were not birds of passage, but citizens of these countries. What was the future for them and their families in the countries they had helped to create and build?'

On the 15 October 1960, *The Economist* described and commented on the findings of the Monckton Commission on the future of the Central African Federation. The previous week, a referendum in South Africa had resulted in a vote by the South African whites to perpetuate apartheid, with its consequences for the divisions between the races. Now in the Federation, both Africans and European settlers were asked to consider ways to perpetuate partnership between the races through ingenious constitutional provisions, leading to a final decision after five years.

What Monckton has tried to do – with courage and considerable insight as well as commendable ingenuity – is to build a psychological bridge over which black and white in central Africa can advance towards each other, if either side has the wish to do so. ... The Commission asks the whites to take a calculated risk; in five years time whatever is done now, the Africans may still say No. But the risk is worth taking, the report argues, because the Africans too are asked to take a calculated risk. ... The African leaders owe it to themselves and their followers to grasp what there is in the majority report before they opt for balkanisation. ... If they read carefully, they will find that the report offers them self-government of Northern Rhodesia and Nyasaland under African control, which would extend over a broader range of responsibilities including education, health, agriculture, and most finance and taxation than the Nigerian regions have today ... it offers them parity in economic, defence and foreign policy matters and a ban on federal independence until the territories are themselves both self-governing and consenting. It offers a Council of State on the Kenya model to prevent racial discrimination. ... It offers a quick end to racial discrimination in Southern Rhodesia and a wide extension of political and economic opportunity there. ... It does not require much imagination to see that such a set of proposals, if put in force, could open the way not merely to African control of the two territories still subject to policy control from London, but, much more glitteringly, to the creation of the second strongest black African state in the continent after Nigeria. The condition is that the Africans must accept the Europeans as partner – if increasingly the junior one ... why should the Europeans consent to concessions which would gradually demote them from senior to junior partner. The immediate result would probably be political suicide for Sir Roy Welensky and the United Federal Party long before the question of secession arose; but the basic answer to the question is surely this – the Europeans in Central Africa ... are in need of finding the best and surest terms on which the Africans may agree in the long term to allow them to exist, prosperous and free as a distinct community at all. ... White supremacy could indeed be continued for a while in Southern Rhodesia under a South African aegis, by force; in the federation its days are numbered ... the choice before the Europeans is a harsh and distasteful one; it is whether to seek to work their passage with African nationalists in a liberalised federation that bows to the verdict of African events; or to take Southern Rhodesia into the South African laager for whatever time it would buy them at a cost which would be very steep. ... If the Monckton prescription is ruled out, even as a basis for discussion, by blacks or whites, or both, they will have acknowledged that the experiment in partnership has irretrievably failed and that racial cooperation is impossible; that the strongest must be boss in each petty African backyard.

The parties met in London in December 1960 and as *The Economist* again described it in its edition of 3 December, the Africans had not taken the trouble to read the Monckton proposals carefully and seemed to reject them viscerally; the Europeans had not yet realized 'that if the settlers cannot govern by consent, the settlers will not be able to go on governing. Fitness or unfitness to govern is ceasing to be relevant. Either the Africans are going to be set now on the road to power, or they are going to reach for power themselves.'

(Monckton did have the effect of galvanizing the leaders of the three territories to think further about their future and take further steps through constitutional negotiations with Britain, and the holding of further elections. However, the federal idea died; Nyasaland opted out and though Dr Banda held out the possibility of re-entering a federation, the notion of sharing power did not appeal to him. Northern Rhodesia, under the leadership of Kenneth Kaunda, accepted a new constitution in 1962 and had a go at a plural form of government, with at least three multiracial political parties and considerable good will. There was residual goodwill towards the possibility of some form of federation.)

On 25 January 1961, *The Guardian* published a report of a speech made at a lunch in New York City of the Pilgrims Trust by Sir Patrick Dean, the British representative at the United Nations. He again urged the United States not to take action on colonialism before the UN which would make Britain's task more difficult.

> The United States and Britain were the natural friends of nations wishing themselves to be truly free and increasingly prosperous ... the object of British policy was the creation of new nations undivided by ideological, racial or tribal differences ... we would think it to the great advantage of all the free world for you to speak out in support of those policies in these matters wherever, in the exercise of your understanding and judgement, you consider these sound and well-conceived in the interest of the colonial peoples concerned ... if you think we are wrong on any particular question we think that you should tell us so quite frankly in one of the many informal exchanges which we are always having.

On 12 February 1961, *The Observer* published a report of moves being made at the time of constitutional negotiations between the British government and representatives of Northern Rhodesia, but outside the negotiations themselves. A delegation of the Northern Rhodesian Mine Workers Union, representing European miners on the Copper Belt, but not represented at the talks, told a press conference 'an adjournment was the only hope ... if constitutional terms unacceptable to the African delegations were imposed there would be violence ... more time was needed for both Europeans and African delegations to formulate their policies ... there was plenty of room for negotiation ...' the delegation saw the Minister of State to seek assurances that Colonial Office would not depart from the basis of non-racial representation in Northern Rhodesia laid down in the 1958 White Paper.

On 6 October 1961, *The Guardian* published a report by Patrick Keatley of talks held in Accra between Nkrumah and Duncan Sandys, Commonwealth Secretary. 'The Ghanaian leader has agreed to go on the record as recognizing the sincerity of the British government's approach to the colonial issue and also agrees that Britain's colonial policies had set an example to some other nations having dependent territories overseas. The communiqué includes the comment from Sandys that accusations against Britain of neo-colonialism were therefore not justified. ... But the joint statement is also remarkable in the British government's bold concession to the virtues of non-alignment in international affairs as practiced by Ghana and other Commonwealth nations. It represents a very considerable public commitment in terms that differ markedly from present policies in Washington towards neutral nations. The key phrase in the text states "that Britain fully understands and respects Ghana's wish to remain unaligned in the Cold War."' This coincided with a report in *The Observer* which, while reporting on the discussions, also reported the arrest of numerous members of the Ghanaian Opposition United Party, including Dr Danquah and Appiah, under the Preventive Detention Act of 1958. However David Holden, reporting on these issues in *The Guardian* a few days later concluded that the apparently good relations between Nkrumah and the British government were unlikely to last long, though everything would be done to avoid unpleasantness prior to the Queen's visit the following month. For within the last two months 'Ghana had taken one more step sideways towards the Left and two more steps downwards towards effective dictatorship'.

The press coverage of colonial concerns continued through the 1960s, though few new issues arose. In November 1961, for example, *The Guardian* covered a debate in the House of Lords on Kenya and measures needed to reassure European farmers who were so critical to the future of the economy and to ensure that investment in the country continued in the years before and after independence. On 8 December 1961, *The Guardian* gave prominence to the great agricultural potential and the rich mineral resources of the Congo, the large dividend which the mining companies were paying to Tshombe, and the problems the breakaway province of Katanga would experience in getting the product of its mines to market. On 31 July 1962, *The Guardian* featured a debate on the new Southern Rhodesian constitution, which many felt placed too many qualifications and barriers before Africans wanting to participate in the elections. On 7 September 1962, *The Guardian* addressed the issue of scale in the countries becoming independent. There was a case for distinguishing between self-government, which might be encouraged for any small territory, and independence which would be impracticable for the smallest ones. On 3 December, *The Guardian* again addressed the linked questions of the future of the Katanga and Northern Rhodesia about which talks were taking place both in London and at the UN. On 20 December, the paper returned to the issue of the Central African Federation by covering a debate in the House of Lords. Lord Listowel said 'For the first time since the Federation was set up, all three territories were against it. How could we maintain the Federation in those circumstances? Once the issue of the Federation had been settled, the leaders of the three territories would be able to get together to plan their future relationships on the basis of their most important common interests'. ... Lord Salisbury pointed out that the only Central African politicians who had stood throughout for true non-racialism – Sir Roy Welensky and Sir Edgar Whitehead – had been driven into the political wilderness. On 31 May 1963, *The Guardian* featured a review of a book by Patrick Keatley on Central Africa, in which the reviewer argued that the principal responsibility for the difficulties in Central Africa could all be traced to successive British governments which failed to be clear about the situation of the settlers and HMG's insistence, made much clearer in East Africa than in Central Africa, that they viewed themselves as trustees for the Africans who would one day assume the role of government. In the absence of such clarity, the attempt to build multiracial societies had failed.

Conclusion

As a commentary on the debate which occurred within Britain and the Colonial administrations on the process of decolonialization, a selection of press reports of the kind presented earlier has merit and serves to add some of the immediacy, the drama and the political conflict entailed in the process. However, it is necessarily selective and depends upon the ability of newspaper reporters and editors to distil fairly and accurately the essence of the issues as they arose and avoid acting as a mouthpiece for particular interests or groups. My view is that they succeeded remarkably well and were able to express well the opinions and reservations of most interests.

What they did not do, or attempt so far as I can see, is to represent in any way the emerging opinions of African writers and academics, mainly because few had had much to say up to the 1960s when decisions were being taken. In any case, the whole process of decolonization was shot through, for all the parties concerned, with practical issues of the most immediate kind, requiring pressing, early answers. Intellectual or philosophical debate about colonization and decolonization was a luxury available to future writers and thinkers, with few consequences for those involved, but not to those enmeshed in the complex problems of government and the transfer of authority in the colonies. The history of the British Empire is replete with practical men and women hammering out solutions to the problems, mistakes and opportunities confronting them. It is sad that the pressure for early decolonization was such that there was too little time in Africa to complete the job as it could have been done.

Chapter 8

Retrospective on decolonization

The quotations which introduced the Preface illustrated the 'trade-offs' which were implicit in the timing of 'decolonization'. The longer the time available, the better the prospect of senior posts being filled by men and women of knowledge, experience and competence, and the greater the chance of the independent state working effectively in the interests of the people at large. On the other hand, a slower process would have delayed achievement of the aspirations of some (though only a small minority) of Africans. In the event, there was little time and the Public Service in most colonies at independence was still weak, in some cases very weak. It is truly shocking to find that nine months before the independence of Tanganyika only 13 per cent of the senior posts in the Public Service were held by Africans. How could Nyerere, Twining, Turnbull and McLeod imagine that the country would be able to run itself competently with such inexperience in the Public Service?

The objective of decolonization from the perspective of the British government, as frequently articulated and repeated and demonstrated over the years, was to hand over to the people of the newly independent states functioning state institutions, educated and experienced functionaries, a social and economic structure which was viable at an attainable level and a society which was broadly at peace with itself. These objectives were spelled out again to ministers as late as 1957 by the British cabinet secretary, Sir Norman Brook. Given the starting point for all the colonies with their complex tribal affiliations and obligations, with the low level of educational attainment and economic and social development, this was always going to be difficult to achieve and was also going to require time, especially time.

Over a period of four decades from 1920, British policy was broadly unchanged – namely to achieve self-government and independence of the dependent territories at a time to be determined in due course. As Sir Ivor Jennings stressed in his 1955 BBC talks (Annex 2), delivered before any of the African colonies had achieved independence, what Britain is trying to do is to overcome the local

> difficulties in the way of 'freedom' and 'independence'. The essential condition is that the people should be able to govern themselves. ... Lincoln in his Gettysburg address linked freedom and democracy ... a people's democracy which allows no freedom is not a democracy and the people do not govern.

Jennings further argued, 'The real problem in any country, not least in a country which is moving towards self-government, is not to draft a Constitution or to make laws, but to find men and women capable of running the machinery of government.' It is clear that in most colonies that condition was not adequately met. There were two fundamental requirements for an effective government, governing in the public interest, namely a strong and capable Public Service and an independent and courageous judiciary. In most colonies both the Public Service and the legal and judicial professions were short of fully educated people at the time of independence and the level of experience of most was insufficient to the task. In the absence of strength and capability in these fields, the constitution was in danger, the possibility of politicians using the state in their own or their group's interest was increased and officials were liable to be suborned.

As indicated here it was always going to take decades for a cadre of well-educated Africans to emerge to fill the positions in the Public Service being created in the new states and for them to acquire experience. Ibadan University in Nigeria produced its first graduates in 1952, only eight years before Nigeria's independence; Makerere, about the same time; the University College of Rhodesia and Nyasaland produced its first graduates in 1960, only three years before the independence of the three member states of the Federation. Only Gold Coast and Nigeria in Africa had created a Public Service Commission (PSC) before 1950. In the others, there was no PSC until just before independence. Most countries had staffing plans of some kind, encompassing Africanization, but in many cases they had not reached the stage of creating a formal PSC process to plan future training needs and give emphasis to the appointment of Africans to the Public Service. Botswana and Malaya set their face against over-rapid localization of the Public Service, to their undoubted benefit. Most African colonies rushed ahead far too quickly, with overambitious appointments, often of inadequately qualified staff.

Until at least 1945, it was expected that self-government of the African colonies would require decades. Though it was sometimes quite difficult to balance administrative and technical quality with the aspirations of the inhabitants of the colonies with their natural wish to run their own affairs, there is ample evidence that most members of the colonial service considered that the process was in practice too fast, too hurried; that a much better outcome was possible with patience and the colonies ought to have been given more time before independence. The example given of the opinion of the provincial commissioners in Kenya is typical – they feared the outcome of the rush to independence but could not think of any way to slow it down. We have to conclude that their fears were fully justified.

It seems to me that Elspeth Huxley got it broadly right in her Foreign Affairs article of 1949, referred to earlier in the text, in which she emphasized the scale of the societal changes required, and taking place, in African countries which were a prerequisite for running these new states along modern and creditable lines:

> We do not always realise how much must be destroyed in order to rebuild, or how drastic that destruction must be to the human beings involved in it … the customary way of life of the African is incompatible with westernism. It must go … what must replace it? The strength of tribal life was discipline, loyalty, faith and the sense of community, of working together for common ends … in the new generation we see froth and no body; it is easily led, ignorant yet arrogant, undisciplined and above all self-seeking and unstable … the process of achieving self-government used to be seen as one of gradual evolution, allowing time to learn from experience and to build up a healthy economy and a well-informed public opinion … estimates of time were shunned … but the plan has gone wrong … we now think in terms of decades or even single years … the rising tempo of events has hastened matters … Nigeria has had two constitutions in three years … history has much to say of the results of handing over to a small minority of privileged persons all the powers of government before there is a body of citizens with critical judgement and independent views to keep them in check … this is the road not of democracy, but of tyranny.

And tyranny was soon the result in many former colonies. Subsequent elections in the former colonies have amply demonstrated that given a chance, Africans value the opportunity to vote as much as any people and will turn out in their millions. Sadly, many of them were denied the chance for many years by their post-independence rulers and many still face corruption of the electoral process.

What was the cause of the hurry? There was of course ambition on the part of the rising class of Africans who happened to be the first to have a full education; though they were few in number, they were eloquent in the cause of early independence. But there were no mass political parties such as had emerged in Asia and such countries as Egypt. Even TANU, though without domestic opponents, was not a mass party. The emerging leaders were encouraged along by visitations from the UN Trusteeship Committee and others, many of whom knew and understood little of what was involved. They believed the United

States would support them. The ultimate cause was of course much broader and perhaps best described by Colonial Secretary Oliver Lyttelton in the House of Commons in 1954 as 'the mighty ferment caused by the projection of Western ideas into the continent of Africa over a considerable period'.

Could Britain have slowed the whole process down? We have seen that in a few cases it was slowed down. In Nigeria, the northern emirs delayed the grant of self-government for several years until 1960. Britain said it would not grant independence until all the regional governments requested it. Perhaps it could have been postponed even longer. In Malaya, there was a deliberate decision to slow down the handover of responsibility from British to Malay/Chinese officers. Procedures were adopted to limit the number of members of the Colonial Service who could depart each year. In Botswana, too, Seretse Khama took a stance against the appointment of ill-qualified Africans to replace British staff. In light of the encouragement given to early independence by many of those speaking on behalf of the United States, by often ill-informed officials and diplomats at the United Nations, by the leaders of the states which became independent soon after the Second World War and by anti-imperial zealots, the impetus at the international level for early moves towards self-government and independence of the colonies was substantial. No doubt this encouragement proved to be influential in changing expectations.

In his Oxford interviews in the 1970s, Alan Lennox-Boyd, colonial secretary from 1954 until 1959, said that in his view the British government's conception of its colonial responsibilities changed somehow during the course of the 1959 General Election. He said he could not pin down all the factors at work, but he felt they included increasing British interest in Europe, dissatisfaction with the British economy and a wish to take new approaches in the international economy; and perhaps a sort of weariness on the part of ministers and civil servants with the difficulties of managing the process of colonial emancipation. At any rate in the 1960s the process was speeded up, especially under Iain McLeod. With inadequate will power in London to slow the process, the administrators and leaders in the individual colonies were bound to find it very difficult to slow down. It probably would have required an act of statesmanship by Prime Minister Harold Macmillan to persuade the African leaders and the international community within the United Nations to take their time. Lord Home and Colonel David Sterling toyed with such an idea, but it did not gain traction within the British government and the opportunity was lost.

Moreover, the handling of colonial matters both by the British government and at the local level was essentially pragmatic. A close study of each colony makes it clear that it was the local situation, and the British government's reaction to it, which was decisive in regard to the specific timing of self-government in nearly all cases. Thus we must address this question country by country. Though there were powerful historical forces at work tending towards the retrenchment of empires, dwelling on the strategic level of British policy-making in regard to the colonies does not get you very far in understanding the timing issue.

In the case of Sudan, the poor relations between Britain and Egypt in the 1940s and 1950s proved decisive in the timing of independence. The Egyptians were not particularly interested in the welfare of the Sudanese, but rather their own influence and power. Some Sudanese nationalists facilitated Egyptian agitation and, led by their own ambition, lost sight of the true needs of their country, which were complex and daunting. Others resisted the Egyptian embrace and in the end the country was able to attain its independence in 1954. But the Egyptian agitation and British acceptance of a very early date for independence meant that the Public Service and its institutions at independence were very inexperienced and weak; and the handover of responsibility from British to Sudanese officials was far too quick, even precipitate. There was insufficient time for officials and politicians to learn how to manage the country's numerous problems before independence. The domestic history of the country since independence has been troubled and marred by conflict. The Sudanese government was unable to gain the confidence of the people of the Southern Sudan, now recognized internationally as a new state after fifty years of strife and struggle; and in recent times it has alienated the people of Darfur.

In Gold Coast (Ghana), while Nkrumah and the CPP won two elections before independence, there were already signs of his megalomania which would eventually bring the country to its knees, politically and economically. Faced with Nkrumah's political skill, and his electoral mandate, it would have been difficult for Britain to delay independence after the 1956 (the third) election, though there were many in the territory who would have preferred a slower timetable and a more federal constitution, some of whom later argued their case before Prime Minister Harold Macmillan. It is sad that after independence the country had to endure many years of autocracy and misrule before it could regain some semblance of the representative government it started with.

The independence of Nigeria was delayed for four years at the initiative of the Northern rulers who were realistic about their capabilities due to the lagging educational progress in the North. Was it impossible for Britain to negotiate another five or ten years to give the leaders more time to learn how to operate a relatively weak federal constitution in such a large and complex country? The Nigerians were not keen on Ghana becoming independent before Nigeria and Azikiwe and Awolowo were a formidable pair. But was it not possible for the governor and HMG to appeal to the people at large on the grounds that it would be a mistake to see squandered the good work done on the constitution? The process of arriving at the 1950 Nigerian constitution was excellent, with public consultation at all levels of government, and a national conference at the end to agree its main provisions. There was a large measure of public support for it. But there was inadequate time for the federal agencies, ministers and officials to gain experience in operating the federal system. In retrospect, it may be that the Clifford concept of federation, with fourteen provinces or states, would have suited the country better and it is a pity it was not really examined in detail before the three-region federation was adopted. Lennox-Boyd considered that when he became secretary of state in 1954, the die was already cast and that reopening the issue of the Nigerian constitution would have been very difficult, despite the goodwill on all sides. It is of interest that something similar to Clifford's concept was in fact adopted after the Biafran Civil War, when a much stronger federal government was established to administer a country of twelve states. Since then, many new states have been created with much less autonomy and power than the original three regional governments enjoyed.

In Tanganyika (Tanzania), the government of Nyerere initially agreed to a prospective date of 1969 for independence. Despite this, on Governor Turnbull's initiative in the face of Lennox-Boyd's opposition and McLeod's, and the British Cabinet's evident doubts, the country became independent in March 1962. Tanganyika had had only one national election and the level of experience of its Public Service was woeful – less than 13 per cent of senior posts in the Public Service were held by Africans in July 1961, only nine months before independence. Was it impossible to persuade Nyerere to wait a few more years? McLeod was a formidable negotiator which he demonstrated on many occasions in his political life. Could he not have used these skills to postpone independence, at least until after another election – as in Ghana? TANU was the only political party. What could Nyerere have feared? McLeod considered that by pushing ahead he was avoiding bloodshed. But both the Gold Coast (Ghana) and Nigeria had become independent without serious trouble. What was there to fear in Tanganyika?

The early independence date for Tanganyika put pressure on Uganda and Kenya to push for early independence too. Kenya in particular needed time to sort out the communal issue, on which progress was already encouraging. Tom Mboya, a Luo, discounted the dangers of a dominating political party or group, but the history of the country since independence has shown that he misjudged those dangers which have strongly influenced the country's politics ever since. The Kikuyu have retained power much of the time since independence and have not hesitated to use it to their own advantage, as told recently in Michela Wrong's vivid book on the life and experiences of John Githongo. A saving grace in Kenya was the leavening of settlers who remained in the country after independence, who helped to maintain and expand a functioning economy.

Uganda became independent in 1962 with much goodwill on all sides, but quite soon succumbed to a bout of violence under Obote and Idi Amin which killed many, led to the expulsion of the Asians who were so critical to the modest prosperity of the country prior to independence and set back the promising economy by years. The structure and authority of this new state at independence, especially the judiciary and the Public Service, did not have sufficient strength and cohesion to resist the pull of tribal allegiances and the political personalities; and proved to be incapable of constraining those who seized power.

The East African Common Services Organization, an adaptation of the colonial-era High Commission, did not last beyond 1977. National interests intervened. It is of great interest that consideration is being given to an East African Community today, with the possible addition of Rwanda and Burundi. The rationale for its initial creation is still there.

Perhaps the most regrettable timing decision was that taken by the United Nations in respect of Somalia (previously Italian Somaliland). In deciding to make the country independent in 1960 the weak capacity of Somalia to govern itself was ignored. This decision put British Somaliland under pressure to seek independence from Britain and to merge with Somalia well before it had sufficient trained people and before they could gain experience in governing themselves. It seems likely that this timing decision influenced politicians in East Africa to seek independence prematurely. The governor of Uganda was particularly critical of the Somalia decision. Arguably the current state of Somalia is in some measure a consequence of those rash decisions on the timing of independence.

In Central Africa, there was a failure by the Southern Rhodesian politicians (and the proponents of federation in Britain) to demonstrate convincingly to the Africans by specific measures and social adaptations, especially to those in Northern Rhodesia and Nyasaland, that the federation could be in their interest too. Indeed they never really tried – in most cases the Southern Rhodesian politicians did not even meet the leaders of Northern Rhodesia and Nyasaland until they met in London for the constitutional conferences. This was political ineptitude. The Colonial Office must share the blame for the failure to ensure there was adequate exchange before those conferences between the three parties. The high hopes for the federation which were permissible by the mid-1950s, and its undoubted economic benefits in the early years for all three states, turned to dross. It was short-sighted to place the federal capital (as well as the university) in Salisbury, which was by far the most significant city already, instead of in Livingstone and/or Lusaka (Lennox-Boyd later regretted he did not intervene on this issue). The Africans in the two protectorates, Northern Rhodesia (Zambia) and Nyasaland (Malawi), never had a chance to vote on the federation on the basis of a balanced and complete assessment of its record and of policies demonstrating an intention to make it beneficial to all. All three countries paid a high price for the federation's failure, a price which arguably is still being paid today.

Southern Rhodesia (Zimbabwe) had a good number of competent officials though the country took a wayward approach to its future. The Public Services of Zambia and Malawi, by contrast, had very little experience of government, and it soon showed. They came to be dominated by persuasive political leaders who did not give, or were not able to give, priority to the needs of the people at large but allowed themselves to be distracted by their own concerns and by the various regional conflicts, especially the rising opposition to South Africa under apartheid.

Southern Africa. In view of Botswana's relative success in administering itself after self-government it is informative to look for the reasons. Peter Faucus wrote,

> Botswana's continued success and tranquillity has not been due solely or even mainly to the wealth it has acquired as a result of mineral discoveries. It has been due in large measure to the political stability it has achieved as a result of the attachment of its leaders to multiparty democracy, to the rule of law, to the protection of human rights and the holding of free and fair elections at regular five-year intervals.

It is also noteworthy that from the start, Bechuanaland adopted a simple franchise of one person one vote on a common (rather than a communal) franchise. Further, a House of Chiefs was retained, parallel to LegCo, perpetuating the leadership role performed by the chiefs in the traditional societies – probably nowhere else in Africa did the role of the chiefs survive at the national level in a manner in which they could act independently of the political parties. Finally, Seretse Khama declared that 'We should never sacrifice efficiency on the altar of localisation.' The contrast with the hegemony claimed by leaders in many other former colonies; avoidance of the convolutions of the communal franchises; and the willingness to wait for local people to acquire the necessary learning and experience before they took full control of the administration is striking. Seretse Khama was an unusual man; the country had a small population and it continued to give the chiefs a say in running national affairs. Perhaps these factors were decisive.

Malaya's recovery from the dark days of the communist insurrection was remarkable and a credit to the determination of the rulers and the people, the senior appointments made by Oliver Lyttleton and the consistent and large-scale backing of the British government over an extended period. Education was already quite far ahead of most African colonies even before the Second World War, so the stream of qualified people becoming available was growing well by the time self-government was achieved. The PSC and the Malay government set their faces against the too rapid replacement of overseas officers by inexperienced Malays so that a considerable core of experienced British members of the Public Service remained for a while after independence. Would that other colonies had done likewise?

African or multiracial states

In the Devonshire policy enunciated in the early 1920s in regard to East Africa, HMG stressed that it held the African territories 'in trust' for their inhabitants – the

Africans. Subsequently, and especially after the creation of the United Nations which espoused multiracialism, British policy in the territories which had settlers from Britain, Europe and Asia was more equivocal and shifted in the direction of multiracial solutions. It did so in the face of ardent and rising Africanism, or African nationalism. Such nationalism was perhaps understandable; and it was not confined to Africa. Perhaps this exclusivity is now being reversed.

Freedom of the state or freedom of the individual

When nationalists especially talked and argued, often with emotion, for early 'freedom' they seldom explained what they envisaged – did freedom of the state mean freedom of the individual as well as self-government? As we know from our own history in Britain, reconciling the two is not easy and required goodwill, determination and patient compromise over the very long term. It also required a strong and competent judiciary and a belief in the rule of law. In much of Africa the freedom of the state has come at the expense of freedom of the individual. Colonial governments were the initiators of most new institutions in most colonies. Thus there was a tendency for government to become in many ways all-powerful. The colonial-era constitutions attempted to enshrine protection of civil liberties and individual rights against abuse by the state, but in most former colonies, the centralization of power has actually facilitated the seizure of control by autocratic political personalities or political groups at the expense of individual rights. It is not obvious how this centralization of power could have been avoided – except by federation which was not always appropriate. No doubt some African leaders believed they could achieve more for the people by taking extensive control over them. The fallacy of this belief has been revealed for all to see. It is heartening that in some states there is now a search for ways to enhance protection of the individual, which British experience tells us will be difficult and require persistence over many years.

Thinkers on colonial policy worried that the colonial police tended to become agents of the state rather than independent agents for maintaining the rule of law; and that this was very different from the British tradition of policing which emphasized the rule of law by local magistrates and locally controlled police authorities. Before its independence, a Southern member of the Sudanese National Assembly warned, using Winston Churchill's words, of the danger of 'the people being owned by the state' instead of 'the government being owned by the people'. The warning was widely ignored, not least in Sudan. This issue could not be resolved in colonial days. The independent states will have to continue the struggle to enhance the rule of law and limit the power of the state and its functionaries. The people will have to continue their struggle to reclaim their sovereignty from over-powerful administrations.

In most colonies the government became the prime mover in the economy and tended to centralize economic decision-making and public expenditure – with mining and oil enterprises being notable exceptions. In 1955 the East Africa Royal Commission argued to the effect that 'an important impact of British colonial policy had been to tilt the balance in the economy too much away from economic change and progress and that this needed to be corrected'. *The Economist* reviewing the commission's report fully endorsed its finding. Professor Bauer made a somewhat different critique (see extracts of his letter of 8 April 1958 in the Press Review). The consequence was that at independence governments of former colonies were handed great economic power and powers of patronage, for good or ill. In the 1980s and the 1990s, a major attempt to address this matter and loosen controls was made under the rubric of Structural Adjustment, fostered by the Bretton Woods institutions, the IMF and the World Bank. Again, given the history and the nature of Africa prior to colonization, and indeed the drift of policy in Britain itself during the colonial era, it is difficult to know how this centralization of economic power could have been avoided. There is no doubt that the effects were often deleterious.

It is apparent to me that the rush to independence of the colonies was unfortunate and worked to the distinct disadvantage of most people of most colonies. I don't think the date of independence could have been deferred for very long in any colony as there was a very natural wish for them to be able to govern themselves. However, it should have been possible for the colonial administrations and HMG to make the case for more time and a slower handover by appealing to a broader constituency than the few political leaders with whom they negotiated; and by displaying and highlighting the paucity of experience and necessary skills available in relation to the needs. In the event, as I argued earlier, some colonies never had a chance.

Notes to the Text

Preface

1 *African Affairs*, vol. 49 (20 July 1950).

2 *Foreign Affairs*, 1956.

3 CO 554/400.

4 See *The Times*, 22 October 1994.

Chapter 2

1 Sir Penderel Moon, *The British Conquest and Dominion of India*, Duckworth, 1999, p. 229, ISBN 0-7156-21696-6.

2 Rudolf von Albertini, *De-Colonisation: The Administration and Future of the Colonies*, Africana, 1982, ISBN 0-8419-0603-3.

3 Peter Burroughs, *Journal of Imperial and Commonwealth History*, vol. VI, no. 3 (May 1978).

4 Rudolf von Albertini, pp. 94–6.

5 Hansard, House of Commons, CXVIII (30 July 1919): 2174.

6 D. J. Morgan, *The Official History of Colonial Development*, Volume 1, The Origins of Aid Policy 1924–1945, Macmillan, 1980, ISBN 0-333-28800-7.

7 CO 318/433/1 & CAB 23/94.

8 Ibid.

9 W. M. Macmillan, *Warning from the West Indies*, London: Faber & Faber, 1936.

10 David Goldsworthy, *Journal of Imperial and Commonwealth History*, vol. XVIII, no.1 (January 1990).

11 House of Commons, 7 December 1938; quoted in Charles Buxton, 'The Government of Crown Colonies', *Political Quarterly* (1939): 516.

12 Ibid.

13 Ibid.

14 *An African Survey – A Study of Problems Arising in Africa South of the Sahara*, Oxford: Oxford University Press, 1938; Revised 1956.

15   See CAB 65/5.

16   Winston S. Churchill, by Martin Gilbert, Volume VI; page 1163; and the PM's personal minute M.812/1, of 20 August 1941.

17   Roosevelt and Churchill, Their Secret Wartime Correspondence, edited by Francis Loweheim, Harold Langley and Manfred Jonas, page 74. 'There is no doubt of the President's anti-imperialist outlook – and there are a few examples of it in his correspondence with Churchill. But except for his messages on India in 1942, Roosevelt was reluctant to raise the subject direct with the Prime minister'.

18   Hansard, HofC Debates, vol. 391, Col. 48 (13 July 1943).

19   CO 96/776/31475.

20   Arthur Creech Jones, *New Fabian Colonial Essays*, The Hogarth Press, 1959.

21   See John W. Cell, 'On the Eve of De-Colonisation: the Colonial Office's Plans for the Transfer of Power in Africa. 1947', *Journal of Imperial and Commonwealth History*, vol. VIII, no. 3 (May 1980). See also Anthony Kirk-Greene, *On Crown Service*, London: I.B. Tauris, 1999.

22   Ibid.

23   CO 847/13/16, 15/11,17/11.

24   Hansard, 20 July 1949, pp. 1397–444.

25   Ibid.

26   *African Affairs*, vol. 49 (July 1950).

27   'British Aims in Africa', *Foreign Affairs*, vol. 28, no. 1/4 (1949/1950).

28   'The British Problem in Africa', *Foreign Affairs*, vol. 29, no. 1/4 (1950/1951).

29   'Economic Planning in British Colonies', *Foreign Affairs*, vol. 27, no. 1/4 (1948/1949).

30   *Native Administration and Political Development in British Tropical Africa*, Lord Hailey, 1942; published by HMSO 1951.

31   CO 936/217 No1. The Problem of Nationalism; minute from Sir T. Lloyd to Sir W. Strang.

32   See *The Memoirs of Lord Chandos*, Bodley Head, 1962.

33   Ibid.

34   See Annex 4 and Philip Murphy, *Alan Lennox-Boyd, A biography*, I.B. Tauris, ISBN 1 86064 406 6.

35   CO 1015/1918.

36   CO 1015/1920/285.

37   CO 1015/1920/263.

38   PREM 11/3239.

39   See P. Dignan & L. H. Gann, *Colonialism in Africa*, vol 4, 'The Economies of Colonialism, Cambridge 1975'; P. T. Bauer & B.S. Yamey, Markets, Market Control and Marketing Reform (1968); J. Forbes Munro, Britain in Tropical Africa, 1880-1960, Economic Relationships and Impact, Macmillan, 1984.

40   CAB 134/1353.

41   CAB 134/1558.

42 See Robert Shepherd, *Iain Macleod – A Biography*, London: Hutchinson, 1994.

43 PREM 11/2588.

44 PREM 11/2583.

   See Also:

   Annex 3 Lord Hailey native administration in the British African territories

   Annex 6 The political objectives of British policy in the African dependent territories

   Annex 7 Summary of a speech made by the prime minister, Harold Macmillan

   Annex 9 The advisory commission on the Central African Federation (The Monckton Commission)

Chapter 3

1 Report of Major Vischer to the Colonial Office of December 1924.
   CO 1045/431.

2 Education Policy in British Tropical Africa, Cmnd 2374, March 1925.

3 Cmnd 3573, 1930.

4 CO 847/3/2, no 3.

5 *Annals of Tropical Medicine and Parasitology*, vol. xxx, no. 2 (1936).

6 J. H. Oldham & B. D. Gibson.

7 Education in Somaliland by R. K. Winter; CO 535/119/3.

8 Annual Report of the Department of Education, Sudan Government, 1937 FO 371/23351.

9 Higher Education in East Africa, 1937; SOAS Library VA/34556.

10 Ibid.

11 *Catholic Times*, 15 October 1937 & letter to the Catholic Times from the Archbishop of Westminster, 1 November 1937.

12 *An African Survey*, Oxford, Hailey, 1938.

13 BW 90/19-20.

14 CO 822/116/1.

15 Report of the Commission on Higher Education in West Africa, June 1945; SOAS Library; VST 378/47876; BW 90/19-21; CO 1045/337; See also 'Higher Education in West Africa', *African Affairs*, Vol. 44, (October 1945), Higher Education in West Africa.

16 Examinations in West Africa; CO 554/170/1.

17 FO/371/80584; CO 859/166/3.

18 CO 859/137/5.

19 'Education in British Africa', *African Affairs*, vol. 53 (April 1954).

20 'The Challenge of Education in British Overseas Territories', *African Affairs*, vol. 57 (April 1958).

21 Annual Report of the Sudanese Department of Education, 1947; FO 371/69154.

22 Colin Wise, *A History of Education in British West Africa*, Longman; SOAS: VM 370/107743.

23 CO 554/1107.

24 CO 554/2372.

25 CO 544/2372.

26 CO 554/2029; CO 554/1378.

27 The Ashby Report; CO 1045/720.

28 The Carr-Saunders Report on Makerere.

29 CO 622/369.

30 CO 691/207.

31 CO 822/1153.

32 CO 822/1208.

33 CO822/2419.

34 CO 822/2675.

35 Ibid.

36 Report of Working Party on Higher Education in East Africa, 1958; BW 90/72; CO 822/944; CO 822/2419.

37 'Education in East Africa', *African Affairs*, vol. 57 (July 1958); CO 847/73.

38 BW90/72.

39 CO 1045/1096.

40 CO 1015/1142; BW 91/799.

41 Ibid.

42 CO 1015/1129.

43 CO 525/203/2.

44 CO 525/203/1.

45 CO 1045/785.

46 CO 1045/1426.

47 CO 1045/785 (Reprinted from *Nature*, vol. 172 (July 1953)).

48 CO 691/202.

49 CO 1045/1142.

50 CO 1045/1426.

51 BW 91/799.

52 CO 1045/1426.

53 CO 1045/829.

54 CO 1045/1426.

55 CO 318/459/, no 67.

56 CO 859/132/1.

57 CO 1045/1188.

58 CO 717/194.

59 CO 876/139.

60 Advisory Committee on Education in the Colonies; Report by the Hong Kong Director of Education, 1948; CO 859/132/1.

61 Personal Information.

62 See Cmnd 6647 of June 1945, The Commission on Higher Education in the Colonies.

Chapter 4

1 Numerous passages in the following text referring to Africa draw on Lord Hailey, *An African Survey* (Revised 1956), Oxford, 1957; Revised 1956.

2 Sir James Robertson, *Transition in Africa – From Direct Rule to Independence*, London: C. Hurst & Co, London, 1954, ISBN (UK only) 0 903983 060.

3 Letter Sir Hubert Huddleston/Sir Miles Lampson, FO 371/31587, no 5145.

4 See correspondence in FO 371/53255, FO 371/53261/53576 and in PREM 8/1385/1&3.

5 FO 371/63052, no 2096.

6 See Robertson, *Transition in Africa – From Direct Rule to Independence*.

7 FO 371/90111, no 11.

8 Hansard, HofC Debates, vol. 493, cols 1177–80.

9 *African Affairs*, Adbes tatto Royal African Society, 16 July 1953.

10 See Curtis R. Nordman, 'The Decision to Admit un-officials to the Executive Councils of British West Africa', *Journal of Imperial and Commonwealth History*, vol. IV, no. 2 (January 1976).

11 Ibid.

12 Report of Commission of Enquiry into Disturbances in the Gold Coast, 1948; Colonial 231, 1948, HMSO.

13 'Address to the Royal African Society', *African Affairs*, 21 November 1957.

14 Statement by HMG on the Report, Colonial 232, 1948, HMSO.

15 CO 554/254, no 10.

16 See Page 27 of Chapter 2 – note of Prime Minister Macmillan's visit to Ghana.

17 CO 554/805; Letter from Arden-Clarke to Gorell Barnes, 2 September 1954.

18 CAB/129/83; Secretary of State to Cabinet, 29 August 1956.

19 CAB/128/30.

20 *African Affairs*, vol. 50 (January 1960).

21 Sir James Robertson, *Transition in Africa*, London: C. Hurst & Co, 1974.

22 Robert D. Pearce, *Sir Bernard Bourdillon*, The Kensal Press, ISBN 0-946041-48-3.

23 *African Affairs*, vol. 54 (April 1955).

24 CO 583/244/22; CO 583/261/30453.

25 CO 583/261/8.

26 CO 583/255, 261, 263.

27 See R. D. Pearce, 'Governors, Nationalists and Constitutions in Nigeria, 1935-51', *Journal of Imperial and Commonwealth History*, vol. IX, no. 3 (May 1981).

28 For an excellent discussion of the varied and changing constitutional concepts in Nigeria at this time see John P. Mackintosh, *Nigerian Government and Politics*, London: George Allen & Unwin, 1966, Library of Congress Catalogue No 66-19844.

29 See Obafemi Awolowo, *Path to Nigerian Freedom*, London: Faber & Faber, 1947.

30 CO 583/296/5.

31 CO 583/286/5.

32 CO 583/299/1.

33 CAB 129/39 CP (50) 44 & PREM 8/13/10, CM30(50)6.

34 Cmnd 8934; CO 554/840, no 1; CO 554/840.

35 (See 28 and 29 above).

36 CO 554/840, no 84.

37 Cmnd 51, London, 1957; CO 554/1140; CO 554/2128, no 9.

38 CAB 133/227, NC(5)(57) 20.

39 CO 554/846, no 10.

40 DO 35/6541, no 43.

41 CAB 129/100.

42 Cmnd 1922, 1923.

43 CAB 24/187.

44 CO 822/114/46523.

45 CAB 129/43.

46 CO 822/1807.

47 CAB 134/1560.

48 Colin Legum, *Must We Lose Africa?*, London: Allen & Unwin, 1954.

49 *African Affairs*, vol. 56 (April 1957).

50 CAB 134/1556.

51 Colin Legum, *Must We Lose Africa?*.

52 *African Affairs*, Twining, October 1958.

53 CO 822/559.

54 See Colin Baker, Exit from Empire; a biography of Sir Richard Turnbull.

55 CO 822/912, no 30.

56 CAB 134/1556; Letter from Governor Twining of 18 June 1957.

57 *African Affairs*, Twining, October 1958.

58 CO 822/1444.

59 CO 822/1448/165.

60 CO 822/1449.

61　CO 822/1449/5.

62　CO 822/1449/229.

63　CO 822/1448/165.

64　CO 922/1449.

65　See Robert Shepherd, *Iain Mcleod, A Biography*, London: Hutchinson.

66　CAB 134/1806.

67　CAB 134/1558, CPC (59) 20.

68　CAB 134/1559, CPC (60) 24.

69　CAB 134/1560, CPC (61) 5.

70　David Throup, *The Economic & Social Origins of Mau Mau*, James Currey Ltd., 1987, ISBN 0-8214-0883-6.

71　KNA Lab 9/304).

72　KNA MAA 8/22) These references are both from David Throup's book.

73　Michael Blundell, *So Rough a Wind*, Wiedenfeld & Nicolson, 1964.

74　Sessional Paper No. 5 of 1959/60 F. D. Corfield.

75　*The Memoirs of Lord Chandos*, Bodley Head, 1962

76　Ibid.

77　Ibid.

78　Ibid.

79　See Philip Murphy, *Alan Lennox-Boyd, A biography*, I.B. Tauris, ISBN 1 86064 406 6.

80　*African Affairs*, vol. 55 (October 1956).

81　Michela Wrong, *It's Our Turn to Eat*, 4th Estate, ISBN 978-0-00-724197-2.

82　CO 822/1806.

83　CAB 134/1556 CPC (57) 35.

84　*African Affairs*, vol. 58 (July 1959).

85　M. F. Hill, *Foreign Affairs*, vol. 38, no. 1/4 (1959).

86　Tom Mboya, *Foreign Affairs*, vol. 41 (July 1963).

87　CAB 129/108.

88　Ibid.

89　CAB 129/114.

90　CAB 129/80, CP (56) 89.

91　CAB 129/80, CP (56) 84.

92　CO 1015/1917.

93　CO 1015/1947; CO 1015/1920/208.

94　CO 1015/1660.

95　See R. T. Rotberg, *Journal of Commonwealth Political Studies*, vol. 2 (1963).

96　CO 968/791.

97　CO 847/23/11.

98 Report of the Nyasaland Commission of Inquiry under Lord Devlin; Cmnd.814 of 1959 (The Devlin Report).

99 CO 525/220/12.

100 CO 525/220/3.

101 CO 795/128/45104/1944.

102 DO 35/3594.

103 CO 1015/553.

104 CO 1015/65, no 165.

105 See 79 above.

106 *African Affairs*, vol. 58 (October 1959).

107 *African Affairs*, vol. 57, no. 229 (October 1958).

108 CO 1015/1129.

109 CO 1015/1045.

110 CO 1015/1179, no 13.

111 CO 1015/1002, no 1.

112 PREM 11/2784.

113 BDEE, Central Africa, vol. 1; Introduction by Philip Murphy.

114 DO 35/4675.

115 *African Affairs*, vol. 59, no 235 (April 1960).

116 CO 1015/2281.

117 CO 1015/2423.

118 CO 1015/256 & 2281.

119 CO 1015/2053.

120 PREM 11/3485/6.

121 PREM 11/3487.

122 PREM 11/3942, PM (62) 3.

123 See 98 above.

124 PREM 11/2783.

125 The Case for Withdrawal of Nyasaland from the Federation, Guy Clutton-Brock; Personal Note of 1959.

126 *The Spectator*, 27 February 1959.

127 CAB 129/100.

128 CAB 128/33.

129 CO 1015/2422.

130 CO 1015/1740.

131 See *The Economist*, February 1960.

132 See Peter Fawcus, *Botswana: The Road to Independence*, with Alan Tilbury.

133 CO 1022/444.

134 CO 1022/489.

135 CO 1045/1426.

136 CO 273/667/1, no 5.

137 CAB 66/50, WP (44) 258.

138 CAB 65/53, CM 8 (45) 8.

139 CAB 128/1, CM 27 (45) 3.

140 CAB 21/1954.

141 WO 203/5642, no 74/16/45.

142 CO 537/1528, no 40.

143 CO 537/1528, no 44.

144 CAB 128/5, CM 19 (46) 7.

145 CO 537/1529, no 104.

146 CO 537/1529, no 110.

147 CO 537/1543, no 110.

148 PREM 8/1406/1.

149 CAB 21/25/10, no 5.

150 CO 537/4741, no 83.

151 CO 537/6026, no 10.

152 See 79 above.

153 *The Memoirs of Lord Chandos*, Bodley Head, 1962.

154 CO 1022/22, no 1.

155 PREM 11/639, ff 20–22.

156 CO 1022/86, no 3.

157 CO 1022/86, no 27.

158 CO 1022/86, no 93.

159 CO 1030/311, no 130.

160 CO 1022/494.

161 CO 1030/30, ff 3–16.

162 CO 1022/22, no 1.

163 CAB 129/79, CP (56) 47.

164 CAB 1131/16; CAB 129/80; CAB 128/30.

165 Col. No 255.

166 Col. No 268.

167 Col. No 254.

168 T 220/360, pp. 59–62.

Chapter 5

1 See A. R. Thomas, *Development of the Overseas Civil Service*, Public Administration (Winter 1958). See also Anthony Kirk-Greene, *On Crown Service*, 38, ISBN 1-86064.

2 The passages referring to India draw predominantly on Sir Penderel Moon, *The British Conquest and Dominion of India*, Duckworth, 1989. ISBN 0-7156-2169-6.

3 See Rudolf von Albertini, Africana, 1982. ISBN 0-8419-0603-3 and Commonwealth Documents 3131 (1928).

4 CAB 24/280.

5 CO 554/100.

6 CAB 129/41; CAB 129/102.

7 FO 371/73468.

8 FO 37169154.

9 See Kenneth Younger, *The Public Service in New States*, Oxford: Oxford University Press, 1960 and FO 371/1019.

10 BW 90/255.

11 CO537/7181.

12 CO 544/399.

13 CO 544/1000.

14 The Times, 18 March 1953, quoted in CO 554/1000.

15 CO 554/400.

16 Barbara Ward Jackson; Foreign Affairs 1953/54; Vol 31, ¼.

17 CO 554/1000.

18 CO 554/399.

19 CO 554/400.

20 CO 554/406.

21 CAB 129/102.

22 CO 554/1001, Nigerianization of the Civil Service, 1954.

23 CO 554/2029.

24 CO 554/400.

25 CO 822/732.

26 CAOG 13/67.

27 CO 822/1807.

28 CAB129/100.

29 CAB 129/97.

30 DO 185/46.

31 DO 185/47.

32 CO 822/732.

33 CO 822/732.

34 CO 822/1050.

35 CO 822/1648.

36 CO 822/1648.

37 CO 822/2689.

38 CO 822/1648.

39 CO 822/2764.

40 CO 522/1951.

41 CO 522/1951.

42 CO 1015/2072/159.

43 CO 1015/2071.

44 CO 1015/2071.

45 Rhodesian Herald, 17 November 1956 (Racial Purity in the Civil Service) See also CO 1015/913.

46 CO 1015/2423.

47 CO 1015/1740.

48 CO 1022/444.

49 CO 1017/ 436.

50 CO 1017/436.

51 Dr Valentin Seidler-Overseas Pensioner 2016.

52 Younger, *The Public Service in New States*.

53 Cmnd Colonial 306, 1954; Reorganisation of the Colonial Service.

54 *African Affairs*, February 1962.

Chapter 6

1 George Bennett, *The Concept of Empire; Burke to Attlee, 1774–1947*, London: Adam & Charles Black, 1953.

2 See *The Manchester Guardian*, 19 April 1960.

3 Pierre Ryckmans, 'Belgian Colonialism', *Foreign Affairs*, vol. 34, no. 1/4 (1955/1956).

4 See H. J. van Mook, 'Indonesia and the Problem of South Asia', *Foreign Affairs,* vol. 27, no. 1/4 (1948/1949).

5 *Oxford History of the British Empire*, Volume IV.

6 Prosser Gifford (ed.), *The Transfer of Power in Africa, 1940-1960*; Tony Smith, *Comparative Study of French and British De-Colonisation*.

7 CO 537/7148.

8 Charles de Gaulle, *La France sera la France*, Paris, 1951, 193.

9 See *The Times*, 18 May 1958.

10 Leopold Sedar Senghor, 'West Africa in Evolution', *Foreign Affairs*, vol. 39, no. 2 (January 1961).

11 J. H. Huizinga, 'Unique Experiment in French Black Africa', *African Affairs*, vol. 58 (January 1959).

12 J. H. A. Watson, 'French-speaking Africa since Independence', *African Affairs*, vol. 62 (July 1963): 211–22.

13 CO 1015/1922.

14 Winston Churchill, *The Second World War*, vol. IV, London: Cassell & Co Ltd, 1951, 181–96.

15 Max Hastings, *Finest Years, Churchill as Warlord 1940–45*, Harpur Press, 2010, 256; ISBN 978-0-00-726364-4.

16 Prosser Gifford (ed.), *The Transfer of Power in Africa 1940-1960*; This section draws on the essay entitled The United States and the Liquidation of the British Empire in Tropical Africa, 1941–1951, Wm. Roger Louis and Ronald Robinson.

17 Ibid.

18 CO 537/7136.

19 CO 537/7137.

20 Cornelis de Kiewiet, 'African Dilemmas', *Foreign Affairs*, vol. 33, no. 1/4 a. (1954/1956).

21 FO 371/113462.

22 PREM 11/3230.

23 PREM 11/3239.

24 Quoted by Deputy Assistant Secretary for African Affairs, Joseph Palmer 2d in a speech given on 16 June 1958 at New York University; to be found in FO 371/131189.

25 FO 371/125293.

26 FO 371/131184.

27 FO 371/137974.

28 Rupert Emerson, 'American Policy in Africa', *Foreign Affairs*, vol. 40, no. 2 (1962).

29 CAB 129/16.

30 CO 936/337.

31 Clyde Eagleton, *Foreign Affairs*, vol. 31, no. 1/4 (1952/1953).

32 Vernon MacKay, *Foreign Affairs*, vol. 35, no. 1/4 (1956/1957).

33 FO 371/137974.

34 FO 371/108378.

35 PREM 11/459.

36 FO 371/137974.

37 CAB 134/1352.

38 Christopher Andrew, *The Defence of the Realm*, Chapters D 7 & 8, London: Allen Lane, ISBN 978-0-713-99885-6.

Attachment 1: Nigeria Public Service senior staff, 1959

Government/Rank	Establishment	Vacancies No (%)		Overseas Officers	Nigerian a/ Officers (%)	
Western Region						
Exec and Tech	1369	430	31	96	843	62
Admin/Prof	650	153	24	159	338	52
Superscale	233	43	19	117	73	31
Eastern Region						
Exec and Tech	669	133	20	102	434	65
Admin/Prof	571	228	40	77	276	48
Superscale	174	41	24	90	43	25
Northern Region a/						
Superscale	221			161	60	27
Federal Government						
Exec and Tech	2437	631	26	575	1231	51
Admin/Prof	1673	426	26	658	589	35
Special Scale	94	45	48	44	5	5
Superscale	626	145	23	410	71	11
Total						
Exec and Tech	4475	1194	27	773	2508	56
Admin/Prof	2894	807	28	924	1203	42
Special Scale	94	45	48	44	5	5
Superscale	1254	229	18	778	247	20

a/ Data are incomplete for the Northern Region.
Source: Kenneth Younger, The Public Service in New States, Oxford, 1960.

Attachment 2: Africanization of the Public Service in Tanganyika

Status on 1 July 1961

Senior Posts by Ministry and Department

Ministry/Department	Total Establishment of Senior Posts	Number of Posts Held by Local Officers			Per cent of Posts (%)
		Africans	Non-Africans	Total	Africans
1. Home Affairs	531	124	10	134	23.3
2. Prime Minister	803	165	18	183	20.6
3. Education	834	79	61	140	9.5
4. Agriculture	818	92	33	125	11.2
5. Health and Labour	630	72	17	89	11.4
6. Commerce and Industry	137	14	5	19	10.2
7. Local Government	90	11	1	12	12.2
8. Comms, Power and Works	434	30	26	56	6.9
9. Lands and Surveys	276	17	8	25	6.5
10. Audit	50	3	1	4	6.0

Ministry/Department	Total Establishment of Senior Posts	Number of Posts Held by Local Officers			Per cent of Posts (%)
		Africans	Non-Africans	Total	Africans
11. Treasury	142	4	8	12	2.8
12. Judiciary	63	–	2	2	–
13. Legal Affairs	42	–	1	1	–
14. Other Departments	37	5	3	8	13.5
Total	4,887	616	194	810	12.6

Analysis of Africanization in Senior Posts

Category of Post	Salary Scale	No of Posts	Local----		Expat.	Vacant Posts	Per cent Local (%)
			African	Other Local			
Admin/Professional	Super	320	1	2	265	52	0.9
Admin/Professional	A	1640	207	79	979	375	17.4
Semi-Prof; Police & Prisons	Various	698	157	7	438	96	23.5
Executive/tech							
Executive	C	255	10	1	186	58	3.9
Technical	C	1059	77	65	646	271	13.4
Accounting	C	125	8	4	94	19	9.6
Secretarial	C	279	1	9	82	187	3.3
Nursing etc	C & N	237	2	4	127	104	2.5
Training Grade	D	274	153	23	–	98	64.1
Total		4,887	616	194	2,817	1,260	16.6

Source: Establishment Circular Letter No 17 of 1961.

Attachment 3: Kenya Public Service Commission, 1962

Appointments to Training Posts	No of Vacancies	Applications Received	Candidates Selected
Junior Lands Assistant	9	40	6
Community Development Officer	12	72	10
Local Government Financial Officer	4	15	3
Survey Cadet	9	n/a	9
Inspector, Weights and Measures	9	42	9
District Assistant	9	n/a	9
Laboratory Technician, Veterinary	5	30	5
Valuer, Dept of Lands	2	12	2
Executive Officer, Trade and Supplies	3	41	3
Mineral Dressing Asst, Mines and Geology	1	6	1
Fisheries Officer	4	17	3
Immigration Officer	11	139	10
Statistical Assistant, Treasury	3	21	3
Game Warden	1	12	1
Assistant Game Warden	5	18	3
Accounts Assistant, Treasury	6	n/a	6
Forester	11	18	11
Auditor	1	52	1

Appointments to Training Posts	No of Vacancies	Applications Received	Candidates Selected
Legal Assistant, Registrar General	1	21	–
Inspector of Explosives, Mines and Geology	1	n/a	1
Apron Marshaller, Airport	2	27	1
Airport Receptionist	5	n/a	5
Technical Officer (Signals), Police	20	183	20
Technical Assistant, Printing and Stationery	15	84	14
Registrar of Titles, Lands	3	18	3
Crown Counsel, Legal Department	6	38	6
Secretarial	14	170	14
Dept of Works Foreman/Inspector	8	20	3
Hydrological Assistant	6	27	4
Executive Officer (Accounts)	8	10	–
Inspector Mechanical	2	4	2
Senior Laboratory Assistant	3	1	–
Structural Draughtsman	1	14	1
Quantity Surveyor's Assistant	4	6	1
Inspector of Works, Electrical	4	11	4
Technical Assistant, Survey	4	23	4
Road Foreman	–	56	–
Foreman, Buildings	6	n/a	6
Total	218	1,214	184

Bursaries approved for Further Study

Bursaries for Study in East Africa	81
Bursaries for Study Overseas	43
Commonwealth Scholarships	11

List of Posts the PSC Advised Should be Filled by Overseas Recruitment

Assistant Agricultural Officer	11
Assistant Surveyor	7
Health Worker	1
Senior Establishments Officer	1
Teachers	60
Information Officers	2
Shorthand Writer, Judicial	1
Broadcasting Engineers	2
Junior Lands Assistant	5
Electrical Inspector, Medical	2
Hospital Secretary	2
Statistical Officer, Police	1
Police Photographer	1
Statistical Officer, Prisons	1
Technical Instructor, Prisons	1
Lithographer	2
Assistant Lithographer	1
Printer	1
Chief Stores Officer, Supplies and Tpt	1
Health Inspector, Veterinary	1
Livestock Officers	7
Ministry of Works Chief Technical Assistant	2
Technical Assistant, Electrical	2
Inspector, Mechanical	5
Materials Assistant	1
Assistant Quantity Surveyor	4
Assistant Surveyor	2
Station Officer, Fire Service	1
Total	128

Source: Annual Report Kenya Public Service Commission, 1962.

Attachment 4: Decolonization – Timing of creation of Public Service Commission and major staff plans

Country	II Date PSC Created	III Major Local Staff Plan	IV Date of Independence	V Years	
				II–IV	III–IV
India	1886		1947	61	
Ceylon (Sri Lanka)	1931		1948	17	
Malaya	1953		1957	4	
Singapore	1950		1965	15	
West Indies	1950s (advisory)		1962	12	
	1959 (Jamaica and Trinidad, executive)		1962	3	
Sudan	1953	1948	1956	3	8
Aden	1959	1957	1967	8	10
Somaliland Prot. (Somalia)		1958	1960		2
Gold Coast (Ghana)	1948	1942 (advisory)	1957	9	15
		1954 (Executive)			3
Nigeria	1949	1954	1960	11	6

(Continued)

I Country	II Date PSC Created	III Major Local Staff Plan	IV Date of Independence	V Years	
				II–IV	III–IV
Sierra Leone		1961	1961	–	
Tanganyika (Tanzania)	1957	1961	1961	4	–
Uganda	1952		1962	10	
Kenya	1954	PSC Annual reports	1963	9	
East African Territories and The EA Community		1953–4			7–9
Southern Rhodesia (Zimbabwe)	1927/44		1964 (1980)	38/53	
Northern Rhodesia (Zambia)	1960		1964	4	
Nyasaland (Malawi)	1960/1		1964	4	
Central African Fed.	1956	1956			
Bechuanaland (Botswana)			1966		2
Basutoland (Lesotho)		1964	1966		2
Swaziland			1968		4

Annex 1: Social and economic accomplishments of African countries

This Annex is based on the 2010 *Human Development Report* published by the United Nations Development Programme. It focusses on just a few of the more important indicators which are particularly revealing for Sub-Saharan Africa (SSA). These are the Human Development Index (HDI), a composite index measuring human development, Life Expectancy at Birth (years), Secondary Schooling enrolment (per cent of secondary school-age population) and Tertiary Education enrolment (per cent of tertiary school-age population). All analytical conclusions contained in this Annex are taken from the *Human Development Report*. For a full understanding of the indexes used, the *HD Report* should be consulted.

HDI has fallen since 1970 in only three countries in the world, Congo, Zambia and Zimbabwe. In the latter two countries, the HIV epidemic was an important cause, as it was in all countries in Southern Africa with slow growth in their HDI. Over the past forty years a quarter of developing countries saw their HDI increase less than 20 per cent (nearly all of them in Sub-Saharan Africa), another quarter more than 65 per cent. These differences partly reflect starting points but half the variation in HDI performance is unexplained by initial HDI, and countries with similar starting points experienced remarkably different evolutions, suggesting that country factors such as policies, institutions and geography are important. The HDI gap between developing and developed countries has narrowed by about a fourth since 1970.

One of the most surprising results of human development research, confirmed in the 2010 *Human Development Report*, is the lack of significant correlation between economic growth and improvement in health and education.

Progress in education has been substantial and widespread, reflecting both the quantity of schooling and increased access for girls. To a large extent this progress reflects greater state involvement, which is often characterized more by getting children into school than by imparting a high-quality education.

The unprecedented flow of ideas across countries in recent times – ranging from health-saving technologies to political ideals and productive practices – has been transformative. Many innovations have allowed countries to improve health and education at very low cost – which explains why the association between the income and non-income dimensions of human development has weakened.

Income and growth remain vital. To conclude otherwise is to ignore the importance of income in expanding people's freedoms. ... Nor do the HDI results negate the importance of higher income for increasing poor people's access to social services and hunger often reflects the lack of means to acquire food rather than general food scarcity; nutrition is an aspect of health where income also matters.

The share of formal democracies has increased from fewer than a third in 1970 to half in the mid-1990s and to three-fifths in 2008. However, of the forty-two African states with a low level of human development, only sixteen (42 per cent) have functioning democratic systems in place.

People in Sub-Saharan Africa suffer the largest HDI losses because of substantial inequality in all three dimensions – health, education and income.

Sub-Saharan Africa has the highest incidence of multidimensional poverty (a new index of poverty). The level ranges from a low of 3 per cent in South Africa to a massive 97 per cent in Niger; the average share of deprivations ranges from about 45 per cent (in Gabon, Lesotho and Swaziland) to 69 per cent in Niger.

Conflict usually stops development. Paul Collier and Anke Hoeffler have estimated that it takes an average of twenty-one years to reach the GDP that would have prevailed without conflict. The people of Sierra Leone suffered a halving of incomes over the eleven-year conflict, while in Liberia the estimated decline was 80 per cent. Several countries that performed poorly relative to their starting points have been affected by conflict – including the Democratic Republic of the Congo and Cote d'Ivoire.

	HDI		Life Expect. at Birth	Secondary Enrolment	Tertiary Enrolment
	1980	2010	2010 years	2001–9 (%)	2001–9 (%)
High Income	0.753	0.878	80.3	100.9	70.8
SSA	0.293	0.389	52.7	34.4	5.5
Gabon	0.510	0.648	61.3	53.1	7.1
Botswana	0.431	0.633	55.5	80.2	5.2
Namibia	–	0.606	62.1	65.8	8.9

	HDI		Life Expect. at Birth	Secondary Enrolment	Tertiary Enrolment
South Africa	–	0.597	52.0	95.1	–
Equat. Guinea	–	0.538	51.0	26.2	3.3
Swaziland	–	0.498	47.0	53.3	4.4
Congo	0.462	0.489	53.9	43.1	3.9
Kenya	0.404	0.470	55.6	58.3	4.1
Ghana	0.363	0.467	57.1	54.1	6.2
Cameroon	0.354	0.460	51.7	37.3	7.8
Benin	0.264	0.435	62.3	36.3	5.8
Madagascar	–	0.435	61.2	30.1	3.4
Mauretania	–	0.433	57.3	23.3	3.8
Togo	0.347	0.428	63.3	41.3	5.3
Comoros	–	0.428	66.2	45.8	2.7
Lesotho	0.397	0.427	45.9	39.9	3.6
Nigeria	–	0.423	48.4	30.5	10.1
Uganda	–	0.422	54.1	25.3	3.7
Senegal	0.291	0.411	56.2	30.6	8.0
Angola	–	0.403	48.1	17.3	2.8
Djibouti	–	0.402	56.1	29.5	2.6
Tanzania	–	0.398	56.9	6.1	1.5
Cote d'Ivoire	0.350	0.397	58.4	26.3	8.4
Zambia	0.382	0.395	47.3	51.8	2.4
Gambia	–	0.390	56.6	50.8	1.2
Rwanda	0.249	0.385	51.1	21.9	4.0
Malawi	0.258	0.385	54.6	29.4	–
Sudan	0.250	0.379	58.9	38.0	5.9

(Continued)

	HDI		Life Expect. at Birth	Secondary Enrolment	Tertiary Enrolment
Guinea	–	0.340	58.9	35.8	9.2
Ethiopia	–	0.328	56.1	33.4	3.6
Sierra Leone	0.229	0.317	48.2	34.6	2.0
C. Afric. Rep.	0.265	0.315	47.7	11.9	2.3
Mali	0.165	0.309	49.2	34.8	5.4
Burkina Faso	–	0.305	53.7	19.8	3.1
Liberia	0.295	0.300	59.1	31.6	17.4
Chad	–	0.295	49.2	19.0	1.9
Guinea-Bissau	–	0.289	48.6	35.9	2.9
Mozambique	0.195	0.284	48.4	20.6	1.5
Burundi	0.181	0.282	51.4	17.9	2.5
Niger	0.166	0.261	52.5	11.0	1.3
Congo D. Rep.	0.267	0.239	48.0	34.8	5.0
Zimbabwe	0.241	0.140	47.0	41.0	3.8

Annex 2: The approach to self-government – Sir Ivor Jennings, KC, KBE: A synopsis

Sir Ivor Jennings was a constitutional lawyer, was principal and first Vice-Chancellor of University College, Ceylon, 1940–54, participated in the drafting of the Ceylonese independence constitution, was constitutional adviser and chief draughtsman of the constitution of Pakistan, 1954–5, and was a member of the Malayan Constitutional Commission 1956–7. He became Master of Trinity Hall, Cambridge, and Vice-Chancellor of the University of Cambridge 1961–3. In 1955 he gave a series of talks on the BBC titled 'The Approach to Self-government' which can hardly be improved on as a commentary on the complexities involved in drafting constitutions for colonies becoming self-governing states and in the handing over of authority to an independent state. This annex seeks to provide a synopsis of his talks, delivered before any of the African colonies achieved independence.

The problem

Every constitution has to be a product of history, even when it comes straight from the draughtsman's pen; it is a product of the manner in which the country concerned emerged as an independent state, of the conflicts which preceded that emergence and of the forces that have played upon it. What this means is that every people is unique, and accordingly every country must have a constitution to suit itself, a constitution made to measure, not bought off the rack.

We in Britain are very familiar with the idea because we have no written constitution at all but a mass of laws and institutions which determine our form of government, and this form has evolved over centuries. It contains relics of feudal monarchy; it has been profoundly influenced by both Roman Catholic and Protestant churches; it reminds us of acute political conflicts including a civil war; it owes something to Normans, Danes, the Welsh, the Scots and the Irish, as well as the English. It is in short impregnated with our history.

Our political writers have rationalized the process of constitutional change, defended each step and justified each innovation. Their books have influenced thought throughout the Commonwealth and far beyond. The nationalism which develops in a colonial territory is partly a product of individual experience; but it also consists, in very large measure, of a complex of ideas derived from our own history and literature. The combination produces nationalist emotion; it tends to become not the tempered patriotism which is evident in Britain, but the virulent and aggressive nationalism with which British administrators have to deal in the last stages of colonial development. The process is so rapid that the whole cycle occupies less than a century. (Note: In Africa it was effectively about fifty years.)

Let us consider India. What keeps India together is the nationalism produced by British rule. It can misrepresent events; it tends to be aggressive as seen in Hyderabad, Kashmir and Goa; it causes trepidation in Pakistan and Ceylon, but on the whole it is the cement which binds India together. It is, however, a modern development; 1857 is significant in Indian history not on account of the Mutiny, but because in that year the universities of Bombay, Calcutta and Madras were founded. It was the infusion of modern, English education which enabled the nationalist movement to be founded and give India sovereign independence within a century. The first signs of the nationalist movement appeared after one generation (of university education), but two generations were needed to make it a political force; its power developed rapidly in the third generation and led to much conflict in the 1920s and 1930s. It was complicated by the growing antagonism between the Hindu National Congress and the Muslim League, which led to the creation of two states, rather than one, and delayed the attainment of self-government, giving rise to increasing virulence in the campaign. What would have happened if Britain had 'quit India' without leaving successor authorities we do not know; possibly there would have been a civil war, though the Indian Army contained both Hindu and Muslim elements. We do know what happened when Britain 'quit India' leaving successor authorities inadequately prepared to maintain law and order. It is significant, however, that nobody, or hardly anybody, now complains that India and Pakistan were left inadequately organized. There are many in India who regret that Britain's attempt to hold the balance led to the division of India and many in Pakistan who regret that the boundaries were drawn as they were. My point is that this complex of emotions has left its imprint on every page of that enormous document, the Constitution of India. British rule did not seek to force the whole subcontinent into a uniform framework, wherever Britain has ruled, the same characteristics are noticeable, the same process of adaptation of existing entities.

When Pakistan was created, the politics were dominated by the Muslim League which claimed the support of all Muslims of undivided India and then claimed the loyalty of all the Muslims of Pakistan during the eight years since its independence, it has lost much of that support and held only a minority of seats in the second Assembly elected in 1955.

In Ceylon, which had a 2000-year history of Sinhalese monarchy up until 1815, its independence constitution gave the Queen very much the same role as does the Australian constitution, though the relationship between the Crown on the one hand and the Ceylonese Ministers on the other was different.

The problem now is to develop self-governing institutions in other parts of the Commonwealth – in Malaya, Africa and the West Indies. Will the experience of India, Pakistan and Ceylon have any relevance to the problems in those colonies? This country has been remarkably successful in propagating British constitutional ideas throughout the Commonwealth. Everywhere are to be found village Hampdens, politicians as eloquent as Burke, lawyers as tough as old Coke, financial experts who know every piece of red tape and why it exists. There are reasons for this success. The freedom and tolerance which flowed from the Civil War, the Restoration and the Revolution of 1688 have made Britons very independent and given their administrators a strong sense of justice; they can be trusted to be fair. Moreover, the self-government which the nationalist politician wants for his own country is the self-government we have in our own country. The phrase often used is 'responsible government', where the Cabinet is responsible to an Assembly, in our case to Parliament, in other words, to the representatives of the people. India and Pakistan were provided with constituent assemblies and meanwhile were governed in accordance with the Government of India Act of 1935, suitably modified to permit self-government. In the end the Indian constitution was based on the 1935 Act. Though India is a federal republic, there are 'responsible' governments both in Delhi and in the states.

In the case of Pakistan, however, there were greater difficulties because Pakistan was created out of three complete states and parts of two other states. Many of the public employees, being Hindu, migrated to India; there was at first no Pakistani army and the police were disorganized. The new central and provincial administrations had to be built up from a miscellaneous collection of people from all over united India. After Jinnah died and Liaquat Ali Khan was assassinated, there were few outstanding personalities to lead the nation and the Muslim League progressively lost legitimacy. Thus Pakistan's constitution had to reflect the fact that there were a variety of parties and provision had to be made for continuity while the parties put together the coalitions required for government. Thus its constitution has fixed four-year terms as in the United States.

The Indian constitution also includes a Bill of Rights, which does not exist in the British constitution. The American Bill of Rights was intended to protect the principles of personal and political liberty which had, it was thought, been ignored by the Government of the George III. Thus every phrase of the American Bill of Rights is redolent of British constitutional history. In addition, the Indian Bill of Rights reflects Dicey's Law of the Constitution, which is very familiar to Indian lawyers. The Pakistan constitution is less ambitious and has left more to common law and to the normal working of political institutions.

It is a rule of English constitutional law that when a territory becomes one of the dominions the local law remains unaltered until it is amended. We have a series of precedents so vast that hardly anyone knows all of them. 'When a member of a Drafting Committee or Constituent Assembly asks a question about the means to overcome a local difficulty, it is as if he puts a coin in a slot machine. Out pops a precedent; perhaps not exactly in point, but near enough to suggest a line of development'. However, it must be remembered that a draft of an amendment of any constitutional problem is not the end of the matter. For the institutions to enforce the law are men and women; not only men and women who rule but the men and women who are ruled; for in a democratic system there is constant interaction. The real problem in any country, and not least in a country which is moving towards self-government is not to draft a constitution or to make laws, but to find men and women capable of running the machinery of government.

The people

Abraham Lincoln in his Gettysburg address during the American Civil War gave the most famous and most apt description of democracy. He expressed the hope that 'this nation, under God, shall have a new birth of freedom, and government of the people, by the people, for the people, shall not perish from the earth'. Thus he linked 'democracy' and 'freedom' in the same sentence. A so-called people's democracy which allows no freedom is not a democracy and the people do not govern. We in the Commonwealth are busy extending the area of free democracy. In 1920 there were six free democracies within the Commonwealth; thirty-five years later we have added five more. We also know that it is the policy of Her Majesty's Government to raise all colonial peoples to self-government; and nowadays, I think, that objective is rarely doubted. It is not always appreciated that what Britain is trying to do is to overcome the local difficulties in the way of 'freedom' and 'independence'. The essential condition is that the people should be able to govern themselves. This is where the difficulty arises, the fact that one can find twenty university graduates capable of forming a Cabinet does not imply that the responsibility for governing their country can be forthwith handed over to them; that is not 'Government by the people'.

In a colony the population is rarely homogeneous and the majority are poor and illiterate; they often do not speak the same language; they may have had little commerce or contact among them; the impact of newspapers and radio is new and quite limited. There is no larger patriotism, but a mass of local patriotisms. In this situation, the notion of public opinion is fractured, meaning that the impact of the personality, family, race and religion of politicians is more significant and that of their policies less so. In a dependent territory, we have to create institutions by legal enactment which will, one hopes, meet the special conditions of the country and its people. No doubt the basic human material is everywhere the same, but the process of self-government depends upon the accumulated wisdom of centuries of development. When I was in Zululand in 1953 I felt it would not be difficult to sit down with the Zulu elders and an interpreter and work out a constitution for Zululand. Unfortunately, Zululand does not seem to be a political unit except as part of a broader South Africa. Our task in East Africa is to produce a 'partnership' of African, European and Indian; it is a beautiful phrase and solves the whole problem until the constitutional lawyer is brought in to work out the franchise, the number of seats, the methods of election, the rules of parliamentary procedure, the workings of a Cabinet and the thousand other details are needed to define a partnership. Then we shall discover, as we discovered in Asia, the meaning of the phrase 'communalism'.

The unit of government

In united Canada the division between English and French was based both on language and religion. In Ceylon the division is based on 'race', language and religion, but it is difficult, if not impossible, to make it a political division also. In undivided India the fundamental conflict was in respect of religion and that conflict caused the separation of India and Pakistan. Within both countries, however, there are divisions of 'race', language and religion which complicate the problem of government. In South Africa there are roughly 2 million Europeans divided between the English-speaking and the Afrikaans-speaking. There are a number of Indians and a number of 'Cape Coloureds' Eurasians and Eurafricans of mixed descent. Finally, the majority of the population consists of Africans, speaking different varieties of the Bantu languages. The South Africans have made no attempt to solve this problem on acceptable lines, for the South African theory of 'Apartheid' and racial discrimination could not be accepted elsewhere. My point, however, is that it would be extremely difficult to solve it along acceptable lines. Questions of race, language, religion, economic status and educational development are all involved. In any case it is evident that a unit of government which is socially homogeneous is impracticable (this was written before the phrase 'rainbow country' had been heard).

I have mentioned three methods of solving the communal problem. The first, which is adopted in Ceylon and South Africa, is to achieve a balance between communal ideas, and also to form a single state which does its best to develop the larger patriotism. The second method, adopted in the partition of British India into India and Pakistan (and considered in Palestine, hitherto without success), is to create separate states based on communal differences. The third method, illustrated in Canada, India and Pakistan, is to create a federation of states in such a way that the separate states can stress their communal loyalties. This brings us, however, to a very practical problem. What is the effective unit for the purposes of government? It is not very easy to give an answer, because several factors are involved and different persons emphasize different factors.

In the first place, an independent state must be an economic unit, with its own currency and the means for controlling economic life. However, no state can be economically independent for we are all engaged in trade and other forms of commerce. Second, a self-governing people must provide for its own defence and maintenance of its external affairs, though the financial impact of this depends upon the geographical location of the state, its diplomatic relationships and its willingness to take risks. Some states can never expect to defend themselves militarily without assistance. Third, the territory must be such that the country can govern itself effectively, be it 'city state', island, collection of islands, small area or large area. In all cases, the array of governmental authorities created under a constitution must be in proportion to the population and resources of the state. Each case is different. Finally, the country must be able to secure the loyalty of its citizens. Fortunately, history has shown that it is possible for people of different races and religions to work together if stable institutions can once be established and a common loyalty developed. These generalities help to illustrate the complexity of the problem but they do not help much when a practical problem has to be solved. President Wilson enunciated an apparently appealing doctrine, that of self-determination but who are the people to make the self-determination? The principle of majority works well when there is a homogeneous population, but less so when this homogeneity is absent. However, there is no problem of government that cannot be solved with goodwill; and if the goodwill is lacking, one must take steps to create it.

A Bill of Rights

The idea of a Bill of Rights derives from the first country to leave what we now call the Commonwealth – the United States of America. We do not have such a Bill in Britain. When the Constitution of the United States was referred to the states for their ratification, several of them expressed apprehension that it contained no provision limiting the power of the Congress of the United States. Accordingly, the first Congress passed a resolution submitting twelve amendments to the states. Ten of these were accepted and make up the Bill of Rights. This was in 1789. Three later constitutional amendments deal with the consequences of slavery. By that time, slavery had been abolished in the British Empire; indeed slavery was abolished in England in 1771.

It is sometimes alleged by nationalist politicians seeking the freedom of their country, and still more by communist agitators, that British practice in the colonies differs from that in Britain and to anyone who has seen colonial government at work, however, it is quite remarkable how British officials carry into their own administrations the principles they have learned at home, though it is not easy in a colony moving towards freedom, where the officials are publicly denounced as agents of imperialism, exploiters of the local people, toadies of the Governor, arrogant exponents of colour prejudice and every other epithet which frustrated nationalism or personal or political ambition can invent, for them to behave tolerantly and justly and adhere to proper procedures of constitutional government. The fact that these epithets can be used openly and without penal consequences is in itself proof that the constitutional principles are being observed. It is only when abuse goes beyond abuse and becomes incitement to disorder that action is taken. More important still is the fact that nationalist politics and public opinion generally become imbued with these same constitutional principles. The lessons that have been learnt in the Inns of Court and Westminster Hall have spread around the world and are illustrated every day in arguments at the Bar and by pronouncements from the Bench.

The constitutional expert ought to know something of the social and economic conditions of the country with which he is dealing, but he cannot be expected to be omniscient. In any case he does not possess the gift of prophecy and therefore cannot know what problems are likely to arise in the future or what legislative devices may be required to solve them. Therefore the less one puts into a constitution the better, and in particular the fewer restrictions there are on legislation the more likely it will be that successive generations of legislators will be able to solve the country's political problems. However, this principle must not be carried too far; in Britain we have carefully preserved the independence of our judges and we do not require a constitutional provision to protect them; free elections and political liberties are part of our tradition and do not need to be embodied in laws; we do not fear coup d'etat or revolution; we have no laws against discrimination because our laws do not discriminate; we can share our experience and history with the colonies, but we cannot guarantee that colonies which have not had such experience will necessarily acquire the intuition which enables us to react almost by instinct to defend our fundamental liberties. It may not therefore be desirable to prevent new legislatures from passing some kinds of laws which the British Parliament could enact, but does not need to.

In particular, the main constitutional structure must be protected. No constitution can prevent revolution and the modern technique is for a small revolutionary junta to ally itself with democratic parties, to get key institutions like the army, the police and the radio into its hands and then push out its allies or browbeat them into collaboration. Others seek to overawe sections of the population by threats of violence and generally make the machinery of government run down. This has to be met by exactly the opposite of constitutional guarantees, for the government must be entrusted with wide discretionary powers of an emergency character to be used if the constitutional construct itself is threatened.

Though such powers may be incorporated in the constitution, the best way to protect democracy is to ensure democratic elections. This involves an autonomous Election Commission charged with responsibility for delimiting constituencies, compiling electoral registers and running elections. However, even such provisions can be subverted by potential tyrants or dictators and it is therefore important to recall that democracy does not require us to give legal protection to those who seek to overthrow democracy.

Another institution which requires protection is the judiciary. Thus judges should hold a commission 'during good behaviour' and their salaries and allowances should be a charge not on a departmental budget but on the consolidated funds of the state. These provisions are to enable judges to avoid being suborned by politicians, and must be protected by the judges and the legal profession itself. The public opinion developed in this way is I think more important than constitutional provisions.

The conclusion to be drawn from the experience of India, Pakistan and Ceylon is, I think, that one should not attempt to deal with the problem of minorities by constitutional guarantees in a Bill of Rights. One should try to find where the shoe is likely to pinch and to provide the necessary flexibility at that point. It must nevertheless be remembered that a constitution ought to be acceptable to the great mass of the people. What the draughtsman has to do is to provide a constitution which will work; and it will work if it is acceptable to public opinion.

The legislature

In the Commonwealth, opinion is almost unanimous that some kind of second chamber is required. There are several reasons for this. First, the larger plural societies must have federal constitutions in order to maintain unity in diversity, or more properly diversity in unity. The general principle adopted in the United States is then generally followed. The first chamber represents the people; the second chamber represents the constituent units (states or provinces) of the federation. By varying the composition of the second chamber, and weighting the powers of the two chambers, it is possible to achieve a communal balance.

Second, even where a unitary constitution is involved, the second chamber may produce a different communal balance from the first. Thus in South Africa, the House of Assembly represented the population of the Union, while the Senate was designed to represent the Provinces. Since two Provinces had an Afrikaaner majority and two Provinces an English majority, the balance was important. However, it was then destroyed by recent legislation designed to give the nationalist government a two-thirds majority at a joint sitting, so that the constitution could be amended without the support of the opposition. Usually, the principle applied in the first chamber is what in Canada was called 'Rep. by Pop', or representation according to population. In the second chamber equality of representation is more easily accorded. The problem then is to achieve a balance of power between the two chambers.

Third, it is unusual to find the ablest persons in the country taking an active part in politics, because they prefer to go to the universities, or the professions, the public service or business. Thus it is often necessary to devise ways to ensure that access to expertise and experience is made available to government by other means. The second chamber can often help to solve this problem, by according it a revising rather than a primary role in the passage of legislation, by limiting its hours, limiting the access of members to the ministerial office and by other means, including appointment rather than election.

Once it is agreed that there ought to be a second chamber, it then becomes possible to consider the system of representation as a whole. This is the kind of problem which requires local knowledge. There are at least two aspects to the problem, the problem of franchise – that is who can vote and how they can vote – and the problem of representation – single-member territorial constituency, communal representation and the problem of minorities – how are they to be represented when they would always be outvoted by the majority. In the United States the latter problem is partly overcome by giving each state two senators, whatever the population of the states. Communal representation presents many difficulties, and should be avoided if at all possible, but where necessary a system of weighting or electoral colleges may help to reach a solution. There may sometimes be a case for nomination to a representative body of people who would otherwise not be represented. This was done in Ceylon, where the Governor General could, on advice of the Prime Minister, appoint six persons to the lower house to represent Muslims, Indians and the 'Burghers'.

Administration

The pattern of the public service varies from country to country and even from colony to colony. For example, Ceylon had the lowest level labourers engaged on public works, irrigation, the railways and so on. Though literacy levels were high in Ceylon, many of these people could not read or write. Above them were people engaged in low-level administrative tasks which required some education but limited levels of responsibility. The next group were the clerks who could read and write English and carry out routine administration under supervision. Most of them had taken public examinations and among them were the Chief Clerks who were key functionaries, some of whom were admitted to the administrative grades, with much greater levels of responsibility. Finally there was the Administrative grade to which admission was by public examination after university education. Something similar existed elsewhere.

It is obvious that if self-government is to be meaningful, the administration as well as the political leadership must be of the territory. This is largely a matter of education, though experience is also vital. There is also a financial incentive for the government to replace expensive expatriate officials by local officials. Localization is inevitable. In the simplest form of the changeover to responsible government, the official becomes responsible through the head of his department and the Permanent Secretary to the Minister. Indeed the Head of Department may be dispensed with altogether. Ministerial responsibility is very different from official control, even if the official is senior enough to sit in the Legislative Council. The latter feels he has a job to do; the Minister has to show himself to be successful, because he wants voters to vote for him and he may seek a more important ministry from the Prime Minister.

The replacement of expatriate officials by local officials requires time. A young man of twenty-five years, with an excellent university record, can rarely replace an administrator of thirty years' experience. If there is enough time, the process of substitution of local staff for expatriates can take place naturally as young officials are promoted and older men retire. But generally there is pressure to go more quickly. This happened in Burma where experienced British and Indian officials with pre-war experience were replaced by Burmese, few of whom had much experience. In India, the services had been in large measure Indianized by 1947, but a great many senior officials still had to be pensioned off and professional experts were kept on for only a short period. Pakistan recruited a number of British officials who had served in undivided India. In Ceylon, some of the younger expatriates sought and were transferred to other colonies, and the older men were pensioned off. In any case very few expatriates had been recruited to Ceylon after 1934, fourteen years before independence. It will be clear that the problem of substitution is in the first instance one of education, though experience is equally necessary, and this can only be acquired over time. The time allowed may not be sufficient because the up-and-coming politicians are rarely interested in waiting.

Educational development

Self-government is one of the inevitable consequences of education, not one of the objectives of education. Generally speaking, education was left to the missionaries and to local initiative, though grants were often paid from public funds. Though a small minority obtained a good education, initially the mass of the population received no more than the missionaries could provide. Furthermore, very little was done about technical education. The result was not only an unbalanced educational development but also a strong nationalist movement led by the English-educated, before the educational system was sufficiently developed to enable self-government to be granted. Africa is advancing more rapidly than Asia did, but experience in Asia suggests that nationalism becomes prominent in the third generation of the English-educated.

A complete education system cannot be created in one generation, even if all the funding and teachers required are available, which they never are. It is not always recognized either that each level of the education system depends upon the level above. The primary schools need teachers educated in high schools; the technical schools need teachers educated in the technical colleges; the high schools and technical schools need teachers educated at the university. On the other hand, it is also true that the higher level depends upon the level below. It is an old problem; there are no eggs without hens and there are no hens without eggs.

If self-government is to be attained in the remaining colonies quicker than it was in India and Ceylon, more funding is required and this has now been made available through the Colonial Development and Welfare Acts by which the British taxpayer is providing large sums for development assistance. In the context of providing education for those who will become members of a competent public service, high-quality staff are required at all the levels of the service summarized earlier. Thus not everyone needs to be educated at the university level, though highly trained specialists in various disciplines are also required, not merely administrators. But in fact the most pressing need in most countries is for more and better teachers at all levels, for without them, the education system cannot meet the needs and cannot be expanded. However, the premature development of universities, as occurred in India, is not wise, because the entry levels will fall and that takes a long time to remedy. (See Chapter 1 for a more detailed discussion of this matter).

Executive government

Executive government tends to be created in the years prior to self-government. What is not created, and in fact can only be created with the experience of self-government, is an opposition, without which the dominant party could either lose its vigour or become a dictatorship. But that is not reason to delay self-government; rather the transitional period should be pressed ahead, for experience has shown that it cannot be delayed much without the colonial administration and the politicians falling out.

The dilemma of representative government

The difficulties which arise in the operation of representative government are not new. They arose in the eighteenth century in the American and West Indian colonies. The practice then was to empower a Governor to summon an assembly elected on a narrow franchise, which in effect gave control to the wealthier sections of the population. The Governor retained executive authority in his own hands, working with an Executive Council consisting of the chief officials and eminent local people. This worked reasonably well in the West Indies, even up to the twentieth century, though it broke down in some colonies. Even in America, the revolutionary war did not arise on account of conflicts between the Governors and their assemblies, but because the British government tried to get the Americans to pay for their own defence. In the newer colonies this system began to fail when nationalist movements arose, since their loyalty, if it existed at all, was to their own country, and indeed – and this is the critical point – the people of such a colony will never be able to govern themselves until they develop a patriotism which extends beyond the traditional loyalties of race, religion, caste or tribe. Thus the slowing down by the colonial power of the handover of authority to local politicians serves the purpose of encouraging the national patriotism necessary for a country to govern itself. Though this notion was not really articulated in this manner at a policy level, over and over again colonial administrators, faced with a divided country, slowed things down until such divisions began to sort themselves out into something resembling a national patriotism.

From a practical point of view, the problem is how to maintain friendly relations between the colonial government and the nationalist movement in the difficult period of representative government, while the nationalist politicians spend so much of their time 'blaming the British' for every perceived ill or slight. There is no real solution to this problem except the exercise of tact and good relations by those in positions of authority, as did happen in many cases – for example, Lord Irwin in India and Governor Arden-Clarke in Ghana. After 1945, when the objective of self-government of the colonies was explicitly stated as the British government's objective, this became easier to accomplish.

The transition

Lord Durham in Canada in the 1840s said that opposition between government and the legislature was almost inevitable; and the experience of a century has not proved him wrong. However, full responsible government cannot be conferred until all the problems discussed above have been reasonably settled. I hope I have made it plain that perfect solutions cannot be expected. Various constitutional devices, some of which I have mentioned, can be invented to minimize the risks; but some risks must be taken. Even so there must be a transition. The electors have to get used to the exercise of the franchise; communal claims have to be sorted out and be incorporated in the larger patriotism; a public service, staffed largely by local people, has to be developed; the parliamentary majority has to learn to accept leadership; and persons capable of functioning as ministers have to be discovered and encouraged.

Effectively what happens is that powers previously reserved to the Crown or the British government are gradually handed over to the colonial government, though some powers may be reserved to the British government or the Governor until independence. These powers are only rarely used but were, for example, in Jamaica, Malta, Newfoundland and British Guiana when the local constitution was suspended until a problem could be resolved. Typically Governors have retained some powers over salaries of expatriate civil servants, over budgetary control and other issues though such reserved powers will be rarely exercised and then only after strenuous efforts have been made to reach an agreement with the Legislative Council. The system of dyarchy used in India and Ceylon was another approach to this intermediate stage. But this stage cannot last for long, for it can prevent or disrupt the very exercise of power which is the essence of good government and for which the previous years have prepared the colony.

Sir Ivor Jennings, 1955

Annex 3: Lord Hailey native administration in the British African territories

Following his monumental survey of Africa published in 1938, Lord Hailey followed this with an equally vast analysis of 'Native Administration' in ten British colonies and protectorates, contained in a book published by HMSO in 1951. The findings of this analysis were deeply relevant to the search for ways to develop 'self-government' as a prerequisite for independence of the various territories, which is alluded to many times in this volume. I feel the best way to show that relevance is to reproduce here a review by Martin Moore of the book which appeared in the *Daily Telegraph* of 9 May 1951:

To his great 'African Survey' Lord Hailey adds today an equally vast marshalling of facts about native administration in ten British colonies and protectorates. This study of the day-to-day domestic rule of 55 million Africans is fundamental to any consideration of political and constitutional developments.

Here in all its diversity is the human material portrayed in the conduct of its own affairs. It ranges through all gradations from native authorities which are already discharging many functions of local government, as in Nigeria, to others which can only understand the relative costs of different items of expenditure when they are depicted by heaps of stones of varying sizes.

The picture which emerges from more than 900 pages of detailed facts is of communities intimately associated, under guidance, with the administration of everything which touches their daily lives, yet almost totally unprepared for representative self-government.

Native authorities assess and collect their own taxes and control their land. Health and education come within their purview. Native police or 'tribal messengers' deal with all except major crimes; native courts try the overwhelming majority of criminal and civil cases. What the colonial government has done is to reinforce customary authority with statutory powers.

The indigenous authorities who exercise such wide control are basically democratic in that they depend upon the acquiescence of the community. Autocratic or authoritarian rule is, as Lord Hailey points out, rare in Africa.

Today this traditional system of local administration faces a challenge. Upon it has been superimposed the modern demand for self-government on a national scale. Can local rule, as at present practised, offer a workable basis? Can it produce the men for national tasks or – more important – train a potential electorate in democratic method?

The question is not so much whether Africans are ready, but whether they are even being realistically prepared for the democracy of the ballot box. Acknowledging the training they have been given in the management of their affairs, Lord Hailey adds:

> It has often been claimed that this has also afforded them a training in the practise of self-government in the political sense. But this does not necessarily follow. The conduct of political self-government, as the term is understood, demands experience in the practise of selecting representatives charged with giving expression to policies approved by the community, and its success depends on the ability of the public to hold them to account if they fail in their duties.

By this criterion, we are only at the beginning of the first stage in preparing Africans for self-government. The logical evolution would be from customary rule, through local government institutions, to national self-government. Lord Hailey shows both the difficulties of taking this intermediate step and the peril of being rushed into skipping it altogether.

Many native authorities, as he records, have been given wider responsibilities though none has as yet a measure of autonomy comparable with that enjoyed by a local government body in Britain. But 'if the Governments are now to be pressed to make more radical changes, in order to accelerate the rate of political advance, they may be faced with the consequences of giving a political objective the priority over measures designed to secure ordered progress in the field of Native administration'.

The main practical difficulty which Lord Hailey sees in creating African local authorities with executive and financial powers is, as might be imagined, the lack of personnel.

> There are numerous areas in which there is at present no adequate material for the purpose. ... There are many other areas where the difficulties may appear to be less pronounced, but where nevertheless the creation of local government bodies of the class suggested would be ineffective, not merely because popular opinion still acknowledges only the authority of the

traditional leaders, but because the other elements which would go to form the proposed bodies, are simply non-existent.

In towns, which should offer more promising materiel for democracy, municipal institutions have been discouraging.

It is particularly noticeable that where there has been an electoral system, little interest has as a rule been shown by the African public in the elections. It is sometimes suggested that service on these municipal bodies has not attracted Africans of standing because the range of their activities has been unduly limited … but African elected members have very seldom shown themselves willing to face the responsibility of increasing taxation in order to finance and extension of these functions.

Lord Hailey also points to a difficulty more fundamental than lack of personnel to man and elect local government bodies. In gaining autonomy, they would inevitably have to shed some of the functions, such as maintenance of law and order and the provision of tribunals, which native authorities now exercise. Self-government would thus break the unity of the community's intimate association with the management of its daily affairs.

Clearly a local government body cannot just step into the place of a native administration based on tradition. Lord Hailey therefore urges that decisions should be made now about the future of the whole system; 'not merely in its relation to possible constitutional developments but in the light of existing administrative requirements'.

Self-government has long been the objective of our colonial policy, though opinion has differed about the period within which it should be realizable by the various territories. Now we are everywhere under pressure to revise even the most optimistic estimates of this speed.

There would be reason enough for misgivings if policy were merely being forced unwisely fast along a well-surveyed path. But it is worse than that because there is no certainty about either the path or the kind of self-government to which it should lead.

Whether self-government can most suitably find expression in Parliamentary institutions on the British model is, as Lord Hailey remarks, a 'most debatable issue'. His analysis of the practice and prospects of local government makes it seem equally debatable whether British democratic institutions even on this lower level, can be widely transplanted to Africa.

He shows that the existing native administration based on customary rule will in any case have to be recast if it is to develop into a system of local government. With the practicability of local government itself uncertain, policy is indeed in the melting pot.

In reshaping it, two essentials are the collation of widely varying experience of native rule in the different territories and continuity of administration on the spot. To the first essential, Lord Hailey's own work is a monumental contribution.

As a means of maintaining local continuity despite the frequent changes of British personnel, he suggests the appointment of African assistants to district officers. This would afford valuable training in the administrative duties which are too often forgotten in the clamour for political responsibility and it would also put Africa's readiness for self-government to a practical test.

For, as Lord Hailey adds, 'if Africans are not prepared to accept the exercise of administrative authority by other Africans, this materially reduces the prospect of the extension of self-government'.

He also calls for a decision or policy on the native's right to pledge or alienate his land which, if unrestricted, may darken Africa's future under whatever system of government she evolves.

In an agricultural community there is no graver source of unrest than a system of tenure which may subject the peasantry to exploitation by a landlord or moneylender. There is no graver menace to society than the dispossessed landholder who can find no alternative livelihood in industry. These are the features of agrarian life which have hitherto had no analogy in the African indigenous economy, but unless due regard is paid to development of a suitable form of land tenure, they are now likely to become common in those areas of Africa which have a high population or an intensive form of cultivation.

The importance of the economic approach to Africa's vast and complex political problems is one of the major lessons to be drawn from Lord Hailey's survey. While he utters the warning against creating a class of discontented cultivators who would be prey for 'those who are interested in bringing about a political upheaval' he is equally sure that the path to political maturity is through economic betterment.

On the basis of his experience in India as well as Africa, he declares that 'nothing is more convincing than the rapidity with which an improvement in material conditions is followed by an increase in the initiative and capacity of individual members of the community'.

Annex 4: Alan Lennox-Boyd, minister of state, Colonial Office 1951–2 and Colonial Secretary 1954–9

Alan Lennox-Boyd (Lord Boyd) was formally interviewed at Oxford in December 1974 and February 1975, fifteen years after he left office.[1] The interviewers were Sir George Sinclair (on Cyprus), Kenneth Kirkwood (on Central Africa), Anthony Kirk-Green (on West Africa) and Alison Smith (on East Africa). In each interview Lord Boyd commented also on general matters relevant to his period of office. This annex does not address Cyprus and the minor territories.

Lennox-Boyd interested himself in the empire and colonial matters from the time of his undergraduate days at Oxford, when he won the Beit prize for an essay 'The Development of the Idea of Trusteeship in the Government of Backward Peoples'. He said the notion of trusteeship was uppermost in his mind from that time onwards. After his election to parliament in 1931 he was influenced by Leopold Amery, colonial secretary and subsequently secretary of state for India. Later in the 1930s and 1940s he was also influenced by Oliver Stanley, who was the foremost conservative politician on colonial matters and who encouraged him to attend the meetings of the Colonial Affairs Committee. Stanley also wanted him to become a spokesman on colonial matters and in due course indicated to him that he hoped he would take over from him as colonial secretary. He eventually became minister of state at the colonial office under Oliver Lyttelton for a period of six months in 1951/2, but then served as minister of transport until 1954, when he succeeded Lyttelton (Lord Chandos) as colonial secretary within Winston Churchill's last administration. Thus by the time he became secretary of state he had been thinking about and studying colonial matters for nearly thirty years and was exceptionally well qualified for the position. He had an extravert character and by all accounts much charm. He befriended many people in the colonies, entertained them when they were in London and had them to stay at his substantial house in Chapel Street, Belgravia.

West Africa

Boyd felt that the 1949 Watson Report on the Gold Coast disturbances degraded the role of the tribal chiefs, unintentionally but definitely, though the balance was somewhat restored under the Coussey constitution. He regretted that Secretary of State Creech Jones had in 1949 made a virtual promise of independence – he deplored such undertakings as they changed the behaviour of everyone involved. He was surprised on visiting the Gold Coast for the first time at the extent of tribal tension and jealousy. He found both the governor, Charles Arden-Clarke and Nkrumah viewed federation as being impossible. Though he was drawn to a federal solution for the territory, he did not receive advice to seek that approach either from the governor or from colonial office officials. He felt that the die was cast constitutionally by the time Oliver Lyttelton became secretary of state. He feared that Nkrumah would undermine the safeguards built in to stabilize the constitution. From the time of independence, this is exactly what Nkrumah did; he destroyed local assemblies, threatened the chiefs and sacked or de-stooled them. Lennox-Boyd found Nkrumah very vain and very worried about threats to him when he visited Britain.

He found that Arden-Clarke did not like to have the secretary of state visit the territory and he had to insist on it. He thought Arden-Clarke had worked out what he thought was the only possible and tolerable constitution and was rather worried that he (Boyd), with a natural concern for minorities and the armed forces would come in and disturb the pattern he had worked out.

In regard to Nigeria, Boyd thought at the time that there was no chance of it moving to independence as a unitary state, but agreed that the federal solution with three large and powerful regions which had grown up since Governor Bourdillon was rather weak. He regretted having overruled the recommendations of Willinck in regard to minorities. He said that he did not think that at the time he was in office he had seen Miles Clifford's memorandum to Bourdillon of 1941/2 in which he advocated a federation of fourteen provinces/states, including Rivers Province, abolishing the regions and re-adjusting the existing boundaries along ethnic and traditional lines, or natural boundaries; and foresaw that the Ibos were potentially de-stabilizing in any case. Clifford also advocated a good deal of delegation and more representation. The interviewer (Kirk-Greene), who was serving in Nigeria at the relevant time, recorded that he had not seen the memorandum either. Boyd and Kirk-Greene agreed that Bourdillon must have decided that Clifford's suggestions should be left to the Royal Commission then planned. In the event perhaps it was overlooked after Bourdillon's retirement.

It is of interest that Clifford's recommendation was very similar to the 1967 re-arrangement of the federation adopted by the military government after the Biafran War, which provided for twelve states under the Government of Nigeria. Boyd felt that by 1957 when the pre-independence constitutional conference was held, it would have been very difficult to move to a federal solution such as this, even supposing it had been accepted in Nigeria, as it would have meant postponing independence, which no Nigerian politician would have supported.

Boyd recalled that in 1956 he had stated that he 'was not prepared to fix a date for self-government for Nigeria as a whole', the more so as the Northern delegation, representing over half the population, was unable to depart from its policy of 'self-government when practicable'. He said he had had to defend this statement without being able to reveal all the reasons given to him by the Sardauna of Sokoto. He recalled that Nigeria had dragged its feet over a defence agreement with Britain at independence because the intention had been for the agreement to apply to Commonwealth forces, not merely British ones. Neither the Sardauna nor Prime Minister Abubakr was willing to allow Nkrumah to land military planes in Nigeria.

Boyd thought Robertson had been a good governor, who stood up to both British and Nigerian ministers. He could also say 'No' to the Treasury.

East Africa

Kenya. Boyd said that the first time he visited Kenya, Governor Mitchell did not want him to speak anywhere. Mitchell was rather aloof and failed to take seriously the rural reports reaching him prior to the outbreak of Mau Mau. Boyd recalled that in a personal letter to him Baring said how Kenyatta dominated the funeral of Chief Waruhiu at the beginning of the emergency. Baring described in his letter how at the funeral Kenyatta would turn round so that the carved head of the stick he carried would confront a group of Africans, and how they immediately stiffened when he was looking at them in particular; and then he would move it round a bit to another group. By then the administration was already coming to think that Kenyatta was behind the murder. Boyd said that at first Baring did not take the settlers seriously; he did not like pressure groups. Boyd decided early on in the Emergency that Africans in senior positions should never be left alone and be expected to obey the rule of secrecy. It was essential that they should have another African with them at all times with whom to discuss events and decisions. Boyd very much admired Governor Baring's attempt to continue with the Swynnerton plan for agricultural development despite the Mau Mau emergency.

Boyd recalled how he took to the Cabinet in London the language which was to be used in regard to the Mau Mau 'irreconcilables':

We speak as men who have religious faith and believe we hold the view that no one is irreconcilable; but on behalf of the British Government, I give you this assurance that the irreconcilables, the founders and managers and organisers of Mau Mau, will not be allowed to return to their homeland as long as they remain irreconcilable.

The report of the Bottomley/Elliot Parliamentary Mission to investigate Mau Mau, which was based on the confessions of Africans involved, was published. However the Confidential Annex on the demands which were made on young and middle-aged African men and women before they were initiated into Mau Mau was so shocking and revolting that the Cabinet decided to place it in the libraries of the House of Commons and the House of Lords, but not to release it to the public. The major task was to find ways to bring people back to a sane approach and discard all the outward symbols of Mau Mau. Many dedicated people spent a long time engaged in this trying and difficult work.

Boyd said that the imposition of the death penalty during the Mau Mau Emergency for anyone found carrying weapons received widespread support among the Africans. He did not think he ever came under any pressure to commute a sentence of death.

Boyd described the difference of view between the government and the Kenya Police Commissioner Arthur Young, which caused the latter to resign. Both HMG and the Kenya governments considered responsibility for law and order should lie with the local administrators (District Commissioners and District Officers, supported by the Home Guard) and that the responsibility of the Kenya police was to investigate crimes and bring offenders to justice. Young considered the police could not do their job in the emergency, and retain public respect for the law, if the Home Guard who, in his view abused their powers, were not responsible to him.

Boyd regretted some of the things he had said about the prospects for European settlers in East Africa, which induced some of them to burn their boats as a result, even though he was careful to make no commitment without first clearing it with the Colonial Policy Committee or the prime minster. He also said that he and Governor Baring had found ways to meet Tom Mboya without anyone else knowing and that they had achieved more in two hours talking with him than all the time spent in the formal negotiations at the colonial office.

Uganda. Boyd said he would never have appointed Andrew Cohen to be a colonial governor. He thought he was too anxious to work out his own theories without due regard to the circumstances or the areas where he was in charge. He considered him a dangerous governor and deplored the way he handled the issue of the Kabaka.

Tanganyika. Boyd said in retrospect he was mistaken in extending Twining's term of office as governor. He became over-confident and careless, ('as I did myself by 1959'). Boyd said that the United Nations' missions to Tanganyika were nearly universally mischievous, and by encouraging Nyerere to pursue impractical objectives rendered poor service to the country. Ministers listened carefully to both Twining and Turnbull, but he personally thought that Tanganyika self-government came far too early.

Central Africa

The Labour minister, Patrick Gordon Walker, and Leopold Amery gave Boyd the greatest possible encouragement in regard to Central Africa. 'I dreamed like many others of a non-racial state in Central Africa.' This, of course, required a federation; amalgamation was a non-starter. Lyttelton had invited representatives of the African Representative Council of Northern Rhodesia and the African Protectorate Council of Nyasaland to visit London for informal discussions before the formal negotiations on the federation began. They came but, under pressure from the two African National congresses, were not willing to participate in the official negotiations. By contrast the two Southern Rhodesian representatives did participate.

Boyd said, 'then and thereafter I wished that the capital of the federation could have been Livingstone in Northern Rhodesia (instead of Salisbury), and if I had stayed on as secretary of state I would have pressed for this. I had a feeling that the fate of the federation might turn on where the capital was.' He considered that the federation did have accomplishments:

- By 1959, health expenditure in Nyasaland had trebled and capital expenditure increased fivefold.

- Education expenditure in both protectorates had increased from 5 per cent to 10 per cent of the budget, which was itself larger.

- Savings by Africans had risen substantially.

- European ownership of land in Nyasaland had halved.

- The University College of Rhodesia and Nyasaland had been launched under the inspired leadership of Walter Adams.

There was however something in Welensky's complaint that so long as the colonial office was the ultimate arbiter in the two northern territories, they could never build up loyalty to the federation, though Welensky exaggerated when he had said that the Africans looked on HMG as a sort of opposition to the federation.

Governor Benson of Northern Rhodesia told Lennox-Boyd he would not be able to meet the members of the political parties during his first visit. He (Boyd) had had to insist on seeing them as that was the purpose of his visit.

Boyd considered that the tribal chiefs played an indispensable part in Africa and he wanted to see that the position of those on whom the people had relied for so long as a source of wisdom and authority should not be suddenly undermined; he tried to create a bridge between the old Africa and the new.

Boyd said he had the greatest difficulty with the white trade unionists in the Northern Rhodesian copper belt, who deeply resented the prospect of Africans taking their jobs. He had virtually no help from the British trade unions on this issue.

Boyd said that Garfield Todd was thought to be a liberal but he never appointed an African to the Southern Rhodesian government. Boyd thought he was a bit phoney.

Boyd said that he was in the air from Aden at the time of the declaration of the Emergency in Nyasaland and that had he not been so tired he would have flown straight on to Nyasaland to address the issue on the spot before conceding the request for emergency powers.

He was asked if federation was imposed on an unwilling majority of the African people. He agreed with this but pointed out that federally minded people in Southern Rhodesia did not want Nyasaland in the federation. It was HMG which insisted on its inclusion.

General

Boyd said that on the whole the colonial office and ministers were deeply resentful about the American attitude towards colonial issues and although they spoke to them repeatedly and often, and sometimes had the satisfaction of pointing out their treatment of the Indians and the released slaves, we were never on terms with them about the speed of self-government. However, once their own interests were affected, for example in the Caribbean, the Americans would change their views. He recalled John Foster Dulles saying that America could not tolerate an independent British Guiana.

Boyd thought that those who took the view that only Britain was capable of being an effective colonial power would, in the light of subsequent history, have to modify their views. He thought the French handling generally of Africa in the 1950s, particularly under de Gaulle, was in many ways inspired.

Boyd was asked if he thought decolonization was precipitate. He considered that it clearly was in so far as it came from the home government. The interviewer said that it had been suggested that Britain as a country, its senior opinion in government, the city, among opinion formers, and elsewhere was of the view that the colonies ought to be brought to an end; that there was a weariness and a willingness to give way to importunate pressures in the struggle; or a lack of resolution to continue it. Boyd concurred with this view and said he thought it happened during the 1959 general election. He felt there was a view that the country ought to turn its attention to Europe. There was also a prevailing view that we ought to become again a trading nation. However, he said that Macmillan subsequently changed his view and deeply regretted his decision to appoint Iain McLeod as colonial secretary. He recalled that Macmillan was a 'profit and loss' man, never an imperialist like Churchill; nor did he have the genuine sense of trusteeship and obligation that Anthony Eden had had.

Annex 5: Synopsis of notes prepared by T. Neil, permanent secretary, Kenya Ministry of State for Constitutional Affairs and Administration, July 1962

These notes were prepared by Neil in advance of an interview with the HMG Economy Commission in 1962. They shed an interesting light on various aspects of the localization programme and the constraints government had to contend with. The synopsis retains the first person of the original.

I think it might be profitable to make a few general comments about the organization of the Kenya Government, pointing to some avenues which might be worth the further exploration of the Commission both in regard to expenditure and revenue.

As an example of the growth of the government, there are now nearly as many staff in my ministry as there were in the whole of government twenty years ago. It will have occurred to the Commission that perhaps the scale and scope of such services will ultimately be beyond being sustained by a country which relies for the most part on the export of agricultural produce, and then only on a limited scale, and in a country where so much of the agricultural land is marginal. In many areas of Kenya the natural wealth of the country is negligible and is represented by a few hundred thousand heads of scrub cattle and goats which are of no economic value except in the traditional estimation of their owners.

Thus, for example, in Kenya we have the Turkana District with an estimated population of 100,000 where the people are still for the most part as unaffected by modern progress as they were fifty or sixty years ago, but which nevertheless, as part of Africa, must be administered, policed, provided with medical facilities and in bad years prevented from dying off by the massive injection of free relief.

The Turkana live off their useless cattle and over the years they are fortunate if they receive one meal a day, usually of milk, and perhaps one meal a week of meat. The Masai and the coast hinterland, the Samburu and other parts of the Northern Province all fall within what may be termed poor and biologically unbalanced areas. How then can we sustain the highly elaborate, skilled and, if I may say so, for the most part devoted civil service which has been so carefully built up since we introduced the cabinet system of government under the Lyttleton Reforms of 1954? The people want medical services, education, they feel they are moving with the world, and yet all this has to be done on a per capita income of about £26 per head ... economic emphasis will no doubt shift from the European farms to the African peasant agriculture and the first steps in that direction have already been taken in the Central Province where, under the direction and inspiration of the provincial administration, a total and complete agricultural revolution has been carried out since 1953.

Despite political criticism to the contrary, it has always been the aim of the colonial administration in Kenya to see that all parts of the territory were administered as uniformly as the condition of the people and the limitations of geography, climate, natural resources and temperament would permit. This despite the fact that per capita costs of the administration alone varies from about Shs 1.80 per head in Nyanza to as high as Shs 6.00 per head in the Northern Province. In Kenya we have no less than sixteen ministries to deal with services in a country where many of these, such as Transport, Customs, Income Tax, Civil Aviation, Post and Telegraphs, are organized on an inter-territorial basis. These ministries are by their nature expensive not less than £25,000 for each ministry.

Following the Lancaster House Conference earlier this year we seem now to be committed to a system of Regional Government and, however impeccable may be the reasons for embodying Regional Government within the Constitution, one cannot set aside the thought that we shall shortly be embarking upon yet a further layer of expensive government. No serious examination of the cost of government in Kenya can be realistic without some fresh appraisal of what the country can afford by way of Legislative Assemblies, Upper and Lower Houses, Regional Assemblies, Ministers and so on; can we look for a more simple and less sophisticated form of government in what is basically a poor country?

Reports coming in from all over the country indicate that a very large proportion of the expatriate officers will leave this country at independence and since it will be quite impossible for the successor government to either have trained replacements immediately available or to recruit replacements elsewhere in the professions where there is also a great scarcity of skilled personnel, such services will have to be cut to suit the staff positions; it may well be necessary to close hospitals because doctors and nurses are not available; it might appear to outsiders that our accounting procedure, for example, is unduly elaborate but it has been built up over experience and unless we have strict accounting and auditing procedures the loss of revenue and general misappropriation of government funds would rise sharply. If I may express a personal opinion, I feel that recent Salaries Commissions in Kenya have set the salaries at too high a level in relation to the economy of the country and the general background of standards of living and expectancy of the people concerned. Clerks and executive staff, for example, have established a standard of living quite beyond that to which they aspired when they joined the service or which they enjoyed in their countries of origin.

The establishment of the Provincial Administration at July 1961 was as follows:

Chief Commissioner	1
Provincial Commissioners	6
Officer-in-Charge, Nairobi District	1
Senior District Commissioners	27
District Officers	236
District Assistants	174

Local officers include 76 of the District Officers and 110 of the District Assistants. To enable localization to proceed at a faster pace in the District Officer cadre, the Limited Compensation Scheme was invoked in the latter half of 1961 and fifty-seven expatriate District Offices are going on voluntary retirements under the scheme. They are being replaced by local officers. Thirty local District Officers will be appointed by next September, taking the proportion of local District Officers to about 50 per cent. Further localization cannot be contemplated for the present because the remaining experienced staff is already barely sufficient to handle the political and constitutional development, settlement schemes and the forthcoming census, and to train local officers, it is surely better to give an increased number of local officers a little training under the remaining expatriate officers rather than wait until Independence when the bulk of the expatriate officers is likely to leave. Fortunately there is no shortage of applicants with sufficient educational qualifications for either District Officers or District Assistants, although it is not always possible to find candidates with outstanding character and personality; nevertheless, the standard is adequate.

The problem arising from the loss of expatriate staff can be summed up in the word 'inexperience'. Only one African now has more than three years' experience. Of the 100 plus African District Officers who will be in service by next September, over half will have been appointed since 1 January this year. The first four African District Commissioners were appointed in February and a fifth will be appointed in August. Only one of these District Commissioners will have more than three years' experience as a District Officer and against this must be set the fact that it has taken an expatriate officer on the average ten years to become a District Commissioner.

Under the African Courts (Amendment) Bill 1962, to be enacted this year, the African Courts are to be transferred to the Judicial Department. These courts hear far more cases than do the subordinate courts of the Colony and the Justice Department is not in a position to supervise the African Courts yet, so specialist expatriate officers will have to be retained for this purpose for some time to come. It will also be necessary to provide an avenue for promotion of District Registrars to Provincial African Courts Officers. This should not be and cannot be hurried so that the integrity, independence and efficiency of the Judiciary are not impaired.

In the Chief Accountant's Office, there are at present two expatriate Accountants and I could almost guarantee that if these two officers were taken away, the Branch would begin to degenerate within forty-eight hours. There is only one qualified Kenyan Chartered Accountant and he is employed by an oil company. Out of a staff of ninety-four in the Finance and Establishments Branch, eight are European expatriates and hold key positions. The subordinate staff are largely Asian and they would be promoted if the Europeans were to leave, for there are no African staff with the necessary trained capability. We are training staff in the Institute and will graduate 100 Africans this year after a three-month course; they will be followed by others. But a three-month course is no substitute for experience in what has to be meticulous work. We cannot supervise district and provincial staff from the centre and must rely on Provincial and District Commissioners to maintain day-to-day control over revenue and expenditure.

I would strongly recommend that HMG should be quite adamant that all Grants-in-Aid towards the recurrent budget should be brought to an end at the end of the current financial year. The new Africa must learn to cut its cloth according to its income and a first step in national education is a balanced budget. I would go further and suggest that HMG should use the threat of cutting altogether development money unless and until the recurrent budget is balanced.

Annex 6: The political objectives of British policy in the African dependent territories

The following is the text of a paper submitted to the State Department in Washington by the British Embassy, as part of the briefing for the Bermuda Conference between the United Kingdom and the United States in July 1957. It was prepared jointly by the colonial office and the foreign office in London.

1. The central purpose of British policy is to guide the dependent territories to responsible self-government within the Commonwealth in conditions that ensure to the people a fair standard of living and freedom from aggression from any quarter.

2. The objective is to create stable states in which individuals feel both free and secure. That is, however, by no means an easy task. When we arrived in Africa, its inhabitants were in a transitional state halfway between that of purely tribal inter-warring groupings, and that of the emergence of autocratic rulers or oligarchic groups who were succeeding in forcing their rule over something more than a purely tribal area.

3. The sense of association with the tribe is still infinitely stronger, in East Africa, for example, than the sense of identification with the geographical areas known by the names of the present British territories. The possibility of establishing a unit of self-government which has inherent stability is directly conditioned by the extent to which tribal sympathies and affinities can be merged in a wider feeling of community and mutual interest.

4. Experience has shown that the strength of such developments is related to the length of time during which the influence of the central government

introduced by the administering power has been able, by the establishment of common institutions and a common framework of educational and social policies, to create a sense of community. In West Africa, such success as had been achieved is the result of two centuries of this sort of influence. The Gold Coast is now embarking on self-government as a unitary state: but it is to be noted that even here a resurgence of older and narrower loyalties among the people of Ashanti and the Northern Territory, which threatened to divide the county on the eve of independence, called for a great last-minute effort to produce an acceptable constitution which maintained unity while meeting regional susceptibilities.

5. In East Africa, this influence has been at work for little more than fifty years. In that area also the pattern is further complicated by the fact that communities with more advanced civilizations have established themselves in a number of our territories; some (e.g. the Arabs on the East Coast of Africa and some of the Indians in East Africa) before our arrival, and some (e.g. the Europeans and most of the Asians in Kenya) since our arrival.

6. Before the United Kingdom can abandon control, we must be reasonably certain that we shall not be handing over a territory or an area either to autocratic or oligarchic dictatorship, or to a virtual state of anarchy. When it is possible to be reasonably sure of that in any particular territory or area must depend on the circumstances of that territory or area. It will depend in particular on the homogeneity of the population, the prosperity of the territory, the respective levels of educational and technical advancement of various sections of the community, and similar factors.

7. For such reasons, the optimum rate of advance of the relatively homogeneous and prosperous territories of West Africa is plainly very different from that of the much poorer and more backward plural societies of East Africa. The fact that there is a difference in rates reflects no inconsistency in policy, but is a reflection of the factors which govern the rate at which, in given circumstances, a stable and healthy free society can be brought into existence.

8. The alternative to a steady and orderly development, determined by the evolving facts of the situation in each particular territory, is a disorderly and precipitate slide towards the assumption of power by individuals or groups who lack the ability or experience to use it wisely and the confidence of large parts of the population that they can and will do so. The consequence is likely to be maladministration, corruption and chaos leading to serious internal strife, presenting a golden opportunity for Soviet machinations. In one sense the work of the bloc

would already have been done for it, in that the territories concerned would in effect by these very developments, have become politically, economically and morally denied to the free world.

9. In the ideal situation, the rate of political advance of given territories should be determined solely by the developing capacity of the local population to discharge satisfactorily more and more of the responsibilities of government. So far as concerns the British dependencies it is the policy of HMG in the UK to foster the development of that capacity, by education and by the improvement of the necessary economic and social substructure as well as by political and constitutional changes. There will however always be some to whom this process may seem too slow, and if these voices gain widespread support, then a rate of advancement may as a matter of practical politics have to be accepted which is in fact too fast for the circumstances of the territory, and for the interests of the free world.

10. An important factor in this respect is the extent to which local political leaders gain 'outside' support, which means to a very large extent support in the United States and in and around the United Nations. That extent is affected by the attitude of the United States Government and its representative more than by any other single influence. It is essential, therefore, if developments in the dependencies are to follow the steady course which is desirable on all counts that the US government in its actions and in the utterances of its spokesmen should consider the bearing of such actions and utterances on the attainment of the agreed objects of policy set out above. These considerations apply particularly to utterances at the United Nations and in the Trusteeship Council. For example, the uncritical advocacy by the United States Representative in the Trusteeship Council of set timetables for political advance in Tanganyika has played a significant part in disturbing a situation previously characterized by racial harmony and well-balanced political progress.

11. The attainment of 'independence' by a territory has little meaning or value either to its own people or the rest of the world if it is accompanied or followed by oppression and misgovernment, poverty and civil disturbance. The external independence of states is in fact worthwhile only to the extent that it is a condition of the internal freedom of individuals within the states. The central problem of policy in relation to dependencies is to prepare for the day when the cause of individual freedom and security will thenceforth be best served by political independence, and to judge correctly when that day has come.

Source: FO 371/125293

Annex 7: Summary of a speech made by the British Prime Minister Harold Macmillan to the Parliament of the Union of South Africa, 3 February 1960

After courtesies and observations about the close ties between Britain and South Africa, in peace and in war; after recognizing the striking material progress achieved; after noting that two-thirds of the foreign investment in South Africa had been financed with British capital; Macmillan went on to talk about Africa more generally.

In the twentieth century, and especially since the end of the Second World War, the processes which gave birth to the nation states of Europe have been repeated all over the world. We have seen the awakening of national consciousness in peoples who have for centuries lived in dependence upon some other Power. Fifteen years ago this movement spread through Asia. ... Today, the same thing is happening in Africa; the most striking of all the impressions I have formed since I left London ... is of the strength of this African national consciousness. In different places it takes different forms, but it is happening everywhere. The wind of change is blowing through this continent and, whether we like it or not, this growth of national consciousness is a political fact. We must accept it as a fact and our national policies must take account of it ... and we and the other nations of the Western world are ultimately responsible. For its causes are to be found in the achievements of Western civilization, in the pushing forward of the frontiers of knowledge, in the applying of science in the service of human needs, in the expanding of food production, in the speeding and multiplying of the means of communication and perhaps, above all, the spread of education.

As I see it, the great issue in the second half of the Twentieth Century is whether the uncommitted peoples of Asia and Africa will swing to the East or to the West. The struggle is joined and it is a struggle for the minds of men. What is now on trial is much more than our military strength or our diplomatic and administrative skill. It is our way of life. The uncommitted nations want to see before they choose.

What can we show them to help them to choose a right? Each of the independent members of the Commonwealth must answer that question of itself. ... We may sometimes be tempted to say to each other 'mind your own business', but in these days I would myself expand the old saying so that it runs 'mind your own business but mind how it affects my business, too'.

Let me be frank with you, my friends. What governments and parliaments in the United Kingdom have done since the war in according independence to India, Pakistan, Ceylon, Malaya and Ghana, and what they will do for Nigeria and other countries now nearing independence, all this, though we take full responsibility for it, we do in the belief that it is the only way to establish the future of the Commonwealth and of the Free World on sound foundations. All this, of course, is also of deep and close concern to you for nothing we do in this small world can be done in a corner or remain hidden, What we do today in West, Central and East Africa becomes known tomorrow to everyone in the Union, whatever his language, colour or traditions. Let me assure you, in all friendliness, that we are well aware of this and that we have acted and will act with full knowledge of the responsibility we have to our friends.

We have tried to learn and apply the lessons of our judgement of right and wrong. Our justice is rooted in the same soil as yours, in Christianity and in the rule of law as the basis of society. This experience of our own explains why it has been our aim for the countries for which we have borne responsibility, not only to raise the material standards of living, but to create a society which respects the rights of individuals, a society in which men are given the opportunity to have an increasing share in political power and responsibility, a society in which individual merit and individual merit alone is the criterion for men's advancement, whether political or economic.

In countries inhabited by several different races it has been our aim to find means by which the communities can become more of a community. This problem is not confined to Africa, nor is it always a European minority. In Malaya, though there are no Indian or European minorities, Malays and Chinese make up the bulk of the population. Mr Selwyn Lloyd, the Foreign Secretary, set out our attitude in the United Nations. 'In those territories where different nations or tribes live side by side the task is to ensure that all the people may enjoy security and freedom and the chance to contribute as individuals to the progress and well-being of these countries. We reject the idea of any inherent superiority of one race over another. Our policy therefore is non-racial.

The problems which you as members of the Union Parliament have to address yourselves to are very different from those which face the Parliament of countries with a homogeneous population. These are complicated and baffling problems.'

Annex 8: Sir Charles Phillips CBE

Sir Charles Phillips was formally interviewed by the staff of Rhodes House in January 1971. The following is a synopsis of what he said at that time. I have retained the First Person of the original interview record.

I arrived in Mombasa, in what was then known as the British East Africa Protectorate, in 1908, as an employee of the British-American Tobacco Company. I operated throughout East Africa, including Kenya, Uganda, what was then German East Africa and Zanzibar. At that time, Kenya produced very little and was in receipt of a Grant-in-Aid from the British government. I served on many official or semi-official bodies, including initially the Mombasa Township Authority and as Uganda's representative on the Harbour Advisory Board. I became president of the Mombasa Chamber of Commerce and the Mombasa Sports Club.

Government policies encouraged African participation in cash crops, tea coffee and cotton; maize was introduced about 1922 and this became one of the staple crops, with Kenya exporting surpluses. Wheat was encouraged in the Highlands. Sisal became a valuable crop both in German East Africa and Kenya. Coffee production began with outside capital and cattle and sheep were brought in by settlers from Britain, to create a dairy and meat industry.

When Britain accepted the League of Nations mandate for Tanganyika in 1919, no other country was willing to contribute to the cost of recovery from the First World War. Creating a viable economy was a very slow process and by 1938 total trade (imports and exports) had reached a figure of only £7.6 million. Though there was land suitable for European settlers, few came partly because the future of the country seemed uncertain under the mandate system. By contrast, the growing number of settlers in Kenya contributed to rapid growth of the economy and in Uganda the growth of small-scale cotton and coffee production contributed to growth there. In 1936 I took up residence in Dar es Salaam. At that time, opinion in Tanganyika was that HMG was giving too much economic and industrial emphasis to Kenya. In addition, Nairobi was already the undisputed capital for all inter-territorial purposes, including the location of the Central Legislative Assembly of what became the High Commission of East Africa.

I was the only unofficial on the Tanganyika Economic Control Board (ECB) established prior to the outbreak of war in 1939, which had five members, and I held its chairmanship until the Board was abolished in 1948. The ECB had complete control of the economy; the only appeal was to the Governor. Wholesale and retail prices were fixed and imports and exports controlled. All essential food and transport were controlled. I represented the ECB on coordination meetings with the other territories.

At that time, the private sector, as represented by the Tanganyika Unofficial Members Organisation (TUMO), considered the East African territories comprised a single, and consequently more valuable, unit from an economic and industrial viewpoint, than if each territory stood alone. But politically, any closer union was not considered to be practicable because Kenya was a colony, Uganda a protectorate and Tanganyika a trust territory. Thus closer ties were limited to such matters as customs, income tax, railways, some research and the post office. The Central Legislative Assembly provided a useful forum for debate on these matters. The private sector and some officials considered that HMG was proceeding towards self-government in Tanganyika at a pace which was against the interests of the country as a whole, though we recognized that HMG was under great pressure on this timetable, especially from the USA and the UN.

When the Tanganyikan African National Union (TANU) was created, a number of non-African residents had considerable influence on its policies and some emphasized how important it was to have majority rule. This was demonstrated very forcibly when Julius Nyerere went to the UN on behalf of TANU and I was there on behalf of TUMO. The basic idea of a multiracial society, however fine it sounded, was obviously not acceptable to the Africans. I had realized before TANU came into existence that 'Africa for the Africans', and some form of socialism nearly allied to communism, was the real objective of Africans and few paid more than lip-service to the idea of a multiracial state. Many people at home (in Britain) in responsible positions and with considerable influence, really believed that a multiracial country was possible under an African independent state. Today, it is clear that not one multiracial state exists in Africa.

When I first went to East Africa in 1908, the currency was the Indian Rupee, most of the laws were adaptations of the British Indian laws, and the only direct shipping service to Mombasa was from Bombay, by the British India Line. Thus Asians were quite well established in East Africa before many European settlers arrived. I can say without a shadow of doubt that the Asians formed an essential link between the importer and the consumers and provided most clerical services. They became permanent residents whereas most commercial Europeans in East Africa were expatriates. Without the small Asian shopkeeper, who was already established in remote areas, the viability of the territories would have grown more slowly. The disadvantage was that their efficiency meant there was little opportunity for Africans to enter trade or clerical work, though it has to be said that in my experience it is very difficult to train Africans as traders or clerks before they were educated. It is also to be said that in the early days most Africans lived in their tribal groups on the land and were not interested in going too far outside their tribal area except to work on plantations or large farms. Now the whole position is changing owing to the attitude of the independent African states and the Asian's contribution to the economy will disappear through the policies now being adopted. Many Asians were in close contact with rural Africans who did not participate actively in the growing forces of nationalism. In the towns, they were much more aware. When the British government offered British citizenship to the Asian communities, most of them had little thought of leaving East Africa. However, this changed when they became aware of the Welfare and Social services in Britain.

I consider that the constitutional changes in the 1950s, which led up to self-government and eventually to the formation of a republic, were too rushed. It seemed quite clear that neither administratively, nor economically nor politically were Tanganyika or any other East African territory ready for this drastic change. It would have been more advantageous if self-government had been delayed for another few years with the Africans taking an ever-increasing part in the administration. More training was needed so that a much larger number of Africans could be ready to assume the responsibilities needed to run a country. With regard to racial aspects as such, these became noticeable during the 1950s and were aggravated by the procedure followed by the UN visiting missions. Pressure to speed up the transfer of power was constant. Quite naturally, this influenced the African members of LegCo and ExCo.

Nyerere to my way of thinking appeared to have a dual nature to his character. It is clear he had very strong personal integrity and where the finances of the country were concerned, his endeavour to prevent dishonesty generally and to control the widespread misuse of public funds by Ministers and others was admirable. On the other hand, despite repeated assurances to foreign investors, he nationalized all banks and the leading businesses. The 1964 mutiny of the KAR units, when he disappeared until British forces restored order and disarmed the mutineers, upset him a lot; he felt that if he had remained at State House and faced up to the situation, he could have settled it. A more rapid Africanization policy was generally expected but it was effected in a manner that showed that the early statements of a policy regarding a multiracial community could not be taken seriously. I think Nyerere and his ministers have looked outwardly to create an image internationally in the UN and the OAU, instead of inwardly to bring prosperity to the country and thereby raise the standard of living of all the people.

Annex 9: The advisory commission on the Central African Federation (The Monckton Commission)

The Act of Parliament establishing the Federation of Central Africa in 1953 provided for a review of the federation, its accomplishments, its constitution and its relations with the three territories which comprised it, seven years after it was established – that is, in 1960. The findings of the Monckton Commission provided the briefing material and agenda for the review.

As previously mentioned, the Africans, especially of Northern Rhodesia and Nyasaland, were always opposed to the creation of the federation, largely on the grounds that they did not think they would receive fair treatment by the predominant European community in Southern Rhodesia. This belief played a large part in the outbreak of violence in Nyasaland in 1959 which was examined by the Devlin Commission.

Nevertheless, the economic benefits engendered by the creation of the federation were considerable and the commission's report describes these. Rather than try to describe all the accomplishments of the federation up until 1960, and its failings, the following summarizes the principal findings of the Monckton Commission and describes the changes required in its view to enable the federation to thrive in the future. The Commission explicitly addressed the possibility of secession from the federation by individual territories, as a means of encouraging all parties to contribute to the Commission's collection of fact and opinion.

Summary of conclusions and recommendations

The dilemma and conflict between the numerous, varied and deep-seated criticisms of the present arrangements, and the clear evidence of the economic, material and also political advantages of federation lead us to conclude that while the federation cannot be maintained in its current form it should not be abandoned either. Since 1953–4, federal expenditure on social services has increased from about £8 million in 1953–4 to about £15 million in 1959–60. The territorial governments are now spending twice as much as six years ago. The non-racial University College of Rhodesia and Nyasaland has been established in Salisbury. The federation can maintain its independence and protect its peoples far more effectively as a single entity than if it were to be divided between three separate states. Several other functions can be better performed by the federation than would be possible by three separate states. If the federation were to be broken up, markets would contract and opportunities for employment diminish; the creditworthiness which has made the advances possible would disappear. One of the greatest arguments in favour of the continuance of federation is the fact that it exists, and has existed for seven years.

Specific conclusions and recommendations made by the commission included the following, though there were minority opinions at variance with them:

1. If some form of federal association is to continue, Africans must in the immediate future have a much higher proportion of the seats in the Federal Assembly. The franchise should remain qualitative and there should be no devalued or weighted votes. A committee should be appointed to work out the details of the franchise.

2. All members of the Assembly should be elected on a common roll, though the Commission could not agree on the principles which should govern the proportion of seats as between Africans and Europeans. They put forward three alternatives for decision.

3. The Speaker should be appointed from outside the Federal Assembly.

4. HMG should declare as soon as possible that further constitutional advance towards self-government will be made in the near future in Northern Rhodesia. Most of the Commission considered that there should be an African majority in LegCo and an unofficial majority in ExCo.

5. Nothing should be done to diminish the traditional respect in which chiefs are usually held by their communities. All possible steps should be taken to stamp out the intimidation which is undermining the authority and status of the chiefs.

6. Matters which affect the day-to-day life of the inhabitants should be territorial subjects. No subject should be divided between the federal and the territorial Governments on a racial basis. The federal government should be responsible for all matters connected with external relations.

7. Non-African education, all roads and prisons, and probably health and non-African agriculture should become territorial subjects.

8. The Loan Council should control both internal and external capital issues.

9. Revenue can be divided on a percentage or on an annual grants basis.

10. Territorial surcharges on income tax should continue with a limit expressed as a money sum per £1 of income or profits.

11. The proceeds of customs and excise, and of income and profits taxes, should be pooled for division between the federal and territorial governments.

12. The machinery of consultation between the federal and territorial governments should be strengthened, with regular inter-governmental meetings being held by rotation in all three capital cities.

13. The constitution should provide for the setting up of an advisory economic development council, with two ministers, one of whom should be the finance minister, from each government.

14. Racial discrimination exists in all parts of the federation, but is more rigid and more comprehensively entrenched in Southern Rhodesia. No form of association between the territories is likely to succeed unless Southern Rhodesia is willing to make further and drastic changes in its racial policies. In particular, the Pass Laws, discrimination in local government in urban areas, in the public services and in industry, and the Southern Rhodesian Land Apportionment Act should be removed or amended.

15. Governments should take the lead in removing discriminatory practices in social, economic and commercial relations, and in all agencies and activities which require the sanction of the state.

16. A Bill of Rights should be included in the federal constitution and in each territorial constitution in accordance with the traditions of the English-speaking world and the current practices of the Commonwealth. The Bill of Rights should provide for a right of appeal to the Judicial Committee of the Privy Council.

17. They advocated the setting up of federal and territorial councils of state on the Kenya model, with the membership to exclude legislators. The provisions relating to the Bill of Rights and the Councils of State should be specially entrenched in the federal and territorial Constitutions.

18. The federal capital should remain in Salisbury, but the federal legislature should meet in all three territories in turn, the first two meetings to be in Lusaka and Zomba.

19. The term 'federation' has in itself become a serious political liability and the new association should start with a new name.

20. The governments should without delay put in hand a comprehensive review of the terms of service of all civil servants with a view to unifying conditions of service for all.

21. At present the expansion of higher and secondary education is more essential than universal primary education on account of the need to find sufficient qualified applicants for jobs in both the public service and the private sector.

22. It should be made clear before the Review Conference that the question of secession is entirely open. HMG should explicitly commit to permitting secession of any of the territories if so requested after a stated period of time or at a particular stage of constitutional development, and this would have a very favourable effect.

23. A seceding territory should accept responsibility for its share of the public debt of the federation.

24. The commission wanted to see a customs union continue in being after secession on terms acceptable to all parties.

25. There were also a range of other measures recommended though many of them were technical or subsidiary to other recommendations or events.

March 2011

Annex 10: Robert McNamara on Africa, 1990

In June 1990, Robert McNamara addressed a meeting of the Africa Leadership Forum in Lagos, Nigeria. Speaking on the topic of Africa's development crisis, he reflected on the condition of Africa several years after he had stepped down as President of the World Bank, and twenty-five years after most of the colonies had achieved independence.

McNamara was downbeat in his analysis of the then current development situation in Africa, though upbeat about the availability of solutions and eloquent on the need to apply them. He quoted Chairman Obasanjo as saying 'African leaders have squandered 30 years'; and 'The bald fact is that Africa is a continent in dereliction and decay. We are moving backwards as the rest of the world is forging ahead'. There was a crisis of institutional competence and skilled management.

Speaking on African agriculture McNamara said 'a fundamental factor for the decline (in agriculture) has been the failure to modernize African agricultural practices ... the slash and burn system worked with a low density of population ... increases have made it unviable'. He went on 'the failure of African agriculture reflects the low priority accorded to farming by Africa's post-Independence policy makers and government. Malaysia allocated 25% of their budgets to agriculture in the 1970s ... the median for Africa was 7.6%'.[1]

McNamara quoted President Julius Nyerere, speaking at FAO in 1985, 'Until the last few years, Africa regarded environmental concern as an American and European matter. Indeed there was a tendency to believe that talk of the environment was part of a conspiracy to prevent modern development on our continent ... environmental concern and development have to be linked to be real and permanent'. McNamara further quoted Nyerere as saying 'conservation was resented in Africa as a colonial imposition on rural people ... indeed, it was used as a springboard for nationalist opposition during the pre-Independence period'.[2]

Speaking on the topic 'Building African Capabilities', McNamara said, 'A single concept cuts across all the items on Africa's strategic development agenda: the imperative of building local African capabilities. Whether in agriculture, industry, education or natural resource management, Africa lacks the necessary skills and well-managed public and private institutions for long-term, sustainable growth'. This was twenty-five years after most African colonies became independent.[3]

Speaking on the question of governance, McNamara said:

Outsiders should not attempt to impose on African countries any particular political system. ... However, there is a palpable popular demand for more accountable systems of governance ... outlays which do not go for development are not just wasted; they deprive needy sectors and programs of vital support ... military spending in the mid-1980s consumed more than twice Africa's spending on education and three times the spending on health ... the price tag for non-productive expenditures and for poor governance in Africa has become increasingly visible and can no longer be ignored ... the citizenry sees the elite as self-serving and clinging to political power for their own gain. Only six out of more than 150 national leaders in post-colonial Africa have voluntarily handed over power. The winds of change are again beginning to blow through Africa and the peoples of Africa are growing increasingly impatient with the old ways.

Notes to the Annex

Annex 4

1 See Boyd Papers, Rhodes House, ref PBM, Mss Eng, c 3433.

Annex 10

1 In her Foreign Affairs article of 1949 (forty-one years earlier) Elspeth Huxley had written of African agriculture, 'their first need is to raise the pitifully low productivity of their peasant holdings and to arrest a hastening decline in soil fertility … the yield from a scientifically managed plot is four times that of the peasant holding … Africans can see the difference by looking over the fence (of an experimental station), but they follow the old ways' (see Chapter 2). Thus the diagnosis had been available all that time, but it had been largely ignored and in the main the solutions had not been applied.

2 Perhaps he was referring to Kenya (see Chapter 4).

3 The need to enhance African capabilities had been well known and understood; indeed it was obvious and pointed out before decolonization in the British House of Commons, at the metropolitan level, and more widely at the local country level (see Chapter 2).

Index